Princess
Pamela

Also by Ray Russell

Princess Pamela

BEING
THE PERSONAL JOURNAL
OF

Miss Pamela Summerfield

OF
BERKELEY SQUARE
MAYFAIR
LONDON

ॐ

edited, with an Afterword
by

RAY RUSSELL

HOUGHTON MIFFLIN COMPANY BOSTON 1979

Library of Congress Cataloging in Publication Data
Russell, Ray.
Princess Pamela.

I. Title.
PZ4.R9663Pr [PS3568.U77] 813'.5'4 79-9242
ISBN 0-395-28210-1

Printed in the United States of America
v 10 9 8 7 6 5 4 3 2 1

Note

Although I have given myself the title of Editor, I have not cut or otherwise tampered with the diary, except to regularize some inconsistencies of spelling. I have taken the liberty of supplying each month with a subtitle ("Secret Letters," for example) suggested by its content. I have resisted the temptation to add footnotes to the text and have reserved all commentary for the Afterword, which appears at the end of the book.

R.R.

Post Scriptum

I interrupt the forward flow of this journal, and turn back the pages to this fly-leaf, to set down some thoughts here, at a point before the beginning.

Half a year ago, when I commenced to write in this book, I was a child. Now I am a woman: I have been made so, not merely by the act of flesh, but — of far greater importance — by life; by joy; by adversity; by stunning enlightenment in things of which I would have preferred to remain ignorant; by tragedies both personal and national. As I turn the early pages of this volume, and live again my girlish occupation with frocks and fabrics, teas and balls, I smile ruefully, for I can scarcely recognise the frivolous child who wrote those lines. It was but a few months ago, and yet it seems as if it were a lifetime.

Who could have foreseen the terrible event of last month and its even more terrible effect on our country? In my most extravagant imaginings, how could I have dreamt of Mamma's startling disclosure; of Phoebe's fate; of Willy's unexpected behaviour and his subsequent self-sacrifice; of the court-room drama I would witness; of the scandals that would surround me; of constables invading the sanctity of our house to make an arrest; of pistol shots in the dead of night; of plots and poisonings; of suicide; of the loathsome horrors that festered — and no doubt fester still — behind that padlocked black door?

And love: who could have predicted its deliciousness, its radiance — or its crushing disappointments and betrayals? Not I, for all the cleverness I am pleased to think that I possess. Not even those strange and omen-laden *tarot* cards of my long-dead gipsy uncle — remarkably prophetic though they proved themselves to be — could have foretold all the multitudinous glories and terrors of these months.

Having experienced those glories and terrors (with many more of both surely ahead of me), I am more than ever firm in my faith that we are not without one great and powerful Friend who wishes our eventual good, who guides us if we will but open our hearts and heed Him, and yet whose ways often seem cruel and capricious, because they are beyond our puny understanding. There are those who do not agree with me — one adamant dissenter in particular, for it is his belief that Man is alone, sufficient unto himself, and needs no higher Being's help to attain greatness and purity of spirit.

But — despite, or perhaps because of, the tribulations of these months — I know better, dear Heavenly Father.

Pamela Summerfield
Saturday, 1 July

In the Year of Our Lord

&

1837

January

❦

"SECRET LETTERS"

ᴔ *Sunday, 1 January*

Why am I awake? The dawn is only just beginning to stain the sky outside my bedroom window; all the house is fast asleep; not even the servants are about below-stairs; and yet here am I, wide of eye, my blood as lively as that champagne I drank last night — the first I'd ever tasted — how it *hissed* in my glass, like a serpent!

I should be tired, but I am not. Papa permitted me to stay up past midnight to see in the New Year, and, although I retired to my bed soon after, my mind was buzzing so, like a hive of bees, that I did not fall asleep for a time. It may have been one o'clock. It may have been two. And yet I am the first awake. Of course, it is not the first time I have welcomed the New Year, but it is the first time I have "officially" done so, with Papa's sufferance and sanction. In other years, I have seen it arrive whilst I was all alone in my bedroom and was assumed to˙be sleeping; or in the company of dear Phoebe, the most trustworthy confidante, the finest sister a girl ever had. O Phoebe, why did you have to marry and go off to live in the Midlands? It is too bad of you. I have nobody to talk to now, no-one in whom I can confide and whisper my little secrets — except old Sophie, who tries to understand, but can not. Papa is a dear, of course, and so is Mamma; even brother Willy is a good chap, in his way; and I love them all, but they

5

are not the same as an elder sister — they are not the same at all.

I must, then, turn to you, dear Diary, and set down all my thoughts, my fears, my foolish conceits, all those things I used to prattle of to Phoebe. And all my questions, too. But you — dumb, silent, inanimate object that you are — will not answer me, as Phoebe did. You will not slake my girlish thirst for knowledge of worldly things, as she did. You will not check my wilder, whirling fancies, either, nor will you correct my misconceptions. By the same token, Diary mine, you will not scold — as dearest Phoebe did, though rarely, when I'd been vain and naughty.

If I may pay you a compliment, Diary, you are a rather handsome article, and my positive favourite amongst all the pretty gifts I received last week at the Christmas celebration: the lace, the bottles of scent, the book of sermons, the *tarot* cards, etc. Your pages are large and smooth and creamy — I may say *virginal* in these private writings which no eyes but mine will see (Mamma would frown and look severe if I spoke the word aloud, for she will not even refer to Elizabeth as "The Virgin Queen" in my presence, but will call her, instead, "The *Maiden* Queen"). Your binding of fine watered silk is exquisite to the touch of my finger-tips, and its colour, a kind of ivory, most pleasing to the eye. Best of all are the words stamped in flowing gold-leaf script on your cover: *Princess Pamela's Diary*. When Papa presented you to me, he said, "I make of you but one request, Princess: that you set down in this book only those things that are good and moral and true." I answered, "Yes, Papa," and kissed his cheek, for I am a dutiful daughter.

But O! dear Diary! how am I, in my green youth, lacking Phoebe's counsel, to *know* what is good? what is moral? and, most particularly, what is true? Did not Pilate himself ask that latter question? And does not Goodness exist, as Mr. Hume said of Beauty, in the mind which contemplates it? Besides, if one may not set down, from time to time, one's fleeting little *wicked* notions and silly questions, what then is a Diary for? Even so, I said, "Yes, Papa" — but I will keep you *hidden*, Diary!

For, as Shakespere has rightly written, "Though I am bound to every act of duty, I am not bound to that all slaves are free to. Utter my thoughts? Why, say they are vile and false? Who has a breast so pure but some uncleanly apprehensions keep leets and law days?" (Papa calls me his "little philosopher," and Mamma says I am too young to crease my brow with frowning thoughts.)

I begin to hear sounds of stirring in the household. The servants are up and about, and soon I must dress and be off to Sunday worship with the family. The New Year has truly begun. What unforeseen events will it bring? What joy, what pain? What births and deaths? What milestones of history?

The day looks to be fine and clear, with some light clouds in the sky, and still some snow remaining on the ground. Happy New Year, Diary! I am off to church. I hope the sermon will not be *too* dreary.

P.S. It was!

ॐ *Monday, 2 January*

I deem it fitting, as this new year opens, to say that I think it is a glorious thing to be living at this time, and in England. As Mr. Wordsworth has written, in another connexion (I paraphrase, changing the tense):

> Bliss is it in this dawn to be alive,
> But to be young is very heaven!

For I do think of this epoch in Britain as a kind of dawn. The villain Bonaparte was defeated at Waterloo just four years before my birth, and died on St. Helena when I was a toddler of two. All of Europe lay in ruins, exhausted by the Napoleonic wars; all save England. We alone were whole and strong, and have continued to grow stronger. Not even the Roman Empire of old could boast the far-flung sweep and sway of our British Empire. Asia, Africa, North and South America, Australia — in all those distant lands our influence is felt, and it is

7

a benign influence (for has not the evil of slavery been abolished in our Colonies four years since? Our American cousins continue to foster this barbarity).

And here on our home ground, thanks to the richness of coal and iron with which God has blessed us, a great burgeoning of industry and prosperity has flourished. Our ships transport a huge share of the world's goods: Britannia rules the mercantile waves. Papa says that England has passed unscathed through a period of revolution which has thrown most other European countries into turmoil. King William is the only contemporary European monarch to survive what Papa calls "the juggernaut of democracy."

Truly, in the words of the song, Britons never will be slaves — unless the ravens of the Tower of London, which have been there since antiquity, suddenly take it in their little heads to leave. Then, as legend has it, England will fall. But I think that no such a thing is likely to happen. The Tower had its ravens even before the lions and leopards of the Royal Menagerie were brought there in the Thirteenth Century — indeed, the ungainly black birds may have been there always, even before the Norman Conquest. (Speaking of the Menagerie, I was so unhappy when those handsome beasts were removed from the Tower three years ago. I always regarded them as the high point of our visits there.)

England's glory is by no means confined to material things: we are not derelict in our offerings to the Muses. Mr. John Field is an internationally lauded pianist and composer. Mr. Constable and Mr. Turner (among others) are brilliant painters admired the world over. And think of the fine writers established in our midst — Wordsworth, Landor, Carlyle, Bulwer-Lytton, Southey, Hunt, Disraeli, De Quincey, Sir Terrence Dickson, Tom Moore, and others, such as Mr. George Borrow, who so graciously gave me his book of translations from the Russian poet Pushkin. (What a service Mr. Borrow has performed in introducing this great artist to English readers.) Then consider the new writers just beginning to make their mark, such as Tennyson, Macaulay, and Dickens; and this century's dead: Keats, Shelley, Blake, Lamb, Hazlitt, Byron, Coleridge, Scott.

On the subject of Scott, I still remember vividly an experience from the last opera season. My parents and Phoebe and I attended the Opera, where we heard Donizetti's *Lucia di Lammermoor*. It had the most moving story, drawn from the novel *The Bride of Lammermoor,* by the late Sir Walter. Lucy, or Lucia, as she is called in Italian, is forced by her horrid brother to marry a man whom she does not love (*she* loves her brother's sworn enemy). The poor girl becomes demented, goes quite mad in fact, kills her husband, and then takes her own life. At the sight of her funeral procession, her true love, Edgardo (the tenor *rôle*), then takes *his* life. All this was set to music of the most melodic and exciting kind imaginable. I am still humming those soaring airs, and I will not be satisfied until I have a copy of the published score so that I may play them over and over again.

And oh, the brilliance of the costumes, the settings! The eyes as well as the ears were overwhelmed by that surfeit of magnificence. Phoebe loved it, too. She always accompanied us to the Opera when she lived with us here. Our box will seem quite empty and odd without her. I wonder if her husband, Mr. Braithwaite, is a gentleman who takes pleasure in music?

For a moment in the last act, I was confused by my imperfect command of the Italian language. Edgardo, in a flash of anger at his beloved, at one point sang, *"O barbara!"* I asked myself: Why does he call her Barbara, when her name is Lucia? Luckily, I soon recollected that he was, in fact, saying, "O barbarous one!"

A rather strange and chilling thing happened — quite outside the tragic events of the opera. When the lights were brightened for the first interval, I looked in the direction of the adjoining box, straight into the single living eye of the man who sat there. He had been staring at me; but he did not lower his gaze or turn away: it drilled into me, arrogantly, voraciously. His expression, though cold, was filled with rapacity and raging appetite. It was an unpleasant, frightening moment, and mortally insulting. He was a man in his middle years, lean and gaunt, and, even though seated, appeared to be unusually tall. His face was hideously ugly, wolfish, with a wild tangle of beard and a ferocious scar that extended out of that thicket to the very rim of the socket of his ghastly, distorted dead eye. If ever I have seen a candidate for Madame Tussaud's wax museum — the Chamber of Horrors section — here certainly was one. A lady sat at his side.

I turned, blushing, from his relentless, Cyclopean scrutiny. But curiosity overcame me, and I whispered to Phoebe, asking her if she knew the identity of the man in the next box. She replied in a voice so soft that I could scarcely hear her, and she was forced to repeat: "Cumberland."

"So!" I said to myself. "It is the most disreputable of Victoria's several disreputable uncles who insolently disrobes me with his eyes: the notorious Ernest Augustus, Duke of Cumberland. Small wonder that Phoebe speaks his name low."

But I was not to know till later precisely *why* the Duke is so disreputable and notorious.

ॐ *Tuesday, 3 January*

It occurs to me, Diary, that I have not properly introduced you to this family. Let me do so at once.

We live in one of the most attractive houses in Berkeley Square. From our windows, we can see No. 45, where Lord Clive lived: it is a handsome house, but ours is even more handsome, I think.

We are what is known as well-to-do. Papa, who is highly respected in London and elsewhere, is that same Summerfield of brewing fame: Who has not heard of Summerfield's Golden Lager? He is fifty-nine years of age, becoming a bit portly now (*port*-ly is precisely the word I want, for Papa is fond of his glass after dinner), and the most good-looking man I know. I think he would be even better-looking if he would relinquish the moustaches and side-whiskers he has grown in latter years: they make him look older and so severe, shot with grey as they are. They are greyer than his hair, which, however, is getting rather thin on top. He is plain *Mister* Wilfrid Summerfield now, but there is hope in his heart that when the next Honours List is announced — or the List after that — the King will make him *Sir* Wilfrid. Papa would be so proud! He goes into the City to his office six days a week, for he is very industrious, although he works only half a day on Saturdays, usually returning well in time for our Saturday afternoon at-homes.

Mamma is some eight years younger than Papa and is still a beauty, probably the best-looking of us all. Before marriage, she was Melissa Worthing, daughter of the bishop of that name, who, alas, went to his reward when I was in my infancy, and as a result I do not remember him. Mamma has a multitude of duties to keep her occupied. She must keep an eye on the staff and see that they waste nothing (servants can be so lax: after all, it is not *their* money that is being spent). Store-cupboards and linen-cupboards have to be kept locked, and she is the Keeper of the Keys. She made all arrangements for tutors when we were children, and is still in charge of paying Signor Olivo, my music teacher. She supervises all meals, as well as Mrs. Pruitt's making of marmalade, jam, pickled walnuts, ginger preserves, etc. (Mrs. P. is our cook). The nursing and watering of all potted plants is under Mamma's supervision, and much of it she does herself (I sometimes help her). It is she who must keep up most of the family correspondence, writing long letters to friends and relations (Aunt Esmie, Uncle Roger, Willy when he is away at Oxford, et al.). The planning of dinner parties is her province, of course, as is the ritual of calling upon friends and leaving visiting-cards — almost an occupation in itself. What else is there to say of Mamma except that she is the dearest lady alive?

Phoebe I have already spoken of. She is only four years my senior, but has always seemed so *much* older and wiser. If *she* were writing in you, Diary, what pearls of perception would illuminate your pages!

Then there is Young Wilfrid (he *hates* to be called Willy, and, of course, I do so all the time). In appearance, he is a younger replica of Papa, although with Mamma's fine eyes. He is two years my senior, but I think I am cleverer than he. But I am likewise naughtier; so perhaps that balances things. Willy is a very good boy — how should it be otherwise, seeing that he is a divinity student at Oriel College? He was recently home for the holiday, but has now returned to Oxford. I wish I could say that I miss him, but I have sworn to be truthful in these pages, and I am bound to admit that Willy has always been a trifle boring, even when we were children, and even more so, now that he has become immersed in theology. There simply has not ever been the tiniest scrap of *mischief* in him. Old Sober Sides we called him, even as a child. I need hardly say that the volume of sermons I received as a Christmas gift last week was from him. He is my parents' only living son (two children died in infancy, a girl and a boy), and I think — nay, I know — that Papa has always been disappointed that Willy decided to prepare for holy orders. He would have preferred him to take up "the business." But Mamma stood up for Willy and told Papa, "The boy has the call, like his grandfather the bishop. Sanctity is in his blood, in his heritage. You shall not stand in his path." However, even Mamma was disconcerted to learn that, of all the Oxford colleges to which Willy might have applied (every one of them teaches divinity, of course), he had set his heart on Oriel — that maelstrom of dissension and upheaval! It is hardly a fashionable college since John Henry Newman left it so dramatically a few years ago; and his rebellious influence still permeates its halls. Not really suitable for the grandson of a bishop and the son of a man who longs to be a knight. Still, there it is, and we must all make the best of it.

And now, how shall I limn myself? I stand five feet, five inches, without shoes. It would be vain to say that I am pretty. It would be wicked to tell you of my large eyes, as green as the sea; of my honey-coloured hair; of my cream-and-strawberries complexion; of my rounded bosom, narrow waist, delicate ankles and feet. It would also be untrue. I fear I am less ornamental than Phoebe, who is an absolute goddess of perfection in both face and form. (I have sketched her in pencil many times, and rendered her in water colours, too, but even my skill, which is considerable, has never captured her ethereal beauty.) I am not downright *plain,* you understand; but I seem not to have inherited the finer physical qualities of either parent. I think I am tolerably pleasant to look at; and yet I could wish my eyes to be a trifle larger and my nose and feet to be a trifle smaller. My hair is not precisely the colour of honey, as I have hinted; it is closer to the brown of treacle.

The delicate ankles referred to above are, perhaps, a bit sturdier than I have tried to suggest. However, my waist *is* narrow; my eyes *are* green; I *do* stand five feet five (not tall, but taller than Princess V.); and my bosom *is* reasonably rounded (what else should it be: cubical?). My neck is too long.

Perhaps I should explain to you that I am not a princess; it is just a name that Papa has always used for me, ever since I can remember. The reason, he has always said, is that I was born on the same day as our dear Princess V., on the 24th of May, 1819. She was born at a quarter past four in the morning, while I, according to Mamma, came noisily into this world some hours earlier, a few minutes after midnight, so I am just the tiniest bit older than she, as well as somewhat taller.

Mamma says that I was born in typical early summer weather — "A bit chilly, and a light rain falling, really very pleasant after the dreadful heat we had endured all that month right on through to the day before you were born. Then the weather broke, as if it were a sign of a happy birth, and indeed it was, child. But as my father, the bishop, said, God's purpose is seen in all things, and perhaps if it had not been for those weeks of unseasonal heat, Mr. Keats would not have been inspired to give us his 'Ode to a Nightingale,' which he composed during that period."

Although Mamma is kind enough to call my coming into the world "a happy birth," I know it was a troubled and dangerous labour for her, nearly causing the loss of both our lives, and rendering her incapable of bearing more children. She says, "It was God's way of telling us, Enough, Mr. and Mrs. Summerfield; you have replenished the Earth quite sufficiently, thank you, and I am well pleased. This pretty little girl-child shall be your last-born and best-beloved."

In May of this year, the Princess and I will both become eighteen. But I will still be a pretty little girl-child, while she will be a woman, for the reason (which Papa has explained to me) that royal personages reach their majority at that age, unlike other folk. I think it is lamentably unfair. I *feel* like a woman; I *look* like a woman; and yet a silly law made by silly men says that I will not *be* a woman for some years yet to come.

Do not misunderstand me, Diary: I bear no ill-will towards

the Princess. I love her and wish her well. She had no hand in the making of that stupid law, although she benefits by it. She will succeed to the throne when King William dies, which I hope will not be for a very long time, God bless him. He is a good man — they say he loved to roam the streets alone and mingle with the mob even after he ascended to the throne, the dear old booby, and had to be rescued from the embraces of pedlars and prostitutes who clapped him on the back and kissed him, in their love for him — but I am not ashamed to say that I will be pleased when a woman, and a woman of my own age, sits on the throne of England.

To complete my self-description: I am good at needlework and *very* good at drawing; I play the pianoforte better than passably and sing a little better than that; I have some French, less German and Spanish, *much* less Latin, no Greek at all, and just enough Italian to hobble haltingly through Dante and Boccaccio and to sing the airs of Rossini, Bellini, et al., when Signor Olivo comes here for my weekly lesson.

The youngest (and yet the oldest) member of our family is Sophie, a lovely, loving King Charles spaniel I received as a puppy at Christmas-time some dozen years ago. (I mean *she* was a puppy — although I suppose it might be said that I was, too!) Papa says that she is now eighty-four years old in human terms, poor old dear. I think that she is the finest, sweetest person in this house.

ॐ *Wednesday, 4 January*

To-day I met the most beautiful man I have ever seen!

Mamma and I took tea at Lady Merlyngton's, for this is her at-home day. I had first thought of staying away, for I had a small headache and I do not find Lady M. a fascinating person; but her guests are often tolerably amusing, so I attended.

We were introduced, for example, to Mrs. Trollope, the authoress, whose book, *Domestic Manners of the Americans*, made such a sensation when it was published four or five years ago and is still read avidly. She told many colourful anecdotes about the coarse customs of the Americans — scenes etched in acid — and entertained the company most admirably. With her was her son Anthony, who seemed to be just a few years older than I, and a pleasant, sociable sort, although not excessively attractive in a physical way. I asked him if he, like his mother, were a writer, and he said he was not.

Also among the guests was Mr. Thomas Attwood, who composed the coronation anthems for George IV and our own King William. He played for us at the pianoforte, and very well, too, for such an elderly gentleman. The pages of the music were obligingly turned for him by another guest, the appropriately named Sir Gregory Page-Turner, a delicious coincidence which amused me greatly, although nobody else appeared to see the joke.

Lieutenant Giles Ormond is the name of the beautiful man. So stunning in his uniform (he is in the 18th Light Dragoons), and so attentive to this humble diarist! He is very tall, with the broadest shoulders I have ever seen, and classically muscular thighs in tight-fitting military breeches, to say nothing of his long, straight calves in gleaming leather boots. He has wavy dark brown hair and a small moustache; his eyes are deep brown, almost black. I judged him to be about twenty-five. He noticed me immediately I entered Lady Merlyngton's drawing-room—and, needless to say, I noticed him.

"Miss Summerfield," he said, soon after we were introduced, "I am your most ardent admirer."

"Indeed, Lieutenant!" I responded, pleasantly surprised. "And precisely how long have you held this admiration?"

"Oh, for a very long while," he said. "Ever since the moment you walked through that door."

An empty compliment, perhaps, mere flattery — but pretty, and what woman would disdain to hear it? I laughed, but not derisively, for I did not wish to discourage him, and I gave him permission to bring me tea and cake.

In the mean while, Mrs. Trollope was holding forth. "Do not visit America, Mrs. Summerfield," she advised Mamma, "unless you wish to be jostled in the streets and addressed, in the most revoltingly familiar fashion, as 'Old Woman.' "

"Dear me!" exclaimed Mamma. "I should not like that at all!"

"Nor did I," Mrs. Trollope assured us.

"I saw an American once," I said. "Do you remember, Mamma? He was in some way a business acquaintance of Papa's, here on holiday, and we were obliged to invite him to dinner. He was an amiable enough person, but he spoke in an impenetrable accent, and he ate in the most peculiar way. After cutting his meat, he put down his fork and immediately picked it up again *with his right hand,* speared the meat, and carried it to his mouth. Then he put the fork down, picked it up in his left hand once more, and repeated the ritual. Over and over again, with every bite. It looked to be the most tedious hard work. Can it be a custom they have learned from the Red Indians?"

"I shouldn't be surprised," said Mrs. Trollope. "They are a savage people, whether red or white. For example, the so-called Grand Hotel at Memphis — that is in Tennessee — is a kind of damp barn, smelling of wet plaster. The manager of that primæval establishment refused to let me have tea in my room unless I could satisfy him that I was *ill!* Have you ever heard anything to equal that? And, in the dining-room — if the draughty barrack can be dignified by that name — I was actually forced to sit at the same table with my *footman!"*

"Insufferable!" said Lady M.

"It may be, ma'am," interposed a voice lightly touched with the brogue, "that the poor man was likewise flummoxed to be sitting at the same board with *yourself."*

Mrs. Trollope looked up at the speaker with disapproval. He was a man not quite so tall as Lieutenant Ormond, of about thirty years, thin as an anchovy, and dressed in the fashion: sleeves very full, gathered and pleated at the arm-holes; coat with high collar and spreading lapels, worn well open to display a satin waistcoat, tight at the waist, over wide-topped trousers, diminishing to small ankles. The coat was black, almost a clerical black, cut away with tails, and the trousers were of plum-coloured fabric. His cravat was also plum-coloured, covering the shirt front and collar, and clashing, I thought, most dissonantly, with the colour of his hair, which was like an orange bonfire. His skin was clear, but pale; his eyes, chips of blue ice. He had a grim, thin-lipped mouth, turned down at the corners; troubled eyes, webbed round with premature wrinkles; and there was about him an air in part monastic, in part Satanic, which gave him the look of an unfrocked priest.

"Pay no mind to Mr. O'Connor," Lady M. advised Mrs. Trollope. "He thinks that he can say anything at all, simply because he is Irish."

At this, he laughed, shewing rows of irregular but very white teeth, and transforming his appearance from *mauvais prêtre* to that of *poète maudit*.

"Faith, and I'm even more fearsome than that!" he said. "'Tis half-Irish and half-Irish and half-Welsh I am. Me mother was a Griffith, spelled G-R-U-F-F-Y-D-D."

"Papa's mother was a Fanshaw," I said, "spelled F-E-A-T-H-E-R-S-T-O-N-E-H-A-U-G-H."

"What occupation do you follow, Mr. O'Connor?" asked Mrs. Trollope.

"I'm an observer of contemporary life, ma'am," he replied.

"So are we all, I think," she said, "but can it truly be called an occupation?"

Lady Merlyngton explained, "Mr. O'Conner means that he is a writer."

"Heaven defend our tribe!" said Mrs. Trollope, laughing. "I think you are quite right, Mr. O'Connor — my poor footman seemed to be just as much discomfited as I."

"A writer?" I said. "Are you really?" We had strolled a little apart from the rest of the company, and were talking together.

"Lady Merlyngton is too kind," he said. " 'Tis primarily a journalist and pamphleteer I am."

"To which papers do you contribute?"

"Only the most radical of them. None that yourself would be reading. Although I occasionally contribute to *Fraser's Magazine*."

"Why, I am devoted to *Fraser's!*" I declared. "I read the whole of Mr. Carlyle's *Sartor Resartus* there."

"A magnificent satire, that," he said. "But I think that he will surpass it with his historical book, promised for this year."

"*The French Revolution,* you mean."

"Why, yes. You are better read than most young ladies of my acquaintance."

"And yet I do not recollect seeing your name in *Fraser's*. O'Connor, is it?"

"Rhys O'Connor. I'm a member of Billy-Be-Damned's Round Table."

"Billy-Be-Damned?"

"Me own private name for him. Billy Maginn, the editor of *Fraser's*. A brilliant Irish rascal, and a skin-'em-alive satirist. There is a group of us that meet periodically under Billy's leadership in the back room of James Fraser's, in Regent Street. Thackeray, Churchill, meself, and others. We drink enormous quantities of whisky punch and collaborate on satires which Billy publishes over the signature of 'Oliver Yorke.' That is why you've never seen me name in *Fraser's*. Of course, I write pamphlets and broadsheets, too, but these are likewise signed with pen-names."

"Well, now, I find that exceedingly interesting, Mr. O'Connor, or Mr. Yorke, or whatever name you choose to be called by. *My* name, by the way, is Pamela Summerfield."

"Oh, I know the name well. 'Tis the younger of Wilfrid the Wolf's two pretty daughters you are."

"Wilfrid the — what?"

"Forgive me. We pamphleteers tend to think in caricature, and I couldn't resist the alliteration. Sure, and it becomes a bad habit."

"But there are other alliterative words you might have used: Wilfrid the Wise, for instance, or Wilfrid the Wonderful. Why did you call my father a wolf?"

"I think that you don't really want to know."

"I do."

"Very well, then," he said, setting down his cup. "Because he and others of his kidney have grown rich on the sweat of children — pardon me: in this genteel assemblage, I expect I should have said 'perspiration.' "

"Not at all," I replied, my face hot with anger. "Shakespere, who was surely a far better writer than *you,* referred to sweat a great deal. Fifty-seven times, in fact. I have studied him closely, you see. He used it as a noun sixteen times and as a

18

verb twenty-three times. He used 'sweating' nine times, 'sweats' five times, 'sweaty' two times, and 'sweaten' and 'sweatest' one time each. Not once did he use 'perspire' or 'perspiration.' If *he* said 'sweat,' so may you. The choice of word does not matter, Mr. O'Connor, but your slander of my father *does* matter. It matters very much!"

"Slander?" he said, calmly (and I could see that he was both impressed and amused by my Shakesperean scholarship). "No. A slander is a lie. And, you may deny it if you will, but I have seen little ones, no older than five, labouring fourteen hours a day in your dear da's brewery."

"Would you rather they starve?" I said. "They earn their living there. Is my father to be blamed for granting them employment?"

"You have voiced the burning question of the age, Miss Summerfield," said Rhys O'Connor, "and I suggest that you seek the answer in your own heart."

With that, he bowed, and walked to the refreshment table, where he commenced to stuff himself.

What an offensive person! I soon attached myself to Lieutenant Ormond and young Trollope, who proved to be far jollier companions for the afternoon.

Mr. Trollope, inspired by Mr. O'Connor's overheard sentiments, made what I thought to be a sensible and well-expressed remark: "I do, in part, share Mr. O'Connor's sympathies," he began. "The gates of one class should be open to the other. *But* — and it is a very important *but* — neither to the one class nor to the other can any good be done by declaring that there *are* no gates."

Hearing this, Mr. O'Connor said, "I have never denied the existence of those gates. I see them all too clearly. 'Tis me aim in life to smash them down."

My beautiful lieutenant, somewhat contemptuously, asked, "All by yourself, O'Connor?"

The pamphleteer smiled. "Me name is Legion," he replied.

Before the afternoon ended, Lieutenant Ormond asked me what day the Summerfield family was at home. I told him that he must, more properly, speak to Mamma on that subject. I believe — I hope — that he did.

Thick fog this morning, but a happily rapid thaw. The old dirty snow is fast melting away, and is nearly gone.

I so admired Lady M.'s *coiffure* yesterday that I asked the name of her hairdresser; and this morning that gifted artisan, a Mlle. La Grange, attended me in my dressing-room. Last year, I wore my hair plaited in wickerwork fashion on the crown of my head, with flowers added for the evening; but now, inspired by Lady M.'s attractive tresses, I asked Mam'selle to arrange my hair in those pretty side-curls which the French, for some reason, call *"anglaises."* (I suppose it is for the same reason that a soldier absent from his regiment without permission is said, by us, to have taken French leave, while the French call the same thing English leave.)

Speaking of soldiers, I confess that I cannot get Lieutenant Ormond out of my mind. We are at home on Saturdays, and I do so hope that he will call upon us on the day after to-morrow.

I asked Mlle. La Grange, "Is it true, Mam'selle, that Frenchmen are more adept in matters of love than others?"

She shrugged and looked at me in the mirror as she combed my hair. "Men are the same the world over, I think."

"You have never been married?"

"Not as yet, Miss."

"But you have . . . known men?"

"Oui, naturellement."

"Many of them?"

She laughed and said no more than *"Oh, la, la!"*

"Have any of them been military gentlemen?"

"Les soldats? Ah, oui, beaucoup!"

"How do they differ from civilians?"

She sighed. "In the uniforms only. When the, how do you say, the *fine feathers,* come off, it is as I have said before — men are the same the world over."

I had not intended the conversation to turn to the subject of naked men, but seeing that it had done so, I said, "Are they the same, *truly?"*

She shrugged again. "Oh, some are thin; some are fat. Some have the smooth skin; others are all over covered with hair . . ."

"Like Jacob and Esau," I said, and a little shiver passed through me. "Covered with hair! I think I shouldn't like that! Isn't it like hugging a bristly great bear?"

She sighed again, but this time as if in happy memory. "*Oui*," she said softly, "*vraiment . . .*"

"And are there no other differences amongst them?"

She frowned at me in the mirror with mock solemnity. "Your *maman* must speak to you of these things," she said.

I laughed. "Oh, come, Mam'selle, you know what mothers are. They tell us nothing! I insist that you answer just *one* more question."

She sighed yet again, this time an eloquent sigh of resignation, tinged with just a touch of annoyance -- indeed, Mlle. La Grange is a *virtuoso* in the Art of Sighing. "*Eh bien*," she said, "but only one."

I chose my words with care. "In the act of . . . well, on the wedding night . . ."

"*Non!*" snapped Mlle. La Grange. "I have told you — these things must be spoken by your *maman*."

"Dear Mam'selle," I said, persisting, "I meant to ask only if the . . . if both partners share equally in the *glory* . . . the *joyousness* of love?"

"You mean . . . *le plaisir?*"

"I suppose I do."

For a moment, Mlle. La Grange was deep in thought as she tended to my side-curls. Then she said, "Sometimes, Miss, you will feel the most terrible itching in your ear, *comme tout le monde*, no? You will do like so, *n'est-ce pas?*" In the mirror, I saw Mlle. La Grange insert her little finger in her ear and vibrate it vigorously for a second, pantomiming exquisite relief.

Although puzzled, I laughed and said, "Yes, of course."

"*Alors*," she said, "when you do this thing, which part feels the more *plaisir* — the finger? *Or the ear?*"

I required a moment to comprehend this parable, and when I did, I said, "Then you are saying that we *women* feel —"

21

"I am saying nothing. I am speaking only of scratching the ear."

After Mlle. La Grange left, I pondered her words. I wondered if that is all there is to love — a kind of scratching of the ear? Is love no more than an itch, then? There lies dear Sophie, curled at my feet, from time to time waking to bite at a flea: Is love no loftier than that? If it is not, then how may we account for those who have suffered and died for love? How may we explain Romeo and Juliet, Héloïse and Abélard, Orpheus and Eurydice? Is it all mendacious nonsense? Is all the great love poetry of the world a lie? All the great music and painting and sculpture? Have the most inspired artists of the centuries plumbed their souls and brought forth rhapsodic works of genius — all in service of an itch?

Can a flea-bite impel us to sacrifice and self-denial?

No, I most emphatically think *not!*

But perhaps that is mere girlish silliness and childish idealism. When I am older, perhaps, like Phoebe . . .

In the mean time, I will continue to think of love in the most elevated and poetic terms; and dream of Lieutenant Ormond in his thrilling uniform; of his deep brown eyes and darling moustache; and wonder whether he is smooth of skin from head to toe or covered with bristles like some enormous and terrifying bear!

ஒ *Friday, 6 January*

I have the most oppressive headache to-day, and other general aches, and my face looks chalky and puffed, and I am so cross that I even shouted at poor Sophie. Yes, I fear That Time is coming on again for me, probably to-morrow. How tiresome it is to be a woman!

It must be fine to be a man. No monthly ailments, no corset stays. Of course, they must be shaved every morning. But even that is not a strict necessity — they can always let their beards grow. How would Lieutenant Ormond look in a wavy brown beard, I wonder? I think it would feel soft as sable to the touch. I might rather like that.

I dreamt of him last night. It must have been provoked by my conversation with Mlle. La Grange, for he appeared in the dream *sans* uniform! He was not all hairy like Esau, but smooth like Jacob. (Or is it the other way round?) And this was most singular: *below,* he was exactly like the "David" of Michael Angelo that we saw on our visit to Rome last year — and when I say *exactly* like, I mean that those parts of him were made of marble! Dreams can be so contrary.

I suppose the reason lies in the fact that, except for those carved in marble, I have never seen a naked man. Well, "never" is not quite accurate. On family trips to Brighton, when we were children, there were occasions . . . Do you know, Diary, I have always thought how curious it is that gentlemen, on holiday at the sea-side, bathe as bare as God made them, while we women must needs wear long bathing-dresses, usually in the most dreary dark blue, fastened with strings round the ankles. Mixed bathing is, of course, impossible under the circumstances, and each sex must occupy its own stretch of sea-side. Phoebe and I, when we were naughty little girls, would sometimes perch on the cliffs near to hand and, equipped with Papa's collapsible telescope, spy on the shivering gentlemen and giggle at their white bottoms and shrivelled other parts. How Mamma scolded when she caught us at it!

Oh, this headache! I would ask for laudanum, but I shall never forget the profound fear I experienced a few years ago when I was leafing through Papa's old bound volumes of the *London Magazine.* How I shuddered to read Mr. De Quincey's account of his terrible addiction! Eight thousand drops of laudanum a day! Thank God he mastered himself and is now one of our most respected writers. He must possess a will of iron.

And yet a drop or two could do no harm and would dispel these exasperating aches and pains. Perhaps I *will* ask Mamma to send one of the servants to the chemist's shop for a small bottle. Laudanum brings pleasing dreams, too — of a certain Dragoons officer, perhaps!

I can write no more. I shall go to bed. I must be at my *best* to-morrow.

P.S. I have risen from my bed to pen a question that I fear I may forget if I wait until to-morrow. It is in regard to men;

that is to say, the bodies of men, as seen in classical paintings or statues or as in my dream of Lieutenant Ormond. Diary, why in the world do men have *nipples,* like us? I have often wondered. It seems so contrary of the Creator to have given men something of no use to them whatever.

Back to bed.

&0 *Saturday, 7 January*

Devastation! Double devastation!

To-day being Saturday, we are at home to guests in the afternoon. Our drawing-room is well known and admired, and we are justifiably proud of it and like to shew it off at these gatherings. Especially well-spoken-of are such touches as our polished steel grate and marble chimney-piece and the glass over it, which has Sphinx heads on its pilasters, with an admixture of Greek ornament. Of course, it was Bonaparte's campaign in the Land of the Pyramids that heightened interest in Egyptian design — which may be seen again in the patterned paper on our drawing-room walls. The chairs and sofa are in black with gold lines; and these colours are repeated in the carpet. Sufficiently off to the side is our six-octave pianoforte, of rosewood, with brass inlays. It was made for us by Mr. Thomas Tomkinson when I was only a year old. Mamma played upon it (and still does), then Phoebe, and then I. I think I am the best. On the whole, an attractive room.

The guests were a varied assortment. Sir Oscar Fenton came to call, with his prodigiously fat wife. Lord Henry Stanton was also present, and bestowed upon us his latest garland of poems, a volume as thin as Sir Oscar's wife is fat. He is an incorrigible peripatetic, is young Lord Stanton, and is off to Italy in the morning. Mrs. Ridgely put in an appearance, with her twin daughters, Sarah and Clara, both with their noses haughtily in the air and cherry-red from colds. I have disliked the Ridgely sisters ever since we were children. One of them — I never knew which — glued together the pages of my favourite Mother Goose book, one day long ago when Mamma was entertaining Mrs. Ridgely at tea, and the young-

24

sters were sent off to play in the nursery. At any rate, that completes the roster of our guests to-day.

For, oh Diary — Lieutenant Ormond was notable only by his *absence!*

I tried to put on a brave face for our guests; I smiled; I played the pianoforte; I read aloud from Lord Stanton's new book — but inside I felt so empty, so cold, and my heart was a rock in my breast. Afterwards, I locked myself here in my bedroom and wept.

He had seemed to be so very favourably impressed by me. He had paid me such pretty compliments. He had made a point of asking when we were at home. And now, when the day arrives, *he* does not!

What am I to think? Is he all smiles and sugared words? Is he not, officer though he be, a man of action?

As if that were not enough, a disturbing letter arrived by post for me. Do disappointments never come singly?

The day after Christmas, I wrote to Phoebe. I miss her terribly, and did so most particularly at Christmas-time. I felt certain that she and her husband would visit us for the holiday, but it seems that he insisted they visit *his* family. And so I wrote to her, and this morning I received her reply. I will copy out a few extracts:

". . . But pray do not be in a great rush to marry, dearest Pam. What is called wedded bliss is held out to us as if it were a golden prize. We are put in a state of anticipation and expectation about it all our lives, until we are worked up to a veritable froth of eagerness, like exercised young mares. We can not wait to be wives.

"And when the time comes, we may find that we have been sold a hollow *bon-bon* — all sweet and pretty on the outside — empty within . . .

"It is not that Mr. Braithwaite is not a good man. He is very good. It may even be that he is *too* good. He is always pleasant and courteous; he never raises his voice; he treats me with the utmost respect. He engages me in conversation on a variety of subjects. We go riding. We play draughts together often of an evening. Sometimes I read aloud to him from a

25

book or periodical. Nor are we recluses: we pay visits to other houses, and his friends come here to tea and dinner — they are all good people. Our cook provides an excellent table.

"Perhaps that is all one should ask of marriage. It is not a bad life. Many would envy it, I suppose. But where, I wonder, is that *magical* element we were led to expect? Where are those transports of unparalleled rapture? . . .

"Oh, Pam, your sister is so *desperately unhappy!* And *afraid* of what is yet to come . . .

"If you answer this letter, write nothing of these matters. Restrict yourself to other things. Tell me what gifts you received for Christmas. Did my lace arrive in time? Mr. Braithwaite does not open my letters, I must assure you, for he is no tyrant; but he is so attentive and so interested in every article received by post, so full of polite questions, so eager to share *his* letters with *me,* that he will be hurt and puzzled — and, indeed, suspicious — if I do not shew him *your* letters . . .

"I beg you to say nothing of this to our parents. Let it be our secret. Do not leave this letter lying about. It would be best to burn it, I think . . . ."

Phoebe's letter now is blackening and curling in my fireplace. The words are gone but they ring in my mind and fill me with distress. Dear Phoebe unhappy? — *"desperately"* unhappy? Why should this be? What a terrible injustice that such an angel should be made unhappy. And what on earth can she have meant when she said that she is afraid of what is yet to come? Why *afraid?*

Mr. Braithwaite surely is not beastly to her; he can not beat her or be harsh and stern — she says he is courteous, pleasant, attentive, and never so much as raises his voice to her. Of what, then, can she be afraid?

The thing that perturbs me most is how our positions — Phoebe's and mine — are now as if reversed. Until but recently, it was I who poured out my heart to *her.* Now, she turns in her despair to *me,* as if I were the elder, wiser sister. But how can I comfort or advise her? I am such a goose! I know nothing of the world, or of men, or of marriage.

Even if I were as wise as Solomon, I could not give her solace, for she has forbidden me to refer to the very things that are tormenting her. I am thus censored and frustrated, knowing that my most intimate sisterly words will no doubt be read by the *pleasant, courteous* Mr. Braithwaite! Well, I say *damn* you, Mr. Braithwaite; and damn your pleasantness and courtesy; damn your goodness; damn your damned draughts and your teas and suppers and excellent table; damn everything that has made Phoebe unhappy and afraid!

And yet, knowing that I must answer her letter in some way, I have done so. It was not an easy thing, to write for her eyes as well as the eyes of her "too good" spouse, peering over her shoulder; to write and yet avoid all the very things I long to say, the questions I yearn to ask. Here is a copy of my response:

"Dearest Phoebe, —
"Your letter was delivered by this morning's post, and was most welcome. (Yes, the lace indeed arrived — did I not say? — and is beautiful. Thank you!)

"It was fascinating to hear all the delightful details of your life in Warwickshire: how you go riding, and entertain, etc. I wish I had your letter before me as I write, but that naughty Sophie got hold of it and tore it to tatters — I fear it is quite destroyed! No matter — I have all but committed it to memory and carry *every phrase in my heart.*

"How blissful and full your days must be, to hear you tell it. How wonderful to be a married lady. How fortunate to be the wife of a man like Mr. Braithwaite — for, from your description of his qualities, which amounts to a panegyric, he appears to be a paragon. Pray tell him that I remember him in my prayers.

"Your dear letter is evidence that real life is far different from the wild romances of our novelists, where everyone is woe-beset and tempest-tosst. I was reading one of them only to-day (such rubbish that I threw it on the fire), in which the heroine, a young matron married to a seeming *nonpareil* of a gentleman, lived in a condition of such dire despair that she was mortally 'afraid of what was yet to come.' A dramatic device, no doubt, designed to tempt readers to read on and on (but *this* reader resisted the temptation). One longed to ask the heroine: *why* are you afraid? of *what?* of *whom?* What manner of menace threatens you? One wondered, as one read, if the poor girl spoke literally, or was indulging in metaphor? *Answer me, girl!* I wanted to shout. *Answer or I shall go mad!* Such are the silly fancies we are stuffed with by scribblers.

"Mamma and I took tea with Lady Merlyngton on Wednesday. We met Fanny Trollope, the writing lady, and *I* was quite taken with a young lieutenant in the Light Dragoons, who has *broken my heart* by failing to appear at our at-home today. I am very piqued. Lord Henry S. paid a call, too, and presented us with a book of his verses. His lyrics are pretty, with pleasant rhymes and rhythms, but I think he is not a poet of the first rank. I do not believe that he could ever conceive of images like those of Mr. Wordsworth, flashes of inspiration such as —

> A perfect woman, nobly planned.

or —

> A spirit, yet a woman too!

or, in the pathetic vein —

> Maidens withering on the stalk.

And so many other lines from here and there in the mighty *oeuvre* of this great master of our time; such lines as —

> How does the meadow flower its bloom unfold?
> Because the lovely little flower is free
> Down to its root, and, in that freedom, bold.

and —

> Give all thou canst; high Heaven rejects the lore
> Of nicely calculated less or more.

"But goodness, how I prattle! This screed of mine has ceased to be a letter and has become an anthology! I do hope, by the way, that Mr. Braithwaite loves good poems, as you and I do? Pray answer this, and other questions, in your reply by *immediate* return of post.

> "I remain,
> "Your loving sister,
> "Pam"

I hope she will apply those lines of verse to herself. I hope she will know I mean to assure her that *she* is a perfect woman, nobly planned; a spirit, yet a woman, too. I want her to be, like Mr. Wordsworth's meadow flower, *free* down to her roots and, in that freedom, *bold*. I want her life to be something better than a nicely calculated less or more. She must not let herself become a maiden withering on the stalk — no, not my dear Phoebe!

Well, that has been my day, Diary. Disastrous from first to last. Sharp disappointment in my perfidious Dragoon; that upsetting, puzzling letter from Phoebe; the snuffling Misses Ridgely (from whom I hope I have not caught a cold); and — O lamentable lot of poor weak Woman! — this debilitating, inconvenient, cramping, aching, gory time of month that has given ironic new meaning to those lines penned by Mr. Tennyson a few years ago —

> "The curse has come upon me," cried
> The Lady of Shalott.

The laudanum has begun to have its effect on me. I feel languid and drowsy; I long for my cosy bed and a sleep I hope will be free of dreams — yes, even of pleasant ones.

ࣴ *Sunday, 8 January*

I have already told Mamma that I will not be accompanying her and Papa to church this morning, but mean to spend the whole day in bed. Mrs. Pruitt sent me up a bowl of barley soup, but I could take only a few sips. The rest I gave to Sophie, who lapped it up most gratefully. The dear little crea-

ture is curled up on my bed at this very moment, sound
asleep.

I had drifted into a doze, and when I awoke, Mamma was
sitting at my side. She and Papa had been home from church
for almost an hour, she told me.

"Whilst we were gone," she said, "a letter was delivered for
me, by hand." She shewed me the outside: I did not recognise
the writing. "The messenger," she continued, "according to
Rutledge, was a young soldier. The note is from that
Dragoons officer we met at Lady Merlyngton's last week."

My heart seemed to trip and stumble! I tried very hard to
contain my emotions. "Ah, yes," I said languidly, "I think I
remember him. He had red hair."

"No, that was Mr. O'Connor," said Mamma. "The lieutenant has dark brown hair and a moustache."

"Oh, *that* gentleman."

"Yes. Shall I read his note to you?"

I shrugged. "If you wish, Mamma. It is of no great matter
to me."

"Well," she said, rising, "if you are feeling tired and poorly,
perhaps I shan't bother you with such trifles. It is neither here
nor there."

"Still," I said quickly, "it is so horridly tiresome and boring
here in bed all day. Perhaps it would occupy my mind and
divert me from my ailments."

"Oh, it's only a very *short* note," said Mamma. "It would
not divert you for very long. Better I should read to you from
Mr. Cobbett's *Rural Rides?* Or perhaps from Mr. D'Israeli's
Curiosities of Literature."

"No, please —"

"But I thought you were particularly fond of those books?"

"I am —"

"And his son Benjamin, they say, may be elected to Parliament this year. Such a clever gentleman. The son, I mean. Although, of course, *both* are —"

"Mamma, *please* read Lieutenant Ormond's note!"

She smiled. "Ah, you remember his name now, do you?"

"You spoke it a moment ago."

"In point of fact," said Mamma, "I did not. But no matter." She opened the letter and read it to me:

"Dear Mrs. Summerfield, —

"I was so sorry to have missed your at-home yesterday afternoon, for I had been looking forward to it. Regimental duties required my attention, and, of course, these must take precedence over social activities, no matter how delightful or how eagerly anticipated.

"I will make every effort to visit you next Saturday, and sincerely hope that I shall be welcome at that time.

"Please convey my high regards to Mr. Summerfield, whom I hope to have the great pleasure of meeting, and to your daughter, whom I look forward to meeting again.

"Until Saturday, then, I remain,

"Truly,
"Giles Ormond
"Lieut., 18th Light Dragoons"

This time, my joy must have shown in my face, for Mamma said, "You are feeling better, I see?"

I could not dissemble. "Yes, Mamma, much better."

"No more laudanum?"

"Oh, no! Perhaps you could ask Mrs. Pruitt to send me up something."

"Broth? Milk toast?"

"Oh, not such pap as that! A cold game hen, I think, and one of her puddings and some hot muffins with butter; and do you think I might have a glass of claret?"

"A small glass, perhaps," said Mamma, leaving behind the note, which now resides under my night-gown, pressed to my heart.

P.S. A word about Rutledge, mentioned above in passing. He is our butler and has been with us longer than any of the other servants, even longer than Mrs. Pruitt (and both of them have been with us since long before I was born). He is about

Papa's age, or perhaps a year or so younger, and he stands very straight, and, although he is not as good-looking as Papa, he has a much fuller head of hair, once brown, quite grey by now. His nose is of generous proportions, and his eyes are heavy-lidded. He can be formidable when he frowns and is stern — I was frightened to death of him as a child, and can still hear his voice, saying, "Miss Pamela, your parents will hear of this," when I'd done something naughty. He is the only servant who calls me Miss Pamela — all the others call me Miss Pam. He smiles *very* infrequently, but sometimes his eyes crinkle at the corners in a decidedly human way, and it is then that I know he is amused.

Monday, 9 January

I am feeling so much better.

But I confess that I would feel even better if Lieutenant Ormond's note had contained a warmer reference to me. I have read it over many times since yesterday and find it less satisfactory each time. He mentions me only at the very last, *after* asking that his regards be conveyed to Papa, almost as an afterthought: ". . . and to your daughter, whom I look forward to meeting again." Does he truly look forward to meeting me again, or is that merely an empty turn of phrase? He could have said, ". . . and *most especially* to your daughter" or "look forward *with great pleasure* to meeting again" — or, better still, both. But he did not.

Am I making too much of a hastily dashed-off note, written by a busy officer? Is his reticence no more than proof that he is extremely proper and well-brought-up? I realise, of course, that it would have been most unseemly for him to have addressed a letter directly to me, nor should I have expected that. It would have smacked too much of the rake.

The word "rake" puts the Duke of Cumberland in my mind again. I remember an incident some five years old or less, involving two young sisters with the curious surname of Perfect, who, whilst strolling along a path by the Thames near their home at Hammersmith, were frightened out of their wits and nearly run down by a galloping horse. The rider, who merely laughed at their fear, was Cumberland, although it was later given out that it had been not the Duke but one of his equerries. *The Times* printed a poem by Mr. Tom Moore which began, "The Duke is the lad to frighten a lass," and which ended:

> And as no nymph is
> Fond of a grim phiz,
> Fly, ye new married,
> For crowds have miscarried
> At sight of this dreary Duke.

Last season, the day after we heard *Lucia,* Hester (the head parlour-maid) was in my bedroom, and I drew her out on the subject of the dreary Duke. Hester is a cornucopia of information, particularly of the scandalous variety, and I knew that she would be my best source.

"The Duke of Cumberland!" said Hester, her eyes going wide. Her plump little figure quivered all over, like a dish of aspic. She made a large intake of breath. "Oh, Miss Pam, that gentleman, some say, is the most hated man in England — and the most feared."

"But what has he done to deserve such a reputation?"

"Dreadful crimes, they say. Murdered his valet in a fit of rage. And he's said to have been *too fond* of one of his sisters, if you catch my meaning."

"How horrible! Are you sure?"

"It's what I've heard, Miss."

"Only rumour, then."

She nodded, and resumed her gossip with exuberance. "His wife is no better, I've been told."

I recollected the lady who sat next to the Duke in the box at the Opera. "And what of her?" I asked.

"Well," Hester said in a rush, "she's been married I don't know *how* many times. Prince Louis of Prussia first. When he died, the Duke of Cambridge courted her and asked her to marry him, and she accepted, but at the very last moment she *jilted* him! Made the poor Duke that unhappy, it did. And then she married the Prince of Solms-Braunfels, in *secret*. He died,

33

too. They *do* say that one of her husbands, I'm not sure which, was *helped* into his grave, so to speak, by Her Nibs."

"You don't mean to say that she *murdered* him!"

"I only tell you what I've heard, Miss Pam. But they're well matched, the pair of 'em. Like to like, you might say."

"Good gracious! I thought Cumberland was no more than a bit of a rake."

"It gives you a turn, Miss, when you think that just *one* delicate life stands between him and the throne."

"Princess Victoria."

"Exactly, Miss. And don't he know it! They say he was dining with his brother the King, and after proposing the King's health, he followed it up with another toast: 'The King's heir, and may God bless him.' Oooh, His Majesty was *that* angry, the way I heard it. 'The King's heir, God bless *her,*' he said."

"Amen to that," I remarked.

"Yes, Miss, but —"

"But what?"

"Well, Miss, the Princess ain't in the best of health, they say."

"Nonsense. She's as sound as a horse."

"She's had her ailments, God bless her. Her feet, for one thing."

"What's wrong with her feet?"

"Cold as ice all the time, they say, and when she was just a little bit of a girl, they thought she'd never be able to walk on 'em. And then there was that bilious fever she was took with last year, or the year before, in Ramsgate. Pulse of a hundred and thirty, as I heard it. Her poor mother was in a panic."

"But she recovered."

"Yes, Miss. Will there be anything further?"

"Thank you, Hester, no. That will be all."

Ever since that day, I have had long thoughts about the Princess and her health. Phoebe had once said that Sir John Conroy was the perpetrator of those rumours; that it was to his advantage to have the Princess thought too ill to reign; for then, upon the death of the King, the Princess's mother, the Duchess of Kent, would almost surely be made Regent —

34

which would mean that Conroy, her adviser (and, it is hinted, somewhat more) would, in effect, be the King of England.

That would be a calamity, indeed; but not so great a calamity as it would be for the crown to sit on the head of the Duke of Cumberland.

ℰ Tuesday, 10 January

"It would not necessarily be a calamity," Papa said at dinner this evening when, purely to stimulate conversation, I brought up that hypothetical possibility.

He went on, between bites of beef: "A British sovereign must abide by the laws and limitations of our custom, our tradition. He — or she — must reign as a constitutional monarch. Remember, Princess, that we have a Parliament, a Prime Minister, and all manner of other checks and balances. Any sovereigns who have tried to reign as absolute monarchs have not been tolerated. They have been forced from the throne. I speak, of course, of relatively modern times, not of antiquity."

"Indeed," I interjected, "one might say that, in many ways, *antiquity* and *iniquity* are synonymous." (Papa smiled at my *bon mot*.)

"Do not forget," he continued, "that a monarch has various advisers. These are learned men, of much experience and skill, capable of compensating for any lacks in the monarch's training or capacities."

"But can not advisers sometimes give bad advice? What about Ethelred? I read recently that it is an error to call him 'The Unready.' He was known as the *unræd*, which in Saxon means 'ill advised.' "

"Our little scholar," Papa said, with another smile. "Ethelred lived a very long time ago, in what was almost a different world. I am not saying that everybody in our Government is perfect. It is made up of men, and men have failings. But, for the most part, they are men of sense and conscience and devotion to duty, and they are more than a match for any incompetent or unsavoury monarch."

35

I persisted. "But that is like saying it makes no difference who sits on the throne."

"In some ways, that is true."

"A man, a woman, old, young, brilliant, stupid, moral, immoral — it is all the same, then?"

"No, not exactly . . ."

"Alfred the Great was no better than horrid old King John or Richard the Third?"

"That was another age. In our own time, a John or a Richard would be forced to relinquish the crown. On the other hand, the brilliance and compassion of a genius such as Alfred would leave its mark. His influence would be felt."

"Despite the constraints of Parliament and the Ministers?"

"Yes."

Rutledge served the sweet. After a moment, Mamma said, "There does appear to be a contradiction in what you say, Wilfrid."

"I see none," Papa replied.

"If the bad influence of a John or a Richard — or a Cumberland, as Pam has suggested — can be checked by our constitutional form of government, why may not the *good* influence of an Alfred also be held in check, and not permitted to flower fully? A *good* absolute monarch could surely accomplish more in the way of humanitarian reform, let us say, if he were allowed to rule unhampered."

"My dear," Papa said with a tolerant chuckle, "the Government do not wish to hamper *good,* only evil and incompetency."

I quickly asked, "Can you be sure of that, Papa?"

"It is common sense," he said patiently. "What kind of government would deliberately wish evil to flourish?"

"An evil government," I replied.

"Balderdash!"

"Perhaps," I added, "we should first define evil."

"Perhaps," he said, "we should enjoy our coffee in the drawing-room and converse on subjects which you are better equipped to understand."

"Yes, Papa," I said, meekly.

Papa is very wise and a dear; but when he sees that he is in danger of losing an argument, he usually changes the subject.

I suppose that may, in part, explain why he is such a successful man.

The weather was warmer to-day, but the sky was overcast.

It was one week ago to-day that I met Lieutenant Ormond. Can it have been truly only one short week? It seems much longer. I must try to put him out of my thoughts; yet that will be an act of insurmountable difficulty, I know. I shall see him again, the day after the day *after* to-morrow. Till then, I must rein in my impatience.

To occupy my mind, I have been playing with the pack of *tarot* cards which Aunt Esmie sent me from the Cotswolds as a Christmas gift. She is Mamma's eldest sister, almost seventy by now, and a widow. She married a man named Cooper, who, some say, was part gipsy. "It is a common name among English gipsies," Mamma once told me, "and he *was* very dark-complexioned." He died before I was born.

Aunt Esmie sometimes likes to pretend that she is a witch, but Mamma always scolds her at such times for "putting nonsensical ideas into the child's head." I know, of course, that my aunt is not truly a witch; and I am glad that she is not, for I should then liken her to the witches in *Macbeth,* who are so evil and repulsive. Besides, it is decidedly grim to think that it was less than eleven years before I was born — in October of 1808 — that the last punishment for witchcraft was administered in England. How shudderingly primitive, and *recent,* that seems.

The *tarot* cards are very old and quite beautiful. Each is a little work of art, expertly drawn and coloured in a quaint, archaic style. In her most fascinating letter, which accompanied the cards, Aunt Esmie says they had belonged to the late Mr. Cooper, handed down to him by his mother. "They were in his family for how many generations the dear Lord only knows," my aunt writes, "and, in view of the fact that Mr. Cooper and I did not have progeny, I wish *you* to have them, and to pass them on to your own first-born." She then explains the meanings of the cards and how one is to read them.

The remainder of her letter is of great interest to me, and I will copy it out here:

"The *tarot* is rich in mysteries, my dear Pamela, and the greatest of these is its source, which is unknown. Throughout the centuries, men have striven zealously to trace it to its beginnings, but the secret has always eluded mortal quest, remaining hidden in the thick shadows of impenetrable antiqunity. The very word '*tarot*' defies etymological analysis and is, to this day, inexplicable.

"The *tarot,* as you see, is a pack of 78 cards, 22 of which represent the Greater Arcana, the remaining 56 forming the Lesser Arcana. These lesser cards are the ancestors of the common playing cards we use to-day; our King, Queen, and Knave may be found there, in addition to a Knight, which has disappeared from modern playing-cards. The Coins, or Pentacles, of the *tarot* have been elevated into our Diamonds; the Wands, or Cudgels, have become Clubs; the Swords have become lowly Spades (reminiscent of the Biblical injunction to beat our swords into ploughshares); while the suit known as Cups has become — in a puzzling change typical of the *tarot*'s mysteries — Hearts.

"But the cards which have truly captured the imaginations of men are those of the Greater Arcana. For untold generations, these two-and-twenty evocative, disturbing, cryptic little pictures have tempted us with the suspicion that they contain — in symbolic, allegorical form — the inmost secrets of life, love, destiny and death.

"The cards of the Greater Arcana picture all of life. They show us an assortment of human characters: The Pope, The High Priestess, The Emperor, The Empress, The Magician, The Hermit. They show us, also, grim allegorical personages, The Devil and Death. The cardinal virtues of Justice, Strength, and Temperance are depicted, and the astronomical elements of The Sun, The Moon, The Star. Two of the cards relate to fatality in human life: The Lovers and The Wheel of Fortune. Four more depict elements of cosmic fatality: The Chariot, The Judgment, The World, The House of God (sometimes known as The Lightning-Struck Tower, which many assume to be the Tower of Babel). The twenty-second and last card of the Greater Arcana is unnumbered, and is called The Fool.

"I have singled out one card for your special attention, Pamela. It is the twelfth card, the strangest of all, The Hanged Man. Its meaning is obscure, buffeted by controversy. In most versions of the *tarot,* he hangs by one foot from a cross or gibbet, head down, not dead but alive, his face usually expressionless, sometimes suffering, but in some *tarots* almost blissful. In at least one version, his head is surrounded by a glowing nimbus, much like a halo. In another version, his hands are holding two cloth sacks (do they contain money or something else?). One *tarot* scholar insisted that The Hanged Man only *appears* to be hanging because the card has traditionally but erroneously been held upside down: in reality, he is standing on one foot, and the other foot is shewn in mid-air whilst the man carefully considers whether or not he should take the next step.

"Although *tarot* cards can be used like any other cards to play mundane games of chance, their true worth is seen in the art of cartomancy, whereby gifted persons, attuned to the mysteries, may divine the course of future happenings. A famous cartomancer of our own time is Mlle. Le Normand, twice imprisoned by the brute Bonaparte, who used the *tarot* to foretell the Empress Josephine's divorce. Josephine said of this divination, 'It told me that from the moment Napoleon left me, he would cease to be happy.'

"Unlike tea-leaves, the crystal ball, common playing-cards, or other aids to prophecy, the *tarot* is steeped in, among other things, a certain fleshliness, a subtle, understated physical quality. Without being overtly erotic, undraped male and female figures, their privates unhidden, are pictured in many versions of the cards called The Lovers, The Devil, The Star, Judgement, The World. The Ace of Wands is sometimes quite shockingly obvious in its symbolism, and among the meanings attributed to it are virility, creation, and birth.

"We will never know when or where the *tarot* was born, but its devotés are generally agreed that it will never die. It must not be dismissed as a fad, for the *tarot* has survived the shifts of fashion, the scorn of sceptics, the persecution of Church and State, often content to remain in the background while the *simooms* of controversy or cynicism rage, keeping its secrets safe, emerging again whenever we have most need of it.

"Enjoy this little gift, dear Pam, and from time to time remember —

"Your loving aunt,
"Esmeralda Cooper"

How deliciously *sinister* Aunt Esmie makes the *tarot* sound! And how naughty (I am thinking of the "fleshliness" she mentions, and her talk of "privates"). She has always been the most outspoken of all my relations, and for that reason I suspect that some of them do not approve of her.

But I have always loved her best of all my aunties.

A sharp drop in temperature to-day, but fine and cloudless.

ഇ *Thursday, 12 January*

No, Diary, I have not forgotten Phoebe; nor can I erase from my memory the despairing outcry in her recent letter. You are the only one to whom I can speak of it, for she forbade me to say a thing to Mamma and Papa.

I do not pretend to be a fortune-teller (despite my *tarot* cards!), but I have to confess to you that I was not surprised to learn that she was unhappy in marriage. I had always thought Mr. Braithwaite to be all wrong for her, long before the wedding took place. I never understood — still do not understand — why on earth she married him.

He had paid court to her for quite some time, coming to our at-homes, etc. I always thought him to be a singularly bloodless piece of goods, and certainly not a man to stir the heart of a girl, although I suppose he has regular features, no outstanding blemishes one can see, and he can not, with justice, be called ugly.

The most curious thing is that, for some time, I had suspected Phoebe of being in love. I would come upon her, in her bedroom or just returned from a shopping afternoon, and find her fairly *glowing* with happiness. The rose would be in her cheek, and her eyes would sparkle like our New Year's champagne. I have read enough novels and poetry to form the assumption that she had been seeing somebody she deeply adored.

I could not believe that the "somebody" was Mr. Braithwaite. If it was indeed he, then Phoebe would have had to be the greatest actress of our age, a dissembler to put even the late Mrs. Siddons in the shade. For those shining eyes and heightened colour were never to be seen in her face whilst she was pouring tea for Mr. Braithwaite or passing him the cake. She was courteous to him; no more; and she did not laugh at his jokes, because he did not tell any. Not what I would call jokes, at any rate; academic parodies, full of Latin and Greek, which would occasionally cause Papa to smile politely.

And then — suddenly — for seemingly no reason —Phoebe accepted him, on what must have been his fourth or fifth offer of marriage. A lightning-bolt could not have stunned me more. *Phoebe?* To marry Mr. *Braithwaite?* "For Heaven's sake, *why?"* I asked her.

"He is an excellent match," she said.

"But — but — he's so stale, flat, and unprofitable!" I wailed, remembering my *Hamlet.*

"Hardly unprofitable," replied Phoebe, "for he is the heir to a considerable estate, which includes a magnificent mansion in Warwickshire."

"You cannot *love* him, surely!"

"I admire and respect him. Love is a plant which grows, given proper care and nurturing."

"That's something you've heard from *him!* It sounds exactly like him. It does not sound like you."

"Pam, sweet, do not carry on so. Remember, he is my husband-to-be. You must not speak ill of him. I can not allow it."

"Oh, Phoebe, Phoebe!" I broke into tears. "I simply don't *know* you any more!"

Mr. Braithwaite had, at first, been of the opinion that a long engagement was desirable (no ardent lover would have held such an opinion!); but Phoebe hinted to him that a protracted delay in the nuptials might afford her the opportunity to change her mind — and this caused a sudden *volte-face* in his thinking.

I was her bridesmaid — I caught the flung bouquet — but nothing could make me feel happy on the day of that wedding. Not even the joyous, lively wedding march which followed the ceremony lifted my spirits (the organist played the new music Mr. Mendelssohn composed for *A Midsummer Night's Dream*). I think that Phoebe was not happy, either, although she smiled constantly, too constantly: it was a fixed grimace that never wavered.

And so, when that terrible letter of hers arrived on Saturday last, it only confirmed the suspicions of my heart. She had made a dreadful mistake, and now she profoundly regrets it.

This afternoon, I had my singing lesson with Signor Olivo. We had missed our lessons for the past few weeks, because he had made a trip to Italy, to spend the holiday with his mother. He did not appreciate the light snow that fell to-day; but, then, he always complains of our English weather, comparing it unfavourably with that of his sunny homeland.

I told him that I should perish if he did not bring me the *Lucia* score to play and sing. He said he would do so in the near future, but that in the mean time we must make do with a little Bellini: "From-a *Norma,* no? The *bellissima* duet 'Mira, o Norma.' "

"Oh, Signore, have you forgotten? Phoebe is no longer here to sing with me."

He slapped his brow with the palm of his hand — so hard that I feared the oil might fly in droplets from his hair. "*Si!* I forget! *Stupido!* The *sorella,* she is-a get married. *Ebben* — then I, Olivo, will sing-a with you."

I tittered. "But the duet is for two sopranos, Signore!"

He shut his eyes and haughtily drew himself up to his full height (about five feet, four inches, I should judge), and informed me that anything which can be sung by a soprano can be sung by a tenor. And, indeed, he is a very able tenor who has appeared at the Opera, albeit in minor *rôles*. So we sang the duet, with Signor Olivo replacing Phoebe.

(Ah, Phoebe, if he could but replace you in all other ways, as well!)

꩜ *Friday, 13 January*

I am dashing off these few lines immediately upon waking. If I were superstitious, I should fear some frightful blow to fall, for it is Friday the 13th, day of evil omen. But what could have been worse than receiving that heart-breaking letter from Phoebe on the same day as my heart had already been broken by Lieutenant Ormond? And yet those things happened on Saturday the 7th.

Of course, I know I am tempting Fate by saying "what could have been worse?" The blackest day can seem, from the bitter vantage point of a later, blacker day, to have been almost sunny. When tragedy strikes, we wish to turn back the clock to one day, one hour, one *minute* prior to the calamity; for *then,* we tell ourselves, we were happy! But were we truly happy in that earlier time? Were we not, perhaps, afflicted by vexations and melancholy that seemed insupportable?

This day of evil omen is still young. Perhaps it will, indeed, bring terrible tidings.

In the mean while: shopping with Mamma. More to be added later.

Mlle. La Grange came to dress my hair this afternoon.

"I have been giving much thought to the subject of ear-scratching," I told her, not without a dash of mischief.

"Ah, oui?"

"But it seems to me, in my experience, that what you call *le plaisir* is less important to women than to men. Is it possible for it to be less important and yet of greater intensity? Is that not a contradiction?"

"Oui, Miss. It is a, how you say, paradox. But life is full of such paradoxes, no?"

"I have observed men at teas and balls and parties of all kinds. Even the politest of them, if they have red blood in their veins, not milk-and-water, fairly *devour* a pretty woman with their eyes. To stand before such eyes is like standing before an open grate, singed by the heat of the flame."

"*Oui, c'est vrai!*" Mlle. La Grange agreed, with a smile.

"Women are not like that, as a rule. We are more passive. I have seen male dogs staring at little Sophie through the garden windows downstairs. The look in their eyes is the same. But I have never known female dogs or cats to stare with the same fixity at males. It is so curious that human males and females should comport themselves in the same manner as those dear, dumb little beasts. Am I talking nonsense, Mam'selle?"

"No, Miss, what you say is *la verité*. It is all part of *la nature*."

"Then Nature is a very odd lady. Why should the initiative be so one-sided? How did Mr. Keats put it? — 'What men or gods are these? What maidens loth? What mad pursuit? What struggle to escape?' *Why* should maidens be loth, Mam'selle? *Why* should we struggle to escape — if, as you say, *le plaisir* is greater for us?"

Mlle. La Grange shook her head and waved the comb in an eloquent gesture of philosophical acceptance that seemed very French. "*Je ne sais pas,*" she confessed, with a gentle sigh.

"But," she added a moment later, "there is an old French saying. In English, it would be said something like 'The man, he offers love in exchange for *le plaisir*. The woman, she offers *le plaisir* in exchange for love.' "

"Very nicely put," I said. "But it does not really explain anything. Why should not men and women offer each other love for love — or *le plaisir* for *le plaisir?* That would seem to be much more sensible, would it not?"

"*Oh, la, la!*" responded Mam'selle with a tinkle of laughter. "Of all the things in this world, Miss, do you expect of *l'amour* that it be SENSIBLE???" (She uttered the word in capital letters; and I have written it so.)

"Perhaps not," I said. "But I don't see why love should not proceed along reasonable lines, like anything else. And you French are supposed to be such practitioners of *logique!*"

She laughed again. "Not when we are in love. Then, it is: *Logique, adieu!*" She kissed her finger-tips, as if bidding a lover farewell.

I suppose that says it well enough — *Logique, adieu!* It is even more succinct than that jewel of a *pensée* by Mlle. La Grange's illustrious compatriot M. Pascal — *Le cœur a ses raisons que la raison ne connaît point.* The heart has its reasons, which reason knows naught of.

And my own heart, throwing reason and logic to the winds, is beating quicker at this very moment, as night draws on and the morrow approaches ever nearer. Each hour, each minute, brings Saturday closer, brings Lieutenant Ormond closer. When I sleep to-night, shall I dream of him again? Will he be *au naturel,* as before? I suppose he will not dream of me. Or perhaps he will? Indeed, I *hope* he will. Does he wear a nightcap when he sleeps? Does he keep his moustache tidy during the night in one of those funny little cloth devices such as Papa uses?

Until to-morrow, Diary — *demain, domani, mañana, morgen!* (You see how silly are the bugbears of superstition? Friday the 13th has come and gone, bringing no evil with it.)

ᘒ *Saturday, 14 January*

This morning, before breakfast, I asked Mamma's maid to draw a hot tub for me. I poured almost half a bottle of lavender water into it, lowered myself cautiously into the steaming water — it was close to scalding! — and, with sponge and soap tablet, scrubbed myself all over for fully half an hour, till I was pink as a cherub from top to toe. (I was careful not to disturb Mlle. La Grange's *coiffure* during these ablutions.) Then I splashed more lavender water all over my body — *everywhere.* Finally, I wrapped myself in the yellow silk dressing-gown Mamma gave me for Christmas, and sat here at my desk to write.

But I shall not write for long, because I am too excited, too full of anticipation. To-day — unless he is *again* occupied with regimental duties — Lieutenant Ormond will be in this very house!

I shall report *all.*

You are eager to know, dear Diary, about our at-home this afternoon. And so you shall.

I made particularly sure to put on my best attire: my new gown of delicate white net, with flounces edged in pink, over white satin. Cut rather low in front, to make the most of my best features: my rounded bosom and my long neck ("Like a giraffe's," I once lamented. "Like a swan's," said Papa).

Our guests, arriving singly or in pairs, presented themselves in the following order:

Lord and Lady Merlyngton. She, you have already met, Diary. He is a man of perhaps sixty years, with a ruddy face, a full beard as white as a fresh snow-fall, and no hair at all. The top of his shiny, rosy head *gleams* like a lamp. He calls me his dear girl, or gel — "m' d' gel" is the way it sounds. I think he is a pompous person, but I do not find him absolutely loathsome.

Mrs. Trollope arrived next, without her son. She told more amusing anecdotes about life in the United States. It sounds like a positively awful place. I think I should not like it at all.

Mr. Cargrave paid a short call, *with* his son, Robert, who is only a little boy but quite charming and very bright. He told me he intends to be a man of medicine, like his father.

Mr. and Mrs. Alfred Randall put in an appearance. He is a business associate of Papa's. Their daughter accompanied them, a little girl, even younger than Master Cargrave. I think her name is Maude. A pretty little thing but shy.

The last to arrive — almost as if he were teasing me — was . . . Yes! Giles Ormond! More handsome even than I had remembered! But a lieutenant no more.

Noting his new braid, I congratulated him. "I see I must call you Captain Ormond now."

"I should much prefer that you call me Giles," he said, with the most heart-melting smile imaginable.

"Are you as bold as this on the field of battle?"

"I hope I shall be, whenever my King calls me into action."

"Well said, sir," I replied.

"I hope that you have been well, Miss Summerfield?"

"Yes, thank you. And you?"

"Well enough, but I very nearly did not arrive here this afternoon, because of an unpleasant encounter."

"Indeed!" I responded, my curiosity piqued. Remembering my duties, I asked him if he would take tea or sherry.

"Sherry," he said, "unless there is something stronger to be had."

"I'm afraid Mamma keeps the whisky under lock and key in the tantalus until later in the day. If you wish, I could risk her wrath and ask her to break the rule."

"Pray don't," he said, with a laugh. "As a soldier, I have a healthy regard for rules and regulations. Sherry will do very nicely."

I had one of the maids bring him a glass, asking, "What was this unpleasant encounter?"

"I dropped by my father's club," he said, "just to pay my respects to the old gentleman, and I ran into that chap O'Connor. You met him at Lady Merlyngton's. He's not a member, thank God; he was there as somebody's guest. I couldn't cut him dead, of course — I had to be civil — so I said how-de-do, and before I knew it, I was engaged in a conversation with him."

"That doesn't seem to be so terribly unpleasant," I said.

"It didn't become so until, for some reason, O'Connor remarked upon what he called the military mentality. 'Do you know why men go to war, Ormond?' he asked me, and then answered his own question: 'Because the women are watching.' "

"Ah! And that set you off."

"No, I let that go by. It was, after all, my father's club, and I had to be on my best behaviour . . ."

By this time, our other guests had turned in our direction and were listening to Captain Ormond with unconcealed interest:

"The burthen of O'Connor's harangue was along these lines," he continued. "I'll not attempt to reproduce his brogue, however. 'The Duke of Cumberland's regiment, the Fifteenth Dragoons, is the *only* one in which picketing is still practised.' "

"Picketing?" I enquired.

"A punishment," Captain Ormond explained. "A chap's forced to balance himself, on one foot, on the end of a stake driven into the ground."

"How unpleasant," I said. "For how long?"

"Quite long, sometimes. Then O'Connor said, 'And consider Cumberland's brother, the late Duke of Kent —' Well, I can tell you that I was not prepared to hear any disrespect towards the father of the lady who'll one day be our Queen! 'What about the Duke of Kent?' I asked. 'He was the incarnation of the military mind,' O'Connor answered. 'They were obliged to ship him out to Canada because he had been so brutal to the men under his command at Gibraltar. Disgraced himself over there, too, by his incompetence. And when they put him in charge of Gibraltar again, he was such a despot that he provoked a mutiny.'

"I reminded O'Connor that the Gibraltar garrison at that time had been allowed to get completely out of hand, and stern measures were required. 'Stern, perhaps,' he replied, 'but not fiendish. Kent's idea of discipline was the horsewhip.' I immediately said, 'Some men deserve to be horsewhipped' — and I glared straight at *him* as I said it! But he went right on:

" 'Do they deserve a hundred lashes, for trifling offenses? Have you ever *seen* a man's back after it's been cut by the cat a hundred times, Ormond? It's not a pleasant afternoon's caning by the head-master! And that was the *least* number of lashes ordered by Kent. He ordered floggings of four hundred, five hundred, *seven hundred* lashes. One poor wretch, who couldn't bear the severity of Kent's tyranny, deserted. But Kent tracked him down — he led the hunting-party himself, I need hardly tell you — and when he dragged the man back to the garrison, he ordered the *maximum* number of lashes permitted under the infinite mercy of the Mutiny Act. Are you cognisant of that fine humanitarian bit of legislature, Ormond? Do you know where it draws a line? It is very tender-hearted; it coddles the mutinous malcontents; it says we may *not* sentence a man to a thousand lashes. How kind! How Christian! And so, the Duke of Kent — that good soldier, that observer of the letter of the military law — ordered the deserter to receive *nine hundred and ninety-nine lashes!* The Duke watched every single one of them. Can you imagine the blood, the flayed skin, the flesh hanging in red strips from the white bone? Can you imagine the *screams?* That was Kent's idea of entertainment. What price

48

Nero, eh? The miracle is that the man lived. Another one did not: soon after, a Sergeant Armstrong died under the lash, and Kent was relieved of all active military employment. He was, however, promoted to Field Marshal. That, my dear Ormond, is the military mentality: not only the demon-mind of Kent, but the maggoty brains of his imbecile superiors, who granted him a *promotion,* rather than giving him a taste of his own medicine, to the tune of nine hundred and ninety-nine! And *that* was the remarkable swine who spawned the next sovereign of England!' "

Lord Merlyngton grew quite purple to hear this. "Outrageous!" he said. "The fellow sounds like one of these Nihilists. What's his name, d'you say? O'Connor? Hmph! Small wonder! Irish! Rebellious lot, all of 'em."

Captain Ormond concluded his story: "I could have struck the fellow. Under other circumstances, in another place, I should have done so. But I merely said, 'You are a guest in this club, sir. So am I. Propriety forbids my responding to you as I should like. But if you would care to repeat your remarks about our Princess and her father elsewhere, I should be happy to oblige you with the answer you deserve.' "

"Oh, very good, lad, very good!" said Lord Merlyngton.

"And what did he say to that?" I asked.

"He laughed," said Captain Ormond. "He simply laughed. And then he said, 'I am not a cow, Ormond. I don't chew me cud twice.' And he walked out!"

"Bounder!" Lord Merlyngton said, with a snort.

"Not a cow, perhaps, but a coward," said Mrs. Trollope. There was general appreciation of her witticism.

Well, Diary, it is late and I am tired — deliciously tired. I can barely hold the pen. I must go to bed and dream of *Giles.* (I may use that name to *you,* but to him I dare not . . . yet!)

ஐ *Sunday, 15 January*

I am, at this moment, returned from church with Mamma and Papa. I think I can be said to be a person who is tolerably devout — certainly, I think many passages in Scripture absolutely exciting, inspiring, and testimony to the heights the human spirit can attain — but why do I find Sunday worship so tiresome? Is it some lack in me, some want of piety? Why do clergymen seem to obey a kind of Eleventh Commandment: Thou Shalt Be Dry as Dust? Henceforth, Diary, you may assume that I attend church on Sundays unless I inform you to the contrary; but I shall not record the fact except in the event that I find it uncommonly uplifting. (He Who sees into our hearts, and over my shoulder as I write this, knows I mean no disrespect to *Him*.)

What a rude and ungentlemanly person is that Mr. O'Connor! And how proud I am of my Giles, who stood up to the rogue in that manner, and figuratively flung the gauntlet in his face. And what a craven churl was Mr. O'Connor to ignore the challenge and slink away.

Notwithstanding these feelings of mine, I can not but wonder if there was any substance to his *tirade* on the theme of the Duke of Kent. If even half of it — a tenth of it — was true, then it must "give us pause," as Shakespere says. It throws a strong, harsh light on the Princess's father. Kent's brother, Cumberland, is said to be a monster (if Hester is to be believed). Another brother, Wellington, has been called a damned millstone around the neck of the Government. Yet another, the Duke of York, had a mistress, Hester told me, who sold Army commissions and promotions with the full complicity of the Duke. Still another, Cambridge, while not evil, seems to be an idle fellow who spends his time playing the violin and singing. They say he wears a blond wig. He is not a rake, but one might almost wish he were, for at least that would be manly: he has never married and has never kept a mistress. They are a sorry lot, those sons of George III. Even the best of them, our beloved King, sired no less than *ten* children out of wedlock when he was still the Duke of Clarence, so he can not be said to be moderate in such matters. And all those royal Dukes are closely related to the Princess. One was her father, and the rest are her uncles.

Is profligacy a thing of the blood? Can it be handed down, father to son — or even father to daughter? Could it be that Victoria nurtures deep in her soul a dormant ember of lust and cruelty that might be fanned into life by her accession to the throne, and burst into raging, all-consuming flame, transforming her into a Messalina?

Our British Empire has been compared, in some respects, with that of the Romans, but only as regards our wide-spread influence and power. Can there be other resemblances as well? The Duke of Cumberland appears to have been modelled after Caligula. And of the Duke of Kent, who watched men tortured to death, Mr. O'Connor said, "What price Nero?"

Of course, he is an unscrupulous journalist of the inflammatory school and must not be taken seriously. "I knew he was no gentleman," Giles said yesterday, "but I thought he was, at least, a man. And had he agreed to meet me, like a man, I should have given him the sorest skin of bones in London!"

֍ *Monday, 16 January*

A note from Phoebe to-day, quite short:

"Dearest Pam, —

"A line or two, merely to thank you for the *clever* and *poetic* letter, which Mr. Braithwaite enjoyed every bit as much as I did; or perhaps I enjoyed it more than he simply because I know you better and can almost hear your voice and *read your thoughts* in every line. It is good to have an *understanding* sister who shares my deepest feelings, even though we are now separated by distance. Would we could play our innocent nursery games again! Do you recollect the puzzles and conundrums we were taught by our governess, Miss Newsome, as well as those simpler pastimes we learnt from Nurse?

"*Phoebe remembers every game, Newsome's and Nurse's, tenderly.*

"With fondest affection,
"Phoebe"

It is not like Phoebe to write such a short letter. I can think only that the ubiquitous Mr. Braithwaite was standing over her as she wrote. But, at least, she has managed to convey to me that she grasped the veiled meanings of my letter and of those lines of poetry embedded in it. The underlined words in her first paragraph confirm that, and shew her to be no less clever than I.

But there is such a feeling of desperate yearning in her final sentence, so poignantly underlined, as if it were an outcry. No married lady should live a life so empty of joy that she yearns, with such piteous urgency, for the games of her childhood.

I do not know how to answer her. Everything I say must be set down with indirection, to hoodwink the hawkish eyes of Mr. Braithwaite. I must become another Bowdler, and Bowdler-ise my own intimate letters to my own dear sister — how ignominious! It was hateful enough for silly old Dr. Bowdler to chop away at his betters, such as Shakespere, "to exclude whatever is unfit to be read aloud by a gentleman to a company of ladies" (I recall how my dear Uncle Roger laughed when he read to me that pompous phrase, and urged me to "take Shakespere neat or not at all"); but for a private correspondence between sisters to be subjected to such indignity — oh, it is insufferable!

What shall I write? "Yours received and contents noted?" That is virtually all I *may* write!

More and more, Diary, I see hypocrisy all about me. Phoebe must pretend to be happy. I must pretend — in my letters, at least — to believe her. I may not speak of her sadness to our parents. I am urged to burn her letters. Mendacity and hypocrisy are seen in even the most common customs of our society. A caller is announced. We do not wish to receive him. Our servant is instructed to say that we are "not at home." Who is deceived by this? No one. It is a lie which the caller *knows* to be a lie; but he pretends to believe it, thus piling lie upon lie, and compounding the hypocrisy. Or, if we feel obliged to receive the uninvited caller, we greet him with a different lie: "I am glad to see you." Papa — and most other men of commerce — sign their letters "Your servant" or "Your obedient servant" or even "Your obedient and most humble servant," meaning not a scrap of it. "Thank you for the lovely book of sermons," I tell Willy at Christmas-time, although he and I *both* know that I will never so much as open the dreary volume. "What a pretty frock!" I say to one of the Ridgely girls, thinking, "What a frump she is!" Mamma says to a lady of her own age, "You grow younger every day." To an ill or even dying friend, we say — in the most cruel and ineffectual lie of all — "How fit you look!"

And this domestic hypocrisy is writ large in the greater world that surrounds us:

Yesterday, as we stood outside the church, exchanging pleasantries with Lord and Lady Merlyngton, this general hypocrisy struck me forcefully. Lady M. was remarking upon the Society for the Suppression of Vice, of which she is a prominent member. She said: "I addressed myself to the Reverend Mr. Sydney Smith for aid and possibly a monetary contribution, thinking that the aims of our Society would be approved by a man of the cloth. Do you know what he replied? 'Madam,' he said, 'your organisation does little, I think, to suppress vice in the upper classes. It would do better to call itself the Society for the Suppression of Vice in Persons Whose Income Does Not Exceed Five-Hundred Pounds per Annum.' The impudence of the man! And a clergyman!"

But *I* say, Hurrah for Reverend Smith!

Another part of the post-worship conversation took place between Papa and Lord Merlyngton, supposedly out of my earshot. But my hearing is keen, and I absorbed almost every word of their dialogue:

LORD M.:
The spread of immorality among the poor is absolutely disgusting, Summerfield. In the poorer sections of London, only a tenth of the couples living together are married. The other nine-tenths live in open concubinage.

PAPA:
Perhaps they can't afford the fee.

LORD M.
(*ignoring Papa's remark*):
I addressed a meeting of the Society for the Suppression of Prostitution recently. [So many Societies for the Suppression of This or That, Diary!] Don't believe I saw you there, Summerfield. Well, I gave 'em something to hear, I can assure

you. Told 'em that, exclusive of the City, London has a thousand houses of accommodation and no fewer than a hundred thousand prostitutes!

PAPA:

That many.

LORD M.:

At least. A gentleman can't stroll anywhere now-a-days without being accosted by these creatures. Step outside your club, and they rush out like pigeons. "Are you good-natured, Charlie?" They address everybody by that name. Insolent baggages! Should be horsewhipped! [Nine hundred and ninety-nine times, Lord M.?]

PAPA:

The spread of disease must be shocking.

LORD M.:

As for that, my dear Summerfield, I hold that diseases of that kind are a blessing.

PAPA:

A blessing!

LORD M.:

Yes, indeed. The diseases ought to be encouraged, not checked. They are inflicted by the Almighty upon the sinful, to act as restraint. A restraint and a punishment. Mark my word: if I could work my will, I'd send to the gallows all of these doctors and scientific chaps who are trying to seek out a cure for the venereal diseases. For if they should ever succeed in finding it — and I pray that they won't — decency and morality may as well be consigned to the dust bin!

There's Christian feeling for you, Diary: thousands of poor women whose crime is less debauchery than destitution, and thousands of men whose only sin is a weakness in regard to the natural urgings of their flesh, must suffer the torments of ravaging disease, if Lord Merlyngton could but work his will. And all in the much-maligned name of the Almighty.

54

There was a drunken man in church yesterday: he had to be removed after he stood up and shouted, in a North Country accent, "Talk to us no more about thy Goddle Mighty, for there isn't one! Go to Yorkshire, and look for Him there! You'll not see Him, but I'll tell you what you *will* see — lassies, as young as seven, as old as twenty-one, sweating as hurriers in the mines! Stripped naked to the waist they are, working alongside naked men! 'Tis not lewdness in them, but the only way they know to keep from fainting with the heat! Nay, there be no God in Yorkshire — but there be the Divel, and there sure be Hell!"

Diary, I am such a little goose! How could I not have seen it instantly? The last sentence of Phoebe's letter — about our childhood games — the stiltedness of the phrasing should have alerted me — there is a hidden message in it!

One of our favourite games, when we were children, was the writing of little notes which, on the surface, said one thing, but under the surface said quite another. Newsome taught us the trick. They were acrostics: the first letters of each word, when strung together, surrendered the concealed meaning. One of my best efforts I still remember, to this day: "If lace over veils enhances prettiness, let's use more, surely." The hidden message was: "I love plums." It was not as difficult as it may seem, and one became more and more adept with practise. I was very good at it, and Phoebe was even better.

It took me but a moment to decipher the true meaning of the sentence, *Phoebe remembers every game, Newsome's and Nurse's, tenderly.*

The single word hidden in that sentence is: *Pregnant.*

ʘ Tuesday, 17 January

I hardly slept at all last night.

Part of me rejoiced at Phoebe's happy news; another part of me was fairly bursting to tell it to Mamma and Papa; and yet another part was puzzled at Phoebe's need to relate the glad tidings to me in childish cypher.

This, of all things, could be written about, surely! Written and shouted from the roof-tops! This can not be a thing to be kept from Mr. Braithwaite — there is no need for *this* to be a secret between sisters!

Here, at last, is the joy and fulfilment that Phoebe has missed in her marriage. From this point, her life will begin anew and her unhappiness will be forgotten.

It is for this reason that I find her latest letter even more baffling than the one which preceded it. How can I answer her? I want to shower her with felicitations on the coming event. I want to ask her *why* she is being so furtive about it. But I can say *none* of this in a letter.

Written later. I have just now finished writing to Phoebe. I thought about it all day — hardly ate my meals — scarcely heard what people said to me. "Pam, are you ill again?" Mamma asked me. I assured her I was not. "Then eat your dinner, and reply when you are spoken to."

Here is what I have written to my sister:

"Dearest Phoebe, —

"Thank you for your note. Although it was very short, I devoured every word. Indeed, I *am* an 'understanding sister,' for I have completely understood everything that you wrote.

"Let me ask your opinion of a piece of verse I have composed. It is a sonnet, addressed to the handsome lieutenant (now captain) of whom I spoke before. When I say 'addressed,' I mean only that it is mentally directed to him, for I know I shan't have the courage to send it to him. For one thing, my metaphors about swords and scabbards, etc., might shock him, for he is *very* proper. For another thing, I fear that it is just not good enough. In it, I have tried to manage a military paradox: the vanquished as victor, the war which is won by both sides — hence the final couplet, in which I attempt to reconcile an image of defeat (the forfeiture of the blade) with an image of victory (the taking of spoils). I can not tell if I have got it right. You know how much I trust and respect your judgment and your taste, so please read it *very closely:*

Be sure, sweet Captain of my girlish dreams,
Ruled as you are by Duty's stern command,
Ardent in bold defence of that which seems
Virtuous in our saintly, sinning land:

All of your strength will be reduced to naught,
Weak as a new-born kitten you'll become,
Hot with the raging fever you'll have caught.
Yet will you march — but to my softer drum.

Surely the god of War defers to Venus?
Even the sharpest sword its scabbard seeks.
Cannon and muskets shall not stand between us.
Ruffian Mars is dumb when fair Love speaks.

    Elegant officer, forfeit your blade —
    Take, as your spoils, this militant maid!

"I must close now — these literary labours, poor though they may be, have quite drained me! Please answer *soon,* and let me be privy to your opinion of the above.

"All my love,
"Pamela"

I do hope that Phoebe will know that my sonnet is a direct response to her single-word message, *Pregnant,* and that she will, by reading the first letter of each line, discover my message: *Brava! Why secret?*

🙰 *Thursday, 19 January*

"If it is agreeable to Miss Summerfield," wrote Giles in a note received by Mamma this morning, "and if she has no other engagement, I ask that I be permitted to call on her this afternoon at one o'clock, to take her riding for no longer than an hour in a hackney-cab which I would hire for the occasion. My respects to you and to Mr. Summerfield. May I ask you, please, to give your reply to my batman, who delivered this note and who awaits your answer."

"Oh, Mama, may I? *Please?*" I wheedled when Mamma read the note to me at breakfast.

She asked Rutledge to bring paper, pen, and ink. When he had done so, she wrote a very short note which she shewed to me. It read:

"Dear Captain Ormond, —
"Because my daughter is only seventeen, I think that she should not be seen riding alone through the streets with an officer of Dragoons. However, if you would care to take tea with us quite informally this afternoon, we should be glad to receive you.

"Respectfully yours,
"Melissa Summerfield"

"Thank you, Mamma," I said, not very effusively, because, although I would be happy to see Giles at tea, I should have so much preferred spending an hour with him alone.

Mamma folded the note and handed it to Rutledge. "Give this to the young man who is waiting for it," she said. When he left the room, Mamma said to me, "Captain Ormond is a very respectable person, and I think him incapable of a dishonourable action towards you, but we must think of the appearance. You understand, I'm sure, my dear. Some people are such gossips."

"People like Lady Merlyngton," I said.

"We need not specify. To be candid, Captain Ormond more properly should have asked *both* of us to go riding with him. Or, if Phoebe were still living in the house, he might have asked you and her. But not you alone."

"Mamma, it is *I* in whom he is interested."

"That is precisely why you must not be seen with him alone." She smiled. "During tea," she added, "it is not entirely impossible that I may step out of the drawing-room for a few minutes, to have some words with Rutledge and Mrs. Pruitt about this evening's dinner."

(She is such a dear!)

"Mamma," I said, "could a message be sent to Mam'selle,

asking her to dress my hair this morning or early this afternoon?"

"Is she not scheduled for to-morrow?"

"Yes, but with Giles — Captain Ormond — coming to tea
this afternoon —"

"Very well. Crewe can take a note to her." (Crewe is our
footman.) "But she may be engaged by other ladies all day,
you know."

"I know, but we can at least try."

"Try?" said Papa, emerging from behind the newspaper for
the first time all morning. "Try what?"

"Nothing at all, Wilfrid," said Mamma.

"Well," he said, folding his paper and putting it beside his
plate, "I must be off to the City." He rose, kissed Mamma on
the cheek, then kissed me, and left.

When we were alone, Mamma said, "On the subject of riding with young men, we must remember the example of
Princess Charlotte. When she was your age or thereabouts, she
went driving with her lady-in-waiting, Lady de Clifford, in an
open carriage through Windsor Park. A young officer soon
appeared, riding alongside. Lady de Clifford, who knew him,
made the mistake of introducing the Princess to him and allowed him to continue riding alongside their carriage. Very
stupid of her. Soon, it was happening every day. Before long,
notes were passing between him and the Princess. Eventually,
they were *meeting*, not without the complicity of the Princess's
mother, that awful Caroline woman. That is what such things
can lead to. Finally, the lady-in-waiting grew so alarmed at the
state of affairs that she told the girl's father about it — the
Prince Regent. Naturally, he put a stop to it."

"Yes, Mamma," I said. "You won't forget about
Mam'selle?"

"I'll give Crewe a note directly."

Mlle. La Grange was able to amend her schedule to accommodate me, and whilst she was attending to my *coiffure*, I told
her about Giles and about Mamma's reply to his note.

"Your *maman*, she is very strict," she said.

"Yes," I said, with a sigh. "I know she is thinking only of
my welfare, but when such restrictions are placed on young la-

dies and gentlemen, how are they *ever* to know each other well enough to pledge their hearts?"

Mlle. La Grange shrugged. "Oh, there are ways."

"What ways?"

She smiled and would say no more.

By tea-time, I had worked myself up to a perfectly tremulous state of anticipation. My whole insides seemed quivering and molten. My face was flushed. I found it hard to breathe. If he had come upon me in that condition, and had but *touched* me, had but placed a gloved hand on my arm, I know I should have fairly *dissolved* in one long swooning sigh of what Mam'selle calls *le plaisir*. I felt he could make any demand of me, and I would eagerly comply, forgetting every warning, every teaching, every restraint.

To calm myself, I took the merest ruby drop of laudanum. It was most soothing, and quietened my racing heart.

Tea went pleasantly. My captain was very charming to Mamma, and I do think she has taken a fancy to him. He and I drank *quantities* of tea, and he devoured an entire plate full of cucumber sandwiches by himself, apologising for his appetite by saying that the press of regimental affairs had kept him from his luncheon. At length, Mamma excused herself and left the room to speak to the servants about dinner.

"Your mother is a gracious lady," he said. "I can not tell you how much I admire her."

I smiled and lowered my eyes, but said nothing.

"And yet my admiration for her," he went on, "is as nothing compared with the high esteem in which I hold *you.*"

("Hold *you . . .*" Heavenly choice of words! *Yes,* I wanted to say, *hold me, dearest Giles! Hold me in your arms!*)

"You are too kind, Captain," I said.

"Not half so kind as I might wish to be. Do you . . . reciprocate my esteem . . . in any small fraction, Miss Summerfield?"

"I think . . . that you are very agreeable," I said.

"I'm glad to hear it."

"I think," I continued boldly, "that you are by far the *most* agreeable gentleman I have ever met."

He seemed overcome with feeling. "Oh, Miss Summerfield!" he said in a low voice that was little more than a sigh. "If you might only know what your words mean to me!" He took my hand in both of his.

Something like a lightning-bolt — oh, the very sweetest of all lightning-bolts! — flashed up my fingers, to my heart, searing my whole body with delicious fire. At that moment, he could have had his will of me — he could have taken me, there and then, in the drawing-room, cleaving to me like Adonis to Venus in the paintings, without shame.

It was *all I could do* to remove my hand from his. I did so very gently.

My mouth felt dry; my voice was hoarse when I said, "I think I have some idea . . . what my words mean to you . . . Captain Ormond."

"Think of me as Giles, I pray you! If you can not speak the name aloud, then utter it silently in your heart!"

"You must not ask me . . ."

"I do not ask; I beg."

"Please . . . Mamma will be returning soon . . ."

"Promise me only that you will think of me as Giles."

"I think of you already by that name . . . Giles."

"Dearest Pamela!"

He reached for my hand again and would have held it to his lips, I think; but we heard Mamma approaching the room, and so we drew apart, and I poured him another cup of tea.

ॐ *Friday, 20 January*

The mind, as it hovers on the brink of waking, can paint a little miniature for us — a by-gone scene from childhood, a forgotten street, an unremembered room, a rolling field of green, limned in sharp detail.

This morning, just before I opened my eyes, I felt as if Phoebe and I were children again. The nursery where we used to play appeared exactly as it was in that time: toys, pictures on the walls, long gone, long forgot, were resurrected, vivid and solid, precisely as they had been. Phoebe looked as she did in those long-ago days; so did Newsome. The very feel of the stuff of my frock was the same to my finger-tips. Everything looked and sounded and smelled the same. I heard the tune our old music-box played — "Alas, my love, you do me wrong, to cast me off discourteously . . ." The sun slanted through the window-pane in a way it has never done since: it has never again been quite that warm tint of gold, and the little motes of dust suspended in its glow have never again been held in the air in precisely that way; that filmy, floating, dreamy way; like a thick, soft plank of glittering fog.

Phoebe's childish voice, sweet and fresh, sang along with the music-box: ". . . For I have lovèd you so long, delighting in your company . . ." Every word, every note, each tinkling tiny chord in the mechanical toy came to me clearly out of the labyrinth of far time.

It was a perfect instant, preserved for ever, lifted whole from the vanished past, and bestowed upon me as a gift. I savoured it as I would savour a rare wine tasted once a millennium ago in another life and never thought to taste a second time; knowing, as the inexpressible sweetness of its bouquet caressed my soul and body, that it was a precious, delicate thing; a fairy-web that, in the twinkling of an eye, would be gone again, never to return.

Good-bye, rare bright eternal moment.

 Saturday, 21 January

Mamma returned from shopping to-day just in time to preside over our at-home. Giles was on hand, and it was, of course, heavenly to see him; but, although he was here for over an hour, it was not near so satisfactory to us as those few moments on Thursday afternoon, when Mamma had left us to ourselves.

He longed to take my hand; I longed to let him. There were so many unspoken things locked in his eyes; I yearned for him to say them aloud. But all round us were the other guests, glaring at us like basilisks (or so it seemed); and Mamma, Argus-eyed, who misses nothing; and Papa, who is her opposite and *notices* nothing.

Papa had not been present at last Saturday's at-home, so I

took this opportunity to introduce to each other the two most beloved men in my life.

"Ormond, Ormond," said Papa, tasting the name. "Not related to Creighton Ormond, the banker?"

"Yes, sir, he is my uncle."

"Why, I know him well. His bank has a considerable investment in my brewery. We are on excellent terms. I greatly like him. Perhaps we might lunch one day, the three of us, at my club?"

"That is kind of you, Mr. Summerfield, but I fear there is bad feeling between my uncle and my father, and so —"

"Say no more, Captain. I understand. These family disputes can be ticklish. Your father, then, is —"

"Percival Ormond. He deals in tea."

"I think I have heard the name. He is Creighton's elder brother?"

"Younger by a year and a half, sir."

"So he has had to make his own way in life."

"Yes, sir."

"Even so have I! More credit to both of us, my boy."

I could see that Papa had taken a liking to Giles, largely because of the second-son badge which he shares with Giles's father. It has always been a source of pride to Papa that he has made more of his life than my Uncle Roger, who, being older, inherited the bulk of Grandpapa's small estate, and was content to live on his inheritance and not stir himself in the great world. Uncle Roger lives for (and lives *in*) his library, happy amongst his beautifully bound books and rare editions. I do think he is the sweetest old thing, and I love to visit him in the rambling family house which Grandpapa built in Suffolk. Papa is the slightest bit condescending to him, I think, for he believes him to be an idler who has thrown away his opportunities and wasted his life. But I love him, and I attribute my own bookish bent to him.

"You and your father and I must lunch one day, then," Papa said to Giles.

"We should both like that, sir."

Later, when our guests had left, Papa said, "Likable young man, that Ormond. Seems to have plenty of go. He'll amount

63

to something one day. Not like that other fellow with the curious name, Strumpet or Harlot or whatever it may be . . ."

"Trollope," I said. (Mrs. Trollope's son had called, briefly, without his famous mother this time.)

"Peculiar person. Do you know, I actually caught him napping? Standing up, like a horse. Leaning against the wall, just over there, arms folded, eyes closed, fast asleep."

"Perhaps he is overworked," Mamma suggested.

"I dare say. Do you know what he does? He told me. He's a junior clerk, working for the general post-office. Miserable position; no advancement; low wages; been at it since the age of nineteen. I gather he hates it. Wants to be transferred to Ireland, can't think why. A travelling allowance, I expect. He has the most extraordinary idea — wants to hang little boxes on pillars all about town."

"Whatever for?" asked Mamma.

"To facilitate the posting of letters, he says. The boxes would have openings in them: one would apparently walk by and drop the letters into them. Presumably, they would be collected at regular intervals and sent on their way."

"A sensible notion," said Mamma.

"Hm? Yes, I suppose it's not half-bad, at that. But I can't believe that the post-office will pay him for the idea. He'll probably not see a farthing. What's the use of being bright if you don't get paid for it? Eh?"

Papa said all this whilst stroking Sophie, who had leapt upon his lap, now that she had been admitted to the drawing-room (she had been exiled whilst our guests were here). "Getting old, are you, old girl?" he said to her, scratching her behind the ears. "Stiff in the back legs. Quite an effort to leap onto Papa's lap." Smiling at me, he said, "Do you remember how limber she was, Princess, as a pup? Full of the very devil. Ran off with my carpet slippers all the time. *Didn't you? Eh?* Good old bitch."

"Wilfrid, such language!" said Mamma.

"It's a perfectly honest word for what she is," Papa replied. "This isn't America, after all, where they call a cock a *rooster*. Ridiculous. All fowl roost, male and female. Puritanical lot, the Americans. Still . . . they're damned good at business. I have to give them that. Plenty of go."

&& *Sunday, 22 January*

Thinking of Uncle Roger yesterday, as I was, brought back the pleasant memory of a visit we made to his house last spring.

I love to journey through the countryside, drinking in the beauties of hedgerow and woodland, meadow, stream and lane. Such masses of green leaves, in every shade of that hue: emerald, apple, olive, sea; and the coppices, in spring, change their colours from day to day. The delicate leaves of the birch first are seen; then the full expansion of the ash. Is there anything lovelier than the bed of a coppice bespangled with primroses and blue-bells? With the coming of the birch leaves, comes also the crowing of the pheasant, as if at a signal; and the whistling of the blackbird; and the song of the thrush. Just when the oak buds turn red, and not a single day before, thousands of finches open their little throats in song from every bough; and larks, in joyous emulation.

Summerfield House — "the ancestral mansion," as Papa jocosely calls it — shows the influence of one of its chief architects, Mr. James Wyatt. Summerfield House has battlements on its roof, and quatrefoil windows set high, in addition to pointed ones with wooden frames. There are strange twisted chimneys, and a round crenellated tower with square windows.

Inside, the house is a medley of Gothic styles, but all done with imagination and invention. There is a monastic hall and a great staircase. Recesses are fan-vaulted. In the library — my favourite room — the recessed bookshelves are elaborated with pointed arch and Gothic tracery, making them look somewhat like holy-water stoups. The shelves are separated by pillars and crocketed finials, and these also adorn the fireplace and reach up almost to the high flat ceiling. All around the circumference are painted knights in armour, riding caparisoned horses. It is very grand, but it also manages to be cosy and charming — possibly owing to the presence of my uncle.

As usual, I spent considerable time in this room, some of it with him.

He shewed me, among other treasures, Dr. Johnson's great dictionary: two immense folio volumes, as large as lectern Bibles, the whole amounting to over two thousand pages. "A monument of our language and literature," Uncle Roger called it. "Nine years of work, and he did it single-handed. Oh, he had copyists, of course, but it is the labour of one man's mind. This is the first edition. Over eighty years old, now. Passed down to me by your grandpapa. I suppose it has its eccentricities — Dr. Johnson was an opinionated fellow. Look at this entry, under *Excise:* 'A hateful tax levied upon commodities, and adjudged not by the common judges of property, but wretches hired by those to whom excise is paid.' " Uncle Roger chuckled. "You see, Pamela," he went on, "Dr. Johnson's father had had some trouble with the excise officers, which may explain his son's lack of impartiality.

"I particularly admire these passages from his Preface: 'The dictionary was written with little assistance of the learned, and without any patronage of the great; not in the soft obscurities of retirement, or under the shelter of academic bowers, but amidst inconvenience and distraction, in sickness and in sorrow . . . I have protracted my work till most of those whom I wished to please have sunk into the grave, and success and miscarriage are empty sounds: I therefore have little to fear or hope from censure or from praise.' Good phrase, that; perhaps an unintentional rhythmic echo from Shakespere — can you guess where? No? Do you recollect your *Macbeth?"*

At that hint, I said, "Banquo to the witches! 'Speak then to me, who neither beg nor fear your favours nor your hate.' "

(You will have learnt, from even this brief introduction to him, two things about my Uncle Roger: firstly, that he is the least crotchety of old gentlemen; secondly, that he is in love with the English language. Indeed, his only crotchet is an impatience with anybody who uses the language in a slovenly way. Even the innocent ampersand offends him; he says, "We shew contempt for a great language when we do not take the small time and trouble to write out the word 'and' in full. It is such a very *little* word, after all." I have eschewed the ampersand in this diary, out of respect for him.)

He next brought out from a cupboard two small crystal glasses and a decanter of a golden cordial. "I don't offer this to everybody," he said, "but I rather think you'll like it." He filled both little glasses, and added, "See the thin layer of green on top? I've never known what it is — a trick of light, an illusion? I like to imagine it's somehow an essence of the grass from the hillsides where the flowers were picked to make it. Shall I say a little toast? May you have your heart's desire, my dear. Now taste it."

It was sweet and pungent — unpleasant, at first; but a moment later, exhaling, I sensed the most delightful after-flavour behind my nose. "Oh, Uncle, I can taste the flowers!"

He smiled. "Yes," he agreed with delight, "they say that the blossoms are distilled in old brandy, and only after a passage of time is the original flower-scent released again. It's made by Carthusian monks. The story — it may be only legend — is that the monk who invented the process, centuries ago, got the secret from the Devil, and subsequently went quite mad, sitting about his cell all day singing bawdy songs whilst his fellow-monks prayed for his soul."

"How awful! What's it called?"

"The monastery, up there in the mountains near Grenoble, is known as La Grande Chartreuse — The Big Charterhouse — so the *liqueur* is called 'chartreuse.' There are three kinds — green, yellow, and white. This, of course, is the yellow. I like it best."

"It's heavenly!"

"Or infernal — eh? — if that Devil story is true."

We sipped the *chartreuse* and leafed through other books. After a time, made bold perhaps by the cordial, I said, "Uncle Roger, may I ask you a rather personal question?"

"You may ask me anything you like, child. And I may choose to answer, or not."

"I can not understand why you have never married. You are such an amiable gentleman. I love you so much, and other ladies must have done, too."

Uncle Roger smiled and poured a little more into our glasses. "Your father is not unhappy with my bachelorhood, I dare say. When I die, this house and the rest of Grandpapa's estate will go to him. I'll leave no widow, no children."

"But *you,* Uncle Roger; are *you* happy?"

"I have been happy, for the most part, all my life, Pamela. I am happy with my books, my pictures. I attend concerts and enjoy myself immensely — Mozart, Haydn. Not that Beethoven chap you admire so much — a touch too boisterous for my taste. I have a happy life. I am content. 'And this the man who in his study sits.' Can you identify that quotation?" I shook my head. "From *Dr. Faustus,* by Christopher Marlowe. He was a bachelor, too. More interested in poetry and tobacco than in the opposite sex. Died young. Killed in a duel, a tavern brawl. Stabbed through the eye by a man named Ingram Frizer. We shouldn't know his name to-day if he hadn't slain Marlowe. He became immortal . . . by killing an immortal."

"But, Uncle, have you never —"

"Persistent little minx, aren't you? Have I never loved; that's what you want to ask, isn't it? Young girls are obsessed by thoughts of love. Well, Pam, love is a curious passion and it takes curious forms. I expect Dr. Johnson has an interesting definition of it; we might look it up later on. Most men love women, it is true, and I have admired many fine women in my life; and some men love money, or art, or other things. The Good Lord made us all different, you see, and He didn't mean *all* of us to marry. Most of us, yes; that's the course of Nature, and it's all well and good. But not all men are suited to marriage, you see —"

"Yes, mean-spirited, hard, cold, hateful men. But you are not one of those, Uncle. You are a dear."

"Bless you. But a man need not be hard and cold to be unsuited to married life. Some of us — we are a minority, I grant you — have no *need* of women, in the way that other men need them. We may like women, admire them, even love some of them, in the way that I love you, for example. But they are not an urgent daily requirement of our lives. I have sometimes thought that your brother is of that kidney. I may be mistaken. How is he, by the way?"

"Oh, Willy is very well. Of course, we don't see him as much as we should like, now that he is away at Oxford. He's very pious, you know — I expect he'll be a bishop one day."

"Your mother would like that."

The following day, Uncle Roger and Papa went fly-fishing

on the bank of the stream near by. Willy used to accompany them in other years, and I would sometimes watch the three men, in their tall hats, casting their lines into the water. This time, however, I stayed behind with Mamma and Phoebe, enjoying the time-steeped beauty of the old Summerfield mansion, and the charms of Uncle Roger's clock garden. This is cunningly planted with flowers whose nature it is to open or close at certain hours of the day. They are arranged in the form of a large, sectional dial, in the following order: spotted Cat's Ear, which opens at six in the morning; followed by African Marigold, Scarlet Pimpernel, Field Marigold, Red Sandwort, and Star of Bethlehem, which open, respectively, at the hours of seven, eight, nine, ten, and eleven. At noon, Ice Plant opens, and this is followed by Purslane, which opens at one. From two until four, the following flowers successively *close:* Purple Sandwort, Dandelion, and White Spiderwort. Then, at five, Jalap opens, and finally, at six, Dark Crane's-Bill opens. This, at least, is what the clock garden theoretically is supposed to do — and perhaps there are days when it all goes off without a hitch — but it requires the full compliance of our English sun, and he, of course, is not noted for his reliability.

All in all, it was a most satisfying visit, even though I still do not truly understand Uncle Roger's attitude towards my sex. It all seems quite odd.

When we returned to London from Suffolk, I composed a little poem, which I will copy out below. No, Diary, there are no hidden messages in it; no tricks. The only cunning I have employed is in the rhyming scheme, which is my invention, I believe. Note how the second stanza rhymes with the first, but in reverse order of lines. I think it is very clever.

> The brothers gathered hillside blooms,
> Steeped them in ancient brandywines,
> To make a glowing golden dew
> Crowned by a sheen of grass, of green.
> After it reached a certain age,
> That dew released the flowers' scent.
>
> The monk who first distilled it went
> Insane, they say — the awful wage
> Of Devil-work — became obscene,

Singing the foulest songs he knew.
The other monks and high divines
Prayed for him in their stoney rooms.

A terrible crime was reported in the newspapers this morning: a young scullery-maid, Mary Wood, was found yesterday in a Hyde Park street, strangled to death. To make matters worse, she had been raped. And, to compound the horror, the medical examiner stated that he had reason to believe that the act of rape had taken place *post mortem*. In a way, I suppose, that was a mercy, grisly though it may be to think about; for, at least, the poor girl had been spared *that* experience.

Monday, 23 January

A light rain all day and into the evening.

If marriage is much in my mind — marriage in the abstract, as well as reveries in which I am the principal character, with Giles as my consort — it is no doubt due to the weight of emphasis placed on the subject by Phoebe's unhappy married state, as contrasted with Uncle Roger's happy *un*married state. Surely these two examples are enough to convince one that marriage is not always a gateway to bliss, and the celibate life not necessarily a vale of woe.

Tuesday, 24 January

Papa stormed into the house this evening, positively vermilion with rage.

"Wilfrid, whatever is the matter?" asked Mamma, who was sitting in the drawing-room with me.

"*This* is the matter!" he growled, flinging a crumpled sheet of paper in her direction. As she smoothed it out, Papa called, "Rutledge! Rutledge! . . . Where *is* the fellow?"

Rutledge, imperturbable as ever, entered the drawing-room quietly, not at a run. (Rutledge *never* runs.)

"Ah, there you are. A large whisky, Rutledge, and be quick about it, if you please."

"Yes, sir," Rutledge said calmly, and withdrew.

"Do you see?" Papa said to Mamma, seething. "Do you see what rubbish these radicals are allowed to write? But this time, by God, I'll not stand for it! This time, the rascals have committed libel. Yes, damn it, *libel!* And they shall pay dearly for their insolence!"

"But, Wilfrid," said Mamma, clearly puzzled, "it appears to be nothing more than a piece of doggerel verse. Not very well printed, at that. On cheap, coarse paper. Not even properly signed. How can you possibly bring a suit for libel? You do not even know who wrote it. You can not sue Roc — who or what is Roc? A kind of mythical bird, is it not? You can not sue a mythical bird. Or any bird, for the matter of that."

Rutledge brought in a tray of decanter and glasses, and was about to pour Papa a drink, but Papa impatiently tore the decanter from his hand and filled the glass himself. He then lifted the glass to his lips and drained it in one swallow. With a wave of his hand, he dismissed Rutledge, who left, closing the drawing-room door.

"I know well enough who this Roc person is," said Papa, his voice hoarse from the great draught of whisky he had consumed. "He is well known in the dirtier gutters of Grub Street. The signature 'Roc' is a form of his initials — R.O.C. — Rhys O'Connor, a rebel and a firebrand of the worst, most incendiary kind."

Still, Mamma persisted: "But how can you claim to have been libelled, Wilfrid? Your name does not appear anywhere on this sheet."

"It does," he said, fuming. "Oh, indeed it does. And there are hundreds, thousands of these scurrilous broadsheets being circulated in the City. They are posted on every hoarding and pillar and wall and fence. Urchins pass them out in the streets. Lord Merlyngton had a copy. Perhaps they have even infiltrated the Palace and may be in the hands of the King himself!"

"*Calm* yourself, Wilfrid," said Mamma. "And try to make sense. *Where* does your name appear, pray tell? I do not see it."

"Read it, read it!" he shouted, waving his hand. "Read it aloud!"

"In Pamela's presence?"

"Why not? She'll be eighteen in a few months. She's no child. High time she knew the kind of mud that's hurled at honest men. Read it!"

Dutifully, Mamma read it aloud.

"Obeying the injunction to be fruitful and increase,
Our poor are nothing loth to spew forth children without cease.
'Ah, see them multiply like flowers in a summer field,'
Says Industry, content with the Cheap Labour that they yield;

" 'For, if your numbers did not thus continually soar,
We Moguls of the Mills and Mines would have to pay you more!'
So, kiss and tumble all you will, poor Dwellers in the Dust:
Fat Opulence is in the debt of Lechery and Lust."

"There! Do you see? In the third line — *summer field!* My name, thinly disguised! So *very* thinly disguised that every member of my club knew what it meant, and laughed behind my back!"

"Poor Papa," I said.

Mamma was shaking her head. "Can you be sure he means to single you out? 'Flowers in a summer field' . . . it may not be intentional, merely a coincidence. The reference is so general."

"Ah, that's the underhanded way these blackguards work!" roared Papa. "They don't shew themselves and face you, man to man. They do their dirty deeds by stealth and subterfuge, like footpads, like thieves in the night!"

Papa was pacing to and fro, and Mamma pleaded with him to sit down, but he would not.

"I'll bring an action! I'll have this scoundrel O'Connor in the courts. Barstow will prepare a devastating brief."

"St. John Barstow?" said Mamma.

"Why not? He's my solicitor. He's a member of my club. He's been our dinner-guest I don't know how many dozens of times. Why not Barstow?"

"No reason at all, Wilfrid, except that, in my opinion, Mr. Barstow will not touch a case of this kind."

"The devil he won't!" Papa snatched the broadsheet from Mamma's hand and stormed towards the door. "I'm going to his office at once."

"At this hour? His office is closed, surely."

"Then I'll go round to his house."

"But your dinner! Can not the matter wait till morning?"

"No, Madam, it can not!" And he was off, slamming the door.

"Oh, dear," said Mamma, after a moment or two. "Your father never addresses me as 'Madam' unless he is in a state near to apoplexy. I can not even remember the last occasion on which he did so."

"Was it not when Willy announced his intention to prepare for holy orders and you defended him?"

Mamma nodded, slowly.

The hour is late, and Papa has not yet returned. We dined without him. I must go to bed. Further developments will be reported to-morrow.

ॐ *Wednesday, 25 January*

Papa was more than usually silent this morning at breakfast. His face — in those rare moments when it appeared from behind his newspaper — was frozen in a forbidding scowl. I did not dare to ask him the outcome of his interview with St. John Barstow. But after Papa left for the City, I coaxed the story out of Mamma, and here is my account of what happened, heard at two removes and, of necessity, restored and coloured by whatever small narrative art I may possess.

Mr. Barstow, who is a widower and dines alone, was on the point of sitting down to his table when Papa was announced. He invited Papa to share his dinner, but Papa took only a glass of whisky. As Papa recounted the story of his grievance, and shewed the famous lawyer the offending broadsheet, Mr. Barstow, it would seem, went right ahead with his meal and made very good cheer.

Finally, over coffee and cigars, he asked Papa, "And what do you wish me to do, my dear chap?"

"Find me the most brilliant barrister in England! Drag this

rogue O'Connor into the courts! Sue him down to the last thread on his body! Force him to make a public apology and print a retraction!"

Mr. Barstow, presumably puffing away at his cigar, said, "Let us consider your demands one by one. If you sue O'Connor, you will indeed be suing for threads, for he has no money to speak of and owns little more than the clothes he stands up in. He's a penny-a-liner and, what's worse, an idealist. He doesn't care a fig for money. I confess I don't understand that kind of creature at all, but there it is."

"Then I'll sue his paper."

"What paper? He is not carried on the staff of any paper. He contributes articles, from time to time, to whatever paper will print them. What they call a 'free lance.' And this doggerel of his was not published in a paper — obviously, it was printed privately, on what press we'll never know, most likely at his own expense. That brings us to the apology and retraction. Should he retract his statement that the expanding growth of population among the lower classes has provided our industrialists with a limitless pool of labour? He can not, for it is true. Should he retract the statement that a labour force of fewer numbers would demand and receive higher wages? Again, he can not, for again it is true. Should he be made to deny that carnal congress often results in the birth of babies? If he denied that, my dear fellow, he would be denying Nature. As for an apology, to whom would you have him apologise, and for what?"

"He'll apologise to *me,* by God, for pointing me out as an oppressor of the poor!"

"Your name appears nowhere in this broadsheet."

"Look there! The third line —"

"Yes, yes, I saw it: 'flowers in a summer field.' It's simply not good enough, old boy. You could never prove in a court of law that he was referring to you. He would claim to have used a poet's metaphor, a botanical image of Nature's bounty, and so forth."

"But he meant *me!*"

"I am not entirely satisfied, in my own mind, that he did, to be perfectly frank with you. He mentions Moguls of the Mills and Mines; you are a Mogul of the Breweries. But even if he did mean you, it would be impossible to prove. The man may be a rascal and a trouble-maker, but he's not a fool. He has worded his diatribe cleverly."

"Then what *am* I to do?"

"If you want my advice, you'll do nothing. If you're foolish enough to bring a suit for libel, you'll lose, and be worse off than before. You'll have called attention to his broadsheet — which is precisely what he'd like you to do! — and you'll have all but admitted that you are, indeed, the 'summer field' of his verses; that you recognise yourself in his lines; that you are, in fact, the very personification of Fat Opulence, and in the debt of Lechery and Lust."

"Confound the fellow! He's as slippery as a serpent."

St. John Barstow may have nodded and agreed, adding, "Would have made a damned good lawyer."

And that, I believe, is the beginning and the end of Papa's lawsuit against the insufferable O'Conner, otherwise known as Roc.

ॐ *Thursday, 26 January*

Heavy rain and high winds all day.

Still no further word from Phoebe. Perhaps it is too early to expect it. Perhaps she will not see the question hidden in my sonnet. Perhaps she will see it but will choose not to answer.

The thought of letters brings to mind young Mr. Trollope's plan for attaching boxes to pillars. It is a splendid idea, but will the Postmaster General accept it? He is unalterably opposed to other postal reforms, such as Mr. Rowland Hill's proposal to introduce small adhesive labels, or "postage stamps," which would be affixed to letters by the senders, providing pre-paid postage at a low single rate, such as a penny, rather than our present cumbrous system, whereby postage rates are calculated according to distance and paid by the recipient. In addition to the added convenience, Mr. Hill believes that his system would increase volume and thereby increase revenue.

The opposing argument, however, is sensible and has much

to commend it. Mr. Hill has claimed that his innovation would provide the poorer classes of people with an advantage now enjoyed only by the well-to-do; and while this, in theory, is a laudable aim, his opponents have rightly pointed out that the advantage to the poor would be chiefly hypothetical, because so few of them can read or write. There is surely something to be said for that point of view.

Also, as Mr. John Wilson Croker has warned us, cheap postage would simply make sedition all the easier: rebels and malcontents could send their treasonous and dissenting matter through the post with great ease and little cost. If penny "postage stamps" were to become available to a man like Rhys O'Connor, for example, his influence might grow to alarming proportions. He could spread his inflammatory scribblings all over the British Isles, fomenting discontent and maligning good men like Papa.

Moreover, if such stamps could be bought cheaply by anybody, imagine the floods of rubbish that might pour into our houses! Think of the merchants who might then propel lurid advertisements for their tawdry wares inside our very doors; or political exhortations, extolling this or that M.P.; or announcements of low theatricals and other offensive affairs; to say nothing of endless pleas for contributions to charitable societies, such as those which Lady Merlyngton sponsors!

So, no matter how convenient it would be for me to paste a penny stamp onto a letter to Phoebe or Giles and then pop it into the nearest pillar-box, I must own that my selfish wishes should not take precedence over the general good.

Still, I can not but dream how the writing of penny-stamped notes to Giles would perfectly combine the utmost *facility* with the greatest *felicity*. What if Mr. Hill's proposal had been accepted and were now in effect? And what if I were then to throw aside all propriety and pour out my heart to Giles in letters? What might I write to him?

Would I tell him how I have dreamt of him, naked as a classical statue? No, I should not dare! Would I tell him how my heart pounds so loudly at the anticipation of his visit that I am obliged to calm myself with soothing drops? I think not.

Would I confine myself to those empty, cool, and passionless phrases that we have been taught are proper to the correspondence of young ladies? How could I?

I think I would say —

My darling, —

You are the very sun. When you are near me, I am warmed as by no other star. I turn to you as if I were a flowering plant; I bloom and prosper; I feel the sap of life flow through me, the sweet honey overflowing in my blossoms. You are the shining source of life to me, without which all my world would darken and be overcome with ice; and I should wither and die and fall into decay.

As the ancients, knowing no other, gentler God, fell on their knees to the blazing sun that nurtured them, so I fall on my knees and worship you. I crouch at your feet in humility and awe and unquestioning love. I am your bondmaid and your creature. I turn my face upwards to drink in your golden radiance. I glory in your beneficent heat. I ask no more than that I be allowed to bask, ecstatic, in your rays. I entreat you to burn me through and through with your love; sear my flesh, my heart, down to my very bones; reduce me to ashes in your merciless consuming flame! I wish no better death, no different fate, no other love than yours, my life, my sun-god, my dearly beloved Giles!

୨୨ *Friday, 27 January*

As Mlle. La Grange was dressing my hair to-day, I asked her what precisely she had meant, last week, when — in response to my complaint that young persons are not allowed to know each other well — she had said, "There are ways."

"*Ah, mon Dieu,*" she replied, "you are not stupid, like some *jeunes filles.* You are, how do you say it, *trés sage,* very wise for your years. *Enfin,* you will think of something, no? Is there not a saying in your England — Love will find a way?"

"But, Mam'selle," I said, summoning my most heart-melting tone of voice, "I can never see my dear captain without *hordes* of other people being in the same room! Last week, purely because Mamma had to speak to the servants about dinner, we managed to seize a few moments alone together. It was less than five minutes! What on earth can be done in five minutes?"

"A great deal, *ma chère*," she said, ironically.

"Mamma will not even allow me to go riding with him for an hour in broad daylight. It is so cruel!"

"*C'est dommage*," she said, in sympathy. "*Mais, c'est la vie.*"

"Is that all you can say? Platitudes?"

"*Ah, ma petite,* what would you have me say, eh?"

I pleaded with her. "You are a woman! A *French* woman! How were such things managed when you were a girl?"

"Ah, that was, how do you say, *autres temps,* and I am of a different class, a different country."

"Was your *maman* not as strict as mine?"

"Stricter."

"Then — ?"

Mlle. La Grange sighed and put down her comb. She said, "It is not in my place to give you such advice." She paused. "*Mais . . .*" She picked up the comb and resumed work on my hair. "When I was a girl, more young even than you, there was a boy I wished very much to see. But my *maman,* she kept the eyes on me night and day. Then, one time, we are visited in our house by my mother's, how you say, *cousine.* She is very, well, very *sympathique* to me, yes? Between the two of us, we make a little plan. This *cousine* and I will go shopping for ribbons for the hair. *Maman* is happy to get me out from under-foot for an hour, *compris?* But with a *chaperone.* And this boy of my heart — he works in the bakery next to the ribbon shop."

"I see," I said. "Very clever of you. And you and this boy, in your stolen hour, did the two of you . . ."

"*Mais non!*" said Mlle. La Grange, severely. "The sweet boy and I, we only talk, and look into the eyes, and for one or two short moments we hold the hands, over the warm loaves of bread and the *croissants* and the *brioches* . . . ah, the good aroma of those breads, I can smell them even now."

"How heavenly." After a moment of silence, I spoke again: "Mam'selle?"

"*Oui?*"

"Do you not think I require new hair ribbons? Perhaps in yellow? And some in pink?"

"The ones you have are still good, *non?*"

"But it is so tiresome to wear the same ribbons, day in, day out. And I have *none* in pink, and I do think it is such a becoming colour for me, is it not?"

"Oui, trés jolie."

"I am such a goose about shopping, however. I always need the advice of an older woman. And my dear mother is so busy, and she accompanied me to the shop so very recently. I should hate to ask her again so soon. If only my sister were still here . . . but she is not . . ." I looked up at Mlle. La Grange, in the mirror. "Mam'selle — on Monday morning, or in the afternoon if it is more convenient, do you think you could find the time to go with me to Layton and Shear's in Henrietta Street? They have such lovely ribbons there. It would be such a help to me. I would be ever so grateful. Our family coach could call for you."

"I am all morning on Monday busy with the *coiffures.*"

"The afternoon, then?"

"Ah, Miss . . ."

"Please, Mam'selle!"

"Alors," she said at last, "if the coach can call for me at two in the afternoon . . . *bien"*

"Oh, Mam'selle! You are an angel! A perfect angel!"

And so she is.

How strangely is coincidence woven through and through the fabric of our lives. If, on the 4th of this month, I had not gone with Mamma to Lady Merlyngton's tea — and I very nearly did not, for I had felt the beginnings of a headache coming over me — I should not have met Giles. Indeed, I might *never* have met him! The thought is too horrible even to contemplate! And if, on that same day, I had not admired Lady M.'s *coiffure* and asked the name of her hairdresser, I might never have made the acquaintance of Mlle. La Grange.

On one day, in one fateful hour, I met the man of my heart and learned the name of the dear French woman who would help me to arrange a rendezvous with him.

Is life not exceedingly strange? And glorious?

I was awakened *much* too early this morning by Sophie's inces-
sant barking and a general commotion in the house, combined
with the most curious noises seeming to emanate from the
very walls! Thumpings and scrapings, muffled cries . . . I
could not imagine what was happening. Was the house on
fire? Had foreign troops landed on our shores, marched up our
street, and demanded to be billeted in our house? Was a rebellious mob attacking us?

I shot out of bed, flung my dressing-gown about my shoulders, and ran out onto the landing, still barefoot.

"Child, put on your slippers — you'll catch your death,"
said Hester, as she ran past me and disappeared around the
corner and down the stairs. (She still calls me "Child" sometimes.) But slippers were the least of my concern. "Hester!
What on earth is happening?" I called after her, but she was already out of sight. I began to run after her, and collided with
Rutledge, knocking some of the wind out of him, I'm afraid.

"Sorry, Miss," he said (although it had been my fault), and
began to dash on his way.

But: *"Rutledge!"* I shouted, with stern authority — and, do
you know, he actually froze in his tracks! It was the first time I
have felt really grown-up! "Rutledge, I demand to know what
is going on!"

"It's nothing, Miss Pamela. A climbing-boy . . ."

"What about him?"

"He appears to be lodged in one of the flues in this
wing . . ."

"Lodged?"

"Stuck, Miss."

"Good gracious!"

"Nothing to concern yourself with, Miss. It happens from
time to time. Now, if you will excuse me . . ."

"Yes, Rutledge, you may go."

"Thank you, Miss." And he was off, at a run.

My feet were beginning to feel cold, so I returned to my
bedroom for my slippers; and, in passing my window, I could
see men with ropes and pulleys — Rutledge was among
them — climbing up the side of our house; and I could hear

voices — "Steady on, lads!" — "Gently, gently!" — "Lift 'im up" — "Stop kicking, boy!" The sky was overcast. There was some rain and light wind.

I pulled my dressing-gown more tightly round me — it was quite chilly in the house, for no fires had been lit — and stepped again onto the landing, where I met Rutledge again, somewhat the worse for soot, which he was trying to brush off with his hands — unsuccessfully.

"It's all right, Miss," he said. "The boy has been rescued. They pulled him out with ropes."

"Is he injured?"

"Just a few scrapes. Nothing serious. Those boys are tough, you know. Their skin is made hard by their rubbing it with strong brine, close by a hot fire. The skin becomes quite toughened in that way, like an elephant's, especially about the elbows and knees."

"But how dreadful for them. Does it not hurt?"

"To be sure, Miss. You must stand over them with a cane to make them rub the brine in good and hard, or coax them with the promise of a ha'penny. Ah, but that's nothing, Miss. Many a boy's been suffocated or burnt when he got lost in the flues."

"How awful!"

"Excuse me, Miss Pamela, I shouldn't have spoken of it."

"Indeed you should have. But is there not a movement to forbid employing boys in this work? I'm sure that I've read something to that effect."

"Oh, yes, Miss; for years there's been talk of it."

"Then why is nothing done?"

Rutledge smiled in a way that can only be called sardonic. "The House of Lords, Miss," he said. "Their lordships are far more worried about the state of their homes and their carpets and their furnishings than the danger to a few boys."

"But there are mechanical sweeping devices to do the work. I have heard of them."

"They make too much mess. And they cost more. Boys work cleaner, Miss, and starving boys work cheap." It is the only time I have ever heard a note of bitterness in Rutledge's voice. "Will that be all, Miss Pamela?"

"Yes, thank you, Rutledge."

Later, as I was dressing, I suddenly recalled a remark Papa made many years ago at dinner, when I was a little girl. Rutledge had just left the dining-room, and Papa had said, reflectively, "A good man, Rutledge. He's made something of himself. D'you know, m'dear" — he was addressing Mamma — "he worked for his father till he was ten; then the old man died, and the boy set out on his own. Taught himself manners, how to speak properly, worked himself up, and got into service as a groom in a respectable household. Now he's the most efficient butler in Mayfair — in all of London, perhaps."

"What was *Mister* Rutledge's occupation, Papa?" I recall Phoebe asking.

"Rutledge's father? He was a chimney-sweep. Until he was ten years old, Rutledge was a common climbing-boy."

Giles attended our at-home this afternoon, needless to say. I managed to draw him over to the pianoforte, on the pretext of playing one of the latest ballads for him, and when we were out of earshot of the others, I asked him if he was ever in the vicinity of Henrietta Street.

"On occasion," he replied.

"I shall be there on Monday afternoon," I said casually, as my fingers toyed with the keys. "Shortly after two. In Layton and Shear's, the mercer's shop, looking at hair ribbons."

"How extraordinary," he said. "I have been meaning to buy some hair ribbons to send to my sister. It is her birthday next month. I know nothing of such things. Perhaps you would assist me in my choices?"

"Perhaps," I replied, with a small conspiratorial smile.

ૐ *Sunday, 29 January*

Sunday again. As usual, a day of tedium. Light snow and wind.

Have I told you, Diary, of the Summerfields' religious affiliation? We are quite comfortable within our Church of England, and we are not at all attracted by the radical (albeit dull and dreary) Evangelical movement. Our form of worship is not as Romish as some would wish it to be; we feel at home, as do our friends, with the Anglican service.

The Jewish and Mahometan forms of worship, although I know very little of them, do seem so curious and Oriental, redolent of the desert and camels and olive trees. They are not without a certain fascination, but I think one must be born into those Eastern races in order properly to worship at such exotic altars.

I wonder if I would make a good nun? No, I think not: I am too filled with worldly thoughts. Sometimes wicked ones.

Monday, 30 January

A *near*-calamity! Although Mamma had already given her consent for me to go shopping for ribbons with Mlle. La Grange this afternoon, at the last moment she decided to accompany us! The family coach had already left to pick up Mam'selle and bring her round here, and I was awaiting its return with no little impatience, when Mamma suddenly made her devastating announcement.

I tried to appear unruffled by it, and said calmly, "But you were shopping so recently."

"Yes, it's tiresome, but my best button-hook broke this morning. It belonged to your grandmamma, so I have a fond attachment to it. I must have it mended, and buy another one to use whilst that is being taken care of."

"I can do all that for you when I am out with Mam'selle."

"No, I must speak to the man myself and tell him exactly how I wish the job of work to be done. These people are so slipshod unless one is firm with them. I find I must always attend to such things myself."

I was growing desperate! The coach would return at any moment! "But are you not expecting Mrs. Ridgely and the twins to come to tea?"

"It's only a little past two. We shall be back in ample time."

What could I do? I peeped out the window: our coach, with Mlle. La Grange in it, had just pulled up in front of the house!

And then I saw a hackney draw up behind it, and my father stepped out.

"Here's Papa," I said.

"At this time of day?"

As he approached the door, Mamma opened it for him. "What's the coach doing out there?" He looked at us, in our street clothes. "Are you two off somewhere?"

"Shopping, with Mam'selle La Grange," replied Mamma.

Papa grunted and appeared displeased. He said to Mamma, "Is your business so urgent that it cannot be postponed until to-morrow?"

"Is something wrong, Wilfrid?"

"No, it's nothing, a trifle; but I should like to tell you about it."

"Then I'll stay at home."

With a sinking feeling, I asked, "Shall I stay, too, Papa?"

"No, no, Princess; be off with you," he said. "It's nothing to worry yourself about. A nuisance; no more."

So I quickly stepped out of the house and into the coach.

Giles was already inside Layton and Shear's when Mam'selle and I arrived. "Miss Summerfield!" he said. "What a delightful surprise!"

"Yes, is it not?" I made hasty introductions: "Mam'selle La Grange, Captain Ormond."

"*Enchantée,*" said Mam'selle.

"I find," he said, "that I grow a bit peckish this time of day, and I note there is a rather presentable-looking tea-room in the house at the next turning. Perhaps you ladies will do me the honour of . . . ?"

"*Merci, mon capitaine,*" said Mam'selle, "but I have just now arisen from my luncheon. However . . ." And she turned to me.

"I should be glad to keep you company," I said to Giles, "if Mam'selle La Grange does not mind?"

"*Mais non,*" she said. "I shall busy myself here. There is much to do. Your coachman has been told to return in an hour, yes? I will meet you here at that time."

After a few more polite words amongst us, Giles and I walked out to the tea-room he had mentioned.

84

After we had ordered tea and cakes, he said, "It's such a treat to see you alone like this, Miss Summerfield."

"You are guilty of backsliding," I said, playfully.

"What do you mean?"

"Not too many days ago, you addressed me as Pamela. I call that progress. Now you have regressed to Miss Summerfield."

He laughed. "I apologise for the regression, and promise to use your Christian name, if you will reciprocate in kind."

"I agree to your terms . . . Giles."

"Splendid!"

"And now you must tell me all about yourself. What sort of things do you like? Are you fond of poetry? Music?"

"Well, I do like a good march and some of the new songs. Did you see that ballad-opera at the Saint James's Theatre a few months ago? What was it called? —"

"The Village Coquettes?"

"The very one!"

"Yes, I enjoyed it immensely. It had a *libretto* by that new writer, Mr. Dickens. Do you know his work?"

"I'm afraid I don't have a great deal of time for reading."

"Your regimental duties."

"Exactly."

"It must be a heavy responsibility, being a captain of Dragoons."

"Oh, it's not as bad as all that. We're allowed a certain amount of time that we can call our own. Such as this afternoon, for instance. And I did enjoy *The Village Coquettes.*"

"Wasn't it most awfully amusing? So many times I thought I should never stop laughing!"

"Laughing? I took it all rather soberly. Was I not supposed to?"

He said this so charmingly, so ingenuously, that a bubble of responding laughter rose from my throat. "Oh, Giles, it was a burlesque! A lampoon of the sentimentality of the usual ballad-opera! Surely you knew that?"

His smile was touchingly rueful. "I'm afraid not. I was close to tears at that song 'The Ivy Clinging to the Wall.' I'm rather a dunce, you see."

"Oh no, *no,* Giles! You are a *dear!* It was so sweet of you to be touched by that song!"

"It takes a subtler mind than mine to appreciate satire," he said. "But I'm good at cricket and billiards, and I must say I'm a more than passable dancer."

"So am I! Are you good at the galop?"

"Superb — and even better at the Sir Roger de Coverley! Have you danced the Lancers? It was introduced in Paris last year and is somewhat like the quadrille."

"You shall have to teach me," I said.

"Gladly."

"We have a great deal in common, you see? And I shall tell you a little secret — I am not so bad at billiards myself!"

"You, Pamela?"

"Papa taught me. He has owned a billiard table ever since I can remember, and we often play together. I have got very good at the game. Even better now than I was, for Papa has just bought one of the new tables with a slate bed. Perfectly flat: can't warp or shrink or crack like the wooden ones. The balls roll as smoothly as can be."

"I've never played on a slate table."

"You must play on ours."

"I should like to, very much."

In this effervescent way, time shot by like an arrow, and I found it difficult to believe that our allotted hour had vanished. I arose from the table hastily, and was leaving the tearoom with Giles, when whom do you imagine we saw coming in? The most notorious gossip in London!

There was no avoiding her — we fairly collided — I felt myself blush — I wanted to sink into the floor. But Giles took the bull (the old cow, rather!) by the horns, and said in the most cheery, open manner:

"Lady Merlyngton! Well met!"

"Captain Ormond," she said. "Pamela." (*I* could say *nothing.*)

"Miss Summerfield and I were just speaking of you!" he went on, in such a jolly, innocent way — albeit lying in his teeth! — that I could see Lady M. was flattered. "We were saying what a marvellous hostess you are, how enormously we enjoy ourselves at your parties. You know the most amusing people. That delightful Mrs. Trollope — I never tire of her American stories. And how is Lord Merlyngton? What a fascinating gentleman — the pearls of wisdom fairly drop from his lips. I could listen to him all day, to my profit . . ."

All this time, Giles had been gently guiding me to the door, his hand cupping my elbow, his teeth gleaming in the direction of Lady M. "Well, Miss Summerfield, we must not keep your mother waiting in the mercer's shop. So kind of you ladies to assist a clumsy soldier in choosing ribbons for his sister. Gwendolyn will be quite amazed at my exquisite taste — she always says I can't tell puce from purple, and I dare say she's right! Well, good day to you, then, Lady Merlyngton — a pleasure to see you — please convey my regards to the worthy peer, ha-ha!"

And, with that, we were out the door.

The coach was waiting for us outside Layton and Shear's, and so was Mam'selle. I bade a hasty good-bye to Giles and told him I would have Papa invite him to a game of billiards. Then I climbed into the coach with Mlle. La Grange and returned home, telling Paley, our coachman, to take Mam'selle on to her door.

As I walked past the drawing-room, clutching the little packet of ribbons which Mam'selle had purchased for me, Mamma appeared from the room and reminded me that Mrs. Ridgely and her daughters would be arriving soon for tea. "Step into the drawing-room for a moment before you go up to change," she added. "There is just time to speak to you about something."

(Had Lady Merlyngton's gossip reached her ears so *soon?* I could scarcely believe it.)

In the drawing-room, she said, "I think you should know why your father returned so early this afternoon."

(I had forgotten all about it!)

"It's nothing so terribly important," she went on; "merely an annoyance; but it has to do with that unbearable Mr. O'Connor again."

"Oh, dear."

"Quite. Your father had the bad luck to run into him in the

street to-day, just outside Claridge's. Your father would not have recognised him, of course, never having met him, but Mr. Randall had been lunching with your father, and it was he who pointed him out and identified him. So tactless of Mr. Randall: I feel quite cross with him. Well, you know your father's temper. He walked up to that awful man and spoke right out to him."

"No! What did Papa say?"

"He said, 'Is your name O'Connor?' The fellow nodded. 'Do you write under the *nom-de-plume* Roc?' He nodded again. 'Well, my name is Summerfield, and when I insult a man, I do it in my own name and to his face. You are a damned snake, sir, and a coward, and a spreader of lies.' As if that were not enough, your father then struck him in the face!"

"Good for Papa! But I hope Mr. O'Connor did not strike him back?"

"Of course not. He is a coward, just as your father said, and as we already know from Captain Ormond's account. He merely turned to his companions and said, 'You gentlemen are witnesses to this, and I shall call upon you to give testimony when I bring suit against Mr. Summerfield on a charge of battery. What is the name of your solicitor, sir?' 'St. John Barstow,' said your father. O'Connor said, 'He will hear from my own solicitor in the morning.' With that, he turned and walked away."

I cried out in anger, "So poor Papa will be entangled in a lawsuit with that dreadful person, after all?"

"It appears so," said Mamma. "And, what is worse, as the defendant."

How perfectly beastly!

ꝑ *Tuesday, 31 January*

I have, from time to time, been accused by my parents — and even by Phoebe — of colouring events in my recounting of them, lighting them with theatrical lamps to make the shadows deeper, the high-lights brighter. No doubt there is some truth to this. But I can say, without exaggeration, that to-day I am staggering from the most awful shock of my life.

No, nothing has befallen me directly. Nor has a loved one been struck down by death or fatal illness. I could almost wish it had been so; for one of the dearest people in this world has stood revealed to me as bowed down by an insupportable shame and threatened by a looming fear.

I received this letter from Phoebe to-day:

"Dear Pam, —

"Your dear sonnet is an accomplished piece of work, especially for one of your age, but I agree that it is the slightest bit naughty, with its sword-and-scabbard imagery. Your lines contain the requisite number of syllables (the extra syllables in your feminine endings, *Venus/between us,* are permissible), but do you not find the closing couplet has too fast a tempo — owing to your sudden change from iambs to dactyls? There is a *triple* dactyl in your penultimate line!

"Even so, it is a creditable performance, and I can not hope to better it, although I have been trying my hand at some verses, composed in the *terza rima* form, beloved of Dante. They have met with the whole-hearted approval of Mr. Braithwaite, who, in his modesty, claims to be no expert in things poetical. Pray read them as *closely* as I have read yours:

> Nothing so dear as marriage is to me.
> Other delights turn pale compared to this,
> The sum of all that we are meant to be.
>
> Hell it would be on Earth, such joy to miss,
> Impious to avoid this happy state:
> Surely high Heaven can not match such bliss.

> "Your devoted sister,
> "Phoebe"

Oh, Diary — by this time I do not have to tell you the acrostical trick employed by my sister to answer my question about why she is keeping her pregnancy secret even from her husband.

Poor Phoebe! What will be the outcome of all this?

February

"LOVE, NATURAL AND OTHERWISE"

A new month. When I look back upon the turmoil of the first month of this year — Phoebe's awful disclosure; Papa's conflict with O'Connor — I am timorous to dip my toes into the chilly waters of February, much less to plunge my whole being into those waters and swim outwards into their wide, uncharted expanse, not knowing what *krakens* and other monsters may lurk in the darkness of their deeps, lying in wait for me, ready to reach up and seize me and drag me down.

And yet January was not all vexation and distress. It gave me Giles.

I have been pondering what to write to Phoebe, in answer to yesterday's letter. I am torn by contradictions and confusion. If the child now growing inside her is, as her acrostic tell me, NOT HIS — that is, not Mr. Braithwaite's — then whose is it? But even setting aside that question for the nonce, why should she be "afraid of what is yet to come," as, she told me in an earlier letter, she is? I tell myself that if I were a married lady, pregnant with a child not my husband's, I should simply keep mum about it, and he would be none the wiser. How should he know the child to be not his? All babies look much alike when they are born. What is there for Phoebe to fear? Unless . . . it crossed my mind that all babies do *not* necessarily look alike. What if Phoebe's child, when born, were unmistakably the offspring of a blackamoor? But that is a silly thought: Phoebe has hardly even *seen* an African man, much less embraced one. And so the puzzle persists: Why is she afraid of this imminent birth; how will her husband ever know the child is not his?

And so I have not written to her — but it has not been for want of trying. I have started many letters, and torn them up. I tried trivial prattle, going on and on about the scandal I have heard these past few weeks about the Dukes of Cumberland and Kent. But all of that gossip was to no purpose, and so I threw away that letter, unfinished. I then began to apprise her of Papa's skirmishes with O'Connor — that scurrilous broadsheet, and their meeting on the street, and the threat of an action for battery. But why should I distress her with these matters? I tore up that letter, too.

Next, I called her attention to the new form of jingle which Mr. Edward Lear, a very droll gentleman, has been publishing in the popular magazines. I described the strict rules of its prosody, and suggested that she and I might try our hand at writing a few of them. I took the initiative by composing one myself — including, in the first letters of its five lines, the burning one-word question that was the natural response to her shattering announcement, NOT HIS.

> Whenever the late Duke of Kent
> Had to emphasise just what he meant,
>   On a poor soldier's back
>   Sev'ral lashes he'd crack,
> Educating the whole regiment.

Not nearly so good as Mr. Lear's, although it served my *sub rosa* purpose — and yet I asked myself if I truly had the right to put that intimate question to my sister. That letter, too, was consigned to the flames behind my grate.

One old question, at least, had been answered. I now knew the reason for her bright eyes and happy, flushed face, when I would see her returning from what ostensibly had been a day of shopping. It had been a day of love.

Then why, *why* had she not married her lover? Why had she

not married the man who had made her so joyous and had given her a child? Why had she married Mr. Braithwaite, who had never brightened her eyes or brought the roses to her cheeks?

So many questions I want to ask her, that I feel myself fairly bursting with them! I may write none of them plain and clear in a letter that will undoubtedly be scanned by the beady eyes of Braithwaite; and to encypher them all acrostically in verse would require a monumental epic the length of *Beowulf!*

And not only questions: assurances, as well — renewals of my love for her, my faith and trust in her, my sympathy, and my encouragement. I want to say: Phoebe, I do not blame you, for I know what it is to love! I, too, have felt some portion of that heavenly passion that transports the soul and makes our hearts and faces glow with a divine radiance! I, too, would have surrendered myself — happily, as you did — "dissolving in pleasures and soft repose," as in the song. Giles need only ask me — not even that; no asking, no words; only looks and touches and kisses — and I would give him all that I am capable of giving. As you did, Phoebe, to your own true love.

If only I could see my sister, see her alone, so that we could hold each other in our arms and talk, for one short hour, for half an hour, for *five minutes.*

(Curious: I remember Papa saying something much like that when Grandmamma — his mother — died. "I would give anything, Princess, all my wealth, everything, if I could bring her back — just for an hour — less than that, even, a few minutes, so that I might hold her dear hands and tell her all those things I never said to her. Oh, why did I not *kiss* her last night before I left her side? I thought I should see her again this morning — how could I know she would pass away from us so quietly in the night? — and so I wasted that precious moment, threw it away! I would give all that I have if I could hold her again just for an instant and kiss her!")

But, by making this comparison with Papa's words, I seem to be saying that Phoebe is dead. She is not only alive; she is carrying another life within her, so she is indeed alive, twicefold alive.

And yet she is as remote from me as if she were in her grave.

Thick, dense fog all day and into the night.

๑๑ *Thursday, 2 February*

The most astonishing thing happened this evening during the dinner-hour. We were all seated at table, when Rutledge leaned close to Papa and spoke in lowered tones which, none the less, could be distinctly heard by Mamma and me.

"You have a caller, sir. When I told him you were dining, he said he would be pleased to wait until you are through."

"Well, who is he, Rutledge?"

Rutledge was obviously uncomfortable, for he hates any kind of contention or unpleasantness in what, not without a certain justice, he considers "his" house. Hesitantly, he handed Papa a visiting-card.

Reading it, Papa's eyebrows rose. "Unbelievable," he said, passing the card to Mamma. "Oh dear," she said, passing it to me. "What presumption!" I said, for the card bore a Chelsea address and the name of Rhys O'Connor.

Papa slowly placed his fork beside his plate. "I will see him at once. In the drawing-room."

"No, Wilfrid." Mamma's voice cut through the room like steel. "I demand that I be present at this interview."

Gently, Papa said, "This is men's business, Melissa."

"Indeed?" The voice of steel again. "The day you saw his broadsheet, to whom did you first turn to vent your feelings? And the day you struck him and provoked him to the threat of litigation, whom did you ask to postpone shopping so that you might speak of the affair? You have made it women's business, Wilfrid. *This* woman's business. I say we receive him here, in the dining-room."

"But Pamela has not finished her savoury. She, at least, should be spared this vulgar nonsense."

"Why, Papa?" I said, with a hint of Mamma's steely firmness. "I was present when you brought home that broadsheet and heard Mamma read it aloud. And I know all about your striking him. Moreover, Mamma and I have had the dubious pleasure of meeting the gentleman, if we may call him that, at Lady Merlyngton's last month. I should like to stay."

"It may be very unpleasant, Princess. Words unfit for your young ears —"

"The other day, when Mamma questioned whether she should read the broadsheet in my presence, you said I was no longer a child. It is true: I am not; you were quite right. Pappa, I *wish* to remain!"

He looked up at Rutledge, saying, "You see who rules the roost in this house, Rutledge. Very well — shew Mr. O'Connor in here."

With obvious disapproval and pain, Rutledge said, "Very good, sir," and left the room.

Papa muttered, "Wonder what the fellow wants? This is a matter to be thrashed out by solicitors, not flung down on the table in a man's own house. Well, I knew he was no gentleman, so why should I be surprised when he doesn't behave like one?"

Rutledge ushered Mr. O'Connor into the room. His hair was even redder and more wild than I remembered it — a raging fire, whipped by the wind — and his eyes were like chips from a glacier. Fire and ice, each at war one with the other; that is Rhys O'Connor.

"Thank you, Rutledge," said Papa. "That will be all for the moment." Rutledge left. "Now then, O'Connor, will you be seated?"

"I will stand, if you don't mind," he said, with scarcely a trace of brogue.

"Suit yourself. I believe you have already made the acquaintance of my wife and my daughter?"

"I have, yes." He bowed stiffly to each of us in turn. "Mrs. Summerfield. Miss Summerfield."

"Will you take coffee, Mr. O'Connor?" asked Mamma.

"Thank you, no."

"Then out with it, man," said Papa.

"I should have preferred a private meeting," O'Connor said.

"Your preferences are of no concern or interest to me," Papa replied. "I have no secrets from my family."

"Very well," said O'Connor. "I will be brief. I have spoken

to me solicitor, and he tells me that I have an excellent chance of winning a suit for battery — we have witnesses; your attack was unprovoked —"

"Unprovoked!"

"There is no evidence that I have ever attacked or insulted you. What I came here to say is that despite the firm legal grounds of my case and my good chance of winning, I am not bringing suit."

Mamma and I were immensely relieved at these words, but if Papa was, he did not shew it.

"Another reason for my coming," O'Connor went on, "is to apologise to you. Oh, don't expect a public apology or a retraction; this will be a private apology only, for your ears . . . and the ears of your wife and daughter. I apologise *not* for what I said — indeed, I did not say half enough! — but for my timidity in signing the verses with my initials only. You are right in one thing, Mr. Summerfield: when a man launches an attack, he should do it openly and take the consequences."

O'Connor began to pace the carpet, restlessly; then he drew a chair out from the table. "If I may, I think I *will* sit down," he said, and did so.

"There is a reason I did not sign me name," he said. "Call it cowardice, if you will; but I call it caution. Do you remember a man named Accum?"

The name evoked a subtle response in Papa — I could tell that he had heard it before — but he assumed a casual air, and replied, "German chap?"

"I see that you do recall him. Yes, he was German-born. But he had a position of great respect and responsibility as a chemical operator to the Royal Institution. He was obsessed by the analysis of foods, and horrified by the amount of adulteration practised by food manufacturers to increase their profits." O'Connor, by turning first to Mamma, then to me, now drew us closer into the subject. "About sixteen or seventeen years ago, Accum brought out a book that provided proof — irrefutable *scientific* proof — that manufacturers were causing illness and death by adding noxious ingredients to the food and drink they sold to the public. Red lead used to colour Gloucester cheese, for example — a lethal substance. Brick dust in chocolate. Powdered chalk in milk, to make it whiter.

Alum in bread, likewise to make it whiter, as well as weightier —"

"Good gracious!" said Mamma.

Papa said, "What has all this to do with us, O'Connor?"

Our visitor smiled thinly and continued as if he had not been interrupted: "And vitriol added to beer, along with *cocculus indicus,* to give it a falsely stronger flavour and to increase its intoxicating effects. I see no beer at this table — I see claret and Rhenish; I see port and sherry and whisky on the sideboard — but I see no beer. I find this odd, in the house of a brewer. And yet I am glad, for I should never like to see these gracious and lovely ladies stupefied or paralysed or thrown into convulsions, or their respiratory systems stimulated to the point of death."

"This interview is at an end," said Papa, rising from the table.

But Mamma said, "I should like to hear what Mr. O'Connor has to tell us. But pray come to your point more quickly, sir." Papa sat down again, displeased.

"Thank you, ma'am," said O'Connor. "I will. Accum's book caused quite a stir — and the thanks he received was to be hounded out of England by the Royal Institution itself. They trumped up a charge — said that when he was the Librarian for the Institution, he mutilated some books, tore out the pages. The pages were found in his rooms. He pleaded innocence, although the charge was trivial enough even if true — said he had never seen the pages; said they must have been placed in his rooms to discredit him. But they kept after him until he was forced to return to his native land. Anybody with eyes in his head never had any doubt that the powerful food and brewing interests had exerted influence on the Institution in order to get rid of Accum and to drag his name in the mud."

"Are you quite through, sir?" asked Papa.

"Nearly so," said O'Connor. "I am trying to explain the reasons why a man might choose to leave his writings unsigned. Accum signed his — and we may learn from his example that it was a foolish, although brave, thing to do. That is why I have not signed me own writings. I do not wish to be brought down by false evidence trumped up by the vested interests which I attack. Me first piece of anonymous writing was published about seven years ago. I imagine it came to your attention, Mr. Summerfield. It was a small pamphlet with a large title — *Deadly Adulteration and Slow Poisoning Unmasked: or, Disease and Death in Pot and Bottle.* Yes, I see by the expression on your face that you recollect it. But no doubt these ladies never saw it. It was an appeal to end . . . let me see if I recall me own words . . . to end 'blood-empoisoning and life-destroying adulteration.' It was widely circulated, and caused a good deal of talk. I can not boast any degree of originality — most of me facts were culled from poor Accum's book — and me prose style has improved since then, I'm glad to say — but it was a creditable effort. Unfortunately, I made use of irony and satire — it is the Irish in me, I suppose — not knowing that irony and satire are not relished by you solid, stolid English. You tend to dismiss writers who are not sober and serious in dealing with sober, serious matters. Besides, who can take seriously an author who lacks the courage to sign his own words? I sent a copy to the editors of *The Lancet,* and even they dismissed it as the work of a panic-monger. And so, nothing has been done to stop adulteration. They silenced Accum, and I silenced meself by satirical conceits and anonymity."

O'Connor rose from his chair. "Well, it has taken a long time for me to learn me lesson, but I have learnt it at last. I will write no more anonymous pamphlets. From this point, I will put me name to everything. Roc is dead; long live O'Connor! And I give you fair warning, Mr. Summerfield — you have not heard the last of me. Books, pamphlets, articles — they will pour from me pen as beer from your breweries, and they will be enlivened by even more vitriol than you employ!"

"Get out!" roared Papa.

"But here is the difference," O'Connor concluded. "Me vitriol will *save* lives — not destroy them!" And, with that, he turned and strode out of the room.

"Well!" said Mamma, after a moment. "You must admit, Wilfrid, that the man is, if nothing else, colourful."

"So is gangrene," snapped Papa.

The King is not well. That, at least, is the rumour now abroad. I suppose we may have expected it, as he is now over seventy, but it is distressing all the same to think that we may lose him. Some say he is far from brilliant — but he would be the last to claim any extraordinary qualities, for he has always called himself an ordinary man first, a king second. Still, for all his ordinariness — and his eccentricity — he has done much good during his reign. It is thanks to him that the hitherto exclusive Royal Parks have been opened to the people. The Factory Act, which limits the working-hours of children in textile mills, was put through in his reign. So there is much to thank King William for; and we must all pray for his improved health and long life.

If he were to die now, before the Princess comes of age, we would have a Regency of several months, doubtless under the Duchess of Kent and her ubiquitous *éminence grise,* Sir John Conroy — or "King John," as they call him behind his back — and that would be most unsuitable. They say that he is her lover and that he rules Kensington Palace with an iron hand, playing the martinet and despot to his betters, including our future Queen herself. The entire situation is most unsavoury. God protect King William!

Life indeed seems irksome. There are not only the greater worries, such as the health of the King, but the personal ones, as well: Phoebe's strange problem, which gnaws at me; and the insupportable O'Connor person, whose visit yesterday evening has upset me so. The man enters our house under the excuse of tendering an apology to Papa and telling him he is not bringing suit against him — and then proceeds to attack Papa again, accusing him of poisoning the beer he manufactures! Vitriol, he says, and *cocculus indicus,* whatever that may be, causing convulsions and paralysis and death! How absurd! Papa would never hurt anybody! And that dreadful man intends to start a steady stream of his irresponsible scribblings. Thank God there is no penny post to speed them on their way!

Among the many vexations I endure (not even counting That Time, which has come round again):

This afternoon, as Mamma and I were at our needlework, she said to me, "Do you remember, Pam, on Monday last, when I was on the very point of going shopping with you and Mam'selle La Grange — but did not, because your father returned earlier than expected?"

(I certainly did!) "Yes, Mamma," I said.

"A most curious thing," she went on. "If I were a believer in witchcraft or the projection of one's physical likeness to far places whilst one sits at home, I might think I had been suddenly endowed with occult powers. For, even though I did not leave the house on Monday, and merely *intended* to do so, I am told by Lady Merlyngton that I was shopping in Henrietta Street that afternoon."

(My heart dropped down into the pit of my stomach!)

"Yes," Mamma continued, "she was told so by Captain Ormond, whom she met, quite by hazard, in a tea-room in that same street. I suppose the captain saw some lady in a shop who resembled me. That would explain it, would it not? At any rate, to avoid embarrassing the captain, I told a white lie and acknowledged that I was, indeed, in Henrietta Street on that day, and that I am sorry to have missed seeing her."

I thought it best to say nothing and to continue with my needlework.

"Did you also see Lady Merlyngton on Monday?"

"Yes, Mamma."

"And did you run into Captain Ormond, as well?"

"Yes, Mamma."

"Then it must have been a pleasant outing for you."

"Oh yes, Mamma."

"I am surprised that you did not mention seeing those friends of ours."

"Well, Mamma," I said, "you will recollect that, the very moment I returned, you called me into the drawing-room to tell me of Papa's striking Mr. O'Connor. And almost immediately after that, I had to change, because Mrs. Ridgely and the twins were expected for tea. After that, it simply slipped my mind."

"Ah, yes," she said, and spoke no more of the matter. But I knew that she had seen through my little scheme, and this was simply her way of telling me so.

I was the first one down to breakfast this morning. Indeed, one of the new maids had not quite finished laying the fire, dilatory creature. Rutledge, presiding at the sideboard, was unusually cheerful and bright. "Tea, Miss? Coffee? Chocolate?"

"Chocolate, please, Rutledge."

"Here it is, Miss, piping hot. Now then: with what may I tempt your appetite this morning? We have cold joints of lamb and beef, game, some nice broiled fish, sausages, eggs, kidneys, bacon?"

"An egg, I think, and a bit of bacon."

"Nothing else, Miss? The kidneys look good to-day."

I made a face. "I think kidneys are *horrid.*"

"Yes, Miss. As you wish. *De gustibus non est disputandum,* as the Romans said."

"Is that the same as the French *chacun à son goût?*"

"I expect so, Miss. You'll have to ask Mam'selle about that. Toast? Muffins? Butter? Marmalade?"

"A muffin, please. Butter, no marmalade."

"Why, you'll waste away to nothing, Miss."

"On the contrary, Rutledge; I shall grow quite fat if I were to eat all that's offered me. I didn't know you were so learned in Latin."

"Got it all from a book, Miss, when I was younger than you are now."

"I think that is highly commendable. Do you know that Papa considers you a remarkable man? He told us so once."

"Your father is very kind."

"He said you had to make your own way from the age of ten, when your father died."

"That's so, Miss."

"How did you live?"

"As best I could. Slept in doorways or under tarpaulins or in deserted houses. I wasn't the only one, Miss: there were a great many children in the same circumstances, boys and girls alike. The girls sometimes fell into very wicked ways, I'm afraid, especially if they were pretty. As for myself, sometimes a kindly servant would hand me out a crust of bread from the kitchen door, or a bone with some meat still on it." (I recall glimpsing Rutledge passing out scraps of food to ragged children at our own kitchen door.) "I found work where I could get it," he went on. "Worked as a bone-gatherer, a crossing-sweeper, a bootblack; gathered cigar-ends from the streets for a time."

"Whatever *for?*"

"Got ha'penny a pound for 'em, Miss, if they were good and dry. An adult would get anywhere from six to ten pence a pound — I never could see the fairness in that. We sold them to men who used the tobacco to make new cigars, of a very cheap and inferior variety, of course. Do try this bit of fish, won't you?"

"No, thank you, Rutledge. It must be very hard, indeed, to lose one's father at such a tender age. What did he die of?"

"Well, Miss, most chimney-sweeps sooner or later get a sickness in the lungs — it's a natural condition of the work, you see, like miners — and I expect my father was no different and would have died of it in time. But, in fact, he came over queer, all sudden-like, one evening after supper. Doubled over and clutched at his stomach and was dead before morning. Bad beer, they said it was. He was thirty-four. Now what would you say to a nice sausage, Miss?"

"I think not, Rutledge."

I'm afraid his stories quite spoiled my breakfast.

ॐ *Sunday, 5 February*

On Friday next, we will hold our first dinner-party of the year. Mamma planned it and sent out the invitations three weeks ago, and I was present when she gave instructions to Rutledge and Mrs. Pruitt.

"It will be the first time this year we will have entertained," she said, "not counting our at-homes and teas and such, although I like to give at least one dinner-party a month. But the holiday season was such a busy one that I felt quite exhausted by it. At any rate, seeing that this will be our first in some time, I do wish it to be particularly well handled.

"Mrs. Pruitt, I want you to give some thought to the soups

and fish dishes for the first courses. At least two soups, I think, perhaps three, and a like number of fish dishes. Think about it and let me know your suggestions tomorrow. We should have a few light dishes on the side during the first courses, too, such as oyster or lobster patties."

"Yes, mum," said Mrs. Pruitt.

"The *entrées?* Four, I think, will be sufficient, although possibly five would be better. I haven't an idea in my head, Mrs. Pruitt, so I rely upon you to advise me. Some of our guests will prefer white meat, some red; so two roasts must be the absolute minimum. As for the game to follow — oh, the usual: grouse, partridge, pheasant, woodcock, and some kind of domestic fowl for those who prefer it.

"The sweet," Mamma continued, "must call up all your art, Mrs. Pruitt, and after that, when the table is cleared, we will have ices, and savouries for those who want them, and an epergne of little cakes, sweet biscuits, nuts, and dried fruits, to go along with the ices. Coffee and *liqueurs* to finish with."

"Yes, mum."

"Rutledge, be sure we are well stocked with all the necessary wines for the meal — sherry, Madeira, claret, Burgundy —"

"Champagne," said Rutledge.

"Champagne, of course."

"Will you be wanting a whet-cup before, ma'am, or a *coupe d'avant,* as they say? It crisps the stomach before dinner, I'm told."

"Oh, I think not, Rutledge. I know it's the fashion now to drink before dinner, but with all the wines and *liqueurs* that follow . . . Still, if you think . . ."

"Perhaps just glasses of brandy and rum, ma'am, set out for those who might like it."

"Very well." Turning to me, she said, "Pam, you should count yourself fortunate that you are too young to remember the old way of dining, when several dishes were all put out together on the table, with the guests helping themselves out of the platters, and reaching past one another, and asking to be handed this or that, until the table-cloth looked like an artist's palette of gravy and soup and what-not. You remember, don't you, Rutledge?"

"Indeed, ma'am."

"I suppose people may still dine that way in the country, but I am thankful that those of us in good society now use the *service à la française.* It is *one,* at least, of the new fashions of which I whole-heartedly approve."

"Mamma," I said, "may I have a new frock for the occasion? It will be our first grand party of the season, and I shouldn't like to appear in something old."

"I shall require something myself," she said. "There is not a great deal of time, but Mrs. Forbes works very quickly. Rutledge, send Crewe to her with a message, asking her to come round to-morrow with samples of the latest fabrics."

"Yes, ma'am."

Mamma tapped her finger to her chin, to dislodge a hiding thought, then said, "And candles, Rutledge. Plenty of candles. The gas chandeliers are all very well for every day, and they do make the silver and the ladies' jewels sparkle, it's true; but they tend to splutter, and sometimes they fail altogether. Besides, they make the skin look sallow. Ladies' lips look cold and colourless in such light. Young girls like you, Pam, look pleasing in any light; but the older ladies will be in the majority, and we must think of them. One evening I happened to catch a glimpse of myself in a glass under those gas chandeliers, and I resembled the skull of Yorick. Candles are so much nicer, especially the new ones. You don't remember how the old ones smoked, Pamela, and gushed torrents of wax and required their snuffs to be cut constantly — but Rutledge remembers. Tell her why the new ones are so much better — something about the new acids, I believe?"

"Yes, ma'am," said Rutledge. "Stearic and boric acids, discovered in the last decade. The first of them is used as a hardener for the candles — you have no idea how soft the old ones were, Miss — and the second is used to impregnate the wicks, to eliminate guttering. Then there are the new plaited cotton wicks, which are snuffless."

"Quite," said Mamma. "So, plenty of candles, Rutledge. And this will give us an opportunity to use that magnificent new candelabrum your Uncle Roger sent us at Christmas, Pam." She was referring to a grand affair on which a muscular

Apollo clutches Daphne, whose arms are long, curving floral branches in which the candle-holders are set.

"Now, the guest-list," she said. "Pam, be a dear girl and write down these names as I think of them."

"Yes, Mamma." Pen and inkpot were near at hand.

"Lord and Lady Merlyngton. Mrs. Trollope and her son — what is his Christian name?"

"Anthony."

"That's it. Mr. and Mrs. Randall — I suppose your Papa will insist on inviting him because of business connections. St. John Barstow. Lord Stanton is in Italy still, I believe. I would invite the Swinburnes, but she is expecting. You might put down your Uncle Roger, although I doubt very much that he will make the journey. Still, it would be courteous to send him an invitation. No point in inviting your sister and her husband. They won't travel in all the way from the Midlands for a dinner. Mr. and Mrs. Cargrave: some think doctors not suitable for society, but Mr. Cargrave is a most elegant gentleman, and I like to talk to his wife; she's sensible. The Widow Ridgely; and I suppose we shall have to invite the twins, as well."

"Must we, Mamma? They are *so* supercilious!"

"Heavens, child, your words are growing longer day by day. And that's not a nice thing to call a person."

"I meant it quite *literally*, Mamma. Rutledge is a Latin scholar; he can tell us the literal meaning, can't you, Rutledge?"

"From *super cilium*, Miss. Literally, with raised eyebrow. The figurative meaning is less complimentary."

"Well," said Mamma, "raised eyebrow or not, we must invite them; they're not little girls any longer. Put them down."

I did, saying, "I hope they have got over their colds, at least."

Mamma tapped her chin again. "I *know* I am leaving out somebody." I thought it best not to mention her most glaring omission. Suddenly, she said, "Ah! The Fentons! Of course! Put them down, Pam. Sir Oscar and his wife."

"We shall need two chairs for *her*," I said, and, out of the corner of my eye, I saw Rutledge suppress a smile.

"That should be all, I think," said Mamma, and my heart

fell. "How many guests does that total, Pam, and what is the balance of men and women?"

I counted them up. "Fourteen," I said, "not counting Uncle Roger. But we are quite overbalanced with women — it is the three Ridgelys who have done it. There are eight women to six men. And when we add ourselves — you, Papa, and me — it will be no better; ten women to seven men."

"Oh, dear. If we were to delete the Ridgelys *in toto,* what would the balance be, including us?"

"Perfect," I replied. "Seven and seven." (But, privately, I said, Far from perfect without Giles.)

"Then strike out the Ridgelys." (I did so, with three vigorous strokes of the pen.) "There! That's settled!" said Mamma. But suddenly she held her forehead in annoyance. "How forgetful of me. Mrs. Randall is spending a month with her sister in Shropshire. Mr. Randall will have to come without her. That will give us *thirteen* at table! We need another person, but who shall it be? I am *so* vexed at Lord Stanton for being in Italy. He is very amusing at dinner-parties, and always has a new verse to recite."

I was so annoyed at Mamma for avoiding all mention of Giles that I said, rather waspishly, "Perhaps we should invite Mr. O'Connor. *He* writes verses, too."

"Don't be sarcastic, my dear; it makes hard little lines around your mouth, as well as giving you a *supercilious* appearance. I suppose we could invite Mr. Disraeli. But Lord Merlyngton holds such unreasonable views of Jewish people — he *detests* the Rothschilds, for instance — that he might make embarrassing remarks and ruin the party."

"Why not invite Mr. Disraeli and leave out the Merlyngtons?" I suggested.

"Would that we could," said Mamma, with a sigh. "But you know how important Lord Merlyngton is to the brewing industry. Without his influence in Parliament . . . ah, well, we shall just have to solve our problem in another way."

"Begging your pardon, ma'am," said Rutledge, "but if another guest is required, would you be wanting to invite the young captain?" (Bless Rutledge! He is *all-knowing!*)

"A good suggestion," said Mamma, "but should we not invite his father, as well? I believe the mother is dead. We have not met the father as yet, but perhaps it is time we did. Of course, that will give us too many men, but that is all right. If there is to be a slight imbalance at a party, I prefer it is to be on the side of the men. Put them down, Pam: Percival Ormond and his son, Captain Giles."

I did so, enthusiastically!

At precisely that moment, Papa entered the drawing-room. "Are you making up the guest-list for the dinner-party, my dear?" he asked Mamma.

"Yes, Wilfrid."

"Put down Creighton Ormond and his wife. I want to sound him out in regard to investing more heavily in the business. This will give me a perfect opportunity."

"But, Papa!" I blurted out. "Captain Ormond and his father are invited — and you know there is bad blood between the Ormond brothers."

"Simply solved," said Papa. "Remove the captain and his father from the list. Creighton Ormond *must* attend. It is very important to business." So saying, he left the room.

"Oh, Mamma," I wailed, *"must* we?"

"You heard your father," she replied. "And you should know by now that on anything 'important to business,' his word is *law."*

(Business! Sometimes I think it so hateful! Adam Smith was right: a nation of shopkeepers!)

"So strike out Captain Ormond and his father, and write down Mr. and Mrs. Creighton Ormond. And don't *pout* so. We can invite your pretty captain next month."

(But next month is so far away.)

The dress-maker, Mrs. Forbes, came round the next day with samples of fabric for our new gowns. They were all very beautiful. She shewed us Sultane, a mixture of silk and mohair, with alternate *chinés* stripes; and satin *velouté,* which is as rich as velvet and yet as supple as muslin; and Pekin point, a rich white silk, painted with bouquets of flowers, and with a light mixture of gold in the pattern. She then brought out some Levantine *folicé,* a soft, rich silk with arabesque patterns; and Algerine, a delightful twilled shot-silk, available in either green and red, or blue with gold. Finally, she shewed us some Ottoman satin, which is a very rich shaded satin, embroidered with flowers. It was difficult to choose from among that *embarras de richesse,* but at length I selected the Algerine, in blue and gold, and Mamma chose Pekin point. Mrs. Forbes then brought out her pins and tape-measure, and discussed cuts and patterns with us. I insisted on something cut quite low, to display my shoulders and neck; and, after some hesitation, Mamma agreed: "What might be indecent on a woman of fuller figure — myself, for instance — will be proper enough on you, I expect." (Dear Mamma — but I could have *killed* her!)

ॐ *Monday, 6 February*

This morning, there was a timorous tap at my door, and I opened it to Dora, the scullery-maid, who is almost never seen upstairs. "Yes, what is it, Dora?"

"I'm so sorry to trouble you, Miss." She looked over her shoulder, furtively. "Might I slip in for half a moment?"

I stepped aside to let her pass, and she made sure to close the door.

"Mr. Rutledge would throw a fit if he found me abovestairs, Miss," she said.

"Never mind about Rutledge," I said. "What's this all about?"

"Well, Miss, on my half-days, I've been seeing a young man. Walking out with him. A fine young chap he is, and ever so handsome in his uniform. He's a soldier, you see, Miss, in the Dragoons. And, this morning, early, he stopped by the kitchen door — thank goodness Mrs. Pruitt didn't see him! —and passed me this. It's for you, Miss." She handed me a note, folded and sealed, with the inscription *Miss Pamela Summerfield* on it. "It's from his captain, Miss," she said.

"Thank you so much, Dora!" I said in my delight. "I shall remember your kindness, never fear! And thank your young man for me."

"Yes, Miss," she said, and was gone, with another glance over her shoulder.

I broke the seal immediately and unfolded the note, my hands trembling. It read:

"My dearest Pamela, —

"I resort to this clandestine method of delivery in order that I may not give your mother cause to reprimand.

"It is late as I write this, and it is dark and cold. I have arisen from my bed, where I have been unable to sleep. I must tell you that I am in a perfect agony for want of seeing you. Those pitifully few moments we have been together are like scraps thrown to a starving man — they taunt and torture; they but sharpen hunger; they do not assuage it. We are for ever in the midst of other people — whether it be in your drawing-room, or Lady Merlyngton's, or in a tea-room —and in such throngs I may not tell you what is truly in my heart; I may not even hold your hand. And, dearest girl, I wish to do far more than that: to hold you in my arms; to kiss you; to shew you the full and deepest measure of my love. Yes, there, I have written the word — love! Take it as my avowal of all that is true and sincere in my heart, and tell me that you love me in return. Write but a word or two, and your servant will convey your note to my batman, who will in turn bring it to me — where, I assure you, it will be pressed to eager lips and held to my heart for ever. And when you write, my dear, tell me when we may see each other again, and where, and how we may contrive to be alone. If you wish this as much as I, you will bend your mind to it and find a way, for you are the cleverest little lady alive, as well as my sweet, my adorable love!

"Your worshipping
"Giles"

What a dear, *dear* letter! It is before me now as I write this; and every time I read it over, I feel as if the blood burns in my veins.

But, try as I may, I can not hatch a plan whereby we may meet alone. The shopping afternoon with Mlle. La Grange is a thing that will work only once; and even *it* came near to being a catastrophe, for Mamma discovered all. I am not so clever as

Giles thinks I am. I wish I were. And so the note I dashed off to him said only this:

"Dearest Giles, —
"Your darling letter has caused my heart to overflow. I will tell you, in the simplest terms: Yes, my dear, your love is indeed returned! I love you with all my heart, my soul, with every fibre of my being! There is nothing in this world that I desire more than to see you alone; but I am such a goose that I do not know how this may be managed. Can not my valiant captain, so accustomed to sorties and surprises and to plans of action, devise a manœuvre? I beg you to do so; and I will obey every word of your command, like a good soldier.
"Your own beloved
"Pamela"

When I had sealed the note, I carried it below-stairs, for I did not wish to draw attention by summoning the scullery-maid to my rooms.

How I loved, as a child, to venture down to Mrs. Pruitt's fascinating kitchen. The old-fashioned open fire-place, with its array of spits, hanging-hooks, and portable ovens, has now given way to a modern coal-burning cast-iron range. There, on one side of the range, flush with the grate, is the lidded boiler, with a tap for drawing off hot water; on the other side are the ovens. But the old stone sink is the same, with the wooden cupboards below, and the wooden draining-board I remember so well. Also the same is the medley of pots, pans, lids, jugs, and mops standing upon or hanging from those open, scrubbed wooden shelves set in the recess made by the chimney-breast. The stone-flagged floors are uncarpeted, of course, but despite the stone flagging, the kitchen has always been the warmest room in the house in winter.

"Why, Miss Pam," said Mrs. Pruitt. "How good of you to visit us! We haven't seen you down here in an age!"

"I expect you know why I'm here," I said, with my most vixenish smile.

"A nice hot cup of tea and a piece of my Madeira cake, I'll be bound!" she replied, her eyes a-twinkle. "Well, you just sit right here at the table, Miss Pam, and I'll cut you a good big slice. The tea is steeping already, and it will be just right in a minute. Good and strong. Lots of milk and sugar; that's the way you like it. I know!" She walked off, chuckling, and when she was safely out of sight, I passed the letter to Dora, with a pound note and a wink.

Mrs. Pruitt's Madeira cake was exquisite.

ஓ Tuesday, 1 February

All day I waited for some word from Giles; listened for Dora's tap at my door; watched for her in the corridors as I wandered through the house. I did not dare venture down to the kitchen again so soon: it would arouse suspicion and could cause trouble, not only for me, but for Dora, who might lose her place if it were discovered that she is acting as a courier for love letters.

The day seemed endless. By the time the dinner-hour was upon me, I had given up hope of receiving anything from Giles. Perhaps to-morrow, I told myself. Perhaps Dora had not had an opportunity to see her young man.

When I sat down to dinner, I was glum and not disposed to conversation. Listlessly, I drew my napkin out from its ring and unfolded it — and my heart did a little hop when I saw a folded sheet of paper inside! Clever Dora had found a way to convey my lover's message. When Mamma and Papa were not looking my way, I slipped it inside the front of my gown.

A moment before, I had had no appetite because of gloom; now, I still had no appetite, but for an entirely different cause — I was tremulous with impatience; I wanted to dash out of the dining-room, to some private place, where I could tear open the letter and devour it with my eyes.

But I forced myself to remain calm, at least on the surface. I took a little of every dish that Rutledge offered me, although I ate but sparingly of each. At last — after an *eternity!* — we had finished dinner, and I excused myself and walked slowly, sedately, up here to my sitting-room. When I was safely behind its door, I plunged my hand down inside my gown and pulled

113

out the note, almost ripping it in my haste to open and read it. It was very short, and written in a rapid scrawl:

"My dearest girl — in great haste — you have made me the happiest man in the world. Leave the window of your bedroom unlatched tonight when you retire; and wait for — your devoted — Giles."

My heart stopped beating, I swear it. I could not breathe. I was stunned and appalled. *What had I done?*

This is not what was in my mind when I beseeched Giles to "devise a manoeuvre." I was thinking of a guiltless *rendez-vous*, like our meeting in the tea-room — not an assignation in my *boudoir!* How could Giles have thought otherwise? What manner of man is he? What kind of woman does he think me to be? A wanton? How low of him to place me on that level!

And yet, why should I blame him? There was no deception in his letter, had I but eyes to see. He had said he wished to do far more than hold my hand: *to hold you in my arms; to kiss you; to shew you the full and deepest measure of my love.* The meaning was plain: he was seeking that final, physical consummation that should come with the wedding night — and I, in my answer, had granted it! How else should he interpret my reply? I told him: *I love you with all my heart, my soul, with every fibre of my being!* Does that not mean: with all of my flesh, with every atom of my body, from the hair on my head to my toes? I told him: *There is nothing in this world that I desire more than to see you alone.* Is that an ambiguous statement? No: it can have but one meaning, in the heated context of my note. *I will obey every word of your command,* I said, *like a good soldier.* Was that not an invitation to make every demand of me, and a promise that I would comply? What else was the man to think but that I was inviting him to my bedroom and my bed?

I sat down at once at my desk and began to write a note to him, some quick word to correct my error and prevent him from climbing to my window to-night. But even as I was dipping the pen in the inkpot, I knew it was futile. There was no way, at this hour, that the note could possibly reach him in time.

All I can do is to keep my window firmly latched to-night when I retire . . . even though I know that it will break his heart.

Written later. It is quite into the small hours of the morning now, and the thick fog that had hung about all day is gone, and the night-sky is fine and clear and full of stars.

I went to bed at about half past ten, after first making sure that my window was securely latched. I felt miserable and absurd. I knew myself for what I am: a foolish girl, filled with sugary dreams of romance; not the clever grown-up woman I style myself to be. Only a child could not know the true meaning of those impassioned phrases that flowed from Giles's pen and from mine. Only a poetry-drenched, word-besotted virgin, with no knowledge of the world, could be blind to the physical urgency behind the fine rhetoric. I cursed myself for a stupid, simpering imbecile. I could not sleep, or so I thought; but sleep came unbidden and unwanted; and soon I was deep in a dream of Summerfield House, and spring in Suffolk, and walking through the greenwood, hand in hand with a man who should have been Giles, who had in fact been Giles when first we started walking, but who had changed, until now the man who was holding my hand and smiling down at me was the infamous Rhys O'Connor! The curious thing was that it did not *seem* curious in the dream; it seemed the most natural thing in the world that I should be strolling with that detestable person, returning his smile, laughing at his witticisms — which were deliciously clever in the dream, but which I now see were not remarkable at all: reaching up to pluck a plum from a tree, he said, "If lace over veils enhances prettiness, let's use more, surely." It seemed the pinnacle of wit; and as I laughed, Sophie suddenly appeared beside us, barking, and a woodpecker not far off joined us in a kind of counterpoint, tapping away at a tree trunk with its bill, tapping, tapping, tapping . . .

Until I awoke with a start and knew the tapping to be on my window-pane! I turned to the window — I could see the shadow of Giles outlined on the other side of the glass, crouched on the ledge. Sophie (my bold protector!) was bark-ing furiously at him. He had climbed the trellis, tried the latch, found it locked against him, and was now tapping, to attract my attention. I could almost read his thoughts: Damn the girl! She's forgotten!

I felt such a fool. And I felt so sorry for Giles, crouched out there in the winter cold, risking discovery, risking even life and limb if he were to fall. And still he continued to tap on the glass. Could I be strong enough to ignore him, to stop up my ears, to harden my heart to him? "Shush!" I told Sophie.

I threw off the bed-clothes, sprang to my feet, and ran to the window. Cold air chilled me as I unlatched the window and opened it, but I forgot the cold and was bathed in floods of warmth as Giles climbed into the room and into my arms.

I can write no more. The rest must wait till to-morrow.

ஐ *Wednesday, 8 February*

The happenings of last night seem like a dream. It is almost as if the absurdity of walking through a Suffolk wood with Rhys O'Connor had merged with the other absurdity of Giles climbing the trellis and entering my bedroom like a character in a play. Indeed, there seemed to be more reality in my dream of Rhys O'Connor, whilst I was dreaming it, than in the actu-ality of Giles's reckless visit. For the dream was composed of mundane things — a quiet stroll, a wood in spring-time, sun-light, bird-song, idle chatter — whereas the reality was theat-rical, audacious, and like nothing I had ever experienced be-fore.

After that first kiss — the icy buttons of his uniform im-printing themselves on my skin through my silken night-gown — I pulled away from him, lighted a candle, and at-tempted to explain the misunderstanding. "Please, Giles, this is all a mistake, and I am to blame . . ."

"No, no, dearest girl — there is no mistake, no blame . . ." He tried to take me in his arms again, but I eluded him.

Sophie was still barking at Giles, and I was afraid she would wake the house, so I picked her up and carried her into my sitting-room and locked her in. She soon settled down to a low growling, which I could hear slightly through the locked door. I took a deep breath and spoke to Giles in firm, decisive tones:

"I am a silly, stupid little fool, filled with fancies and fine words, but I know nothing of life. A woman wiser than I would have known at once what you were asking in your letter, and would have denied you or accepted you, according to her choice. But, to me, it was all like something in a play or poem: your words of love, and my response to them, were like *arias* in an opera, a love duet . . ."

"And so they are," he said, gently, persuasively. "The most beautiful love duet ever conceived, the truest love song ever sung . . ."

"You do not understand," I said. "I did not *mean* what I said in my note . . ."

He looked wounded, hurt. "You did not mean it when you said that you returned my love?"

"Yes, yes, I did mean *that*, dearest Giles! I *do* love you!"

"Then what is it that I do not understand?"

"I am not . . . the kind of creature you must think me . . ."

"Not the dearest creature God ever created?"

"I am . . . innocent . . . without experience . . ."

"I have never thought of you as guilty and jaded."

"No man has ever before been in my bedroom in this way . . ."

"I rejoice to hear it."

"No man has ever kissed me as you did . . ."

"Better and better."

"No man has —"

"No man has loved you as I do," he said, clasping me in his arms again, with such strength and fervour that I could not extricate myself. "No man has torn out his heart and thrown it at your feet as a token of his adoration. No man has thought of you as you truly are — a woman of warm blood and high passion and the sweetness and generosity of an angel."

"Oh, Giles," I murmured softly. "Let me go, or I shall faint, I shall die . . ."

"Then it shall be the bright and happy little death of love, and we shall die together!"

"Someone will come . . . ."

"They are all fast asleep."

"I will scream . . . ."

"And bring shame and disgrace to yourself, to your family, to me?"

All this time, through all these words, he must have been coaxing me towards my bed, imperceptibly, for now I discovered that we were sitting side by side on its edge, his arms still holding me firmly. I felt helpless — all my strength had fled — my bones had turned to milk — I was completely without defence. Whenever I tried to speak, he stopped me with a kiss, and each kiss was longer and more ardent than the last. I had never before felt the strangely delicious, somewhat outrageous sensation of another tongue inside my own mouth. Soon, mine was inside his, and it was as if our two tongues were kissing each other.

I can not say when it happened that we were reclining on the bed — our intertwined bodies seemed to melt and easily topple towards the sheets of their own accord, without our volition. I do not remember him undoing my nightgown, but he must have done, for he was kissing my throat and bosom, and it was the most heavenly of feelings, and any shame I should have felt was dispelled by bliss.

I think I did not unfasten the buttons of his uniform — I think he must have done so — but I recall my hands on his warm flesh, and my sudden surprise at the oddity my fingers encountered. I had known, from paintings and statues, how men are made, but in none of those artistic representations was the male form shewn in quite that astonishing way. I wondered if Giles were uniquely deformed, or if other men were the same. I asked myself: How can they walk about, encumbered so, and do the business of every-day life? Does it hurt them?

Fearing to irritate further what I thought must be as raw and agonising as the fiercest boil, I drew my hand away, and discovered on my finger-tip a single drop of clear liquid, like a tiny diamond. I rubbed it between finger and thumb, finding it to be slippery, like heavy oil; and then, for I am more curious than a cat, I touched my finger to my tongue, experiencing a delicate, slightly salty flavour, neither pleasant nor unpleasant. Giles took my hand and silently returned it to its former place, and I understood that my touch was no pain to him, but pleasure; and I caressed and stroked that part (not daring to look at it) until it became quite slick with the clear oil; and an Italian book in Uncle Roger's library came to my mind, the *Decamerone* of Boccaccio, which I had often struggled with, trying, with my small knowledge of the foreign words, to translate it; and in particular I remembered the tale of Alibech and Rustico, and the *resurrezion della carne,* the resurrection of the flesh, which I had thought to have a religious meaning only, but which I now knew to be describing this miraculous transformation in the flesh of mortal men; and as that sudden revelation came to me, Giles shuddered in my caressing hand, and said, "Ah! God! God!" in a hoarse, strangulated whisper, as if he were bravely enduring torture; and I said with concern, "Have I hurt you?" and he replied, with a shiver and a sigh, "Oh, no, my sweet; bless you, bless you," and there was a kind of warm tenacious dram of nectar in my hand, not oily like the other, but as sticky as tree-sap, and Giles, with another sigh, his breath exuding an aroma strangely like that of chestnuts, kissed my cheek, tenderly this time, like my mother or sister, not ravenously and ferociously as before, and I sensed that I had made him very happy and contented.

I stole a glance at my bed-side clock: it was well after midnight now, which meant that it was Ash Wednesday. "How curious," I whispered, "that I have tasted a sweet new sin on the very first day of Lent. Must I give it up until Easter, do you think, Giles? No, I shall give up Madeira cake."

We talked in this way for some time, and he paid me many charming compliments. "You're a silly girl to say that your feet are too large. Look: your foot fairly vanishes in my hand. How smooth and white it is, and what a lovely high arch. Such pretty little nails, too, like a row of pearls." He kissed each pearl, and I felt his tongue on my toes in a brief, tickling flicker that sent a spark of pleasure thrilling up my leg and all the way up my spine, setting my very scalp a-tingle. Kisses of this kind continued, in dazzling variation and increasing audacity, until I dissolved into a heavenly state far better than any I have yet attained through laudanum.

After a time, when the fever had passed and my mind was clear again, I began to think soberly of the consequences of our actions, and I grew fearful, and I remembered Phoebe and her shocking message, NOT HIS, and I stammered out my fears to Giles. He merely chuckled, and explained to me that, although we had found much sweetness in each other's arms, and he was grateful for the joy that I had given him, we had not even begun to plumb the deep well of love's fulfilment; had, in fact, but played with love, as children play with toys; and we could look forward to such transports as would take our breaths away and lift us to the very Heavens; but that those raptures would not come to us to-night but must wait upon another time; and when I reached out my hand to him, I discovered that he was no longer the amazing unicorn he had been a few moments before, but was now in a state very like the paintings and statues.

After a few more tender words and gentle kisses, and a fastening of uniform buttons, he opened my window and left as he had come.

In short, Diary, my lover and I have enjoyed *le plaisir;* and yet, if I have understood his words aright, I stand in no immediate danger of pregnancy, and am still, in point of fact, a virgin.

ॐ *Thursday, 9 February*

So a spoon's worth of pungent sauce holds captive, in miniature, a moiety of the next generation — little boys and girls; men and women; benefactors of mankind and villainous blackguards; some of them destined to die at birth; others marked for a life that might stretch into the Twentieth Century; some blessed by happiness; others to be buffeted by grief and ill-fortune to the end of their days. There they are, invisible to the eye, but swimming and thrashing about and jostling one another, competing to be born. That small clinging gobbet of peculiar ichor, that syrup without sweetness, thick and white as Devonshire cream, contains half the secret of Creation; but if it is thwarted of its purpose and denied its goal, those lives are never lived; the benefactor-to-be does not achieve his noble aim; the villain-who-might-have-been is foiled before he can begin to hatch his evil plots.

It is like the toss of a coin. If Giles had accomplished his full intent — as well he might have, in another moment — then one of the next generation might even now be growing in my womb; but if the seed is left to cool and crust over, cupped in the palm of a lady's fragile hand, that clamoring life remains unborn. A throw of the dice, and a human being is either created, or consigned to the grey shadow-land of the unliving.

What if there were another world, a reflection of our own, shimmering unseen beside us, and peopled with another Giles, another Pamela; and what if, in that world — as like to ours as is one pea unto the other — *just one moment* were different, and Giles had achieved his full desire? In that world, from that fateful moment, the endless pathway of the future would suddenly veer in another direction, determined by the deeds-to-come of the newly germinated life.

On such small motes of chance, whole histories are made or marred; empires are built, or toppled into unremembered dust.

Good news! Mrs. Creighton Ormond is ill! Oh, I know that sounds horrid of me, and I wish the lady no harm (I have never even met her), but her complaint is not serious — just a severe cold in the chest. Even so, she can not attend our dinner-party to-morrow evening, and her husband has sent their regrets, adding that he feels he should stay by her side until the ailment has run its course. This development threw Mama's table into disarray again, and so she has invited Giles and his father to fill the gap. They have accepted!

Bad news: I have just learned that Mr. John Field died on the eleventh of last month, in distant Moscow. So far from home! He was a brilliant piano *virtuoso* and a fine composer, admired by Liszt. Chopin is surely in his debt, for Mr. Field invented the "nocturne," of which form he composed twenty, of which twenty I can play three. He was not yet fifty-five years old — younger than Papa. I pray that Chopin will have a much longer life.

ℬ Friday, 10 February

I told Mlle. La Grange, who dressed my hair to-day, that I must be particularly dazzling at this evening's dinner-party, and that she must use all her arts to make me so.

"You are," she replied, "a very attractive *jeune fille,* and need not worry so much about your appearance."

I recited to her the entire catalogue of my physical short-comings. She laughed and said, *"Mon Dieu!* How many ladies would give everything to have this smooth cheek, this beautiful throat, this little nose, *et cette poitrine, douce et ronde . . ."*

"As regards *la poitrine,* Mam'selle," I said in a lamenting tone, "it is too small, and not nearly *ronde* enough!"

"Mais non!" she declared. *"C'est absurde!"*

"I do wish it were still the fashion for ladies' evening-frocks to be reinforced with stays that pushed one *up* and *out.*"

"Oui, c'est dommage," she agreed, "but when I am finished with the hair, I will show you how to wrap strips of towelling under the gown, into the bodice, *here,* to fill you out and push you up *so.*" She demonstrated with her hands. "Your gown will be *décolleté* to-night, no?"

I assured her that it would.

"Bien. Then I promise that when the *capitaine* sees you so, his eyes will, how do you say, pop out!"

Little did she know that the captain had already seen much more of me than can be displayed in *décolletage.* I was tempted to tell her of my recent adventure, but caution forbade the confidence. Still, I managed to make an oblique reference to it, transferring it to an anonymous third person.

"A young lady of my acquaintance," I said, "recently had an assignation with her *fiancé* in her *boudoir . . ."*

"Quelle scandale!" she said, clicking her tongue.

"But the meeting was not . . . not *entirely* consummated,

she told me, and so there is no fear of her becoming *enceinte*."

"That is good."

"It seems that the gentleman in question achieved his satisfaction . . . *dans la main.*"

"Whose?" asked Mam'selle.

"Hers," I replied.

"*Bien,*" she said, with a nod of approval.

"Then this is a common thing?" I enquired.

"It is a not *un*common, how do you say, *possibilité.*"

"There are, then, other . . . *possibilités?*"

"*Oui,*" she said.

"Many?"

"One or two." She laughed softly. "We French are supposed to have invented one of them, but I have known men of many nations, and I tell you we can not claim that *honneur.*"

She had aroused my curiosity, but I knew that I could press Mlle. La Grange only so far, and only by slow and artfully graduated degrees — else she would frown and tell me that she must not speak of such things to me.

"I must say," I sighed, shaking my head ("Hold still!" she admonished), "I can not imagine what those possibilities can be."

"That is good," she said.

"Can ignorance ever be good?" I asked.

"When you are a wife, you will learn of these things," she replied. "*Maintenant,* you have no need of them."

"But let us suppose," I said, "and I am only making an analogy, that someone were to ask your advice on, let us say, the treatment of burns. Would you tell that person that she should remain ignorant of the knowledge until the need of it arose? I think not. You would tell her all you know about the subject so that she would be forearmed against an emergency."

"That is very different."

"Not so different, really. If a young lady were to find herself alone with a man . . . a man for whom she felt the most fond affection . . . a man who could mould her like wax in his hands . . . and if things were to reach a certain stage . . . and she felt powerless to deny him . . . yet feared to become *enceinte* . . . what means might she employ in such an emergency?"

"You are *incorrigible!*" she said, using the French word.

"Ignorance, in such a situation, could lead to shame, disgrace, great unhappiness," I insisted.

Mlle. La Grange shook her head and smiled. "If you find yourself in such a situation," she said, "you could use the *possibilité* you already know, *n'est-ce pas?*" She quickly added, "From the young lady of your acquaintance." (Had she guessed that *I* am that young lady?)

"Yes, that is true," I conceded, "but you said that there are others. What are they?"

"*Non,*" she said firmly. "You would think them *dégoûtantes.*"

"But why? I did not find the first one disgusting."

"Perhaps that is because you did not experience it yourself, but only heard it from the other young lady." (This was said so flatly, that I could not detect whether she was being sarcastic.)

I did not give up. "Nothing that is done with love can be disgusting," I said. "And I am not a child. I have even read Boccaccio."

"Pah! An Italian!"

"And Rabelais."

"*N'importe.*"

"*Please,* Mam'selle La Grange!"

"*Eh bien,*" she said, with reluctance, and began to speak, in a general way, of what she called *les orifices;* and how, of these, only one is involved in making a woman *enceinte.* "But a lady," she said in conclusion, "has more than one, *comprendez-vous?*"

I sat silent, digesting her words and finding them incomprehensible. She almost seemed to be implying . . . no, that was not possible. I looked up at her reflection in the glass. "You can't mean . . ." I began to say, but faltered and could not find the courage to speak the unspeakable. She merely nodded. "But, Mam'selle, how positively *loathsome!*"

She shrugged, and went on combing.

I have just awakened from a refreshing nap; and soon I will dress for the dinner-party. I will write a full account of the party to-morrow.

(Thinking about my conversation with Mlle. La Grange, I now believe that she can not have been serious. Surely she was only teasing me. The French sense of humour is sometimes regrettably coarse.)

ᘒ *Saturday, 11 February*

This morning, shortly after I arose, there was a knock at my door. It was Hester, with a strange request. "Good morning, Miss," she said. "Begging your pardon, but Mr. Rutledge asks if he might borrow a bottle of your Eau-de-Cologne?"

"Whatever for?"

"I'm sure I don't know, Miss."

My curiosity was so aroused that I said, "I will take it to him myself. Hand me my dressing-gown, please."

Picking up a bottle from my dresser, I stepped out onto the landing, where I found Rutledge arranging a tray of bottles, spoon, and wine-glass on the small table. "Here you are, Rutledge. But why on earth do you want it?"

"Thank you, Miss. I'm mixing a cure for your father, and this is an essential ingredient."

"A cure? Is Papa ill?"

"Oh, do not worry yourself, Miss. He's not so much ill as suffering from what is called a sanguineous congestion, brought on by over-indulgence at last night's party."

"You mean he ate and drank too much and now he has a headache and an upset stomach."

"Yes, Miss."

Rutledge pulled the stopper out of the Eau-de-Cologne bottle and poured out approximately three-quarters of a wine-glass full.

"Won't that make him even sicker?" I squealed in horror.

"Ah, no, Miss. It's nothing but pure spirit — much purer than some of the adulterated potations they sell as drink these days." He handed the bottle back to me.

As I watched him tinker with other small bottles, I asked, "What are you mixing in with the Eau-de-Cologne?"

"Two drams of Rochelle salt," he said, suiting action to word, "one dram of infusion of senna, and a teaspoon of tincture of cardamom. There we are!" He stirred it all up with a brisk clinking motion of the spoon. "With your permission, Miss?" he said, merely a rhetorical question, and, without waiting for a reply, he carried the tray in the direction of my parents' bedroom door.

Except for Papa's sanguineous congestion, the party last night may be counted an unqualified success. I suppose *any* party which Giles attends would be considered successful by this diarist, but it was not his presence alone that was responsible. Mamma had planned everything superbly — she is famed as a fine hostess — and Rutledge and Mrs. Pruitt executed the entire affair with admirable care. The dishes were all culinary triumphs; the wines were exquisite; everybody looked splendid in the candle-blaze — even the Ridgely sisters, who, with their mother, had been reinstated on the guest list.

As for me, I think I do not exaggerate when I say that I made a sensation, thanks to Mrs. Forbes's low-cut gown, Mlle. La Grange's artful towelling, and my own natural (albeit abetted) attributes. Giles, being the Compleat Gentleman, did not pop his eyes, as Mam'selle promised he would; but other eyes, if they did not actually protrude, were continually being drawn to my *décolletage* as if it were a lodestone. I think that some of the older gentlemen may have been reminded of the days of the Regency, when "the snowy orbs of nature undisguised heaved like the ocean with a circling swell," and perhaps they sighed for their vanished youth.

Giles introduced us to his father, the tea-importer, whom I found amiable and pleasant. He and Papa appeared to get on very well together. "So, Summerfield," said Mr. Ormond, "you and I are both in the business of beverages."

"Indeed we are," replied Papa, "but yours has the approval of the Temperance societies."

"So it does — but, do you know, I have never understood the objection these people have to a glass of beer or ale. It is healthful, and an aid to digestion, every bit as good as wine in that regard; and it may be drunk by those few unfortunates with whom wine does not agree. 'Use a little wine for thy stomach's sake,' we are told in Scripture, and yet not all stomachs can abide it. Something about the acid. Beer is just the thing for such folk. It is wrong to condemn it — as wrong as it would be to condemn tea."

"I see you are a man after my own heart," said Papa. "We have some few minutes before dinner. Will you step into the library and see my hunting-prints?"

"With pleasure," Mr. Ormond replied, and, turning to his son, said, "Will you join us, Giles?"

"Perhaps later, Father."

"Well," said Mr. Ormond, with a smiling glance at me, "I leave you in good hands. Very lovely little hands."

When we could talk without being overheard, Giles elaborated upon his father's compliments. "You are beautiful tonight. So delicious that one could almost take a fork and eat you, like a plum-pudding!"

"Goodness," I said, laughing, "what a curious simile!"

"Is it? I'm not very good at all that sort of thing. But it expresses my feelings."

"Then it is a perfect simile, as well as the sweetest compliment I have ever received. I am proud to be your plum-pudding, Giles; and, if you wish it, I shall also be your soup, your fish course, your *entrée* . . ."

"Now you are mocking me."

"No, indeed not!"

"You think me a dunce because I can not make pretty phrases."

"On the contrary, you are adept at pretty phrases; I might even say memorable phrases. I am thinking of 'the bright and happy little death of love,' for instance. Or, 'No man has torn out his heart and thrown it at your feet as a token of his adoration.' Why, they might be from a poem or a novel. Or from a play? Were they from a play, Giles?"

He studied the carpet, and I believe he blushed a little. "Perhaps they were," he admitted. "But they said what was in my heart. If I used borrowed words, it is only because I had none better of my own, and they simply leapt to my lips."

"You mustn't think I am scolding you," I assured him, "but

your own words are perfectly acceptable to me, darling Giles
. . . I *want* to be your plum-pudding — blazing with brandy,
if you like!"

Mamma had been quite right not to invite Mr. Disraeli.
During the dinner, Lord Merlyngton dilated, as is his wont,
upon the Jews. "I am of the same mind as Dr. Arnold," he
said. "I believe that the world is made up of Christians and
non-Christians, and that we of the first persuasion should
stand together. Bringing Jews into Parliament would be a
great mistake. The Jews are Orientals, strangers in England,
and have no more claim to legislate for it than a lodger has to
manage the house of his landlord."

The most interesting *raconteur* of the evening, however, was
Mr. Cargrave, whom I had hitherto thought of as a kindly and
accomplished gentleman of no remarkable social brilliance, but
who proved to be *most* interesting when he was drawn out on
his favourite subjects. It started when Mrs. Ridgely asked his
professional opinion of a popular patent medicine known as
Parr's Life Pills. "Dear lady," he replied, "one must view with
suspicion a nostrum that claims to relieve both constipation
and diarrhœa." A remark not perfectly suited for the dinner-
table, perhaps, but honest and well taken.

He went on to say: "These concoctions are all worthless and
not worth the money spent on them. There is one, called
Morrison's Universal Pill, which is claimed by its purveyors
to cure everything, including insanity. I need hardly point out
the absurdity of such a claim. If it could, indeed, cure everything, there would be no sick people at all, and every physician would be out of business." He smiled roguishly. "We
would *never* allow such a panacea on the market!"

Lady Merlyngton asked him, "Do you think there might be
a recurrence of the Asiatic Cholera which afflicted England a
few years ago?"

(I remember it well. It lasted from 1831 to '33. Many thousands died — always in the poor sections, it seemed — and
silly young gentlemen made up a song which they sang to the
tune of "The Campbells Are Coming": "The Cholera's coming, oh dear, oh dear.")

"I can not say, Lady Merlyngton," replied Mr. Cargrave.

"We know neither the cause nor the cure of the disease — we do not even know how it is conveyed from person to person and country to country. *Ergo,* we can not hope to predict the possibility of its return."

Lord Merlyngton then fixed the doctor with his eye and said, "Cargrave, perhaps you can tell us: What the devil is this new formo — or is it chloro —"

"Chloroform? It's not so very new, Lord Merlyngton. Discovered a half-dozen years ago by an American and a German, more or less simultaneously. Curious how often that happens in scientific discoveries. But the name 'chloroform' was coined for it just the year before last by a Frenchman. As to your question, however: I'm afraid I don't know *what* it is. Nor does anybody else. No-one has been able to find a use for the stuff. Mind you, it's not for want of experimenting. Many of us have toyed with it. Not to put too fine a point on it, I held a little chloroform-party in my own house just a few weeks ago. A few of my friends — doctors, chemists, students —and my wife."

"Chloroform-party?" asked St. John Barstow.

"For want of a better name," said Mr. Cargrave. "We sniffed at the stuff, inhaled its vapours — oh, very cautiously, I assure you. It had the same effect on all of us: any fatigue we had felt suddenly vanished; we became quite lively; extremely talkative. It was exhilarating! Until we found ourselves, some moments later, flat on our faces on the carpet — having no memory of having fallen there."

"Heavens!" cried Mamma.

"One of my colleagues, Simpson, came up with the interesting notion that it might be useful in the course of surgical operations, and perhaps child-birth, to render the patients insensitive to pain. I think the lad may have hit on something."

Lord Merlyngton frowned. "Surely, sir, you are not suggesting that we trespass in God's domain? Pain was sent to be endured. If the Almighty had wanted us to be insensitive to it, He would have provided us with the means."

"Perhaps He has," replied Mr. Cargrave, "and perhaps its name is chloroform."

"But in child-birth?" Lord Merlyngton rejoined. "That

would be impious, in defiance of Scripture. 'Unto the woman he said, I will greatly multiply thy sorrow and thy conception; in sorrow thou shalt bring forth children.' "

Mr. Cargrave said, "You are not alone in your views, m'lord, but my friend Simpson, who is a devoted reader of Holy Writ himself, has pointed out — and wisely, I think — that if we look into an earlier chapter of that same book from which you have quoted, Genesis, we shall be reminded that before the Lord God performed what was probably the first surgical operation in the history of the world, He considerately put the patient, Adam, into 'a deep sleep.' May not we healers, and our poor suffering patients, follow the Divine example?"

Lord Merlyngton could say nothing except: "You will face opposition, Cargrave; mark my word."

"Oh, we are accustomed to that. Need I remind you that it was only five years ago that the Anatomy Act finally passed both Houses and received the Royal Assent? It is only in the past five years, therefore, that physicians and surgeons and students of medicine have had a sufficient supply of *legal* cadavers with which to pursue our researches. Priorly, we had all been forced to break the law and make use of corpses dug up for us illegally by paid resurrectionists. I apologise, ladies, for a subject unlikely to whet your appetites, but I think we should not forget that the Anatomy Act might never have been passed, had not some of those resurrectionists grown greedy and provided an abundant flow of fresh cadavers by the simple expedient of murder. Burke and Hare, Bishop and Williams, to name only two of the dreadful teams, may therefore be called benefactors of mankind — indirectly and unwittingly, of course. No, Lord Merlyngton, we are, as I say, grown used to official opposition to any new and beneficial thing. The Government are like a great old sleeping hippopotamus, stuck in the mud, refusing to move, even when prodded. They have to be blown out of the mud by exploding powder — an analogy to the multiple murders of the resurrectionists and the agonised screams of surgical patients. Come with me into the operating theatre some day, m'lord, and I will change your mind for you. There you will see the torture chambers of the Spanish Inquisition re-created in all their horror." So saying, Mr. Cargrave cut himself a generous morsel of roast beef and chewed it with evident appreciation. "Delicious, Mrs. Summerfield," he remarked. "I have always said that you set one of the best tables in London."

Everybody agreed; and a moment later, Mr. Ormond said, wistfully: "Perhaps it is old-fashioned of me, but I sometimes miss the fine times we had during the Regency. I shall never forget how the Prince celebrated the centenary of the Hanoverian accession. Do you remember, Summerfield, how the Royal Parks were thrown open for the celebration? There were gaming and drinking booths in Hyde Park, and a mock naval battle on the Serpentine — a splendid spectacle! In the Green Park, there was a Castle of Discord, they called it, timed to explode precisely at midnight, to reveal a revolving Temple of Peace attended by a choir of Vestal Virgins in transparent draperies (that was the Regent's idea, I'll be bound). They may have been Vestal, but I had my doubt about the other. Perhaps *Di*-vestal might have been a better name for them — di-vested of raiment as they were, or nearly. Charming! And in Saint James's Park, on the bridge over the canal, they erected a seven-storey Chinese pagoda, which also exploded — but accidentally, in the midst of a fire-works display, killing one of the spectators. We all thought it was part of the show! Ah, no, those days will never come again, I fear . . ."

But even though our party could not hope to match such Regency, *fêtes,* except possibly in the splendour of my neckline, I think we can claim that it was a success.

As the dinner's last course was being consumed, Mamma looked round the table at all the ladies, "collecting eyes"; and, on this signal, we of the gentle sex arose and withdrew to the drawing-room, there to spend a half-hour or so in discussing subjects deemed proper for us: frocks and needlework and the rearing of infants and the latest novels. I have often wished to stay behind when the ladies left the dining-room, and to hide under the table, eavesdropping on the conversation of the men. I do not doubt that they tell ribald stories. Once, I denounced to Papa this practise of separating the sexes, calling it barbaric. He replied:

"On the contrary, Princess, it is the most civilised of customs. The ladies and gentlemen mix freely during the dinner, seated alternately and conversing together most amiably. For a brief period after dinner, it is comfortable and courteous to grant the ladies the opportunity to speak together of their own delicate affairs, without the embarrassment of men within earshot. By the same token, the men are then free to talk politics and business and to cloud the air with the smoke of their cigars. After a short time, we extinguish our cigars and join the ladies once more; by then, both sexes are grown surfeited with the exclusive company of their own kind, and welcome the opposite sex with increased felicity. What could be happier and more sensible?"

(And yet I *still* would like to hide under the table!)

         ஐ *Sunday, 12 February*

Mamma received a letter from Willy yesterday, which she passed on to me; but I did not have time to read it till this afternoon:

"Dear Mother, —
"I am sorry not to have written earlier, but my studies have prevented me from doing so. I am in good health, and hope all of you at home are the same.

"I trust you have been able to peruse the issues of *Tracts for the Times,* which I have been sending you. They will help you to understand the thinking of our Movement's founders and you will then be equipped to defend us against our many attackers. As you know, it is our firm belief that the Church of England has gone astray; has forgotten that it is little more than a satellite of the Holy Catholic Church.

"If we Tractarians seem to place undue emphasis on symbolism and ritual, it is only to remind ourselves and others of certain eternal truths that we fear have become blurred by too many years of laxity and materialism in the Church of England. We are criticised for 'Romish flummery,' but so be it.

"Some say we worship Theology, rather than Christ. I deny the charge. Others say we should concentrate our efforts on alleviating the sufferings of the ill housed, the ill fed, the uneducated. Do Man's duties to Man come before his duties to

God? We are condemned for superstition, for bigotry, for our seriousness and the fierceness of our zeal — but John Newman, the most inspired of our Movement's founders, replies that England would be much the better for a religion 'vastly *more* superstitious, *more* bigoted, *more* gloomy, *more* fierce,' and I am in whole-hearted accord with that statement.

"Our detractors are often men of illustrious name, but of mean and unkindly spirit. Mr. Carlyle, for example, has accused our brilliant Newman of possessing 'the intellect of a rabbit.' A remark of that kind, so obviously unjust, unfounded, and envious, need not be dignified by rebuttal.

"Another bone of contention has been the old statute that imposes a shilling fine on anybody not attending Sunday worship: as we all know, this statute is almost never enforced in our lax times, although it has not been repealed. I, and many of our number, feel that it should be stringently enforced, as part of a general return to stricter discipline in all religious matters. A pamphlet which I enclose, and of which I have the honour to share the anonymous authorship, espouses this view. It has been ridiculed in the press by a cynical atheist named Rhys O'Connor, who now insists on paying his fine every week, in the most public manner, in order to advertise his own Godlessness:

> Such freedom (God willing)
> Is cheap at a shilling,

he says, in a set of mocking verses he has been circulating. But we have become accustomed to mockery and defamation; and I, for one, rejoice in it and feel a kinship with the holy martyrs of the past.

"Please convey my love to Father and Pamela, and my regards to all the servants. I shall write to Phoebe separately, as well as to Uncle Roger, Aunt Esmie, et al.

"Your devoted son,
"Will"

Dear Willy: he is *such* a prig. But I do love him, and I admire him for sticking to his principles. Still, I wonder: Why doesn't he, and why do not others of like mind, simply embrace the Church of Rome? I think Willy would not mind being a celibate priest. I think, rather, that it would suit him. (But no celibacy for *me,* thank you very much!)

ϑ9 *Tuesday, 14 February*

The day dawned fine and cloudless, with just a light haze in the air. The sun, blazing through my window, was warming and cheerful.

As I lay in bed, bathed in sunlight, a paradox came to my mind. I thought of the hateful window-tax that has been in existence since the Seventeenth Century: a tax that aggravates the ill health and gloom of poor people by forcing them to board up their windows tightly against the air and sun, lest their meagre pennies be confiscated by the tax-collector. Well-to-do families, on the other hand, proclaim their wealth by spangling their houses with windows, as if to announce "What care we for the window-tax? Tax and be damned! We are *rich!*" The Summerfields are no exception.

The paradox lies in the wealthy folks' custom of *shutting out* that dearly-paid-for sun by the relentless use of blinds, and curtains of Nottingham lace, and heavy plush side-curtains in dark hues, hanging by brass rings from great poles: all these to keep the sun's rays from bleaching the colours from our furniture and patterned wall-paper, our rugs and carpets, our Berlin-work cushions, our oil paintings, water-colours, engravings, silhouettes, samplers; our ornaments and *bric-à-brac* of ormolu and bronze, of sandalwood, lacquer and *papier-mâché;* our painted vases, *bibelots,* silver-mounted ostrich eggs, elephants' feet, stuffed birds under glass domes . . .

The poor, having no finery to fade, could allow the sun to beam into their hovels freely — were it not for the greedy eye of the tax-collector. And so rich and poor alike shut out the sun from their houses, although for sharply different reasons.

How delicious the sun felt to me; how voluptuous, as it moved so very, very slowly up my body, warming first my feet, then my calves, and my thighs, upwards and upwards, bringing my flesh to life as under Giles's kisses, eliciting from my half-parted lips a dreamy purr of contentment, kindling my senses, filling me to the brim, as it were, and past it, until the only words to describe it are those of the Psalm: "my cup runneth over . . ."

A hesitant tap on my door, at that early hour. I left my warm bed and, wriggling into my dressing-gown, ran to open it.

It was Dora, the scullery-maid, again. She said nothing: just smiled conspiratorially, handed me a small packet, and skittered away like a beetle. I closed the door and opened the packet.

A small gold locket fell onto my toes. I picked it up and quickly read the accompanying note:

"Dear Pamela; —

"You have forbidden me to use borrowed words — my own poor ones are good enough, you say — so I will only pledge myself to be your Valentine, to-day and for ever, and beg that you be mine. The locket enclosed contains my portrait in miniature — but at the age of five, because it is all that I have — and, sealed into the reverse side, a lock of my hair taken at the same age. It belonged to my dear mother. Now it belongs to you. As does my heart.

"Your own
"Giles"

I opened the locket with fumbling fingers. There I saw a dear little boy, with huge brown eyes and the face of a cherub. I recognised my Giles at once! The painter had captured that beloved face with admirable skill and art. It was as if I looked upon the face of my own future son, seed of his loins. I turned the locket over, and saw, behind a tiny pane of glass, a curl of sandy hair, so much lighter then. How I wished there were no glass between it and my lips, that I might kiss it! I held it to my lips, none the less, and then to my breast.

I cantered at once into my sitting-room and sat at my desk to write a note that I would later manage to slip to Dora:

"Dear, dear Giles; —

"What a sweet child you were! And how treble-sweet you are now, to make me a present of your mother's locket. It is the best gift I have ever received, and I will treasure it all of my life. Yes — you are my Valentine, and I yours, until the end of the world, and beyond.

"I have no miniature to give you in return — my only portrait is a great enormous thing painted by Mr. Winterhalter when I was sixteen. It hangs in Papa's library. So all I can give you (aside from my undying love) is the snippet of my hair, which I enclose.

"Your adoring Valentine,
"Pamela"

Taking a pair of scissors from the drawer, I clipped off a curl and folded it into the note. Later in the day, I will find a way to pass it to Dora.

Wednesday, 15 February

"I have been meaning to speak to you for the past few days," Mamma said to me this afternoon, "but have been procrastinating." We were in the drawing-room: she was doing her needlework, and I had been practising one of the sonatas of Beethoven on the pianoforte, and finding some of the passages very difficult. I stopped playing and folded my hands in my lap.

"Actually," she said, "it was your father who wanted me to have these words with you — on a subject he would find embarrassing to speak of. It is about your new gown, which you wore on Friday night."

"Yes, Mamma?" (I said this in the most ingenuous tone, as if I hadn't the faintest idea about what she was going to say; but, of course, I knew full well.)

"To be blunt, my dear, your father and I agree that it is entirely too revealing."

I pretended to be surprised. "Really? But you were with me when I chose the fabric and the cut and the pattern . . ."

"I am aware of that. And I remember remarking that a

neckline of low cut would be acceptable on you, although improper on a woman of mature figure. When I said that, I was not fully cognisant of how mature you have become. I have already explained all this to your father, and he has made me promise that you will not wear the gown again —"

"Mamma! I love it so!"

"— until Mrs. Forbes has had the opportunity to close the neckline with a bit of lace or other material."

"But that will spoil the whole line of the neck! And it is so becoming on me!"

"Pamela, I will not tolerate a tantrum. You will either wear the gown as altered by Mrs. Forbes, or you will not wear it at all. I must say I was stunned when you appeared in it on Friday night. But our guests had already begun to arrive, and I could say nothing. I was embarrassed. I'd had no *idea* you'd become so . . . so buxom . . ."

"But *I* was not embarrassed, Mamma."

"Then you should have been, and since you were not, it was my duty, as your mother, to be embarrassed *for* you."

"Dear Mamma," I said, "I am trying to understand. Are you saying that my . . . buxomness . . . was ugly?"

"No, not ugly."

"Then I do not see how it could have given offence. Can beauty give offence?"

"Beauty misplaced can, certainly. A nude Venus by Botticelli or another great master is charming on canvas — but the model for the painting, naked at the dinner-table, would be quite another matter."

"But, Mamma, I was not naked!"

"You were half-naked. It is the exact term your father used when he bade me speak to you about it."

"Very well, Mamma. But I still think I did not offend our guests. Many of the gentlemen seemed quite pleased by my appearance; even the older gentlemen."

"That is to be expected."

"Captain Ormond thought I looked lovely —"

"I am not surprised."

"— and I'm sure his father did, too."

"Yes, I'm sure he did. Mr. Ormond is a respectable enough

man, I suppose, but I can not help saying that I found him just a trifle vulgar."

"Vulgar? Giles's father?"

"I would say that the son has better manners than the sire, in this case. I really do think that Mr. Ormond should not have spoken, at the dinner-table, about hussies in transparent draperies, and made jokes about virgins, and so on."

"I thought his pun on Vestal and Di-vestal rather clever."

"Perhaps, but improper at a dinner-party."

"Was it proper of Mr. Cargrave to talk about diarrhœa and digging up corpses?"

Mamma sighed. "I admit that some of his remarks were unappetising, and I wish he had not made them; but at least they were not uttered with levity. Mr. Cargrave is a sober and dedicated man who was speaking on serious subjects. Mr. Ormond, I fear, is a frivolous person. But he is probably a good man at heart, and I do not wish to blacken his character. Indeed, I had not intended to speak of him at all, until you mentioned his name. I merely wanted to tell you about your gown. I assume you will have no objection if I notify Mrs. Forbes that it requires modification?"

"No, Mamma," I replied, in a tone so drab and leaden that there was no mistaking the intensity of my objection.

೫ *Thursday, 16 February*

At an unlikely hour of the early morning — some time between one and two — I heard, as in a dream, the sound of horses' hoofs in the street below, and coach wheels, followed shortly by the banging of our door-knocker. Indeed, I thought it *was* a dream, for I fell asleep again for several minutes, to be awakened again, this time by Mamma's weeping, followed shortly by heavy footsteps, unmistakably Papa's, walking past my door and down the stairs. Sophie, alerted, was whining softly and sniffing at the bottom of my door, as if her nose alone could analyse the cause of the commotion.

Donning my dressing-gown, I opened my door and stepped out onto the landing. Sophie bolted past me and shot straight downstairs. I turned in the other direction, towards my parents' bedroom. The door was closed, but I could hear Mamma, softly weeping, on the other side. I put my hand on the door handle but hesitated: something told me to leave her in peace for the moment. So I followed Sophie's example and went downstairs.

Sophie stood outside the door of Papa's study, trembling with excitement and wagging her tail. That could mean but one thing: there was someone behind that door whom she knew and liked, but had not seen for a time. Papa had a visitor; a mysterious late visitor.

On tip-toe, I walked silently to the door and listened.

I heard nothing at first. No one was speaking. If it had not been for Sophie's tell-tale behaviour, I should have thought the room empty.

At length, Papa said something, very low, almost inaudible, five syllables which I took to be "Dear God in Heaven." This was followed by another period of silence. Then Papa spoke again, louder this time, to his guest: "Would you like a glass of brandy? . . . No, of course not, I'd forgotten; you don't indulge. Well, if you don't mind, I *will* . . ."

I heard a decanter clink against a glass. After a time, Papa spoke again: "The whole thing is a mistake, of course, isn't it? . . . Well, *isn't* it?"

The other person said nothing, but must have shook his head in negation, because Papa responded, in a tone of disbelief: "You don't mean to tell me it's *true?!*"

A nod of the guest's head now, I assumed.

"But . . ." Papa was evidently dumbfounded. "But . . . I don't understand . . . I simply don't understand . . ."

I heard the brandy decanter and the glass again.

"I have known you," Papa said in a choked voice, "all these years. But it seems I have not known you at all. How could such a thing *be,* without my having some sign, some hint of it before this?"

There was no reply from the guest. The monstrous great clock out in the foyer tolled the hours in two deep, cavernous, metallic tones. It had never sounded lugubrious to me before, but now it did. When those solemn gongs were silent, I could hear the sound of Papa's heavy pacing. Nothing else was said for more than a minute; and what a long minute it was, and cold — I shivered in my dressing-gown and bare feet, and wished I had taken the time to put on my slippers. I tried to speculate as to who Papa's guest might be. Could it be his friend and associate, Mr. Randall, caught out in a swindle or an indiscretion with some lady other than his wife? Could it be Uncle Roger, who had perhaps done something foolish regarding the estate — gambled it away, or lost it through unsound investments?

Papa began to speak again. "What I cannot understand," he said, "is *why?* The very idea is foreign to me. I can not grasp why a person in your position, with your upbringing, is tempted to do such a thing. It is appalling . . . freakish . . . beyond my power of comprehension. To turn your back on every shred of teaching, every moral precept . . . to throw away your reputation . . . your good name . . . to disgrace your family as well as yourself . . . to cause all decent people to lose respect for you . . . worst of all, to lose respect for yourself . . ."

A fear began to hiss at the pit of my stomach. It was Phoebe in there, I guessed. That explained Sophie's behaviour. She had come home, in the dead of night, in disgrace. Her husband had discovered, God alone knows how, that he was not the cause of her pregnancy, and he had cast her from his house.

But why did not Mamma receive her and solace her, instead of staying in her bedroom, weeping? Phoebe should not be shut in with Papa alone, I told myself. If ever a mother's duty was clear, it was surely here and now.

Papa continued to talk: ". . . How could you do it? *Speak! Have you nothing to say? . . ."* The guest did not reply. "Nothing? No remorse? No contrition? Not even 'I'm sorry?' You will just sit there, with your head hanging? . . ."

More pacing on the part of Papa before he spoke again: ` "Very well. But I demand to know the identity of your partner in this abominable affair. *What is his name?* For it is *he* who must bear the brunt of the blame, the one who corrupted you. Such a thing would have never occurred to you, had not some sly devil put the evil notion in your head . . . tempted you . . . hinting at the luscious flavour of forbidden fruit, I'll wager . . . filling your silly head with honeyed words . . . making you turn away from decency, from God, from . . ."

His voice broke off. In a moment, it returned to him, and he spoke more softly now, with sadness and love, "more in sorrow than in anger" —:

"The flesh," he said. "How it trips us up and traps us. Beckons to us with promises of pleasure beyond price. And there *is* pleasure in it, no denying that, but there is also a price. Always, without fail, there is a price: whether it be disease or pregnancy or a life shattered by disgrace, there is a price we all must pay for our moments of pleasure. And what fleeting moments they are. Hardly worth it. Ah, well, enough of this. I'm tired. So are you. You've had a long journey. Are you hungry? No? All right. Now look at me and listen to me.

"Whatever has happened, whatever will happen, we must stand together. I am your father, and I shall not desert you. Go up to your room, now, and try to sleep. Don't speak to your mother or your sister yet — wait until to-morrow — they must not see you weeping. Come, now, no more of that. On your feet. Let us go upstairs now, together . . ."

I quickly scurried away from the door and hid in the shadowed recess under the stairs. The study door opened, and Papa appeared first. Sophie, her tail wagging madly, ignored him and ran past him, happily to greet the crest-fallen, ashen-faced figure of Willy.

ॐ *Friday, 17 February*

Yes, Diary, I know, it's true: I dramatise.

Another diarist either would have written nothing about Willy's return, or would have blurted it all out at once: "My brother has returned from Oxford, and Mamma is in tears." But I, not content with such a simple bulletin, must re-create the event as I perceived it at the time, in the same order, putting in all the apprehension I felt, and even including my mistaken guess about the night-visitor's identity, delaying the disclosure that it was Willy until the very last. But that, you see, is the way that the facts were revealed to *me;* and I think it best and honest to set them down in the same way; and if that is dramatising, so be it.

Willy stayed in his room all day yesterday. Mamma and Papa said nothing at breakfast about him, except that he had arrived in the early-morning hours, and was ill, and had come home to convalesce. I, of course, knew a great deal more than that, but said nothing. "He is resting now," Mamma told me, "and I do not want you to disturb him. His meals will be sent up to him."

Yesterday, I obeyed, but to-day I tapped on Willy's door and heard him say, in a faint voice, "Come in."

He was sitting in his chair, fully dressed, reading a volume of sermons. "Hello, Willy," I said cheerily. "Mamma says you have been ill. You look well enough to me. Are you better, then?"

He put down the book. "Hello, Pam," he said, gravely. "It's good to see you."

"It's good to see *you*, but I'm sorry you're ill."

He smiled thinly, and shook his head. "I'm not ill. That is what Mamma calls a white lie. I can not convince her that a lie is a lie, no matter what its colour."

I pulled up another chair and sat close to him. Patting him playfully on the knee, I said, "But you must not expect others to be as pious and virtuous as you."

He laughed, bitterly. "Virtuous? I'm hardly that. If I had been virtuous, I should not have been sent down from Oxford."

"Sent down!" I pretended to be deliciously scandalised. "Why, Willy! Have you been naughty? Blotted your copybook? *You?*"

"Naughty: that word is too mild," he said. "At Oxford, they said I was guilty of unnatural vice."

"I don't understand," I said (and truly I didn't).

"It is better that you don't," he replied.

"Now, I shall be cross with you if you treat me like a child," I said. "We have always been honest and open with each other, Willy. We have not always agreed, but we have been open. I do not understand what unnatural vice may mean. It sounds a silly term to me, and you must enlighten me. Is not *all* vice unnatural, in the sense that it displeases God, and is it not redundant to add the adjective?"

"Some vices are worse than others," he said. "I may not tell you more."

"But *you*, Willy! Vice? Of *any* kind? Our *Willy?*"

"You know I hate that name," he said, wearily.

"I'm sorry, but I've called you Willy all my life . . ."

"Not quite. When you were *very* little, before you could pronounce 'Willy,' you called me Wee-Wee." And he smiled. I had never known he had such a charming smile. It emboldened me to tell him all I knew.

"I've said we should be honest and open," I began, "so I shall confess that I had my ear pressed to Papa's study door last night. I heard a great deal. Something about the flesh. Something about you and another *man*. That is the part I don't understand, Willy. If you had got a girl in trouble, I would have no difficulty in understanding. But I can not imagine how you can have committed a sin of the flesh . . . with a man. It seems so curious. It seems impossible. It seems . . ."

"Unnatural? There: you see? Now you understand the reason for the adjective. Yes, I suppose it is unnatural. Certainly Papa thinks so. 'I'm no saint myself,' he told me, 'and in my youth I was as reckless as the next one — did things I was later ashamed of. But that was merely part of growing up. High spirits. Wild oats. It was almost expected of one. No importance was placed on it. But this!' "

I shook my head. "I still do not understand. Papa calls it 'This.' But what, precisely, *is* This?"

"Dear little Pam," he said, "you are too young and too innocent to know the details of even the lawful, hallowed congress between man and wife. How can I possibly tell you of . . . this sordid . . . contemptible . . ."

I leapt from my chair and took his head in my hands and kissed his brow. "No, no, Willy, you could never be sordid and contemptible. You must not say so of yourself." I sat down again. "As for being innocent, I am not as innocent as you may think me. Some nights ago . . ."

And I told him how Giles had come to my bedroom. I did not omit *anything*.

When I had finished, he said nothing for a moment. Then he said: "Strange. What happened between Jack and me was precisely — do you understand? — *precisely* what happened between you and your Giles. In our case, Jack was the . . . the recipient, shall we say. But the analogy is not perfect, because he was also the seducer."

"And this seducer," I asked, somewhat waspishly, "is he also reading theology?"

"Jack? Heavens, no! He's at Oriel to read history, like his father and grandfather before him."

"Hasn't *he* been sent down, too?"

"No, he has not; even though he was the instigator, the tempter, the corruptor, if you will — Papa is right in that, at least."

"But why? Why are you the only one who is punished?"

"Because he is the younger boy. An under-classman. They found us together, but because I am the older, it was assumed I was the corruptor. They could not conceive that a young lad like that, no older than you, with such innocent wide eyes and cherub cheeks and sweet pouting lips like a baby, could be the aggressor in such an act, could be the first to suggest it, the first to begin caressing and kissing and . . . *oh, God, it's so damnably vile!*"

I cradled his head in my arms again, and he wept on my bosom. "No, no," I crooned, "no, no . . ."

Kissing his mussed hair, I said, "Willy, do you think *I* was damnably vile — to do what I did with Giles?"

He wiped his eyes on the back of his hand. "You were wrong," he said; "you were, both of you, wrong. What you did was sinful . . . lustful . . . reckless . . . precipitate . . . but it was not vile."

"Then how can what you did with Jack — which you said is *precisely* what we did — how can it be vile? How can the one be vile and the other not, when they are both exactly the same?"

"Because —"

"No, listen to me. Hear me out. Our flesh is weak — we know that. We constantly fight against its temptations; and sometimes we win, and sometimes we lose. My flesh was weak, and so was Giles's; and so we did what we did. Your flesh was weak, and so was Jack's; and so the two of you did exactly what the two of *us* did. Does it matter that I was the younger, or Jack was the younger? *Flesh met flesh,* in both cases. Weak flesh met weak flesh. It is *no more* than that. Your sin is no greater than mine. And our spirits remain untarnished, Willy. The sins of the flesh . . . they quite literally wash away . . ."

He kissed my cheek, which was wet now, with my own tears as well as his. "Thank you, Pam," he said. "You are wiser than any of us has given you credit for. I feel better now."

"Better enough to come down to dinner this evening?"

"Perhaps."

"Dearest Wee-Wee. Do you promise?"

"Very well."

And he did come down to dinner, for Willy has never broken his word to anybody. It was a bit uncomfortable at first, but I chattered so loudly and so continuously on every other subject under the sun, that we managed to get through all the courses in what roughly approximated a normal manner.

ᕙ *Saturday, 18 February*

This morning, at breakfast, Papa said to Willy:

"I have been thinking about your future, my boy. In view of the fact that you have decided to discontinue your studies" — this obviously for my benefit — "I could write you some introductions to associates of mine. There are some excellent opportunities in Canada, for example . . ."

Mamma interrupted, "But, Wilfrid, that is so far from home!"

With a stern look, Papa signalled to her not to interfere. "It is a land where a bright young chap can earn rapid advancement," he went on. "Why, in no time you might become quite a big bug. Even put me in the shade!"

"Thank you, Father," said Willy, as he pushed the bacon about his plate with his fork. "I think it wouldn't suit me,

145

however. As you know, I have never had a good head for business."

"You could learn. You are intelligent, energetic. And you must do *something* with your life, now that . . . you have put Oxford behind you."

Willy nodded. "I have been giving it a good deal of thought," he said, "and there is one part of your suggestion that coincides with my own thinking: the idea of getting away from England. Fresh fields and all that."

Papa said, "Yes, quite right."

"There are a number of small evangelical sects, not associated with the Established Church, and with no formal creed other than a fundamental Christianity. Their missionaries are not required to complete a course of university study or to have earned a divinity degree. They do not ordain."

Mamma said, "But that sort of religion seems at such variance with your own beliefs, as you have written them in letters and tracts."

"Under the circumstances," Willy quietly replied, "it is the best I can do in my chosen line. I have learned that it is folly to fit one's self into a mould with any expectation that one will be allowed to remain there. Life has a way of cracking us out of our moulds and shewing us that we are not the persons we thought we were."

I asked him, "Where will you go?"

"If I can find a sect that will have me," he replied, "I shall go wherever they may send me. The Orient, perhaps. Or Africa."

"Africa! Oh dear!" said Mamma. "You will be eaten by lions!"

"I hope not," Willy said, with a smile, "but if I am, I shall not be the first Christian to be a lion's luncheon."

Papa stirred sugar into his coffee. He said, "I can not deny that I should be happier if you would go into business in Canada. I have many friends there — men who owe me favours. A word from me, and . . ."

"I know that you want only what is best for me," said Willy, "but if my life is to have any purpose, it can not be in the amassing of money. Pamela, what is it that Mr. Wordsworth says about getting and spending?"

" 'Getting and spending, we lay waste our powers.' "

"Yes. I must spread the Word of Jesus, Father. It is the only thing I am capable of doing; the only thing I have ever wanted to do." He turned to Mamma. "I shall never become a bishop, like Grandfather, but I shall be toiling in the same vineyard."

Tears had begun to glisten in Mamma's eyes. "The life sounds so hard," she said, in a tremulous voice. "So few comforts, such privation . . ."

"I will welcome privation and sacrifice. They will strengthen my spirit."

I said, "Africa is so frightfully hot."

"The better to cauterise sin."

Suddenly, I began to respond to the drama of it. "Oh, Willy, I can just see you! All in black . . . standing among the heathens in the shimmering heat of the desert . . . casting out sin . . . redeeming courtesans from their wanton ways . . . like the holy man Paphnutius in Sister Hrotsvitha's play! . . ."

"Nothing so grand and theatrical, I'm afraid. Just a poor sinner, doing his poor best."

"You were always *much* too modest," I said. And that brought the discussion to a close.

During our at-home this afternoon, Willy remained in his room. He missed nothing of interest. Even Giles could not attend, because of family commitments.

ཉ Sunday, 19 February

It was overcast all morning, with a light but steady rain in the afternoon, and a torrential downpour of Deluge proportions battering the roof all evening. It is coming down like a cataract at this moment. Wherever Willy may be, I hope he is warm and dry.

Shortly before the dinner hour, I tapped at his door, and when he bade me come in, I saw that he was packing his bag. "Willy!" I said. "You're not leaving again so soon?"

He touched a finger to his lips, saying, "Shhh . . . I don't want Mamma and Papa to know until after I'm gone." He handed me a folded note. "Here. Give this to Mamma after you sit down to dinner. By that time, I will be well away."

"Well away *where?*"

"Do you promise not to tell?" I nodded. "Very well. Yesterday, whilst the rest of you were busy being at home, I slipped out and paid a visit to one of the evangelical missions I spoke about. I offered to do anything — scrub floors, ladle soup, nurse the dying — if they would only let me stay and be of use. Eventually, I hope to prove to them that I am worthy to be sent abroad to carry the Word."

"Of course you are worthy!" I said, indulgently. "Your training, your devotion, your zeal — all of these make you worthy. You need not *prove* it by scrubbing floors and bandaging beggars!"

"The One Whom I strive to imitate did not disdain such tasks."

"Oh, Willy, don't go all sanctimonious on me!"

He smiled, gently. "I'm sorry. I know I can be such an awful bore. But, really, Pam, a little hard work won't hurt me."

"Where is this mission?"

"You *do* promise not to tell? I shouldn't like Papa coming down to fetch me away."

"I promise."

"It's in Whitechapel."

"Whitechapel! But that's a horrid place! A den of thieves! And please don't remind me Who was crucified between two thieves — I know all that. Willy, Willy, it's a filthy, squalid place, like a running sore, full of misery and poverty and disease . . . I can not bear to think of you there!"

"No harm will come to me. I'll be doing God's work. And perhaps I'll be lucky. They may send me out to Africa or some other such place quite soon."

"You'll visit us from time to time?"

He shook his head. "No, Pam."

"If you are shipped abroad, you'll let us know first?"

"I'll write — after I arrive at my destination."

I wailed, "Willy! You are saying that we shall never see you again!"

He continued to pack things into his bag. "Yes, I suppose

that's true. But it's all for the best. I know Papa would prefer it that way. And he's right. I've dishonoured myself; stained the family name. He'd like to send me away to Canada — but he really doesn't care where I go, as long as it's far away. Africa, the Orient, almost any place will serve. Even my way-station, Whitechapel, is far away: not in miles; but in other ways it is as far from Mayfair as the North Pole." He said all of this with no bitterness. "And yet if Papa knew I was in Whitechapel, he might feel bound by a sense of duty to take me out of it. So you mustn't tell him."

"Mamma will grieve. You will break her heart. You will break my heart, too!" I fell on my knees before him, wrapping my arms around his legs. "Oh, Willy, please don't leave in this way! Not so suddenly, so coldly! I know you think I have never loved you, but I do, and I always have! Even when I was horrid to you, when we were children, I loved you. When I called you names, or hid your favourite toys, or mimicked the way you talked, or tied your stockings into knots . . . oh, I was a beastly little thing, and I beg you to forgive me, please forgive me!"

Willy helped me to my feet and kissed me. "Dearest Pam — there is nothing to forgive. Don't you know you have always been my favourite sister? Never tell that to Phoebe, of course. I love both of you — I always shall — but I have always loved you best."

"Oh, Willy, not truly?"

"I never lie."

"But I was always mocking you . . ."

"I rather enjoyed it. You did it very well."

"Phoebe has always been a much kinder person than I. And prettier."

He nodded gravely. "Yes, that's true. But you were always the jollier. And I think that's why I love you best. Envy you a bit, too. I've never known how to be jolly. And I admire people to whom it comes naturally. It's one of God's gifts. One which He denied me. I rather suppose that's why I was drawn to . . . to Jack. He's such a jolly chap."

"This Jack," I said, but found it difficult to go on.

"Yes? What about him?"

"Papa asked you to disclose his name. Did you?"

"No, and I never shall. You are the only one who knows even the name Jack. And you must not tell it to Papa. As for his last name, I shan't reveal that even to you."

"I shouldn't want you to," I said. "But . . . tell me, Willy . . . do you . . . did you . . . *love* him?"

He grew thoughtful. "Love wears many masks," he said, at last. "I suppose you could say that I did love him. Perhaps I still do. And now, my dear, I must go."

He closed his bag and put on his greatcoat.

"It's *pouring* with rain!" I said. "You'll catch a chill!"

He shook his head. "I shan't walk all the way to White-chapel, never fear. I'll walk just a short way, and then I'll hire a hackney."

I shook my head in confusion. "I'm sorry, Willy, but I still find it so *curious* that you should love your Jack . . . in that way."

"It's one of life's paradoxes. Don't try to understand it. But if it helps you to accept it, let me assure you that there are more of us in the world than you may think, including some of the artists and poets you admire. Shakespere, for instance." I must have appeared shocked, because Willy smiled and said, "Read the sonnets again, a bit more closely. The twentieth, in particular."

Once more, he turned to go, but I kept talking, partly to delay his departure, partly to enlighten myself: "Uncle Roger once told me that there are men who have no need of women, and he said that he was one of them. Do you think that *he* —"

"I'm sure I can not say, but I will guess that Uncle Roger is a person entirely devoid of fleshly interests, whether the flesh be man's or woman's. It is not the same thing. Consider it in this way, Pam: that men like me . . . and like Jack . . . are the victims of an error that was made when we were born. Somehow, the sensibilities of a female were put into the body of a male. Therefore, when we grow fond for other flesh, the female in us yearns *not* for another female — which would be, in a curious way, 'unnatural' — but for a male . . . which feels perfectly right and proper and 'natural' to us. Although not to the rest of the world."

"Then the way you are, if it can be said to be a fault — is God's fault," I said.

Willy considered my statement carefully. "That is a *very* interesting point of theology," he said. He kissed me again and, lifting his bag, walked to the door. "Don't forget to give my note to Mamma."

"I shan't forget."

As his hand touched the handle, he said one more thing. "All that business about tying my stockings up in knots, and so on. You mustn't feel guilty about it, Pam. Do you remember a book of yours, one of your favourites when you were a child, a book of Mother Goose rhymes?"

"Yes, indeed. I was furious at the Ridgely girls because one of them glued the pages together when they were visiting our nursery. But I was never sure whether it was Clara or Sarah."

"It was neither of them," said Willy, with a positively *wicked* little laugh. "It was I."

And then he was gone, into the drenching rain and the dark.

⸎ *Monday, 20 February*

The note which Willy bade me give Mamma contained nothing she did not already know — that he plans to become a missionary abroad, and is off on the first leg of his journey. Mamma and Papa questioned me closely — did I know his whereabouts? — but I was true to my word and said nothing.

It was fine this morning — high winds had blown away almost all the clouds. I hope it is a good omen for Willy.

And yet I entertained fears for him from a hostile quarter; and so I made a bold decision directly after luncheon. I was in luck, for Mamma left the house on business of her own (she would have dissuaded me, had she known of my intention). So, slipping out quietly, I hailed a hackney — not daring to use one of our family carriages lest Paley, our coachman, learn my destination. I gave the hackney-driver an address in Chelsea, and, before long, my heart hammering in my breast, I was knocking on the door of an unmarried man's rooms.

He opened the door hesitantly, as if suspicious of unannounced visitors, and I was surprised to see that he was still in his dressing-gown at that late hour. He, too, was surprised. In a tone of incredulity, he said, "Miss Summerfield?" — as if he could not believe it was I.

"May I come in, Mr. O'Connor?"

He stepped aside without another word, and I entered his rooms. It was cold within: there was no fire. He quickly removed a pile of books from a chair and bade me sit down. I did so, quietly examining the profusion of other books and pamphlets and magazines stacked in piles on every surface. The remains of his breakfast had been pushed to one side of his writing desk, to make room for an open inkpot and an uncompleted manuscript on which he had evidently been working when I knocked.

"How did you find me?" he asked.

"You left your card the evening you paid us a visit."

"Ah, yes, of course. The fire seems to have gone out. I'll start it up again."

"Pray do not trouble yourself on my account. I do not mean to stay long."

He threw his length carelessly onto a well-worn *chaise-longue,* one arm-rest of which was so precariously attached that I feared it might fall away as he leant against it. Fortunately, it did not. He ran his fingers through the flaming thicket of his uncombed hair. "Pray excuse me appearance. I do most of me writing in the morning, and do not dress until the afternoon."

"It is about your writing that I wish to speak," I said.

He proffered me a crooked smile. "Sure, and you could not have chosen a more fascinating subject."

"Mr. O'Connor," I said firmly, "I have come here to ask you to leave off attacking members of my family in your pieces."

"To the best of my recollection," he said, "I have *never* attacked a member of your family. I do not attack persons. I have attacked certain evils. If your family members have been connected with those evils . . ." He shrugged, leaving the rest eloquently unsaid.

"In particular," I went on, "I wish you to let my brother Wilfrid alone. He is an easy target for scandal-mongers, but he is vulnerable and delicate of spirit; and spiteful satires, such as those in which you excel, could kill him."

O'Connor held up a hand. "One moment, Miss Summerfield. I think that you did not hear me. I do *not* attack persons. I have *never* attacked a Summerfield."

He made me impatient. "Oh, stop this pretence," I said. "I have seen your verses, with the clever use of the words 'summer field,' a clear reference to my father and his business. And my brother wrote to us about the way you attacked a pamphlet to which he contributed . . ."

"I assure you, me dear young lady, that the words 'summer field' were not intended to refer to your father — although I was delighted when I learnt that he and some others took them that way. 'Field' was simply the best rhyme I could find for 'yield.' In me first draught, I wrote 'green field,' but it failed to scan — 'green' is only one syllable, and I needed two. I substituted 'verdant,' but this was too florid for my purpose, so I finally hit upon 'summer.' Shall I shew you me draughts? . . . I have them somewhere here . . . you can see for yourself . . ." He began to rummage about in a pile of old manuscripts.

"Never mind," I said. "What about 'Such freedom (God willing) is cheap at a shilling'?"

"My verse on the church-attendance fine. What has that to do with you Summerfields?"

"Do you deny that it was written as a direct response to a tract calling for strict enforcement of that fine?"

"Of course I don't."

"A tract written, in part, by my brother?"

"Your brother! Faith, and how was I to know *that,* pray tell, *when the tract was anonymous?"*

(He had a point: the pamphlet Willy sent us had not been signed. I had quite forgot.)

"Ah! Here 'tis!" he exclaimed, pulling a scrawled-upon sheet of rumpled paper from under a riot of other refuse. He thrust it into my hand, saying triumphantly, "There! Do you see?"

It was, indeed, the original draught of the verses that had so upset Papa. Many words were blotted out and revisions scribbled in their stead. Whole lines were transposed from one position to another, with hastily drawn arrows pointing hither and yon on the all-but-illegible page. As an amateur poet myself, I recognised the familiar throes of creation. And, true enough, "green field" had been emended to "verdant field" and, finally, to "summer field."

I returned the sheet of paper to him. "It appears that I owe you an apology, Mr. O'Connor," I said.

"No need," he replied curtly.

I stood up. "I will take my leave of you."

"Before you go," he said, "it may interest you to know that I recently hired a private chemical analyst to test for adulteration in various foods and drinks, including the beer of several prominent breweries. I received his report yesterday and am now in the very act of writing an article divulging his findings. Among other horrors, he found vitriol in one brewer's beer, strychnine in another's. I shall name them in me piece. I shall also say that Summerfield's Golden Lager, and one or two other varieties, were found to contain no impurities. You may tell your father so, if you like." He held open the door for me. "Good afternoon, Miss Summerfield."

"Good afternoon," I replied. "I . . . I'm sorry I mis——"

"Not another word," he said severely. "I've already told you there's no need for apology. It's only fair to warn you that the Summerfield Brewery is not immune from attack on other counts: working conditions, low wages, child labour . . ."

"My father has broken no laws, sir!"

"Only human lives. To pay for the pretty frock on your pretty back."

I turned and walked quickly away from his door — feeling his cold blue eyes on me all the time.

&* *Tuesday, 21 February*

The longer I postpone writing to Phoebe, the more difficult it becomes. Every new day brings events I could recount to her, if only I could be sure that Mr. Braithwaite did not read my letters. I can not tell her about Willy: his shame must never be known outside this family. I can not describe my visit to Rhys O'Connor: that is none of Mr. Braithwaite's business. I certainly can not divulge any intimate details concerning Giles. I could dilate upon our dinner-party, I suppose, and my new gown, but such things seem so trivial and false when measured against the vital matters I truly yearn to tell her and to ask her.

Despite these misgivings, I forced myself to sit down and write to her to-day, filling the pages with frivolous, shallow chatter. At the end, in response to her bit of verse which spelled out the message NOT HIS, I wrote out my little limerick, originally composed three weeks ago (see 1 February), which acrostically asks, WHOSE? Rutledge posted it this afternoon.

Another strangulation has been reported: again, a young woman; again in Hyde Park; again raped *post mortem*. Her name was Emma Davis. One of the newspapers has taken to calling the murderer The Hyde Park Strangler; another has given him the name The Full Moon Fiend — for both killings took place on a night when the moon was full. Can a merciful God have looked down upon such acts and not taken the part of those poor girls?

࿇ *Wednesday, 22 February*

Signor Olivo was here again today to give me my singing lesson. Perhaps I should point out that his name is pronounced with the accent on the second syllable (thus: o–LEEV-o), and not in the way Papa persists in pronouncing it, like our English word, "olive," followed by an "oh" (thus: OLive-oh). This makes Signor Olivo eloquently wince.

"To-day, Signorina, I make you a little present," he said. (I will no longer try to render his accent — it is much too tiresome to write it down — suffice it to say that he adds a syllable to the end of almost every other word.) With a wide smile, he opened his portfolio and pulled out the score of *Lucia di Lammermoor*.

"Oh, Signore, you remembered! *Grazie! Mille grazie!*"

With a flourish, he placed it on the music rack of the pianoforte. Tapping his forehead, he said, "Olivo, he do not forget when a lady say she want something."

"You are truly the most thoughtful gentleman. I must sing something from it *at once!*"

"No!" he said firmly. "First, the scales, the exercises. Then, Donizetti. But *only*" — he paused dramatically, operatically — "if the scales are good. *Andiamo! Incominciate!* Do, re, mi, fa, sol, la, si, *do! . . .*"

I performed the scales and vocal exercises doggedly and dutifully. Signor Olivo frowned. "Not enough of the practise," he said sternly. "The voice, she is tight, cold. Too much from *here.*" He placed his hand on my throat. "Not enough from *here.*" He placed his other hand on my abdomen.

Leaving both of his hands in those positions, he bade me try an octave scale, but stopped me half-way. *"Here* I feel the voice," he said, his hand encircling my throat and exerting a slight pressure. "But *here* I feel no *thing.*" The hand on my abdomen began to move slowly in a repetitious stroking manner. In anybody else, I should have thought it disallowably familiar; in Giles, it would have been a positive pleasure.

"Ancora," said Signor Olivo, and I sang the scale again. *"Ancora!"* I sang it still another time. He nodded his head and said, "Better, a little better."

His hand rose from my abdomen to a higher position cushioned under, and pressed to, my bosom. "Breathe in," he said. I did so. "More!" I inhaled more deeply, and my bosom seemed to expand in his hand — into both of his hands, which now cupped and supported it. "Breathe out." I forced all the air from my lungs in one long exhalation. He was standing behind me now, speaking into my right ear — or near it, for his lips were actually brushing my neck as he spoke: "Breathe in, *ancora.*" I obeyed, and as I did so, his hands now squeezed my breasts unmistakably and I could feel his warm, moist breath on my neck and the scented oil of his hair on my cheek. *Olio di rosa,* he had called it once, and it did indeed give off the heady aroma of roses.

I must admit that the convocation of sensations — the hands on my breasts, the warm breath on my neck, the floral fragrance in my nostrils — together formed an experience not entirely disagreeable.

Of course, it was not Signor Olivo's intention to give me

pleasure. As with a doctor, these actions, which in others would be considered fondling, were the impersonal necessaries of his work.

His mouth moved from my neck, and I jumped slightly, with a startled "Oh!" for I had felt his tongue flicker instantaneously in my ear — a most curious feeling. *"Scusi,"* he said in curt apology for the accident.

Removing his hands from my body, he sighed and said, *"Ebben.* Now you will sing a little Donizetti, *si?"*

I can not state it with certainty, but as Signor Olivo moved away from me to turn the pages of the *Lucia* score, I could almost swear that I saw the signs in him of what I can only call the unicorn phenomenon (see 8 February). But I think I must have been mistaken.

ॐ *Thursday, 23 February*

This afternoon, while Mamma was shopping at Turner's, the family furnishers, and Papa was still in the City, Rutledge came to me in the drawing-room, where I was playing over some Chopin.

"Lord Granville is here, Miss," he said, handing me a card.

"Do we know a Lord Granville?" I asked.

"Not to my knowledge."

"Which of us does he wish to see?"

"He says he is a friend of the family. When I told him that you were the only family member at home, he asked to see you."

I glanced at the card. It told me no more than: *Jonathan Granville.* No crest, no address; quite simple; but the embossing was of the richest and most costly variety.

Rutledge said, "I took the liberty, Miss, of slipping into the library, on the way to the drawing-room, and looking him up in Debrett's. He is listed as Jonathan Edred Richard Granville, Eighth Baronet and First Baron. His father was —"

"I wish Mamma were here," I said, tapping the card against my hand. "Oh, *bother.* I suppose I shall have to receive him. Shew him in, Rutledge."

A moment later, Rutledge ushered into the drawing-room a

young man of breath-stopping beauty. After determining that Lord Granville required not tea nor sherry nor other refreshment, Rutledge departed, leaving me alone with this Phoebus Apollo. He was *quite* young — about my own age — tall and slim, with a slender waist, delicate hands, and a flood of golden blond curls. His eyes were as close to lavender as I have ever seen. He wore a sky-blue cravat, yards of gold chain, white French gloves, a light drab greatcoat lined with velvet of the same colour, and his breeches — or "inexpressibles," as I have heard them called — were virtually invisible: skin-coloured, and fitting as tight as a coat of paint. The first effect of the breeches was a momentary shock — he seemed to be wearing none at all. I should have to describe him as a fantastick, or, at the very least, a dandy, although an extremely decorative one.

"Miss Summerfield," he said, "it is the greatest pleasure to meet you at last." I expected a childish treble from that face, but what I heard was a luscious barytone of exquisite satin.

"Thank you, Lord Granville. I am glad to make your acquaintance. Will you sit down?"

He did, perching himself on the edge of a chair in the graceful, if not entirely natural, way that I have seen actors seated in a play.

"Did I hear the E-Flat Valse of Chopin as I entered?" he enquired.

"Yes," I replied, delighted to converse with somebody so knowledgeable of music.

"I adore Chopin," he said, "and I adore waltzes. How did Byron put it? 'The seductive waltz . . . the voluptuous waltz . . .' You play beautifully."

"Only passably, I'm afraid."

"Not at all! And I assure you that I am a *connoisseur* — I have heard Chopin himself play, at Carlsbad, two years ago. I was there with Mamma on holiday. We met him. He introduced us to Mendelssohn and Schumann, who were also there that year. And Clara Wieck, as well. He will come to England this year, you know."

"Truly? Chopin?" The news thrilled me.

"Yes. To see a pulmonary consultant whom we recommended to him." Lord Granville tapped his chest. "His lungs give him a deuced hard time. Whilst he is here, we'll introduce him to Mr. Wessel the music publisher — Mamma knows him quite well — and help him to reach an arrangement for the English publication of his works."

"I should *love* to meet him!" I exclaimed.

"And so you shall. I will make it my business to introduce you." His expression grew conspiratorial. "Of course, he'll probably have that tiresome Madame Dudevant on his arm at all times. He's just taken up with her, I hear."

"I believe her name is not familiar to me," I said.

"Unbearable woman. Smokes cigars. Writes rubbishy novels under the name of George Sand."

"In point of fact, Lord Granville, your own name was unfamiliar to me, I must confess, until just a few moments ago. And yet I understand you are a friend of this family?"

"A friend of one of its members, at any rate — and, I hope, a friend of all its members, in course of time. I know your brother, Wilfrid."

"Willy? Then I am doubly glad to meet you!" I said, with unfeigned enthusiasm.

"You are most kind," he responded. "Yes: in fact, I was hoping to find him at home."

I did not know what to tell him. I stammered a bit. "He . . . that is to say . . . I'm afraid you've missed him."

"So it seems. Can you tell me when he'll be in?"

"He won't . . . *be* in," I said, in confusion. "Not for quite a long time . . ."

"Whatever can you mean, Miss Summerfield?"

"He's gone abroad," I blurted out.

"Abroad! When? Where?"

"Just the other night. I don't know where, actually."

"But how devilish curious. *Surely* you must know."

I shook my head. "I don't. Truly."

"I can not believe you. I think you are lying."

"Lord Granville! You go too far!" I stood up, looking at him steadily and sternly. No curly-headed doll of a popinjay would call me a liar. "I must ask you to leave."

Quickly, he spoke in mollifying tones: "No . . . please

. . . I'm most frightfully sorry . . . forgive me . . . don't send me away . . ."

I sat down again.

His stage posture had fled, and he now seemed like a very little boy, his head in his hands, fighting back the tears that were beginning to well in his astonishing eyes. "I beg you to tell me where he is . . . I don't know what I shall do if I don't see him . . . he is my dearest friend . . . my very dearest most beloved friend in all the world . . . and he left Oxford so suddenly . . . without a word to me . . ." He was weeping openly now, the poor young gentleman.

"Lord Granville," I said quietly, "are you sometimes known as Jack?"

He looked up at me with wet and desperate eyes. "Then Will spoke of me? He must have done!"

"He did. He told me . . . everything."

Lord Granville wiped his eyes on a fine lace handkerchief. "He cursed me, I suppose. He had every right."

"He did not curse you," I said.

My guest uttered a short, bitter laugh. "No — Will is far too fine a fellow to curse anybody aloud. But in his heart . . . 'curses not loud but deep' . . ."

"I think he has not cursed you even in his heart," I said. "If you want to know, he told me that he . . . that he loved you."

"Thank you for that, Miss Summerfield," he said softly. "Thank you for telling me that. But you must tell me one thing more . . . you must tell me where he is. You *must.*"

"I must do nothing of the kind," I responded.

He wrung his hands in the most pitiable manner. His beautiful Botticelli face was twisted into a mask of distress. "I know you are not cruel, Miss Summerfield," he said in a kind of groan. "Will has spoken of you in the highest terms. I know you have a generous nature. If you were to see a beast in pain — a dog with a thorn in its paw — your soul would reach out to the animal and you would pluck the thorn from its flesh. Think of me as such a creature — with a thorn piercing my heart. I am in torment; I am in agony. Can you stand by and see me suffer and do nothing? I tell you without exaggeration that if I do not see Will again, I do not know where I will find the courage to go on living. Have you ever loved, Miss Summerfield, and suffered for that love? Have you ever despaired? Ah, dear young lady — have mercy on me and tell me, *tell me* where I may find him!"

He was on his knees before me, like a weeping Cupid, like a fallen angel. How could I refuse him?

"Whitechapel," I said. "An evangelical mission of some kind. That is all I know."

He seized my hand and kissed it. "Bless you!"

Then he rose to his feet, dusted off the knees of his skin-coloured inexpressibles, and composed himself again. Bowing, he said calmly, "Good afternoon, Miss Summerfield. I can see myself out."

"Good afternoon, Lord Granville." But as his hand was on the door handle, I suddenly added: *"Jack! . . ."* He turned to me. "If you find Willy, tell him . . . tell him . . ." Tears began to flow from my own eyes now, and my voice became choked. I could not go on.

"I will tell him," said Lord Granville, "that he is fortunate to be loved by the finest sister a man ever had."

৪৯ *Friday 24 February*

Mlle. La Grange did my hair to-day. I seized the opportunity to ask her something that has been in my thoughts ever since Willy was sent down from Oxford.

"I have heard such a curious thing recently," I said. "I can scarcely give it credence."

"Ah, oui?"

"Someone has told me that there are men in this world who do not ʂeek *le plaisir* from women — but from other men. Can this be true?"

"Oui, c'est vrai," she said, curtly.

"I find it most odd, but if you corroborate the rumour, then I suppose I must believe it."

"The young Miss is becoming so much educated," she observed, wryly.

"Indeed," I admitted, "my education has progressed by

leaps and bounds in *certain* fields these past few weeks." I let the matter rest for a few moments whilst she busied herself with my hair; then I embarked upon the true object of my enquiry. "Mam'selle," I said, "if there are men who prefer men, are there likewise women who prefer women?"

She clicked her tongue and wagged a reproving finger. "Naughty young Miss! Again you wish me to speak of things forbidden!"

"We are quite alone. You have told me — or confirmed — many such things before this. Why should you stop now?"

"All other things," she said, "have been between the man and the woman. But this other, it is against Nature. The Bible, it condemns this thing. *Connaissez-vous l'histoire de Sodome et Gomorrhe?*"

"The Cities of the Plain," I replied, "were smitten by God because of their abominations . . ."

"Oui! Exactement!"

"But Scripture does not tell what those abominations were."

"Ah! You see? Because they must not be spoken of! *Enfin,* I must not speak of them to you."

"But, my dear Mam'selle, I already *know* that such things occur, and you have confirmed it. Anything that you might add would be in the way of a foot-note, no more. Do such things happen between women, as well as between men? You need answer only yes or no."

After a very short silence, Mlle. La Grange replied, *"Oui."*

I turned from the mirror and looked her full in the eye. "They *do?* Truly?"

She nodded.

"I can not believe it."

"Mais, pourquoi? If men —"

"But women . . ." I began to say, and could say no more, because I had no logic to support me. When I looked at it from one point of view, the thing was, if anything, *more* believable between women. Are not women always kissing and hugging each other? Men do not act in that way. Are not women for ever saying that they love each other? that they love certain fabrics or *bon-bons* or flowers or songs? Men never say so; it is only in the greatest extremity of longing that a man will even tell a *woman* that he loves her. Men are restrained; in command of their passions. Women are eternally gushing, like fountains.

Even so, the picture of two women locked in amorous embrace was one that my mind could not conjure up or encompass.

"But, Mam'selle," I said, pressing on into the forbidden territory, "what do such women . . . *do?*"

"*Ma foi!*" she exclaimed. "How am I to know this? Am I such a woman, *moi-même?*"

"No, of course not . . ."

"Do I peep through the keyholes at such women?"

"No, no . . ."

"Then how would I know of such *obscénités?*"

"Simply because you are so wise, Mam'selle, so all-knowing in the ways of the world. You have heard so many things from women of all classes. Your work brings you into contact with them. Some of these may have been . . . inclined . . . in that way. Dear Mam'selle, it is only because I hold you in such esteem that I ask you these things. I look upon you as my oracle, my mentor."

Mlle. La Grange was pacified at this assurance, and resumed the dressing of my hair. After the passage of some minutes, she began to tell me of a woman she had known in France, a beautiful married lady of the aristocracy, a *comtesse,* whose hair was the colour of gold and, when undone, fell to below the lady's waist. The *coiffure* took hours. The lady developed an affection for Mlle. La Grange. She greeted her with sisterly kisses, to which Mam'selle attached no great importance. Before long, however, these displays of fondness became more ardent: the lady would grasp her hairdresser's hands and kiss her finger-tips, her palms. "I was younger then, and *très jolie.*" These caresses soon grew so pronounced that Mam'selle became alarmed, and she protested. "The *comtesse,* she made as if surprised. She said, 'Then you are not a follower of Sappho?' I did not know what she meant. I had never heard of this Sappho. It was then that the *comtesse* laughed and called me *naïve* and explained all to me. She told it to me in this way . . ."

Mlle. La Grange then repeated what the *comtesse* had said to her, word for word. I shall not set it down in these pages, for the simple reason that I think it is untrue. I think Mlle. La Grange has not lied to me; I think the *comtesse* was a wicked lady who teased her innocent young hairdresser by telling her outrageously indecent falsehoods. No two women, no matter how depraved, could commit the acts I heard described this afternoon.

But I think I must read the works of Sappho more closely than I have done. If only I knew Greek!

ॐ *Saturday, 25 February*

Giles, who was forced to miss last Saturday's at-home, was able to attend today, it pleases me to report.

It seemed so long a time since I had seen him — and, indeed, it was over two weeks. There had even been a lengthy interval since his last communication of any kind, for that had been on St. Valentine's Day. Nothing since then!

Seeing him to-day was, therefore, all the more joyous — but it was a joy mingled with pain, for we had not a moment alone to kiss or speak sweet words or even to hold each other's hands. He took my hand and kissed it when he arrived, but with no more outward ardour than he kissed Mamma's. His presence was a delicious agony for both of us.

Mr. Trollope and Mr. Douglas Jerrold were among our more interesting guests. The conversation came round, at one point, to certain pieces of statuary to be seen about London, and Giles observed how curious it was that the statue of George II at Golden Square shows him in Roman costume, "wearing one of those kind of kilt things, with bare knees, and a laurel wreath on his head."

Mr. Trollope said, "Even more odd is the statue of Huskisson in Pimlico Gardens."

"Huskisson?" Giles rejoined.

"Have you never seen it? William Huskisson, a politician. He died seven years ago at the opening of the Liverpool-to-Manchester Railway. Became so excited that he stepped in front of Stephenson's 'Rocket' and was killed on the spot. Surely you remember? At any rate, Huskisson made history by his death, because he is the first person ever to be killed in that way, so they erected a statue in his honour. The odd thing is, he is wearing a toga."

"What a horrible way to die," I said.

"No way is pleasant," Mr. Trollope remarked, "but I think Huskisson's was no less pleasant than most — except to the onlookers, of course. Death must have come almost instantaneously. It has often occurred to me, after learning of that event, that it would probably be a perfect way to commit suicide."

Mamma said, "Oh, for shame, Mr. Trollope!"

He laughed. "Good Heavens, Madam, I am not planning my own demise, I assure you. I was speaking purely in conjecture. But one of these novelist chaps — Dickens, perhaps — might do well to work it up into a scene. Can you not imagine it? Here's this poor fellow, in the depths of despair for some reason — unrequited love, or perhaps he's lost all his money, whatever it may be — and there he is on the railway platform, and here comes the 'Rocket,' puffing and roaring and spouting steam like some great monstrous dragon — and he simply, quietly, without any fuss, steps off the platform into its path — and life is over."

Mamma shivered. "*Too* gruesome!"

Mr. Jerrold said, "Not at all. It makes a good story. You tell it splendidly, Trollope. Why don't you write it down yourself?"

"I am no novelist, sir," replied Mr. Trollope.

"In these times," said Mr. Jerrold, "it seems that most everybody is a novelist, or trying to become one. I was talking to young Branwell Brontë not long ago, during a visit to the Lakes. He told me that all three of his sisters have taken to the pen! Scratching away like hens, the lot of them. Poems, novels, God alone knows what else. I suppose it occupies their time. Of course, it is one thing to write, and another thing to publish; and I hope we may be spared the outpourings of such literary ladies." He looked quickly at Mr. Trollope and added, "I do not include your dear mother, needless to say. She is a lady of much skill and talent. I admire her work immensely. How is she, by the by? In good health, I hope?"

"In excellent health, thank you. She would be here this afternoon, were it not for a prior promise to her publisher, who is eagerly awaiting her next pages."

"I am glad to hear that she is well," said Mr. Jerrold. "It's more than one can say of poor Brontë. He has the look of the consumptive about him; and they do say he is over-reliant on opium. No good can come of that."

"And yet Mr. De Quincey recovered from that reliance," I said.

"He is as one man in ten thousand," replied Mr. Jerrold. "The rest may be regarded as dead, even whilst they live."

In such politely morbid ways, the talk continued, and the afternoon agreeably passed. I played the Chopin waltz I had been practising all week, and it was well received. For a brief moment at the pianoforte, as Giles turned the pages for me, we were able to speak a private word. "I am sorry not to have seen your father to-day," said Giles.

"He tries to work only in the mornings on Saturdays," I explained, "but sometimes the press of business keeps him in the City."

"There is something I want to discuss with him most particularly. Perhaps if I send round my batman with a note early in the week, he would be willing to see me some evening soon?"

"I'm sure of it," I said; and did not dare to ask him about what he wished to speak to Papa; but the slow blush that I felt burning my face and throat may have told him that I had strong suspicions.

℘ *Sunday, 26 February*

> A woman's face with Nature's own hand painted
> Hast thou, the master-mistress of my passion . . .

So begins Shakespere's twentieth sonnet, which Willy bade me read again, and in those opening two lines there is the damning evidence to be plainly seen. How could I have overlooked it before?

A woman's gentle heart, but not acquainted
With shifting change, as is false women's fashion . . .

Then women are weighed in the balance and found wanting, whilst the pretty master-mistress is praised for constancy!
Ah, dear Shakespere, I forgive you! And you still reign as the
nonpareil among poets.

⌒ℯ⌒

"I have had a note from Captain Ormond's batman," Papa
said over the soup. "He wishes to see me to-morrow evening,
if he may. I sent a note back to him, asking him to call after
dinner for a game of billiards. I can not imagine what he may
want to talk about. Can you?"

"No, Papa," I said; but I'm afraid I blushed again.

℘ Monday, 27 February

I simply could not sit still to-day, anticipating Papa's interview
with Giles; so I decided to spend most of the day in the town,
all to myself. I walked a good deal — it is excellent exercise —
and then, rather than hire a hackney, I rode omnibuses.

I love our London omnibuses, and have done, ever since the
very first of them was put into service, some seven or eight
years ago. I love the bright and various colours by which one
may identify them at a glance: there is the yellow and red of
the Paddington–to–Liverpool Street omnibus; the pale blue of
the Fulham–to–Kilburn; the light green of the "Atlas," from
Camberwell to St. John's Wood; the *dark* green of the "Favourite," which travels the London Bridge–to–Hornsey route;
and the delicious-looking chocolate colour of the Chelsea-to-
Hoxton. I have heard some people say that they are vulgar,
but I think that they do much to relieve the drabness of our
streets.

Between walking and riding, I found myself eventually in
Nicolson Street, where, by a stroke of good fortune, Cooke's
Circus is currently regaling the multitudes. I paid the price of
admission and entered. It was a splendid show. Some admira-
bly athletic gentlemen performed the Thessalian Games and
Trials of Skill, shewing — according to Mr. Cooke's printed

bill — "various exercises of the Conisterium or Ancient Gymnasium." How remarkably muscular the performers were, and how accomplished.

I also enjoyed the Fête of Pekin, an exotic and impressive spectacle, "got up with the strictest correctness of costume, emblematic accessories, etc., characteristic of the Tartar Chinese," again to quote Mr. Cooke.

I did *not*, however, like Madame Stevens very much, although I found it difficult to take my eyes away from the unhappy woman. She is called The Pig-Faced Lady, and she looks indeed like a great pig, despite her bonnet and gloves. She simply sits in a chair, blinking, saying nothing, nearly immobile. Sometimes she moves her head from side to side in a doleful manner. I felt sorry for her, and angry with Nature for making her the way she is.

"She's not a lady at-all, at-all," whispered a voice in my ear, and I turned, startled, to find Rhys O'Connor standing beside me, looking at me with a little half-smile. "Neither is she a pig."

"Mr. O'Connor! Do you often frequent circuses?"

"I'm fond of simple pleasures," he replied. "And I seek out fraud wherever I may find it. Madame Stevens, so-called, is an example. I intend to expose her."

"If she is neither lady nor pig," I asked, "what is she?"

"A bear," he replied.

"Surely not!"

"Look again," he said. "The creature's face and forelegs are shaven. The skin of a bear is white, you see. Those padded gloves cover the claws. She is held in the chair by hidden straps. In this half-light, and with that draped table placed in front of her, many people are deceived."

"It seems very unpleasant for the poor thing."

"I dare say it is. All the more reason to expose the fraud, don't you agree?"

"I suppose I do. If you are quite sure of your facts."

"I never set pen to paper," he replied, "until I have marshalled all me evidence. And now that I have denounced Madame Stevens, allow me to recommend the delicious jellies they sell here. May I offer you one?"

"Thank you. I'm partial to strawberry."

"Two strawberry jellies," he said, turning to the man at the refreshment stall.

As we ate them, I could not resist teasing him. "Would you not rather submit these jellies to your chemical analyst, Mr. O'Connor, and wait for his affidavit of purity before eating?"

"Do you think I have not? They are made of fruit, sugar, a relatively harmless dye to give colour, and isinglass."

"Isinglass!"

"Don't be alarmed, Miss Summerfield. Isinglass has uses other than in carriage windows. It's a pure, easily digested substance."

When we had finished our jellies and were leaving Cooke's, he asked if I had come to the circus by our family coach. I told him I had not.

"Ah, a pity. I was hoping I could ride with you to Fleet Street. But no matter."

"I came by omnibus," I said. "I love them."

"Good for you!" he exclaimed. "We share that admiration. It is the only way truly to see London; in particular, the people of London. To travel by omnibus and observe one's fellow-passengers — their faces, their speech, their behaviour — that is a course of study not taught at schools; and an entertainment better than most plays." He tipped his hat. "I will leave you here, then, Miss Summerfield, for we travel in different directions."

"Figuratively as well as literally, Mr. O'Connor."

"Alas."

"Thank you for the jelly."

"It was my pleasure."

Giles arrived after dinner; and, after a short period of conversation amongst all of us, Papa whisked him off to the billiard table for a *tête-à-tête*.

A long time after, Giles left without a further word to me, and Papa, clearly displeased by their talk, walked straight upstairs to bed. When I tried to ask him what had happened, he said only, "It was a most unsatisfactory meeting. We shall speak of it in the morning."

വ Tuesday, 28 February

I hardly slept at all. What on earth had Giles said to ruffle Papa so? When I dragged myself out of bed this morning, I was as tired as if I had stayed up all night. The sky was overcast, in perfect accord with my low spirits.

I had no appetite for breakfast, and Mamma and Papa were unusually silent. When Rutledge had left the dining-room, I summoned up the courage to ask "Papa, why did you say that your meeting with Captain Ormond was unsatisfactory?"

Papa put down his coffee cup. "Because his behaviour resembled that of an adventurer, rather than a gentleman."

"In what way? He always seemed the perfect gentleman, I have thought."

"I, too, had held that view of him, before last night."

(Had Giles foolishly revealed to Papa our *liaison* in my bedroom?)

"Wilfrid," said Mamma, "I think you are perhaps too hard on him." (Dear Mamma: she is on my side.)

"I disagree," Papa replied. "I do not expect a young man — and a soldier, at that — to be a paragon of virtue. I do not demand the impossible. We are, all of us, human and imperfect. But he behaved badly. He marred the favourable impression of him that I had previously formed. He asked things of me he ought not have asked."

"What sort of things, Papa?"

"Money," he said flatly.

"Money!" My spirits plummeted even lower. "I thought he would ask you for my hand!"

"He did." (My spirits rose again — a little.) "It was the first order of business, you might say. It was a quite creditable performance, and did him no dishonour. He spoke of his deep affection and admiration for you. He said he believed the affection was reciprocated. He catalogued your fine qualities, and admitted that he was but a plain soldier. 'And yet,' he said, 'the little that I have is hers, including my life, if you, sir, will

170

consent to our marriage.' It was a very pretty little speech. I took it as sincere.

"I told him that he had my good opinion. I said that I was aware — not being a blind man — that my daughter was interested in him. 'But,' I said, 'Pamela is still a very young girl. She has met too few men of eligible station. I could, without much fear of contradiction, describe her as green, to use the popular word. I must, therefore, oppose her engagement to *anybody* at this time,' and I stressed that I had no particular objection to him.

"He was disappointed, of course. That was to be expected. But still he continued to press me. He spoke of the torment of unfulfilled love, and that manner of thing. I told him that all of us have suffered such pangs in our youth, and that I sympathised with him, but that I must firmly counsel patience. 'It is really only a question of time, my boy,' I said. And it was then that he came out with it." Papa sipped his coffee.

"Came out with *what?*" I asked.

"He said: 'I do not *have* time, Mr. Summerfield. My time has quite run out. I am besieged by creditors. They will wait no longer. If I could but tell them that I am engaged to be married to a daughter of the prosperous Summerfield family, they would be glad to wait. The dowry alone would settle all my debts. But, as it is, I am ruined, sir, *ruined!*'

"I was shocked. I said, 'Am I to understand, Captain, that you meant to marry into this family for financial reasons?'

"He replied: 'No, sir. Of course not. I love Pamela to the point of distraction, and she me, and we should make each other the happiest people in this world. The money is only a part of it — but, I fear, a terribly important part. Money is of *no* importance — when one has got it. When one hasn't got it, it overwhelms all of one's life, taints every corner of one's thoughts . . .'

"He was beginning to gain my sympathy again, in some small part, at least. I said to him: 'My dear young man, it can not be as bad as all that. How much do you owe?' He named a figure so large that I was stunned by it. 'How can you possibly owe such an enormous sum of money?'

"He replied: 'A captain's pay is not very much. Out of it we must pay for our own uniforms, our kit, the mess, and so on. But the truth of it, sir, is that I owe the largest part of it to Crockey's.' "

"Crockey's?" said Mamma. "What on earth is that?"

"Crockford's, the gaming-club," said Papa. "A perfectly unobjectionable place. Good food and drink — they've engaged that French chef Ude. Some of the aristocracy are members. You might see bishops there, and M.P.s and Ministers of the Crown. The Duke of Wellington, young Disraeli, that writer chap Bulwer-Lytton — they're all of them members. William Crockford himself is a decent enough sort: solid; good head for business. Used to be a fishmonger. Made his own way in the world. Plenty of go. There's nothing wrong with Crockey's — for those who can afford it. Captain Ormond can not."

"Poor Giles," I murmured, almost in tears. "I never knew he was in such straits. How horrid for him."

"It is his own fault," said Papa. "He had no business stepping out into deep water when he could not swim. I said to him: 'But surely your own father can cover your gaming-table debts? I know you are on good terms with him, for I have seen you together, here in my own house, and you got on famously.'

"Captain Ormond replied: 'My father is in Queer Street. He may even have to serve a term in prison. That abominable swine O'Connor has published an article exposing adulteration in tea. He had samples of various brands analysed because he had heard that blackberry leaves were being mixed in with tea to bulk it up — not harmful, but fraudulent.'

"I said, 'A man is not ruined and sent to prison for a few blackberry leaves!'

" 'No, I dare say not,' he agreed. 'But in conducting his tests, O'Connor found in my father's product not blackberry leaves but verdigris — added to black tea to give it a green colour so that it could be sold at a higher price, as Chinese tea. Verdigris, apparently, is poisonous, and there have been several deaths which O'Connor and his associates have traced directly to Ormond's Flower of the Orient Fine Quality Chinese Tea. I wish I could say it is a mistake, but I'm afraid that the proof is incontrovertible.'

"I said to him: 'I am most terribly sorry. I do not know your father very well, but on short acquaintance I liked him at once. I can not believe that he would knowingly adulterate his tea in such a way. Surely it must have been carried out by others, without his knowledge or approval?'

"He replied: 'That was my first thought, of course, sir. Not that it would have absolved him of the ultimate responsibility, from the legal point of view. But then, in all honesty, I was forced to ask myself why Father had never allowed his own brand of green tea to be served in our own household.'

" 'Why, there is nothing in that!' I told him. 'I do not serve beer in this house. None of us likes the stuff, that is all! Must a greengrocer's vegetable marrows be brought under suspicion merely because they are not seen at his own table?'

"He replied: 'It is good of you to say that, sir. But it is only *his own brand* of green tea my father has never allowed in his house.'

"I said: 'There must be a satisfactory explanation of the matter. But, to return to your other problem, will not your uncle, Creighton Ormond, help you to pay your gaming debts? He is, after all, a banker.'

" 'I have been to see him,' he replied, 'although I had no real hope that he would help me. He told me what I had expected him to say: that his split with my father had now been fully justified; that, long ago, he had told my father that he could not condone or blind himself to my father's dishonest business practises, which he knew would be his ruination, and that our two branches of the family must have no further contact. Of my own difficulties, he merely said that I am a fool — and I dare say that's true enough — and that I am my father's son. Then he quoted Scripture to me, something about the sins of the fathers being visited upon the sons; and he bade me good day. No, sir, I shall get sweet Fanny Adams from Uncle Creighton.'

"I did not know what to say. It was then that Captain Ormond made an offensive suggestion. He asked whether I would let him have the sum of money he needed — on account, as it were, to be deducted, with interest, from the marriage settlement he was confident would be his on that happy, if somewhat distant, day when you would become his bride.

173

Well, that simply isn't on. I told him that it was an absurd idea, not worthy of the uniform he wore; and I said that, in view of the fact that he had not conducted himself as a gentleman, I would have to ask him to leave my house. At least he had the decency to go without another word."

I was weeping softly, and Mamma had come round to my side of the table to pet and console me. But how could she? What could she say? What can *anybody* say? My world, my universe has been destroyed.

"He plays a damned fine game of billiards," said Papa. "I'll have to give him that."

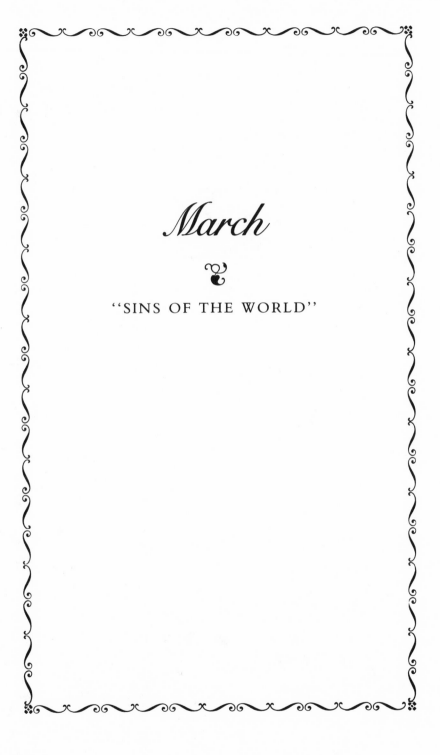

March

"SINS OF THE WORLD"

O'Connor!

I have never disliked a man so much in my entire life! There
has never been a name which, by its sound alone, could cause
my blood to simmer with such rage and indignation — not
Herod, Judas, Nero, Caligula, Bonaparte, Cumberland, none
of those names has ever vexed and distressed me half so much
as that detested name O'Connor!

Time after time he has been the cause of unhappiness to
those dear to me. First, Papa; then, Willy; now, Giles! He is
like some awful Fury, sent to goad us and sting us and leave us
never in peace.

To think that, only the day before last, I let him buy me a
jelly, and that I exchanged light banter with him, and had almost come to think him not a bad fellow, in his way.

Not a bad fellow! This self-righteous, self-appointed Neme-
sis? This destroyer of my very life? Oh, how I hate him! How
I wish him dead! And not a quick death — that would be far
too good for him. Roasted on a spit; broken on the wheel;
boiled in oil; torn by hounds! And then, consigned to the eternal fires of Hell!

How happy were my life at this moment if Rhys O'Connor
had never been born. I think of words I wrote in these pages
some three weeks ago: of that coin-toss of chance by which a

child is born or left unborn; and of that other world I created in my fancy, a world like this one in every respect, save for one fateful moment, from which point "the endless pathway of the future would suddenly veer in another direction, determined by the deeds-to-come of the newly germinated life."

If *this* world, in which I dwell and suffer, could be a world in which Rhys O'Connor had never existed; and if his baleful presence were, at this very second, blighting that other world, squeezing bitter tears from the eyes of another Pamela . . .

But these are foolish, fruitless thoughts.

I have been reading, to divert my mind from my sorrows. Here is a passage from Crèvecœur, in reference to Nantucket: "A singular custom prevails here among the women. They have adopted these many years the Asiatic custom of taking a dose of opium every morning; and so deeply rooted is it, that they would be at a loss to live without this indulgence."

At a loss to live. How I recognise the feeling. Perhaps a drop or two of laudanum will help me to sleep to-night.

৯০ *Thursday, 2 March*

I must try to be fair. I must endeavour to look at this from Papa's point of view. I can understand how Giles's behaviour would seem, to a father, most unpromising in a suitor for his daughter's hand. And yet, taking the larger view, Giles has done nothing for which he should be condemned. He had got himself into debt. Surely he is not alone in that! His father has been accused of adulterating tea. Giles is not to blame. If it be crass to discuss the financial aspect of marriage, then all parents of all daughters of all well-to-do families must be called crass, for the hypocritical phrase "a good marriage" means nothing more nor less than "plenty of coin in the coffers." If to solicit for a loan is ungentlemanly, then many who are taken for gentlemen to-day would have to relinquish that title.

I must own, however, that Giles might have chosen a more tactful way of broaching the subject. To ask for an advance against a marriage settlement when we are not yet engaged — that must be regarded as a breach of taste, although no more than that. I can appreciate Papa's revulsion at what must have seemed, to him, a callous suggestion; but, taking it all in all, Giles is not an adventurer.

I tell myself those things, with full conviction, from one part of my mind. From another small, niggling part, I ask myself if money had been foremost in Giles's thoughts since first we met, in Lady Merlyngton's drawing-room? And later, in our own drawing-room, was Giles too eager to please Papa and charm Mamma? That day in the tea-room in Henrietta Street: the way in which he flattered and beguiled Lady Merlyngton as we inched towards the door — did it shew in him a nature too easily given to sly duplicity and deception?

I am torn in twain! One half of me has faith in Giles and trusts him; the other half harbours these disloyal suspicions of his conduct. It is like being pulled in opposite directions by wild horses.

Later. Dora slipped me the following note from Giles's batman this afternoon:

"My own Pamela, —

"I do not know what your father may have said to you, but I think he can not have told you other than the truth — coloured, perhaps, by his own views. He is a just man, and he would not misrender me, I feel certain.

"Before I leave London" —

(Leave London! Am I to be spared no privation?)

— "I must say that my love for you will never diminish, no matter how long I may live nor what troubles may beset me. No young lady I have ever known has touched my heart as you have done; no other ever will. I have no miniature of you to carry in a locket, but I need no such remembrancer of your dear face — it is imprinted large within my heart; not in dead paint but in all its living, various, animated warmth and beauty. It will glow there for ever, sustaining me in times of turmoil, filling me with hope when my soul is empty and cold and I am in despair."

(Silver words, my Giles; but are they yours, or borrowed?)

"I am resigning my commission. My father's disgrace has cast its shadow upon me, and has made me a pariah in the regiment. I am in Coventry; those whom I thought to be my closest comrades are cutting me dead, looking through me as if I were of glass. Truly they were fair-weather friends, and I see them now revealed as a pack of shallow ne'er-do-wells and snobs.

"I will seek a position where my name — I should say, my father's name — is not known so well. I hope that I may write to you from time to time, and that you will not cast my letters into the fire, but will read them and — dare I ask? — will answer them.

"I leave in a day or two. Until then, I have taken rooms at the address which you see on the cover of this note. Do I expect too much if I express the hope that you will come here to-morrow, if only for a moment, that I may look upon your sweet face one more time? I will wait for you all day. Surely you can slip away for an hour or less? Do not answer this note — do not say either yes or no — just come to me to-morrow and soothe the anguished heart of —

"Your true
"Giles"

Every particle of my flesh and spirit yearns to be with him — he is a magnet, strong and irresistible; I, the helpless needle.

But still I am torn in two ways. Is his letter entirely candid? Is he leaving London solely because his fellow-officers are cutting him — or is the chief cause of flight to escape his creditors? Were it not braver and more honourable to stay in the regiment, stare down his snobbish comrades, and put *them* to shame by his own irreproachable conduct?

I chide myself: inconstant Pamela! so quick to distrust! so soon to suspect!

I look at his letter's cover: the rooms he has taken, and where he's bade me come, are in the vile and hellish sink of Whitechapel.

As I set down these words, just before retiring to a bed that may as well be a bed of red-hot coals, I do not know if I shall visit him or not.

Perhaps purely by chance, I shall see Willy to-day — that was the first thought in my mind as I awoke this morning: for my decision had been made whilst I slept, and when I opened my eyes, I knew with certainty that I would go to Giles in Whitechapel, just as he had asked me to do.

This was the third occasion in a short span of time on which I had been obliged to leave the house surreptitiously and alone; and yet it was the first time I had done so in order to meet my lover. I found a hackney at the next turning. The coachman gave me a queer look when I told him my destination, Hanbury Street, and he said, "That ain't the place for a young lady of quality, Miss. Begging your pardon, but there be hawks on the look-out for pigeons there, if you catch my meaning."

I caught his meaning well enough: the hawks he spoke of are agents for Continental brothels, ever watchful for young girls to be drugged and kidnapped and shipped off to a life of shame. The greater shame is that we have no law to prevent it. I learnt all this, to my horror, by reading an article by Rhys O'Connor last week. "The law protects only girls under the age of twenty-one," he wrote, "and they only if they are entitled to property. It is the property rights of the father to the services of his daughter — her money value — which our English law holds sacred; not the moral, personal, and physical rights of the girl herself."

I was firm with the coachman: "Never mind about that. I am no pigeon. Take me there and be brisk about it."

Even by day, Whitechapel is like a cancer festering on the body of London. I should not like to see it at night. The streets are no better than sewers; there is rubbish everywhere, decaying and fouling the air with its stench. Scraggy, starving children stared at me with hollow eyes as I rode past them; their clothing hung from their bony bodies in shreds — I thought of the line in *King Lear,* "loop'd and window'd raggedness." Drunken men staggered through the streets, not too stupefied to swear indecent oaths. I did not see the painted women one hears of — no doubt they sleep by day and appear only after the sun has set.

The coachman took a side-turning off the High Road and reined in his horse. Calling down to me, he said, "Hanbury Street, Miss." I climbed out and paid him, and, with a crack of the whip, he was soon off — glad to be gone, I think.

I walked along Hanbury Street, looking for the number Giles had given me. The glances I received from both men and women were resentful, when they were not vacant. They seemed to say: Why do the likes of you come here? To gloat at our wretchedness and lord it over us? Go back to where you belong!

An object struck my shoulder, startling me. I turned, frightened; it was only a jeering costermonger's boy, who had taken a potato from his barrow and hurled it at me as an expression of the contempt they all felt for me and others of my station. His elders laughed derisively and praised him. One man added, "But don't be flingin' any more at 'er, lad. It's a waste of good food."

I found the number of Giles's lodgings and opened the street door, entering a dark and frowsty vestibule. I knocked on the first door I saw. It was opened by a woman — old? young? I could not tell in the dim light — with reddened lips and the reek of gin on her breath. "Oooo! Cor blimey!" she said in mocking tones. "Look at 'Er Royal 'Ighness!" Then, laughing, she said, "I expect you'll be wantin' the young swell. Upstairs, Your Grace, and mind the broken stair."

As I began to climb the staircase, she called after me: "Give 'im a kiss for me, dearie! 'E's a luvly lad!"

I tapped at Giles's door. It was opened by him. I was surprised to see him dressed in civilian clothes. He said not a word, but quickly motioned me inside. Only when he had closed the door did he speak. "Dearest girl. I was afraid you would not come."

"O you of little faith," I said.

He took me in his arms and kissed me.

"I'm sorry I can not brew some tea for you," he said, "but these rooms . . ."

"I did not come for tea. But what a wretched place, my dear! Why must you stay here?"

"Because I can afford no better. I must hoard what little money I have, to buy my railway ticket and to see me through. But do sit down — this chair is hard, but it is clean."

I sat on the wooden chair he offered me. It creaked as I did so.

"Why must you go away?" I asked. "Can you not find employment in London?"

"I am known here. The name of Ormond is anathema. But I have tried. I went to see Colonel Charles Rowan of the police force — the man who founded the forces, Sir Robert Peel, used to be a guest in our house. I offered my services; I should have thought that my military training would recommend me. But the opposite is true: Colonel Rowan told me that, following Sir Robert's lead, he rejects all former officers out of hand. 'There will be no officer class in the force,' he said. 'I will not appoint gentlemen, who will refuse to associate with other persons, holding the same offices, who are not of equal rank, and who will thereby degrade the latter in the eyes of the men.' I assured him that I would take no such position. 'I think you could not help yourself,' he said. 'Your breeding, your schooling, your training — all these have moulded your character, and you can not change it in the twinkling of an eye. Besides, I can not make an exception.' I told him I should serve for small wages. He said, 'A sergeant of the Guards at two hundred pounds a year is a better man for my purpose than a captain of high military reputation, even were he to serve for nothing.' "

"My poor Giles," I said.

"I've managed to find temporary work in the North," he said, "with a small private guard corps, but God knows how long I'll be able to stick it. The fact is, I've got fed up with military swagger and had hoped to put all that behind me. I had always thought that if the military life were no longer to suit me, I should take on a post of responsibility in my father's company; but now that may not be. I then had visions of a similar post in *your* father's company; but that hope, too, has been dashed."

"We can not know that for a certainty," I said. "Papa is cross with you now, of course, but that does not mean he will not come round in time."

"Time! Your father said the same thing: 'a question of time.' I told him what I tell you: *I have no time!*"

I shook my head in puzzled worry. "It is all so unfortunate. I *know* Papa held a high opinion of you. I know he would have looked upon you as a son, in . . . in time. My brother, Willy, has always been a disappointment to him, even as a boy. Papa wished him to excel in sport, but he did not. Later, it was Papa's hope that Willy should go into the family business, but Willy chose to prepare for holy orders. And now, Willy has . . . well, no matter. I know that Papa saw in you the kind of son he never had in Willy; a man's man, who sits a horse well and plays a good game of billiards. Somebody to take over the business when he retires. Somebody to carry on for him."

Giles angrily struck his fist into his palm, with a sound like a pistol shot. "What a fool I have been!" he exclaimed. "With a few ill-chosen words, I have spoilt all of my chances and turned your father against me. He was my last hope!"

"Giles . . . please . . . do not say so . . . I can not bear it."

He turned to a cupboard which he opened, and took down a bottle of gin. "Forgive me if I do not offer you a glass of this stuff," he said, bitterly. "It is not exactly the champagne or sherry to which you are accustomed." He filled a tumbler — cracked and none too clean — with the clear fluid and drained it in one draught. He poured another, and drained that as well.

"What I am bound to do," he said, "is to call out that O'Connor fellow."

"Do you mean . . . challenge him to a duel?"

"Of course. He has spread calumny about my father; dishonoured our family name. The choice of weapon will be his, but I am a master of any he may choose, whether it be rapiers, sabres, or pistols. If pistols, I shall shoot him dead with the first ball. If rapiers or sabres, I shall cut him into ribbons, bleeding ribbons . . . slice him, chop him . . . into a gory mess . . . before I despatch him to the devils he serves!"

"No, Giles! You shan't!"

"Why shall I not?"

"Because I forbid you. I tell you that you shall not place yourself in danger of death. If he were to kill you —"

"That coward?"

"— if you were to die, I could not live. I should leap into the grave beside you. Giles, you *will not* leave me behind in a world without you!"

I had sprung from the chair and now was holding his face in my hands. His arms enfolded me. We kissed. We sank onto the bed. The blanket may have been rough and filthy, but I took no note of it. His breath was rank with gin, but it was like the most delicate scent to me. I cannot tell the span of time that passed, but in that span our union was consummated.

Giles had spoken true when, on a certain earlier occasion, he had assured me that we had then but played at love, when measured agains the heights we would later reach. We reached those heights to-day, eventually; but the beginnings were awkward and unseemly and even painful — for me, at any rate. There was, from the start, what I considered to be a disparity of dimension to be dealt with: I saw fully, for the first time, that which I had hitherto but held half-seen in my hand, and I could not believe that I was expected to accommodate the entirety of that which was presented to me. I protested; I resisted; I dilated upon the impossibility of it; but "dilated" is a curiously apt word, for, after a time, a dilation of another kind began to occur (not without his various urgings and proddings and steadfast refusal to retreat), and slowly, patiently, my lover became a longboat cautiously traversing a dangerous strait, easing carefully and smoothly through the narrows. I winced at a twinge of pain, and felt a warm trickle, which I sensed was the blood sacrifice of my maidenhood. I begged him to stop, but he paid no heed; instead, he persisted, pressed on, and I felt myself invaded, filled by him, crammed and stuffed and packed as if from head to toe — and still there was no rapture for me, nothing to equal even the pleasant offering he had made me on that other occasion. There was only discomfort, clumsiness, indignity. But gradually — starting like a far-away melody, almost unheard — I began to be aware of a small distant sweetness, approaching steadily but very slowly. He persevered in his labour of love — now I knew the literal meaning of that figure! the sheer hard grunting *work* of love — his breath deepened, his brow glistened, he toiled strenuously, powerfully, dedicatedly, ever harder and harder, in strict but ever more rapid tempo; and the melody grew nearer, stronger, brighter, clearer; it swelled with orchestration now, and burst into joyous voices; and I pleaded with him to stop not yet, not yet, dear Christ not yet — and the giant sun of noon blazed in my belly, rose to explode in my head, blinding me, melting me down into a river of gold, and I cried out in boundless surprise and a sort of grateful rage, and he cried out, too, convulsed in frightening spasms like a mortally wounded man, and collapsed with all his dear and sweating weight upon me, and I knew that we had become, at last, for ever, in the eyes of God if not of Man, wedded to each other as true husband and true wife.

In the blessed twilight that followed, he whispered gently in my ear, "I shan't leave you behind in a world without me. I'll not call out O'Connor." I was unable to say anything; I could only smile and purr. "Nor do I want to leave you behind in London," he added. "It tears my heart to think of it."

"Mine, too," I murmured.

"And yet I must leave. Life has become impossible for me here. Pamela: come with me."

"With you? . . ."

"We are man and wife, in all but ceremony. Is not a wife's place with her husband? Then stop with me here, in these rooms, to-night; and to-morrow we shall board a train and leave these troubles far behind us. Do not return to your parents' house, even for a bag. Come with me as you are. Tell no-one. Write to them on the train and post the letter from some one-eyed village or other on the way. After some months, write to them again, and say that you are expecting to present them with a grandchild . . ."

"What if it not be true?"

"In all likelihood, it *will* be true. But if it is not, the effect will be the same. They shall urge you to return, and to bring your husband with you. Your father will not *then* object to solemnising our marriage with ceremony."

I eased myself from his arms and sat on the edge of the bed, quite naked. My clothing was piled on the wooden chair. I rose and walked over to it, my bare feet like blocks of ice as they touched the uncarpeted floor.

"Your dear backside," said Giles. "It is shaped like a lyre."

Silently, I sorted out my under-garments from the tangle on the chair: the linen shift, the pantaloons, the several petticoats. I began to put them on.

"Must you dress?" he asked. "And cover up all that loveliness?"

"These rooms are so cold," I said, temporising.

"It is warm in bed."

"I can not stay longer."

"But what of my idea? Stay with me to-night, and then —"

Still dressing, I spoke quietly: "It is a clever plan, Giles."

"I am obliged to agree," he said, with a smile.

"Really *quite* clever. Resourceful. Ingenious. Was it in your mind when you wrote to me and begged me to come to you here?"

"Pamela! Dearest!" He reached out for me from the bed, but I stepped away.

"Was it in your mind even longer ago, when you climbed through my bedroom window? Did you think to get me with child that night and force my father to give you my hand?"

"My own darling! How can you say such things?"

I forced back the tears. I was determined not to break into pieces before him. I continued to dress. "You must really take greater care when you speak," I advised him. "It is true, what you said before: you spoil your chances with a few ill-chosen words. Not only with Papa, but with me, as well. If you had merely said 'Come with me' and said no more, I should have followed you to the ends of the earth. But you had to speak on . . . you had to be devious . . . hatch schemes . . . press me to lie to my parents. Is there *nothing* you will not use for your advantage, Giles? Must you use even love? Even the children of that love?"

"Pamela! —"

I was fully dressed now. Before he could rise from his bed, I was out the door, down the staircase, and into Hanbury Street.

My tears were flowing freely now; they scalded my eyes; they blinded me; I could not see my way. I ran I knew not where, my mind a whirling wheel of pain, until I collided with a large shape that seized both of my arms and chuckled nastily.

I looked up into a sneering, swarthy face. The man who owned it wore a suit of garish but expensive clothing, and his hands were studded with jewelled rings. His breath stank of garlic. "Now then, now then, now then," he said, smiling and shewing a gold tooth. "Wot 'ave we 'ere? A maiden in distress? Poor pretty Poll? Never fear, luv. You're in good 'ands. Just step in 'ere with me . . ."

He began to pull me towards a doorway. I tried to elude him, but his grip was strong, his fingers like iron spikes as they sank into my arms. "None o' that, me doll!" he snarled. "You'll learn obedience before you've seen the last of me!" He slapped my face viciously, and a riot of fire-works blazed behind my eyes.

I knew I was doomed . . . he would beat me into submission and drug me . . . sell me as a slave . . . a prisoner of lust in some foul den across the sea . . . I would never see Mamma and Papa again . . .

Suddenly, his hands released me. Another man had pinioned his arms and now was raining blow after blow on his head. I could not see clearly — the tears; the pain of that slap — but I could see enough to know that my would-be abductor had been beaten senseless to the ground, and then mercilessly kicked by a black boot. I saw the wretch crawl away and vanish into an alley, whilst my rescuer picked up a broken paving-stone from the street and hurled it after him in his wrath.

"Giles!" I managed to sob out. "Thank God you followed me!" (How could he have got dressed so quickly?)

When he turned to me, and I wiped my eyes, I saw that he was not Giles, but Willy.

I am safe now, at home in my sitting-room, wrapped in my dressing-gown, with a cheery fire crackling behind the grate. The slap I received, although a shock, will not discolour my face, and there will be no bruise to raise questions.

I am exhausted — and mortally disappointed in Giles — and I have taken a drop and will now fall into my bed. I will write about Willy to-morrow.

ᗘ *Saturday, 4 March*

As soon as I recognised Willy, yesterday in Whitechapel, he took my arm and gently led me away, saying, "Come along. The mission is just at the next turning."

He escorted me into what appeared to be a little shop. A few destitute people of both sexes, dull of face, sat at long tables, spooning up soup from wooden bowls. He guided me to a corner where we could be very nearly alone. "Did he hurt you?" he asked immediately.

"No. I was terribly frightened, but I'm quite all right now — thanks to you, Willy."

"Nasty bit of work, that fellow. I've seen him lurking about here before. But tell me, Pam, how did you find me?"

"Find you?"

"Surely there is no one *else* whom you know in Whitechapel."

"In point of fact, there is," I said, "or was — for I think I shall not see him again." I told him the whole story.

"You are well rid of him," said Willy.

"I know I am," I replied, and felt the tears start once more. "And yet I love him still. I feel I shall always love him. Against all reason and sense. I can not understand why."

"We do not choose where we love," he said.

"And you, Willy?" I asked. "Are you getting on here?"

He smiled. "Famously. I am now allowed to preach. I would ask you to stay and hear me, but I fear you would be out of place. Besides — you were never partial to sermons."

"I fear you are right," I said, returning his smile.

"We must get you out of this," he said. "I shall find a hackney."

"Not just yet. I want to ask you: Will you be going abroad soon?"

"Perhaps, if they continue to be pleased with my work here. I must demonstrate my willingness to perform all tasks the Lord may require of me. I must shew obedience and denial of self. I pray constantly that I may be sent abroad before long. It is in God's hands."

"Willy, did Lord Granville ever find you?"

He smiled ruefully. "Poor Jack. Yes, he found me — and pray don't apologise for revealing my whereabouts to him. I should have done the same in your place. Jack is a persuasive fellow. No one can resist him."

"He seemed so terribly fond of you."

"His affection is sincere. He took French leave from university to seek me out, and will no doubt be punished for it — perhaps even sent down. I'm afraid he made a scene here: wept, ranted, fell on his knees, begged, threw himself about. He wanted me to come away with him. 'There'll be no lack of money,' he said. 'I have pots of the stuff. We might live in Italy. Or in Greece, like Byron. Somewhere in the warm sun. Somewhere out of this damp, cold, absurd country. This nation of prigs.' I simply could not make him understand that my way lies elsewhere, doing God's work. He said, 'Why must God's work be done only in stinking stews like this, or amongst black savages? Can it not be done in Italy, or in the south of France? Come with me to such places, and you may preach ten hours a day, if that is your wish. I'll help you and pass the collection box.' And he meant every word, I am certain. But I told him it would never do. 'It would be a game with you, Jack, and you would tire of it. You would tire of me, as well, and my pious ways.' He swore he would love me to the end of his life. He said I was the only truly good person he had ever known. 'You are a saint, Will, a living saint, and I worship the very ground you tread upon. Let me stay beside you and serve you. Even in Africa! Wherever you are sent! Do not cast me out; do not send me away.' But in the end, of course, that is precisely what I was forced to do."

"He seems to be not such a bad fellow. I feel sorry for him."

"So do I. When I told him that he should turn to God for solace, he shouted: '*God!?* I *hate* your God! He is a God of pain and filth! He has snuffed out the human warmth in you, and made of you a withered, lifeless thing. You prate about the soul, Will. I am not sure what such a thing may be, but if ever you had one, it is dead in you now. Yes, my dear: your soul is dead, and it was your precious swine-God who killed it!' "

"Oh dear" was all I could say. Willy bade me wait whilst he hunted down a hackney, and within the hour I was home again.

I feel like a victim of the protracted torture known as *peine forte et dure,* slowly being crushed under heavy weights piled gradually upon me, day by day. Mr. George Borrow paid a call this afternoon, for we were at home, and he added yet another stone to the mountain of sorrow that presses down upon me.

"Do you remember my book of translations from Pushkin, Miss Summerfield?"

"I do, indeed. I have read it twice over. I think he is the equal of Byron, if not his superior."

"I have just learned that he died in Russia, early last month. Killed by a pistol shot in a duel."

In a rush, I felt the chill of the early-morning Russian mist and saw the two men, their outlines softened by that mist, raise their pistols. I smelt the pungent odour of wet grass. I heard the shots, I saw the poet fall. I saw Giles fall, as O'Connor lowered his smoking weapon. My heart knotted in pain at the sight of my fallen lover. In the next moment, I felt a twinge of another kind, as I asked myself if Giles truly had intended to call out O'Connor — or had it been bravado?

Great Pushkin dead! So wastefully! All for what Cowper called

> The fear of tyrant custom, and the fear
> Lest fops should censure us, and fools should sneer.

Men are such asses.

There are words in the Roman Mass which have been going round and round in my brain all day. I came across them whilst turning the pages of Beethoven's *Missa Solemnis*. Just three short lines; fourteen syllables; but all the desperate hope of the wretched soul is compressed in them:

> *Qui tollis*
> *peccata mundi*
> *miserere nobis*

This compacted cry becomes looser and less piercing in English:

> Thou who takest away
> the sins of the world
> have mercy on us

— but even so, it expresses the poor heart's yearning; the need to be washed clean and to feel the crusted shames of feeble flesh and craven spirit fall away like filth and scabs under a warm spring rain, leaving us bright and fresh and new-born. It is my prayer for Willy, and Jack Granville, and for Phoebe, and for Giles, and most particularly for me.

The more responsible of our newspapers have been restrained in their reporting of what the buzzing gossips are calling The Ormond Tea Scandal. No date has been set for a trial, and one of the most sober journals has said, "It is to be hoped that it will not come to that; and that Mr. Percival Ormond, who has always been one of our most esteemed and prominent men of commerce, will be found innocent of criminal intent, without being subjected to the Roman carnival of protracted litigation."

The radical papers express no such hopes. They scream for Mr. Ormond's blood, and raise the spectres of his victims, "sped to their final rest by Ormond's *verdigreed.*" (That vicious bit of word-play — need I say? — is from the acid-dipped pen of Rhys O'Connor.) A lurid caricature, drawn by one cunning artist, shews a parody of Mr. Ormond's features (in which, curiously, the resemblance to Giles is more marked than in life), and pictures him with one hand pouring tea from a pot shaped like a skull, and the other hand outstretched to catch the showers of pound notes that are poured into it by a throng of skeletons. A ribbon of speech extrudes from Mr. Ormond's grimming mouth: *"Shall I be Mother?"* The subscription reads: "AFTERNOON TEA AT THE HOUSE OF ORMOND. A VERY GRAVE AFFAIR."

Papa says, "The word in the City is that Ormond's company has been on its beam-ends for some little time, even before this adulteration began to be bruited about. There has been no free issue of new shares for over a year, and the rumour is that the books may have been fiddled, as well. It all points to Ormond deliberately tampering with his tea in order to gain a quick profit and pull himself out of the straits. Of course, appearances can be deceiving, and we must not be quick to judge. I *did* like the chap, at first meeting."

"*I* thought him vulgar," said Mamma, in an I-told-you-so tone of voice.

As for myself, I feel sorry for him. No man should be vilified and caricatured and ridiculed in public as he has been. If the charges are proved false, can the stain ever be removed? On the other hand, what if the charges be true? If Mr. Ormond *knowingly* poisoned his tea in order to sell it at a greater profit, should he not strenuously be prosecuted and punished? Such a man would be no better than a monster, callous and heartless, without conscience, undeserving of pity.

The afternoon post has arrived, and, with it, a small parcel addressed to me, which Rutledge brought up here to my sitting-room. He lingered as I opened it. I tore off the wrapping, to find a thin book, bound in fine leather. Opening it, I was disappointed to see that it was merely a copy of *Hamlet* (which I know almost by heart), and in the detestable edition of Dr.

Bowdler, at that! There was an inscription in ink on the fly-leaf:

"Pamela, here is Shakespere's *Hamlet* — edited, ruined, & expurgated! — Your Uncle Roger."

I smiled, but I still can not imagine why dear Uncle Roger has sent me this utterly worthless book. He knows my opinion of Dr. Bowdler, and he shares that opinion: indeed, it was Uncle Roger who first counselled me to read Shakespere in the original, and not in the gelded versions of priggish editors.

I put the book aside and looked up at Rutledge, who stood there, as if waiting to speak.

"Yes, Rutledge? Is there something else?"

"No, Miss. Will you be wanting anything? Some tea, perhaps?"

"I think not, thank you. Why do you ask? Afternoon tea will be served shortly, and I shan't need anything beforehand."

"No, Miss."

"What *is* it, Rutledge? You are positively fidgeting!"

"It's nothing, Miss. Just something I heard in the town. No doubt you've heard it, too. I fancy it will be in the newspapers to-morrow."

"You are behaving *most* peculiarly. *What* will be in the papers?"

"The young gentleman who called here one afternoon recently. You have not heard, Miss?"

"Which young gentleman?"

"Lord Granville."

"And what of Lord Granville?"

"Of course, it may be no more than a rumour. People do gossip so. It would appear that he's been found dead, Miss."

"Dead!"

"Hanged himself, is what they're saying."

"Dear God, no!"

"A terrible thing, Miss. Such a *young* person."

"Oh, Rutledge, can you be certain?"

He hesitated, and then said, "I should not listen to rumours, Miss, I know; and yet it is my experience that the news that is passed along from the servants of one house to another — not that *I* or any of the other Summerfield staff have ever gossiped about *this* family, Heaven forbid! — but news obtained in that way is usually reliable. More reliable, often, than the sort one reads in the newspapers. For example, Miss, I think that the papers will not say anything about suicide — and yet I do not doubt the truth of it."

"How awful! The poor young man!"

"Yes, Miss."

"How wretched he must have been — to throw away his whole life! What a Hell he must have carried in his heart!"

"Indeed, Miss. Are you sure you'll not be wanting something? A nice hot flagon of mulled claret? It will help to soften the shock."

"Yes. That would be most welcome. I feel . . . chilled."

"I'm sorry, Miss Pamela. Perhaps I should not have told you, but I thought it better than having you come across it all sudden-like in the morning edition. Seeing as you had met the young gentleman, and so recently."

"You were perfectly right to tell me, Rutledge."

"Thank you, Miss. I'll fetch the wine at once."

When he had left the room, I asked myself: How will poor Willy receive this news? For his sake, I hope Rutledge is correct about the papers suppressing the matter of suicide.

Peccata mundi . . . the sins of the world . . . *miserere nobis* . . . have mercy on us. Have mercy on the soul of poor Jack Granville, O Lord! Condemn him not to the fiery pits of Hell. The passion that caused him to sin with my brother — it was of Thy making, Lord; and the torment that racked him so severely that he could not bear to live . . . was it not of Thy making, as well? Forgive him, Lord — and if Thou dost, then Thy servant Pamela may one day find it in her heart to forgive Thee.

8ᴗ *Tuesday, 7 March*

Rutledge was absolutely right: the newspapers this morning all carried small notices of Lord Granville's death, but none of them breathed the dread word "suicide." In addition to being a foreteller of newspaper notices, Rutledge is the soul of discretion. He sensed that I should not wish my parents to know that I had met the dead man, so he said nothing about his visit to our house, even when Papa, looking up from his paper at breakfast, remarked upon the notice: "Young Granville is dead. Just a lad. I knew his late father slightly — he was a member of my club. The boy was the last of the line, I believe. A great pity."

When we were nearly finished breakfast, and Papa was preparing to leave for the City, Rutledge returned to announce "Mr. Wilfrid is here, sir."

"Willy?" I squeaked, in surprise.

"Why, shew him in at once!" cried Mamma, delighted.

Willy entered the dining-room. His face was white. Mamma embraced him, as did I. Papa shook his hand.

"I can not stay," Willy said. "I leave to-day for Africa —"

"Africa!" The word was a cry of grief on Mamma's lips.

"— but I could not go without calling here first to say good-bye."

"Thank God you did, my boy," said Papa. "Thank God you did." There were tears in his eyes.

"I go to replace one of our missionaries who died some few months ago —"

"Died!" Mamma repeated, with a shudder.

Willy said, "Not through misadventure. He was a very old man, over eighty, and he passed into the better world quite peaceably, in his sleep. The natives of that place — I fear I can not yet pronounce it! — are now without a spiritual guide. They are but newly come into the fold, and are in peril of reverting to their heathen ways if a successor does not arrive amongst them without further delay. I shall write to you from there, as promptly as I can. Good-bye, Mother . . . Father . . ."

"You are not leaving so *soon?*" Mamma wailed.

"Won't you at least sit down and take some breakfast?" said Papa.

"I've already had my breakfast, hours ago," Willy replied. "I really *must* go now."

As he kissed me, he said, "Perhaps you will see me out to the street, Pam? I have a hackney waiting."

Throwing on a wrap against the cold, I followed him out to the hackney. He said, "Have you read the newspaper this morning?"

I nodded, my eyes cast down. "You mean Jack Granville," I replied.

"Yes."

"It was a shock," I said. "He did not appear to be ill when I met him."

"He took his own life."

"No! The paper said nothing of that! I do not believe it!"

"I received a letter from Jack this morning — posted before his death. It was quite short. The first sentence read, 'By the time you receive this, I will have left this vile world behind.' I immediately sought out a newspaper, and there I saw his death confirmed. He did not blame me in his note. But I blame myself. I should not have sent him away as I did."

"What else could you have done? Taken him to Africa with you?"

"He offered to go."

"As a kind of game — you were right to have told him so."

"Was I? The greatest error we can commit in this life is to judge others; to under-estimate their spiritual strength. Who am I to tell a fellow-mortal that his offer to help is but a game? What gives me that right? If there is even a chance, the slimmest chance, that a sinner can be saved through sacrifice and good works — must he not be given that chance? But I denied him — I told him he was merely playing at penitence. How could I be certain of that? How could I have presumed to think that I could look into his heart and read his intentions? How could I have been so vain?"

"Willy, you must *not* blame yourself!"

"I do. I am no better than a murderer. All of my life, from this moment, will be an act of penance. I pray that I may be forgiven. I pray that Jack will forgive me. For I can never forgive myself."

"*I* forgive you, Willy!"

He smiled sadly. "Dear little Pam. You have not the power to forgive me. Forgive me for what?"

"I forgive you for . . . for . . ." I searched frantically for words, and then I blurted out, "for pasting together the pages of my Mother Goose book!"

He laughed, just a little. "Thank you, my dear. You are the sweetest person in the world." He kissed me.

"Willy!" I cried, desperately trying to delay his departure. "Can you not stay the night with us, at least? You are breaking Mamma's heart, and mine as well, and Papa's, too. Why must you dash off like this?"

"I mustn't miss my ship," he said.

"There will be other ships!"

"I am needed. And I am impatient to be off. There is something inside me that fears to postpone God's work — every hour, every moment, is precious and must be filled." He seemed to look through me, past me, at distant scenes, and his eyes grew dark and strange and frightening. His voice was peculiarly altered when he spoke again. "I have a kind of presentiment that tells me this world is on the brink of a deep abyss, into which it is in danger of tumbling — all the more reason to brook no delay in spreading the Holy Word. I think of the passage in John: 'I must work the works of him that sent me, while it is day: the night cometh, when no man can work.'" He kissed me again. "Good-bye," he said, and added; "Do you know what that expression means, Pam?"

"God be with you," I replied.

"Yes, that's right. God be with you."

He climbed into the hackney and was gone.

ॐ *Wednesday, 8 March*

Papa returned from the City early this afternoon. I could hear him in Mamma's sitting room, which adjoins mine. Isolated phrases sifted through: "The damned impudence of the man . . . how dare he . . . accusations . . . threats . . . infernal presumption . . ."

Later, he stormed down the staircase with a heavy tread, and I could hear the door of his study slam shut.

Rhys O'Connor again, I *knew* it. Some fresh insult — even after he had assured me that his investigations had uncovered no impurities in the product of Papa's brewery.

198

I knocked on Mamma's door and went in. "What on earth?" I said. "I couldn't help hearing."

Mamma sighed. "It is all most upsetting," she said. "Particularly after that unfortunate incident involving your brother. Children can be such a cross. Sometimes I think that if I had my life to live over again, I should never have had any children at all."

"Please don't say that, Mamma!"

"I do not mean it, of course. I love you all. You know that. But one never stops worrying about one's children, even when they are grown up and gone from the nest. You'll learn the truth of that, one day."

"Whatever has happened?"

"You may as well know," she said. "It will all come out sooner or later." She handed me a letter. "Your father received this to-day, at his office in the City."

Unfolding it, I saw a crabbed, unfamiliar hand. I next looked at the signature. It was signed "E. Braithwaite." Phoebe's husband!

"Are you sure I may read it?" I asked.

"Yes, yes," Mamma replied wearily.

I did so. This is what it said:

"Dear Mr. Summerfield, —

"I write to you in considerable distress. I am not a man easily provoked to anger, but in this matter I feel I have been injured and ill used —"

I looked up. *"What* matter?" I asked.

"Read on," said Mamma, "although I think you will not be much enlightened, and will find it as baffling as your father and I do."

I resumed reading.

"— and I assure you that, if I am forced to the necessity, I will not hesitate to seek the advice of my solicitor. I am certain that you must realise that the law is on my side.

"As you are undoubtedly aware, your daughter — my lawful wife — has left my house. I do not know why she has done so. I tell you with complete honesty that there has never been a harsh word between us. We have had no quarrels. On the contrary, our life together since our wedding might be described as an idyll. She has always given me to believe that she has been entirely happy. Indeed, she has written verses, which she has shewn me, on the heavenly bliss of the married state.

"I assure you, my dear father-in-law, that I am not a brute. I have given your daughter no cause to be unhappy. I have provided her with a fine home. My friends have become hers. She has lacked nothing.

"And yet she has left me, quite suddenly, without a word save the short note which I enclose."

I interrupted my reading of the letter to glance quickly at Phoebe's note. It bore neither salutation nor signature, but it was in her hand, and it read simply: "I am leaving you. I shall not return. Do not try to follow me or bring me back. I fully own that I am in the wrong. I should not have married you. I am sorry to cause you embarrassment." I then returned to Mr. Braithwaite's letter:

"Please do not attempt to deny that she is under your roof at this very moment. Where else should she go? I advise you to return her to her rightful place — the house of her husband — at once. If you do not do so of your own volition, you will force me to exercise my right under the law.

"With respect, I remain,
"Your son-in-law,
"E. Braithwaite"

"But Phoebe is not here!" I said, putting down the letter. "Is she?"

"Of course not," Mamma replied. "That is what is so perplexing. If she is not with her husband, where is she? And why should she leave him in that way, when she has given every sign of being content? I am utterly bewildered. Children!"

I was in a turmoil of divided loyalties. I could not reveal to Mamma things of which Phoebe had written me in confidence. I could not tell her that Phoebe is with child. I most assuredly could not tell her that the child was not sired by her husband. I struggled with myself, and at length I reached a decision. I would shew Mamma only the first of Phoebe's distressing letters, that which I received on 7 January. In that letter, she revealed the extreme state of her misery, and at the same time praised her husband as a good and considerate man. Nothing was said, until later letters, of her pregnant condition. I went to my sitting-room at once and ransacked my desk, looking for the letter, until I remembered that I had burnt it, in accordance with Phoebe's request. But I had copied extracts from it into your pages, Diary, and so I read those passages aloud to Mamma.

When she had heard them, she said, "Then she has been feeling wretched the entire time. And yet I am still in the dark as to the reason. She feels the lack of a 'magical element' in her marriage, 'transports of unparalleled rapture.' What foolishness! She even admits that it is 'not a bad life' and that 'many would envy it.' What on earth is the matter with the girl? I had always thought that she was a most sensible person, but now she has behaved like the silliest feather-head. It is really too bad of her. She has made me quite cross."

"Please, Mamma," I said. "We have not heard her side of this matter."

"*Her* side? She has no side! Mr. Braithwaite is in the right. Even the law recognises that."

"The law is not perfect. It condones many wrongs."

"Where *is* the girl? How is she faring? Does she have any money? What does she eat; where does she lay her head?" Mamma was in tears.

"I wish I knew," I said, kneeling beside her. "If I knew, I would tell you." (And I think that I truly would have done.) "Oh, dear Mamma, please do not weep."

"Where *is* she?" Mamma repeated.

With the father of her child, I have no doubt: that was my silent answer. But who, and where, is *he*?

       ஓ *Thursday, 9 March*

When Papa stormed downstairs to his study yesterday, he wrote a letter to Phoebe's husband. To-day, Mamma shewed me the draught of it. The fair-copy had been posted to Warwickshire yesterday:

"Dear Mr. Braithwaite, —

"I have your astonishing letter before me. It is the first I learnt of my daughter's departure from your house. We are, both of us, gentlemen, I hope, and therefore you must believe me when I assure you that she is not here. I am most terribly concerned for her safety, and my wife is near to distraction with worry. We are as ignorant of her whereabouts as are you, and as anxious. I do not know, at this moment, what I plan to do about the matter. I may inform the police; I may seek the services of a private enquiry agent. I am certain of one thing only:

"If my daughter appears on my threshold, or if I learn by some means where she is, I shall be guided solely by her wishes — by *her* wishes, sir, not yours. If she does not desire to return to you, I shall not force her to do so. Indeed, I shall employ every means in my power, legal or otherwise, to prevent you from taking her back. May I say that I consider the threatening, admonitory tone of your letter to be quite unacceptable, outrageous, and insulting.

"Wilfrid Summerfield"

(Bravo, Papa!)

ॐ *Friday, 10 March*

It is the middle of the night. I awakened quite suddenly, at half past three, prodded into full awareness. Nothing exterior to myself awakened me — no noise or chilly draught or other thing of that kind. It was the prompting of my own mind, telling me something that in the waking state had escaped my attention.

This prompting took the form of a huge character of calligraphy, towering high into the dream clouds and having this shape:

It was nothing more nor less than a colossal ampersand.

I threw off the bed-clothes and lighted a candle from the coals still glowing behind my grate. In the keenest anticipation, I dashed into my sitting-room and took from a drawer of my desk the book I had received on Monday from Uncle Roger. Voraciously, I read again his inscription:

"Pamela, here is Shakespere's *Hamlet* — edited, ruined, & expurgated! — Your Uncle Roger."

By making certain allowances, I quickly discovered what I took to be a hidden message in those words. The allowances were these: first, I disregarded the signature, "Your Uncle Roger." Next, I disregarded the ampersand between the words "ruined" and "expurgated" — if my uncle had spelled out the word "and," I should have had to take it into account; but he had used the ampersand, and he *hates* ampersands. Taking all these considerations into account, and using our old acrostical cypher, I made this message emerge from Uncle Roger's inscription:

PHISHERE

But I was still in the dark. Such gibberish! And then I remembered that Uncle Roger, when resorting to abbreviations in hastily written notes and letters, had always used *P* for my name and *Ph* for Phoebe's. His message now became:

PH IS HERE

My heart felt as if it would leap from my breast! He was telling me that Phoebe was with him, in Suffolk!

I ran onto the landing, Sophie following at my heels, and pounded at my parents' door. I burst into their bedroom.

"Pamela . . . what is the matter?" Mamma muttered. Sophie was barking excitedly.

I turned up the gas. Papa, blinking at the clock, growled, "Do you know what time it is?"

"Phoebe!" I cried. "She's with Uncle Roger!"

"What?" Mamma mumbled, still half-asleep.

"How do you know?" asked Papa.

I shewed him the book's inscription and began to explain our cypher. The words tumbled from my mouth in a tangle.

"Compose yourself, Princess. Am I to understand that, simply because the initial letters of these words spell out the phrase 'Ph is here,' you believe your sister has sought asylum with my brother?"

"Yes, *yes!* I'm sure of it!"

"But this is probably no more than coincidence. Roger is not given to such puzzles and riddles."

"No, but Phoebe *is!* She probably helped Uncle Roger to compose the inscription!"

Mamma spoke. "My dear, I know you are worried about Phoebe, as are we all, but this is surely nothing more than your imagination. Uncle Roger has often sent you books as gifts . . ."

"Not books he *knows* I despise! Uncle Roger, of all people, would *never* send me one of Dr. Bowdler's expurgations! He did so only to alert me to the message — and for that same reason, he used the ampersand, because he knows that *I* know he hates it! But I was such a stupid goose that I did not take the hint until now!"

"If what you suspect is true," said Papa, removing the cloth restrainer from his moustaches and arising from the bed, "why did your uncle not write to *me,* openly?"

"Phoebe must have begged him not to."

Papa, standing there in his long, wrinkled night-shirt and cap and bare feet, looked comical. I have not seen him so since I was a child. "Let me look at that book again," he said, and I handed him the copy of *Hamlet.* He put on his spectacles and perused the inscription closely, spelling out the acrostic aloud: "P-H-I-S-H-E-R-E." He turned to Mamma and said, "There may be something in this." He reached for the bell-cord and pulled it.

"What are you doing?" asked Mamma.

"Waking Rutledge. I want him to tell Paley to ready the coach for a journey to Suffolk within the hour. Mrs. Pruitt can prepare a hamper of food, for I shan't have time for breakfast. I am going to pay a visit to my brother."

"You will not go alone," said Mamma.

"Agreed: it is right that you should come, too."

"And I, Papa!" I demanded.

"No, Princess —" he started to say, but I did not allow him to finish.

"It is *my* book — Uncle Roger sent it to *me* — and the message written inside it was for me. I *insist* upon going with you!"

He sighed. "Very well, very well. Go and dress. We will leave in less than an hour."

I dressed quickly and then scribbled this entry. I hear the coach below. Mamma is calling me.

Saturday, 11 March

Despite the excellent hamper provided by Mrs. Pruitt for our journey, I was famished by the time we arrived at Uncle Roger's house. Almost the first thing I did was to devour two gigantic scones, spreading on them first fresh butter, then damson jam, and, finally, foamy mounds of thick, sweet Devonshire cream — washing all this down with quantities of strong hot tea, liberally sugared.

Uncle Roger was not surprised to see us. He expressed only some wonder that it had taken so long. With a wink at me, he said, "I should have thought that the combination of ampersand and Bowdler would have alerted you sooner. But no matter." He turned to Papa. "I should have written to you, Will, to-day or to-morrow. Phoebe asked me not to do so until a few days had passed. She wanted time to compose her mind. But she had no objection to sending a veiled message to her sister."

"Where is she?" Mamma demanded.

"Upstairs, in her room. When we saw your coach enter the gate, she withdrew and asked me to greet you and tell you what I know. To soften the blow, as it were. She'll be down directly. Will anybody have more tea?"

"Yes, please," I said, although my parents declined.

As Uncle Roger poured, he spoke. "Phoebe arrived here without prior announcement one evening last week, taking me completely by surprise. I had not seen her since the wedding. When she told me that she had left her husband, I was shocked. When she told me why, I was even more shocked."

"Get on with it!" said Papa.

"The first thing you must know is that she is with child."

"Why, that is capital news!" said Papa. Grasping Mamma's hand, he added, "Is it not, my dear?"

Before she could respond, Uncle Roger said, "The second thing you must know —"

"May I have another scone, please?" I said, dreading and delaying the awful revelation I knew was to come.

Uncle Roger passed me the plate of scones, resuming his speech without losing a stroke: "— is that she is fearful of what her husband will do when he learns of her condition."

"Fearful!?" said Mamma. "Why so?"

"Because the moment he knows, he will also know that the child can not be his."

"How can he possibly know any such thing?" Papa demanded.

"More tea?" Uncle Roger asked me; but this time I shook my head (my mouth was full). Smiling at me, he said, "Other girls of Pam's age are perhaps too young to hear this, but you have a very mature daughter in her. She has, after all, read Shakespere unexpurgated."

"Please go on, Roger," said Mamma.

"Mr. Braithwaite will immediately know that he is not the child's father because, in plain truth, the marriage has never been consummated."

Papa was dumbfounded. "But . . . they have been married for . . . for . . . how long has it been? . . ."

"Oh, there has been ample time," said Uncle Roger, "and no lack of opportunity. The lack has been Mr. Braithwaite's. A lack of inclination, let us say; a lack of interest; a lack of . . . capacity."

"Good gracious!" said Mamma.

Papa's face grew grim. "And the impudent beggar had the confounded gall to insist upon his rights! His rights! What of *her* rights? He married her under false pretences! The law is on *her* side! This marriage will be annulled!"

Uncle Roger said, "Not without dragging it through the courts. Phoebe assures me that he would fight you every inch of the way. He is most satisfied with married life. His house has got a charming hostess. He enjoys being thought of as a blissful benedict. He is proud to have your lovely daughter as his wife."

"She is *not* his wife!" said Papa. "He has not made her so!"

"You would have to prove that in court, and no doubt you could do so, with Phoebe's testimony. But she will not allow it. She will not subject herself to public shame, and I can not say that I blame her."

Mamma said, "If Mr. Braithwaite is not the father, then . . ."

"Ah," said Uncle Roger. "That is just the point. She will not say. She will not stand in the witness-box and say in open court that her husband is not the sire — and without such testimony, there can be no successful nullity suit — and she will not say, even in private, who *is* the father. She will not tell me, and she will not tell you. She grows rather theatrical when pressed. 'Tortures would not tear his name from my lips' are her exact words."

Papa groaned. "What a sordid business. Impotence . . . adultery . . . a child out of wedlock . . . infidelity . . ."

"Not that, at any rate," said Uncle Roger. "Your daughter was not unfaithful to her husband. The . . . union . . . took place before her marriage."

"Then why did she not marry her lover?" cried Mamma. "Why did she marry Mr. Braithwaite? I never liked him!"

"I put the same question to her," said Uncle Roger, "but she would not reply. The father's name . . . the reason that she did not marry him . . . she will say nothing about these things. She said only that the man is *not* someone whom we know. None of us has ever met him, she assures me." Uncle Roger toyed with his tea-cup, swirling about the cold dregs at the bottom. "She wishes that her confinement take place here," he said.

Mamma cried, "No! She must be at home, with us!"

"I agree," said Papa. "Anything else is out of the question."

Uncle Roger nodded. "I quite appreciate your feelings, but you will only distress her if you insist upon it. She has her reasons, and they are not unsound. She fears gossip . . . your neighbours . . . your staff . . . After all, you live in a highly populated, fashionable part of London. You receive guests with great regularity. But here, in my house, she is far from all that. The prying eyes, the wagging tongues. The only other house within sight is young Royce's, and he keeps to himself since his wife died. My few servants will be sworn to utter secrecy. There is, of course, no reason why you may not be present here when her time comes. I think she may request it. I insist upon it."

Papa pulled from his pocket the letter from Mr. Braithwaite and the draught of his reply. Handing these to Uncle Roger, he said, "What shall we do about him?"

Uncle Roger read both of the letters and returned them to Papa. "I admire your answer, Will," he said. "The man is obviously an unbearable ass. In response to your question, I should say that the best course would be to do nothing. Wait to see what answer he makes to your letter. Let him come to your house and look about, if he wishes. He will never suspect that she is *here*. He will never find her. Some matters are best left to the passage of time. He may come to admit — if only to himself — that he is at *least* as guilty as she; for if she was wrong to marry him without affection, knowing that she carried another man's child, then he was tenfold wrong to enter into *any* marriage, with anybody. What a blind fool he must be. Did he think that a mere ceremony would make of him what Nature had failed to make? Did he think that a healthy, spirited, beautiful girl like Phoebe could possibly be content with such a travesty of marriage? No, my dears, that silly man is the least in our catalogue of concerns. The only persons who must occupy our attention, who require our love and our understanding, are Phoebe and her child."

"Well said, Roger," Papa murmured.

"May we see our daughter now?" asked Mamma, gently.

"I'll fetch her." Uncle Roger got up from his chair. Before leaving the drawing-room, he turned and said, with a cheerful smile, "Such long faces. Come, look on the bright side. This is cause for rejoicing, not despair. 'Unto us a child is given.' You are about to become grandparents. And you, young lady, will soon be Auntie Pam. I am rather looking forward to becoming a grand-uncle. Don't allow Phoebe to see you like this. Smile. Be pleasant. All will be well."

He left the room.

Very little was said amongst us during his absence. At one point, Mamma said to Papa, "Your brother is a fine man. A very kind and good and gentle man."

Papa nodded. "He is all of that."

The doors of the drawing-room opened. Uncle Roger stepped in, an expression of confusion and dismay on his face. "She is not in her room," he said. "She left this." He read aloud a short note:

" 'Dear Uncle Roger — I can not bear to face my parents. I have disgraced them. I am not worthy of them. I have wronged everybody — my family, my child, the father of my child, even my husband. I beg you all to forgive and try to forget — Your Erring Phoebe.' "

We stayed the night in Suffolk with Uncle Roger and returned to London early this morning. Uncle Roger bade us not to worry, but it was plain to see that he was much distressed.

Although this is Saturday, we were not at home.

ཉ *Sunday, 12 March*

A letter had arrived for me whilst we were in Suffolk. I did not open it immediately upon our return. I saw it was from Giles, and my disappointment in him was so deep that I convinced myself I had no wish to read anything he might write. I came near to throwing it, unopened, into the fire, but could not bring myself to do so. This morning, after we returned from worship, I finally broke the seal and read it:

"My dearest Pamela, —

"As you receive this, I am already on a railway train that is carrying me away from London, putting many miles between us.

"But do not think that you have so easily got rid of me. You left me in anger on Friday last, but that is because you mistook my meanings. The day will come (and that soon, I hope) when you will see that you were wrong. As for the present, I believe it good that we are granted a period of separation and reflection.

"On Friday you made me the happiest man on this Earth, and I thank you for the generosity and graciousness of your gift. In my heart, my mind, my soul, in every fibre of my body, I know you as my true wife, and I shall think of you in that way for ever. Therefore, it is not rash presumption if I sign myself

"Your loving husband,
"Giles"

O subtle charmer! patient as the cobra!

And yet, even as that cynical thought sours my mind, I wonder if I am doing him an injustice. I remember Willy's words: "The greatest error we can commit in this life is to judge others . . . How could I have presumed to think that I could look into his heart and read his motives?"

Ah, Giles, have I misjudged you? Are you true?

Here am I, a wife in all but ceremony; and out there, somewhere, is Phoebe, no wife at all to the man she ceremoniously wed; a wife, instead, to a phantom, a man with neither face nor name.

℘ *Monday, 13 March*

Whilst shopping to-day with Mamma, we overheard two shop-assistants discussing the ill health of the Princess. Mamma immediately asked one of them, "What are you saying, girl? Has there been an announcement from Kensington Palace that I have not heard?"

"Oh, no, ma'am, no announcement," she replied. "Just rumours."

The elder of the two shop-assistants added, "But they do say, ma'am — the rumours, that is — that there may have been something to those old stories that were going about some years ago when the old King was alive."

"Indeed," said Mamma, and the curtness of the word gave notice that she was not interested in pursuing the subject further.

But in the coach, on our way home, I asked her, "What did that shop-assistant mean about 'the old stories,' Mamma?"

"If there is anything worse than gossip," she replied, "it is *old* gossip. I would not for the world repeat those antiquated slanders, and I am thankful that you were too young to hear them at the time."

I was, therefore, obliged to consult my most reliable oracle, Hester. She responded with her customary alacrity:

"Well, Miss, I expect the shop-assistant was referring to those rumours we used to hear during the last years of George the Fourth. About the Duke of Cumberland, you know."

That name again! "What about him?"

"They used to say that the Duke had the old King under his finger. Dominated him, you might call it. And swore that he would one day sit on the throne, and that no slip of a girl would stand in his way. Meaning the little Princess, you see. He's said to have filled the king's ear with stories about her mother, the Duchess of Kent, being far too friendly with Sir John Conroy, if you catch my meaning, Miss —"

"I have heard all this before, Hester. Get on with it."

"Well, the Duke of Cumberland advised King George to remove the Princess from that immoral household; a bad influence on her, he said it was. Myself, Miss, I never believed that the Duchess had anything to do with Sir John in that way, but that's as may be. At any rate, the stories had it that the Duke wanted to remove the girl from Kensington Palace and have her placed under *his* protection — 'protection,' indeed! — where she would be slowly poisoned, and suffer gradually worse and worse health, and at last die."

"Good heavens!" I cried. "That is not to be believed! This is not the time of the Borgias!" (Although I *had* heard that when Princess Caroline had married the Prince Regent, later George IV, the Countess of Jersey, spurred by jealousy, put Epsom salts into Caroline's soup, thus assuring that their wedding night would be marred by indelicate interruptions.) "But do go on, Hester."

"They say that Cumberland persuaded King George to have the Princess taken out of Kensington Palace — the day had been set, the royal order given, and all was in readiness — but the Duke of Wellington, who suspected Cumberland, interceded with the king. And, of course, she never was moved, was she. Wellington was able to keep postponing the move, again and again, until old George died and King William was on the throne. Then Cumberland's influence dropped off, and the stories stopped."

"Until now," I reminded her.

"Yes, Miss. But they do say that even after King George died, Sir John Conroy was terribly fearful of what Cumberland might attempt, and would not allow a crumb to be taken to the Princess until it had been tasted by the very servants who'd prepared it. He was afraid, you see, that Cumberland may have bribed the servants to put something in her food."

I was sceptical. "But, Hester, could not these stories have been started by Sir John himself, to discredit the Duke and to put himself in a better light?"

"There's some as says that," she replied, "and some as doesn't."

"And now all the stories are revived again, simply because the Princess has been feeling not quite the thing of late."

"Yes, Miss."

"Good gracious, Hester, you and I have our days of feeling poorly, now and again. And yet nobody talks of poison!"

"No, Miss."

"So you see how absurd those stories are, and how wicked we are to repeat them."

"Yes, Miss. But, begging your pardon, you and I are not princesses of the royal blood. There is no *reason* to poison us. No motive, as they say."

I must confess that Hester has a point in that.

Cumberland: I see his face still, in my memory, staring at me from his opera box, his eye unblinking, his horrible scar livid, his expression unfathomable. Lust was the passion in those eyes, I'd thought (or so I'd flattered myself), for the Duke's repute in regard to women is decidedly unsavoury, and his appetite recognises no barriers — not even, it is said, the barrier of sisterhood.

But had there been another passion in his eyes that night? Might I not have called to his mind an image of the Princess? I am her age exactly, after all. I was dressed splendidly that night; no princess was ever dressed better. She and I do not resemble each other, but there are some features we share — the hooded eyes, the ample nose, the colour of hair (and my *coiffure,* that night, was similar to a style she has worn). I am taller than she, but I was seated at the time, and the difference in height could not be seen. I am not saying that the Duke actually mistook me for her — I think merely that I may have reminded him of her, and of his own ambitions, and of his smouldering rage at the slip of a girl who stands between him and the throne.

ॐ *Tuesday, 14 March*

I awoke quite early this morning — I still do not know why (unless I had sensed something amiss, even in my sleep). As I arose from my bed, I was struck by the soundness of Sophie's slumber. It had always been her custom to awaken as soon as I did, and to greet me with wagging tail — unless, indeed, she awoke before me and bade me join her, by licking my face. But, of latter days, her sleeps (like those of elderly people) have become deeper, and in the past half-year or so, there have been mornings when I have climbed out of bed and washed my face before she was aware that a new day had begun.

"Lazy little girl!" I said, teasing her. "Time to wake up, you slothful creature!" She heard not a word. I bounced up and down on the bed, but still she did not stir. Next, I ruffled her fur — and it was then that I discovered how cool her little body was. It perplexed me, for she is usually such a warm little parcel. Could she be ill? "Sophie, wake up!" I commanded. She did not respond. I studied her closely. That slow, steady wax-and-wane of her breathing was not discernible. My own breath stopped. My hand flew to my mouth.

In an instant, I was pounding my parents' door and bursting into their bedroom. "Mamma! Papa! Come quickly!" I shouted. "It's Sophie! I think she may be —" I could not utter the awful word.

They were out of bed in a moment and into their dressing-gowns. A moment later, we were, all three of us, in my bedroom. Sophie still lay there, at the foot of my bed, looking for all the world as if she were sound asleep — her head between her two forepaws, her tail curled neatly around her body.

Papa knelt close to her and placed his hand on her silken fur. He carefully lifted one of her closed eyelids. "Good old bitch," he said, softly. "She's gone."

I wailed wordlessly and flung myself onto the bed and wrapped the dear beast in my arms. "Oh, no!" I cried. "No, no, Sophie! You can not be dead! Wake up, wake up!"

Mamma, whose own tears had begun to flow, tried to comfort me. "There, there, my dear. She went peacefully, without pain. One moment, she was alive; in the next, she was dead — and she could not even have known the point when she passed from the one state into the other. You may say that *she* does not know that she is dead; she thinks she is still sleeping."

"Your mother's right, Princess," said Papa. "The little animal did not suffer. Look at her. See how contented she seems."

"I know, I know," I wailed, my eyes streaming, my nose rapidly filling up, "but . . . but . . . ."

"But it is hard," said Papa. "Of course it is."

Sophie was a creature of total loyalty and utter trust; she had no vanity, made no demands, no recriminations. She was unique; she had her own character, her own habits, her own little ways. She was an innocent, more completely than any human being has ever been or can hope to be. She was a furry, wingless little angel. To the end, she was as playful as a pup. And, although it seems curious to say it of a dog, I do believe she had the sense of humour. She had some fears, as well: she feared thunder most dreadfully, and trembled at it, her tail between her legs. It seems fitting that to-day the weather is fine and almost cloudless: no thunder to frighten her hovering spirit as we buried her body in the garden, with all the staff in attendance.

ॐ *Thursday, 16 March*

We had only just finished our dinner this evening when Rutledge announced the unexpected arrival of Mr. Braithwaite.

"Shew him into the drawing-room," said Papa, a dark shading to his voice. Then, addressing Mamma and me, he asked, "I assume that you ladies will demand to be present?"

"Certainly," Mamma and I replied in chorus.

Rutledge ushered Mr. Braithwaite into the drawing-room a few moments later.

"Pray be seated, sir, and take a glass of port," said Papa, and though his words were cordial, his tone was not. Mr. Braithwaite sat down but declined the offer of wine.

"I have received your answer to my letter, Mr. Summerfield," he said, "and I suppose that I am obliged to believe you when you say that Mrs. Braithwaite is not here."

"You are obliged to believe no such thing," Papa retorted. "I do not ask you to take my words on trust — indeed, I should dislike to be in your debt to that extent. You are free to search this house, from roof to cellar."

"I think that will not be necessary."

"Suit yourself — but I refuse to be in your obligation."

Mr. Braithwaite was discomfited and seemed to squirm in the chair. "Will you answer one or two questions, sir?"

"If I can," Papa assured him.

"Have you seen your daughter since she left my house?"

"No."

"Do you know where she is at this moment?"

"I do not."

"Have you received any communication from her?"

"Not directly."

"Indirectly, then?"

"I will tell you this much," said Papa. "Through the good offices of a third party — a trusted member of my family, in point of fact — we have heard that she has left you, never to return. Considering her extraordinary position in your household, it is my judgment that she had every right to do so."

"Every right! Whatever can you mean? May I say, as your son-in-law —"

"Ah, please!" Papa said, wincing. "Let us have these matters out as man to man, not as father-in-law to son-in-law."

"As you wish," said Mr. Braithwaite, "although you can not deny that such is our relationship."

"Oh, I do deny it, sir. I deny it absolutely."

Mr. Braithwaite was taken aback. "What?"

"Consider closely, Mr. Braithwaite," said Papa. "To be a son-in-law of mine, you first would have to be a husband to my daughter — in every way in which a husband is defined by law. I draw your attention to the very word 'law' in the term 'son-in-law.' Are you clear on that, so far?"

"Of course, but —"

"Excellent. Then pray follow: a husband, my dear sir, is not merely one who stands up in the church and repeats some words spoken by a clergyman. A husband does not become a husband simply by slipping a ring upon a woman's finger. The act of marriage is known, I believe, as a sacrament. That means it is sacred: sanctioned by God."

"Mr. Summerfield," said our guest, impatiently, "I am aware of all that."

"You are? So much the better. I am no theologian, Mr. Braithwaite, so you must forgive me if I solicit the assistance of my wife, whose father was a bishop." He turned to Mamma. "My dear, are we taught that Adam and Eve were man and wife?"

"Of course," Mamma replied.

"Were they married in a church?"

"You know they were not."

"Was there no priest or rabbi in attendance? No parson of any kind?"

"Naturally not."

"There was no ring? No ritual? No organ music? They posted no banns?"

"No."

"Then how can they be said to have been married?"

"By the fact that Adam, in the language of the Bible, *knew* Eve."

"But I am hopelessly confused!" said Papa, play-acting great perplexity. *"Knew* her? Good Heavens, Madam, I know many people. I know our guest, Mr. Braithwaite, for example. Does that mean that I am married to him?"

Mamma was enjoying Papa's little game, and so was I. She played up to him admirably. "In the parlance of Scripture, my dear Wilfrid, when a man is said to have *known* a woman, the meaning is that he has consummated the act of love with her."

"Ah! I see! Thank you, my dear! Most enlightening!" He turned to Mr. Braithwaite. "Do you follow, sir?"

"Mr. Summerfield!" our guest exploded. "Is my love for your daughter under question? I have *sworn* to love her, have I not? After the injuries and insults I have suffered, am I to understand that now you doubt my word?"

"Not your word," Papa replied. "Your ability."

"My ability?"

"Your ability to love."

"I love Phoebe most earnestly, I swear to you! I love her with all of my heart!"

"Your heart is not the article under question, sir."

"I do not understand you," said Mr. Braithwaite, appearing to be truly baffled.

Papa scratched his head. "Confound it, man, how plainly must I speak? There are, after all, ladies present. Can it be that you are truly so unknowing of these matters?"

"What matters?"

"Have you been living in cotton-wool all your life? Good Lord, sir, have you no idea what passes between men and women? Do you not realise that you and my daughter are not married at all — in the eyes of God or Man or the law — because you have not consummated the marriage?"

"Consummated . . ." Our guest shook his head in utter bewilderment.

I could endure it no longer. I had remained silent all the while. Now I leapt to my feet and shouted at him: "My father means you never *swived* Phoebe! You never *had to do* with her! You never *had your way* with her! You never *put the devil in Hell!* You never made *the beast with two backs!* Have you not read Shakespere, sir? You never plumbed her *baldrick,* her *bird's nest,* her *charged chamber,* her *chaste treasure,* her *dearest bodily part,* her *flower,* her *forfended place,* her *gate,* her *glass of virginity, nest of spicery, pond, ring, rose, velvet leaves, Venus' glove!* In one word, Mr. Braithwaite, you have never — "

"Thank you, Princess," said Papa, coolly. "You have greatly improved our education. But I fear that our guest remains still in the dark. I advise you, sir, to seek out a good physician and require him to tell you what are sometimes called the facts of life — using illustrated charts, if need be. I will add only this: if you still believe the law to be on your side, then you are in the grip of a delusion. The law is on the side of the young woman to whom — through no actual malicious intent of yours, it may be; through what is perhaps no other than a sad ignorance and incapacity — you denied the act of true love and true marriage." Papa arose from his chair in a stately manner, standing tall and solemn. "And now, sir, you must permit us to bid you good evening."

Mr. Braithwaite stammered as he got to his feet: "I . . . if Phoebe . . . that is to say . . ." With a chap-fallen look and a defeated sigh, he concluded, "Good evening," and he left.

We were all silent for several moments after his departure. Then Papa spoke: "The question that remains unanswered is: why on earth did she marry him?"

"And," I added, "who is the father of her child?"

"And," said Mamma, "where did you learn all those colourful expressions?"

"From the classics, Mamma."

"Indeed. I hope we may be spared another such barrage in future."

Papa chuckled. "Don't scold her, Melissa. Her familiarity with such matters may be unseemly, but it is to be preferred over such ignorance as Mr. Braithwaite's. Besides — she did it in grand style. It was as if Mrs. Siddons were alive again."

⅋ *Friday, 17 March*

This is the day on which the Irish celebrate the patron saint of their nation. I wonder if Mr. O'Connor will wear a shamrock? Or is his Irish blood overly diluted by the Welsh blood of his mother? And is he too much the sceptic and atheist, too much the sneering cynic, to honour a man whom humbler folk revere; a man who was, moreover, a bishop of the Roman Church?

To-night, to take our minds away, however briefly, from thoughts of Phoebe, Willy, and poor Sophie, we went to the theatre to see Mr. Macready, whose performances I always enjoy, particularly when he plays the great Shakesperean *rôles*.

Would that he had chosen such a *rôle* to-night! He is a fine actor, and excels in everything he does, but even he could make nothing of the play, a dreadful piece entitled *Strafford*, which, I am sure, is doomed to failure. What a waste of Mr. Macready's great talent.

The author is Mr. Robert Browning, who has perhaps turned to play-writing after the *débâcle,* two years ago, of his poetic effort *Paracelsus*. I think that this young man will never come to anything as a writer. He would be well advised to seek some other occupation.

It is so dreadfully queer to retire at night without Sophie joining me at the foot of my bed. She had done so for nearly the whole of her twelve-year life. I still reach out for her and look for her and listen for her little bark. It is odd, and a bit frightening, to sleep all alone in the room, after a dozen years of sharing the bed with that dear companion.

When one reaches a certain age, life would appear to become no more than a series of subtractions. Grandparents die; dogs die; others — like Willy and Phoebe and Giles — journey far from us, some perhaps never to return. I find these first losses of my life well-nigh insupportable, and I am not yet eighteen! In the years ahead, what devastating diminutions await me — the deaths of my beloved parents, of course; but how many more?

I suppose there will be some few additions, as well as subtractions: new friends, a husband, children. But, on the tally-sheet of life, will the additions ever truly balance out the subtractions? Will there not be far, far more of the latter, and far too few of the former? Are we allotted equal portions of joy and sadness? Is life a span of happiness, punctuated by occasional points of gloom? Or is it — as I suspect — the other way round?

Perhaps the best thing, after all, is to follow the advice that Mr. Disraeli proffered in his novel of last year, *Henrietta Temple*. In those pages, he causes Count Alcibiades de Mirabel to say "Feel slightly, think little, never plan, never brood." But I could never conform to that regimen: I feel everything too deeply; I am thinking constantly; and I am often guilty of prolonged brooding. These ills, if ills they be, are incurable, I believe.

I have yet another thing to worry me, and I may as well set it down now. Let me say that I know full well that our bodies are not machines and that they are not so precise as fine watches in their workings. Machines are made of hard, inflexible materials; whereas our bodies, built precariously of stuff as soft and vulnerable as jelly, and this mould of jelly filled with insubstantial slime and fluids, the whole hung on a foundation as thin, fragile, and easily broken as a bundle of twigs — these bodies of ours, I say, are far from perfect. It would not do to set one's clock by them. Indeed, in view of their myriad flaws and frailties, the wonder is, not that they often go awry, but that they function at all. They recall to my mind a proverb I heard from Mlle. La Grange, some weeks ago, applied to quite another matter: *"Ça ne s'explique pas, mais ça marche."* You cannot explain it, but it works.

I am, as I have said, aware of all that. Even so, I worry. The plain truth is this: I was due for an onslaught of That Time fully a fortnight ago to-day.

Yes, yes, I know: it has been late before. And I know what Mamma has often told me: in times of sadness or distress, that function is easily thrown into confusion. The Lord knows that there has been no dearth of sadness and distress in this house these many weeks.

And yet I can not help being filled with fear. What if I am, like Phoebe, *enceinte?*

ॐ *Saturday, 18 March*

A pistol shot jolted me awake minutes after I had fallen asleep to-night.

A dream — that was my first thought. A dream of Push-kin's death, perhaps. No — *another* shot followed, unmistakably fired in *this* world, not the world of dreams, and, immediately after, I heard Papa's voice, calling out in stern, commanding tones: "Stop! Stop, I say!"

Fear froze me, and I huddled in the bed-clothes. Somebody

ran past my bedroom door — halted — turned back — the door opened — and a man burst into the room. I could barely see him — but I could hear his laboured breathing. In a hoarse, unfamiliar voice, he begged, "Please, mum, don't let 'im kill me!"

I started to say "Who are you?" — but before the words were half out of my mouth, the door flew open again. This time it was Papa, in his dressing-gown. Even before I saw the smoking pistol in his hand, I could smell the acrid odour of gunpowder.

"If you move," he told the man, "even one inch, I'll not hesitate to shoot you dead on the spot." Papa then turned up the gas, illuminating my bedroom and giving us a clear view of the man.

His clothes were threadbare — not ragged, but worn thin, and patched in spots. They could have been cleaner, and so could he. He was unshaven, and his hair wanted cutting. I could not determine his age — he looked to be anywhere between forty and sixty.

Mamma, accompanied by Rutledge and Crewe, now appeared, all in dressing-gowns. Rutledge was holding a large kitchen knife. "Shall we send for the constables, sir?" he asked.

"Yes," Papa replied; and Rutledge relayed the order to Crewe; but at that moment the man spoke pleadingly:

"Don't 'and me over to the peelers, guv! I'll go to prison — for years!"

"And why should you not go to prison?" Papa asked him. "You broke into my house with the purpose of stealing. We might have been murdered in our beds."

"I wouldn't 'ave 'urt any of you," the man insisted. "An' I didn't break in. The garden door was standin' ajar. I could see it from the street —"

"You made unlawful entry, at any rate. Can you deny it?"

"No, guv. I leapt over your garden wall, an' that's a fact. I saw that door ajar, an', well, I just couldn't 'elp meself. I thought: 'ere's the 'ouse of a swell. I'll just pop in an' nip a bit of 'is silver — 'e'll never miss it, more than likely. Then I'll sell it an' be able to feed me wife an' little ones."

"Very heart-rending, I'm sure," said Papa. "So this is how you make your living?"

"Me? No, sir! This is the first time I've ever been tempted to do such a thing. I've always been an 'ard-workin' man, guv, but they discharged me."

"For what reason?"

"I fell asleep at the job. Couldn't keep me eyes open."

"Then you deserved to be discharged. You're indolent, a sluggard."

The man retorted, with pride, "That I am *not,* sir. It's just that none of us 'as slept properly at night — meself, me wife, the toddlers — ever since we was thrown out of our lodgin's."

"You did not pay?"

"It wasn't that, guv. They pulled down the 'ouse. They've been pullin' 'em down for goin' on two years now, an' they do say they may keep pullin' 'em down for another two years. To clear space for the station, they say."

"The station?"

Rutledge spoke: "I think the man means Euston railway station, sir."

"That's it, right enough, mate!"

Rutledge added, "Some ten thousand persons have been displaced already, I understand, sir, and another ten thousand may be displaced before the station is finished being built."

Mamma asked, "Where do such people go?"

The man addressed her directly. "That's just it, mum. There's nowhere *to* go. We sleep under bridges, in alleys — but a man can't get 'is proper rest that way, an' so I fell asleep, I did, in the brewery."

Papa and Mamma exchanged glances. Papa asked him, "What brewery?"

"Summerfield's. Look, guv, I know I done wrong, but I beg of you, don't give me in charge. If I go to gaol, wot'll become of the wife an' nippers? An' the new one on the way?"

"What is your name?" Papa asked him.

"Bootes, sir. Peter Bootes. I'm a good worker when I'm feelin' meself. I'm young an' strong, just twenty-five —"

(He looked so much older!)

"Listen to me, Bootes," said Papa. "I am not turning you over to the police —"

"Gawd bless you for that, sir!"

"But you must give me your word of honour, as the honest fellow I think you to be, that you will never again attempt a job of work like the one you started to-night."

"Oh, sir, I swear it!"

Papa turned to Rutledge. "Is Mrs. Pruitt awake?"

"Yes, sir. When we heard the shots —"

"Tell her to prepare a hamper of food for this man to take away with him. Bootes, come downstairs to my study. I want to give you a pound note and a pair of letters that I shall write."

"Yes, sir; *thank* you, sir. Letters, sir?"

"Do you know Mr. Quayle?"

"There's a Mr. Quayle at the brewery — I never knew 'im to speak to meself — very important gent, 'e is."

"That's the man. One of the letters will be addressed to him. Shew it to him on Monday morning, and you will be reinstated in your job. The other letter will be addressed to an estate agent called Mr. Travers. He looks after a block of flats I own. He will find you and your family a place to live."

Bootes was dumbfounded. It was obvious that he failed to understand. "Beggin' your pardon, guv," he said, "but why will Mr. Quayle give me back me job just because I 'ands 'im a letter from you?"

Papa smiled ironically. "Come now, Bootes. Confess. You knew full well whose house you were entering, did you not?"

"I, sir? 'Ow could I? I saw that garden door ajar an' —"

"Well, then," said Papa, "God was surely with you to-night and guided your steps. The same God Who caused that garden door to be left unlocked."

"They *do* say," Bootes responded, though still un-comprehending, "that 'E moves in mysterious ways, 'Is wonders to perform."

Later, after Bootes had left with his hamper of food, the two letters, and a pound note, Papa said, "The pity of it is that I can not help the other thousands who are in the same plight as he."

"One does what one can," said Mamma. "One can do no more."

"Oh, Papa!" I cried. "I *do* love you so!" And I threw my arms round him.

PHOEBE IMPERILLED
A dramatic episode in iambic pentameters
By Pamela Summerfield

(A dark, musty cellar in Whitechapel. No furnishings, not even a bed or chair. PHOEBE *is discovered, crouched in a corner, rubbing her arms to warm them.)*

PHOEBE:

My flight has brought me to this wretched place,
The best I can afford, though purchased dear.
Where may she wend who dare not shew her face,
Who hath not friend nor farthing; naught but fear?
Dark, pestilential, stinking hole of Hell,
Thou art the pass to which I've come by strife.
Here, without creature comforts, must I dwell,
And, when my term shall come, bring forth new life.
O babe-to-be, what evil hast thou done?
What fault is thine? The answer, child, is: None!

(She starts at the sound of a rat.)

But hark! What dread companions share my cell?
What watchers of the shadows do I hear?
Sweet author of my shame, I knoweth well
That if thou wert but cognisant and near,
Thou wouldst come gather me within thine arms,
Bearing me hence from misery and harms.

(A door opens, and a SWARTHY MAN *enters. He is dressed gaudily, wears many rings, and has a tooth of gold. In the dark she can not see him clearly.)*

My love! 'Tis thee! — Ah, no, 'tis not, I fear!
Begone, sir! By what right dost thou appear?

SWARTHY MAN:

Now then, now then, now then! Wot 'ave we 'ere?
A maiden in distress? Poor pretty Poll?

PHOEBE:

Withdraw at once!

SWARTHY MAN:

Now, none o' that, me doll!

PHOEBE:

What wouldst thou have of me, presumptuous man?
I am no pigeon for a hawk like thee!
I am a gentlewoman.

SWARTHY MAN:

So I see,
And all the better for my little plan.
Across the Channel, certain 'ouses be,
The naughty needs of which are filled by me,
And girls like you are grist unto my mill.

PHOEBE:

I never shall be subject to thy will!

SWARTHY MAN:

Others 'ave said the same, yet slaves be still.
By dint of drugs, starvation, and of blows,
They all submit, lest I increase their woes.

(*He strikes her, again and again.*)

PHOEBE:

Help me, high Heaven! Shall the Devil win?

SWARTHY MAN:

Another captive for the cribs of sin!

(*Laughing heartlessly, he drags her away.*)

I dramatise. This lurid scene is but a fever of my wild
imaginings, I know. And yet — how *shall* Phoebe fare in the
world, friendless, without money? Might she not seek refuge

in such a place as Whitechapel? And might not a horrid person, like the man who accosted me, seek her out for that very employment in which her beauty would prove no blessing, but a curse? What *does* happen to a young woman alone, outcast, in disgrace, with child? Where might I be *at this moment* — in what vile den — naked in the toils of what slavering lechers — had not Willy come to my rescue? There is no longer a Willy in England to rescue Phoebe.

Help her, high Heaven!

And help me, as well — for *still* That Time has not come! High Heaven, help us both! That is my prayer on this Palm Sunday.

&϶ *Monday, 20 March*

I have been thinking of the wedding of Phoebe and Mr. Braithwaite, and in particular I have been remembering these words of the service:

"I require and charge you — as you will answer at the dreadful Day of Judgement, when the secrets of all hearts shall be disclosed — that if either of you do know any impediment why ye may not be lawfully joined together in matrimony, that ye confess it."

If Phoebe knew, as I think she must have known, on the day of her wedding, that she was carrying another man's child, then she stands guilty of mocking the marriage sacrament by remaining silent at that point of the ceremony.

If Mr. Braithwaite knew that he was incapable of consummating the marriage — if, indeed, he understood the full implications of wedded life at all — then he, too, is guilty by not confessing that impediment.

My inclination is to think that he is truly as *naïf* as he appeared to be in our drawing-room on Thursday evening. Swathed all his life in cotton-wool, to use Papa's words, it may be that he was wholly ignorant of "the way of a man with a maid." It staggers belief that such a thing should be in a man of his age, but perhaps there are more such people about than we know of. And if his ignorance is unfeigned, then he stands guilty of nothing.

By like token, if Phoebe was unaware, at that time, that she was pregnant, then she, too, is not guilty. I yearn to believe it, for her sake, but I can not shake off the conviction that she *knew* — that she married Mr. Braithwaite only *because* she knew — in order that her child be born in wedlock — and that it was her intention to deceive her husband by passing the child off as his own — but that she had not reckoned with her husband's incapacity — and, as the weeks and months wore on, and he did not come to her bed, she knew her secret shame would soon be seen — and that is why she grew "afraid of what is yet to come."

ᨠ *Tuesday, 21 March*

Cause to rejoice!

That Time is here! At long, *long* last — but "better late than never," as is said.

What a great burden has slipped from my shoulders, and how infinitely relieved I feel! I have always thought that these Times were such a cross to bear, and have harboured resentment against them — but no event has ever been more welcome, and I shall never complain about my Times again. This I vow!

That momentous bit of good news is quite enough for one day, I think.

ᨠ *Thursday, 23 March*

Yesterday, Wednesday, was almost the first I have been delinquent in my writing of this journal. When my Time finally came, it came with all the more discomfort. I spent the whole of the day in bed, lulled by my faithful ruby drops. I had not the strength nor the desire to lift my pen.

No dreadful or unpleasant dreams afflict me when those good drops are soothing my pains. I float in a vast, eternal, infinite world, past palaces of stunning beauty whose tops reach high beyond the clouds; and this delicious drifting journey lasts for a thousand lovely years; two thousand; three — for ever.

A great prince clad in snowy silk holds my hand in his. He is Giles. Together we soar through the universe, nodding royally to the stars and moons that whistle past us in their orbits.

Music is the force by which we ride — it carries us along on its broad, warm current, as well as flowing *through* us, taking the place of blood in our veins, coursing melodiously through our flesh, pouring into the tops of our heads, and streaming out from the tips of our toes in a tingling shower of stars: a simple childhood tune, but cloaked in the grandeur of a great and stately orchestra, decked in the dazzling diamond harmonies of Mozart and Beethoven and Mendelssohn.

Phoebe swims into our sight, smiling serenely, as if to say that all is well, her troubles all long past and long forgot.

Sophie is tucked under my arm as I fly: I feel her little heart beating; I hear her tiny bark of happiness.

Even more delightful than all this is the feeling of joyous anticipation that floods us: somehow we know that we are speeding towards a wondrous place, a glorious adventure, an experience a hundredfold more thrilling and fulfilling than any we have ever known, an immersing of our bodies and our souls in a bath of liquid gold, a flowering of our higher natures; and we rush, with exhilarating speed, closer and closer to the sparkling gates of our destiny, which always lie just beyond the next high, spinning, silver orb.

It is like an epic by the greatest poet, set to music by the most inspired composer, on the liberating death of the body and the limitless life of the soul.

The Full Moon Fiend, or The Hyde Park Strangler, struck again last night. His victim's name was Ada Wilkes.

ॐ *Good Friday, 24 March*

I thought it would be particularly appropriate, on this holy day, to do a deed of good work, and so I asked Mamma if I might take a gift of food to the Bootes family. They are now lodged in the block of flats owned by Papa. Mamma granted permission, and Mrs. Pruitt made up a lovely hamper. Paley took me in the family coach to the block, which is new and clean and a credit to the Summerfield name. Luxurious it is not, for these are workers' flats, designed to be leased out at rates well within their wages; but they are as sunny and airy as the horrid window-tax will permit, and if compared with the hovels I have seen in Whitechapel, these flats will seem to be Kensington Palace.

After instructing Paley to wait for me, I climbed the staircase to the third storey and knocked on the door of the Booteses' flat. It was opened by an unsmiling, once-pretty woman whose swollen body told me she was great with child. "Mrs. Bootes?" I asked. She nodded. "I am Pamela Summerfield. May I come in?"

Still saying nothing, her eyes scanned me from head to foot. At the same time, I scanned her and discovered her to be, under the patina of toil and care, quite remarkably attractive, with great dark eyes and hair which, unkempt and unclean though it was, had the colour of a raven's wing. At length, she stepped inside and allowed me to pass through the doorway.

"I've brought you some nice things to eat," I said. "There is a ham and —"

She took the hamper from me and carried it into the kitchen. I followed her. She placed it on a plain wooden table which was without a cloth, and began to unpack it.

"What is your name?" I asked her (I should say I asked it of her back, for that was the part of her that was turned towards me).

"Sally," she replied, without turning around.

"My name is Pamela."

"I know. You said so."

"So I did. May I sit down?"

She pulled a chair out from the table and I seated myself. "How have you been getting on here, Sally?" I asked.

She shrugged — that, at least, I could tell from her back. She said, "Well enough."

"I'm glad to hear it. Is this flat better than the one you were forced to quit?"

"It's better than sleepin' in doorways," she said, sardonically. Then, finally turning to face me, she added, "It's very nice, really. Yes, it's 'eaps better than the old one. Cheaper, too. Do you fancy a cup of tea?"

"Only if you will join me."

"I could do with a drop. I'll just put on the kettle." When she had done so, she sat down at the table opposite me. "It's good of you to bring us all these vittles, Miss."

"Please; it's no more than right that I should. I don't see your children about. Are they outside, playing?"

"Playin'!" She laughed, humourlessly. "Them? Not bloody likely. They're workin'. I'd be workin' myself if I wasn't eight months gone in the family way."

"Where do they work?"

"Why, in your pa's brewery; didn't you know? They go off with my Pete every mornin'. Young Pete, 'e's the oldest, an' Tom an' little Guy."

"How old are they?"

"Seven, six, an' five. Peggy's the baby — she's only two — she's asleep in the next room. Yes, for the first three years, they came along one after the other — one, two, three, regular as a clock. Well, then Peter stayed away from me as much as 'e could, poor sod, an' it slowed down a bit. I 'ad me a bit of a rest before Peggy came along. An' another bit of a rest before this'n." She patted her immense belly.

"Then you and your husband have been married for — "

"Well, we ain't what you'd call properly married, Miss. Never 'ad the parson's fee. I 'ad knowed Pete only a month or two it was, when I missed me time and told 'im I was afeared I'd clicked; but we waited till we was sure — when I was shewin', that is to say — then 'e said, 'Never you mind, Sal, I'll take care o' you.' And 'e 'as, I'll give 'im that. 'E's not a bad sort. There's a lot worse than 'im."

"How old are you, Sally?"

"Twenty," she replied, "an' a bit over."

"Twenty! But —"

"I was just turned thirteen when Pete first 'ad to do with me. 'E was eighteen or thereabouts. Well, 'e couldn't be blamed, could 'e? The men at that age is worse than when they're older, I swear. I was big for me age, an' pretty, they all said."

"You're still pretty."

"For an old woman, eh?" She chuckled, good-naturedly. "Oh, I could 'ave done better, I 'spect. There was them 'oo wanted to take me up, you know."

"Take you up?"

"Ladies 'oo manage fancy 'ouses. Offered to buy me from me mum, an' clean me up an' dress me in fine clothes an' all; told 'er the men would pay 'andsome for the likes o' me. But me mum, she was one of them religious people, don't you know. Didn't 'old with that sort of thing. So I lost me chances."

"Good Heavens, Sally! Lost your chances? I should think you would be on your knees, thanking God that a good man like Peter Bootes found you and loved you! Surely you would not prefer the degraded life of — of —"

"Of an 'ore? What's degradin' about gettin' paid for what I give to Pete for naught? I might be rich by now, and managin' me own fancy 'ouse. As for gettin' down on me knees, I do that right enough every day, scrubbin' the floors. Marriage is all very well for them with no looks 'oo can't do better, but I was *pretty,* I tell you!"

In my shock, I hardly knew how to respond to this. "But your children," I finally said; "you must love them very much."

She shrugged. "I s'pose I do. But do you know, Miss, when I think of 'em — little Pete an' Tom an' Guy, an' baby Peg, an' the one on the way — sometimes I 'ave just one wish for 'em. One prayer. For their own good."

"What prayer is that?" I asked.

"Oh, I know it's wicked, Miss. But look about you at the world. Not your world — my world. An' ask yourself — if you was me — wouldn't you pray as I do for your children? Wouldn't you ask God to take 'em?"

"Sally! How horrible! You can not mean it!"

"Not painful, Miss, not sick an' ailin', or mangled in the machines; nothin' like that. But easy-like, as you might snuff out a candle. Seein' the sort of life they 'as before 'em, wouldn't it be a mercy . . ."

A moment later, she was holding my hands and saying, "Oh, no, please. Don't take on so, Miss, please. You'll make your eyes all red and puffed. You mustn't mind what I say, Miss. My Pete says I natter too much, an' I 'spect 'e's right. 'E says if we 'ad a farthin' for every word I speak in one day, we could live like nobs. I didn't mean it, Miss; truly I didn't. Now you take that fine 'ankerchee o' yours an' blow your nose, good an' 'ard. That's right, luv!"

I left without waiting for tea.

ॐ *Saturday, 25 March*

Our at-homes have been resumed, and one of our guests to-day was Sir David Brewster, who invented the kaleidoscope some twenty-odd years ago. I shewed him our kaleido-scope — the one Phoebe and I peered into for hours on end when we were children — and he exclaimed, "Why, this is one of my very first! Do you still enjoy it, Miss Summer-field?"

"On occasion, I try to catch it out in a repetition, to no avail," I said, "but I'm afraid its place has been usurped in my heart by Mr. Horner's zoëtrope."

"An interesting novelty," Sir David allowed, "but static."

"Static? How can you say so? Its pictures move."

"So they do, but always in the same way. What is it, after all? Merely a slotted drum, with rather crude drawings of fig-ures or animals arranged about the inside, in different phases of motion. Spin the drum rapidly, peer through the slot, and they seem to move — men run, horses gallop, and so forth. Amusing enough, I dare say, but the movement never varies. One should grow weary of it, I should think. I know *I* should. But your kaleidoscope! — ah, my dear young lady, this sim-ple cylinder is a veritable cornucopia of combinations, a source of infinite variety."

"Age cannot wither it, nor custom stale," I said, with the aid of *Antony and Cleopatra*. He smiled at the remark. "But, Sir David, do you not think that there is a great potentiality in the principle of the zoëtrope?"

"Potentiality? In what way?"

"Just imagine: What if it were possible to increase the draw-ings to the size of living figures on a stage — and what if fine

232

paintings, almost as true to life as life itself, were to replace the crude little drawings? Might not whole throngs of people then flock to Cooke's Circus or other shows, to admire such moving pictures?"

"Absurd, Miss Summerfield," said Sir David.

৭৩ *Easter Sunday, 26 March*

There in the dark, he listens to the distant din outside, and the nearer gurglings and thumpings. It will soon be time for it all to begin, and his mind reaches out impatiently, stretches itself through space, through time, and sees the tumult of his life.

More precisely, *hears.*

For he knows, even now, before he is born, that from the beginning it will be not sight that will enchant him, prod him, grip his soul. His world will be one of sound —

The sound of voices, laughing or shouting, long before he will know about words —

The sound of water splashing —

Keys and coins jingling —

Clocks ticking —

Birds and cats and dogs —

The crack of a buggy-whip —

Knives and forks, cups and saucers —

Footsteps —

Rain, wind, thunder —

And, later, the organised sound, the *built* sound that will bloom in smooth and ragged patterns all around him. The rain-wind-thunder of songs and symphonies, brass, strings, woodwinds, drums, cymbals — these will crash and coo, dive and soar, whisper and roar, and he will listen, soaking it up, feeding upon it, gorging himself on sound.

Rooms with no pictures on the walls. Windows opening on barren vistas. He will be content to live and work in such places. He will not hate visual beauty; it will merely be unimportant to him. Only sound will be important; its weights and shapes and speeds, its textures and colours and flavours, the limitless variety of sound.

"If God came down this very minute and said you had to be either blind or deaf, which would you choose?"

It is a question children will ask of each other at their games.

Everybody will say, "Deaf," except him. He will say, "Blind."

He will know, even then, that he could endure a darkened world. But a muted world would be a *nothing;* worse than nothing, death; worse than death, Hell.

As if in punishment, that Hell will come upon him, at the peak of his powers. His universe will be hushed, dimmed to a mocking adumbration of its grandeur. He will curse God. But he will press onwards, against heart-breaking odds, scratching his pen on paper, capturing the silent sounds quickly and desperately and feverishly before they can get away, writing down the evanescent cadences that then will sing only in his brain.

(He stirs, for he feels the nearer and nearer approach of the Moment, that great Moment when he will burst into a place of endless light, and tall sonorities, and love . . .)

Love, real love, will sear him only once. Giulietta the fair, so far above him in rank, but loving him in return. Until her father, the Count, will sunder them for ever, and she will marry a blooded, bloodless ninny, and he will go wifeless to his grave. Wifeless and soundless to the end of his life.

Soundless, to be sure; but he will make up for it by filling the ears of others with sound; furious, fervid, majestic, magnipotent sound; larger and grander than any ever heard before. It will startle and astonish them, crack open their little minds, make their hearts bulge in their bodies, move, shock, enrage them!

His sound will live; yet whilst *he* lives the pedants will call him a madman, and his work they will deem the death of concord.

But he will be praised, too. By the best. Even by Mozart. Poor Mozart, still young but with the chill of death already on him, had heard him play and had told him . . .

Had?

Heard?

Told?

The *past?*

He opens his eyes, looks about, recognises the room, the bed.

He groans. It is all behind him; his life is over. The end, not the beginning. He is old, sick, slimed with his last sweat, smothered in that worst of all things, silence. Suffocating in soundlessness.

He tries to rise, but falls back on his pillow. His breath leaves his body in one long sigh.

All is quite still.

And then the sharp, golden sweetness of trumpets pierces him; and an earthquake of drums; and he clearly hears a mellisonant multitude of men and women — luminous, numinous armies of them — singing:

"Joy, thou lovely spark of Heaven, daughter of Elysium . . ."

The last movement of his last symphony, and the conductor has got the beat just right, for once. "Yes, that's it, that's it, *allegro ma non tanto,*" Beethoven murmurs to himself, smiling in his final sleep.

Again, I dramatise. But who is to say that the death of Beethoven was not somewhat as I imagine it? Ten years ago to-day that great man died: I was not yet eight, and yet it moved me to tears to hear of it.

To-day, on Easter, we celebrate the Resurrection, and affirm once more our faith in the belief that there is no death. A man like Beethoven is resurrected even before the Last Day — he is resurrected *every* day, in the undying glory of his art.

Heavy snow and wind this evening.

⁌ *Monday, 27 March*

The snow continues, and a man who arrived at our house after dinner brushed great quantities of it from his hat and from the shoulders of his greatcoat. His name was Mr. Sparrow — curiously apt, for he had the short, stiff, nervous, somewhat mechanical movements of that bird when it is not aloft; also its drab colouring and hint of furtiveness.

Papa took him at once into his study, where they remained for not much more than ten minutes. Then Mr. Sparrow left.

"He is a private enquiry agent," Papa explained to me and Mamma. "I recently engaged him to help us find Phoebe. St. John Barstow recommended him as one of the best of that breed. He had nothing substantial to report, however. A young woman answering her description was seen in Knightsbridge to-day, but, upon closer investigation, she was discovered to be another person entirely. Mr. Sparrow has men making discreet enquiries in Suffolk, as well, for that is where she was last seen. I instructed him to continue his work and to report any findings to me, no matter how small. In the mean time, we must continue to pray."

"If only my father were alive," said Mamma. "The prayers of a bishop surely would have had superior influence in Heaven."

"The prayers of a loving mother, father, and sister will not go unanswered," said Papa. "They must carry enormous power."

Some words of Juvenal suddenly blazed in my thoughts — I must have heard Rutledge quote them at one time or other: *numinibus vota exaudita malignis* — something about prayers which Heaven in vengeance grants.

The vengeance of Heaven: what an awesome idea.

ॐ *Tuesday, 28 March*

I received in the post this morning a newspaper cutting, with one phrase underlined in red ink. The article, by Rhys O'Connor, dilated (in tones of hot indignation) upon the recent dismissal of charges against Percival Ormond, as regards the alleged malicious adulteration of tea. It was judged to have been "a sad and unfortunate accident, which came about through no deliberate intent." Mr. O'Connor wrote, of this outcome: "Once again we are treated to the pageant of the vested interests gathering to defend one of their own. The spectre of Friedrich Accum — hounded out of the country by the Royal Institution, undoubtedly bowing to pressure from those same interests — rises, along with the ghosts of Ormond's victims, to haunt us and silently to condemn the rot at the foundations of our society."

Near the conclusion of the piece is a paragraph that grudgingly admits that the majority of companies dealing in food and drink purvey reasonably pure products, and he names a representative few of them, including Papa's company, which is the phrase he underlined for my attention.

The cutting was folded into a short note that read:

"Dear Miss Summerfield; —
"Perhaps the enclosed item will be of interest to you.
"I trust that you, and all of your family members, are well.
                                        "Yours truly,
                                        "Rhys O'Connor"

Of course, I was glad to see that he had commended the product of Papa's brewery, but I wondered if there might not have been another motive in his sending the cutting to me. Did he know of my affection for Giles — and was his article, denouncing Giles's father, sent to taunt me? I have misjudged Mr. O'Connor in the past, and accused him to his face of malice, later to learn that no malice had been intended.

I was about to consign his article and his note to the dustbin when I decided upon another course of action. I sat down and wrote this reply:

"Dear Mr. O'Connor; —
"Thank you for shewing me your article, which I am returning herewith. No doubt you keep an album of your pieces, and this may find a permanent abode within its pages.
"All members of this family, to the best of my knowledge, are enjoying good health, I am pleased to tell you. We buried one member recently, whom we mourn, but I think that you and she had never met.
                                        "Sincerely,
                                        "Pamela Summerfield"

Crewe was just on his way out of the house on an errand for Mamma, so I gave him my letter for an early posting.

Imagine the extent of my surprise when, this evening, shortly before dinner, Rutledge tapped on my sitting-room door and informed me that Mr. O'Connor was downstairs and had requested to see me!

"Me?" I said. "Are you quite sure?"

"Yes, Miss."

"Oh, dear. Most peculiar. Are my parents aware that he has called?"

"No, Miss. They are dressing for dinner. And the gentleman did ask for *you.*"

"Shew him into the drawing-room. I'll be down at once."

When I entered the drawing-room, Mr. O'Connor, who had been nervously pacing, turned to me a face pallid and shewing every sign of a distrait man. "Miss Summerfield!" he exclaimed. "I received your letter in the afternoon post, and rushed here directly I had read it. I hope you will forgive me!"

"Forgive you? Forgive you for what, Mr. O'Connor?"

"For what must have seemed the callousness of me note — asking, almost flippantly, if the members of your family were well, at a time when you are suffering a recent loss —"

"But you had no way of knowing."

"I saw no notice in the newpapers — may I ask —"

"It was my dear Sophie. She died peacefully, in her sleep, a fortnight ago."

"Sophie," he said. "An aunt? A cousin?"

"A little spaniel. But she was my companion for twelve years, and I assure you that we all loved her as if she were a human being."

"Of course," he said, visibly relieved. "One can form a close attachment to a pet. Still, it's glad I am to learn that it was not one of the human members of your family. Thank you for receiving me. I will take me leave." He walked to the door.

"It is good of you to express such concern, Mr. O'Connor."

He shrugged. "'Tis a vestige of Irish sentimentality, no doubt. Or Welsh sentimentality, which can be even more mawkish. I shall have to work harder to eradicate that flaw."

"You would do better to cultivate it," I advised him. "Sympathy and compassion are not to be despised."

"Don't trouble to ring," he said. "I can shew meself out."

Angry at his attitude, I fairly spat these words: "Really, sir, you are the most *contrary* man!"

He smiled in that crooked, insolent way I have seen before. "And you, Miss Summerfield, are uncommonly attractive. For a child."

With that, he was gone. A child, indeed! What an exasperating, contradictory, altogether curious creature he is!

§• *Wednesday, 29 March*

Signor Olivo came to-day to give me my music lesson. Together, we sang the lovely duet from the first act of *Lucia:*

> *Verrano a te sull'aure*
> *I miei sospiri ardenti,*
> *Udrai nel mar che mormora*
> *L'eco dei miei lamenti . . .*

When we had finished, he did something he has never done before. He kissed my hand; then pressed it to his heart. "Ah!" he said in a rapturous moan. *"Bellissima signorina!* You have sing the Donizetti *squisitamente!"*

"Thank you, Signore. You sang even more exquisitely."

He still held my hand to his breast. He kissed my fingertips. "No, no," he said. "You sing *come un angelo.* And — please — do not to call me the Signore. It is so cold, so much not friendly."

"But I do not know what else to call you."

"Cara mia, please to call me Agostino," he replied.

"I think Mamma would not approve of that."

His free hand made a quick circular motion of dismissal, and his eyes rolled in a long-suffering way. "Ah, *la madre!* Always the young ladies are afraid of *la madre!"* He sighed. "In Italia is the same. But, *carissima ragazza,* please to call me Agostino when we are alone, *così.* And your Agostino will call you . . . *Pahm*-ell-ah!"

"Oh, my *dear* Signore, when you pronounce my name, it sounds like the title of an Italian opera!" I could not resist smiling.

But my smile merely sent him into another paroxysm of praise, this time for the smile itself: *"Che bello sorriso! Che denti!"*

"Thank you for the charming compliment, Signore, but I fear that I have bad news." His eyes grew wide with alarm. "I can not play the pianoforte any more."

"You can not??! *Ma perchè?"*

"Because it is impossible to do so — with only one hand."

He smiled and kissed that hand which still he held. Then he carefully relinquished it, saying, "I give it to you back. But I will borrow it, *ancora,* another time."

Dear Signor Olivo. He is a charming gentleman and a fine singer; and he is not bad-looking (although I do wish he would not use quite so much *olio di rosa* on his hair). I like him tremendously. But I think that he is beginning to become a problem.

ॐ *Friday, 31 March*

I dreamt last night of the Duke of Cumberland. His scarred face, illuminated as if by harsh, lime-burning lights, was a study in unearthly *chiaroscuro.* He sat in his opera-box, staring into ours. Dissonant music rose, like fumes of acid, from the orchestra.

That was the entirety of the dream. So vivid was the impression it made upon me, however, that it was clear in my mind when I awoke. I thought again of that night last year at the Opera. I thought of my recent speculations concerning that night — how his look may have reflected, not lust for this diarist, but, rather, his hatred of Princess Victoria, of whom he may have been reminded by my slight resemblance to her.

And I had another, more startling, thought:

I recalled the night in sharp detail. I remembered how I had turned from his gaze and whispered to my sister, who sat beside me, asking her if she knew the man's identity. I heard her again, in my mind, reply so softly that I could not understand her answer. I heard myself say, "What?" I heard her repeat the name in a hushed voice not much louder than before: "Cumberland."

Looking back on that episode in the light of other events, I now ask myself if there had been a special reason for Phoebe's hesitancy and her indistinct voice. And I ask: Why did she know his name when I did not? Had she been acquainted with him? Had she been *more* than acquainted with him?

Is Cumberland the father of her child?

April

&

"THE BLACK DOOR"

"Constable died yesterday," Papa said this morning at break-fast, looking up from his newspaper. "The painter chap. He was born in the year that the American Colonies declared their independence. That would make him — let me see —"

"Sixty-one," I said.

"Quite right," replied Papa.

"I am sorry to hear it," said Mama. "His pictures are so pleasant."

"Pleasant!" I repeated. "Mamma, they are superb!"

"I believe he was acquainted with my brother, Roger," said Papa.

"He was," I assured him. "He loved the Suffolk coun-tryside, and he told Uncle Roger, 'These scenes made me a painter.' I adore those dewy, vivid greens of his water-meadows and mills; those fresh, windy skies! It is *too* sad that he will paint no more."

"Don't fret, dear," said Mamma. "We still have Turner."

" 'Airy visions, painted with tinted steam' — that is what Mr. Constable said of Mr. Turner's work. In admiration, I *believe*. Oh, I do revere Mr. Turner, Mamma, but he is not Mr. Constable. Besides, sixty-one, although an advanced age, is not *ancient*."

"I should think not," said Papa. "I am very near that age myself."

The first of April: month of opening, from the Latin *aperire,* when trees begin to blossom anew, and flowers — indeed, the whole Womb of Nature — opens with life. It was fine and clear to-day, with but a few light clouds. There was a brisk wind, however, and the temperature never rose to over 48 degrees. Still, one must not complain. I can remember years when it snowed most cruelly on the first of April, as if Nature were playing a prank on us, in honour of All Fool's Day.

ঽ *Sunday, 2 April*

Our prayers in church to-day were for you, Phoebe, and for your unborn child of ever more suspicious sire. Has my imagination run riot, or can it be that you truly nurture the seed of Cumberland? — tainted seed of cruelty and criminal perversion?

I must try to put the hateful notion out of my mind; must blunt the edge of my thoughts; dull my brain to keep such monstrous suggestions out of sight, submerged, locked deep in some dark dungeon of my soul.

Not another word. To bed.

ঽ *Monday, 3 April*

I paid one of my infrequent visits to the kitchen to-day, chatted a bit with Mrs. Pruitt, and ate a slice of her warm, fresh-baked bread, with butter. My ulterior design had been to speak to Dora and to learn whether she is still walking out with the young soldier who had been Giles's batman. It is my hope that he may have had some news of his former captain — a slender possibility, it is true, but one snatches at straws.

Dora, however, was not in the kitchen. I did not wish to arouse suspicion by asking after her, so after I finished my bread-and-butter, I walked through the servants' quarters to her room.

The door was closed. I was about to knock, when I heard a voice within that was not Dora's. It was that of Crewe, the footman. I could not make out the words, but his tone was soft and melting. It was answered by Dora's voice, even softer, like the fluttering coo of a dove, over and over, in strict tempo, until the cooing exploded into a little whimper of astonishment.

I walked quickly and quietly away.

April, month of opening, indeed!

ঽ◉ *Tuesday, 4 April*

When Sophie was alive, the neighbour cats gave a wide berth to our garden and other surrounds; for her vigilant senses were ever alert to their intrusion, and her sharp eyes, sharp bark, and sharper teeth were a constant caveat to the feline world.

Now that she is gone, they have grown bold. They sense her absence, and two or three of them without fear now vault our garden wall and sun themselves on Summerfield property. One of them walks up to the panes of the garden doors and peers into the house. She is a lovely sleek tabby, with fur striped in shades of marmalade orange. I believe her to be quite wild, for she wears no collar.

To-day, she looked in at me so plaintively and steadily (do cats never blink?) that I opened the garden door and let her inside the house. She rubbed herself ecstatically against the hem of my skirt, and occasionally uttered a tiny syllable that sounded less like "Meow" than "Milk."

I brought her a saucer of milk, and she lapped up every drop of it. Then she indicated a desire to go into the garden again, so I opened the door and she slipped silently out and away.

"Full of fleas, I have no doubt," said Mamma.

ঽ◉ *Wednesday, 5 April*

Mamma's friend Mrs. Swinburne gave birth to a baby boy to-day. He will be called Algernon, unfortunate child.

Signor Olivo, who was here this afternoon for my music lesson, was again guilty of remarkably unpedagogical behaviour. He would not leave off until I reminded him that I could neither sing nor play the piano whilst he was thus occupying himself; and that if Mamma were to become aware of too many stretches of silence, she would surely suspect something.

He saw the wisdom of that. Even so, he held his clenched fist to his forehead and groaned, *"Che miseria!"*

୨୭ *Saturday, 8 April*

"A lamentable thing yesterday at the brewery," Papa said this morning at breakfast. "It was told to me by Mr. Quayle. This fellow Bootes — do you remember him?"

"Peter Bootes: yes, of course," I said.

"His wife had been with child, I understand. But the baby was still-born last week —"

"Oh! What a pity!" Mamma interjected.

"— and now the woman has vanished."

"Vanished?" I repeated.

"Abandoned her husband and her children; gone off no one knows where. Bootes is half out of his mind with despair, I take it, and has not worked for several days — spends all his time looking for her, asking about, wandering the streets."

"What about the children?" asked Mamma.

"They manage as best they can, I expect," Papa replied. "They work at the brewery during the day, and are kept out of harm's way there. It is a regrettable thing to have happen to them: the mother gone, the father out searching for her —"

What's become of little Peggy? I asked myself; but aloud I said: "Are the police of no assistance?"

"The woman has committed no crime. They would have their hands full if they were to hunt for every vagrant woman in London."

"Perhaps a private enquiry agent?" Mamma suggested.

Papa snorted. "Like that chap Sparrow? He was recommended to me as one of the best, and he's turned up damn-all about our Phoebe. Why should he do better with Mrs.

Bootes? Besides, who would pay his fee? Surely I am not expected to do so?"

"To-morrow is Sunday," I said, "and the children will not be at work. I shall go to their flat and see if I may be of help."

"You, Princess?"

"I have been there before. On Good Friday. I met Sally Bootes at that time."

"I had forgotten that," said Papa. "What did you make of her?"

"She seemed to be . . . an unhappy woman," I replied. I thought it best to say nothing of her prayers for the death of her children. That, weighed with the recently still-born child, might feed a suspicion that she had murdered the new baby. I think her incapable of such an act, however.

"If you see Bootes when you are there," said Papa, "advise him to return to work. If he plays the truant for much longer, he will lose his place. There are hundreds of other men, just as deserving, eager to take it up."

At our at-home this afternoon, Lord Merlyngton dilated upon the subject of our future Queen. "She's only a girl," he said, "and the King is not well. I can't say I fancy a child on the throne, and a female child, at that."

"Elizabeth was only twenty-five when she ascended the throne," I pointed out, resentful of his remark.

"There is a great difference, my dear young lady, between twenty-five and eighteen."

Mamma said, "But surely King William may live for several more years — perhaps until the Princess will have matured?"

Lord Merlyngton shook his head. "It is not likely, Mrs. Summerfield. His health grows worse every day, and he is old. I fear he will not last out the year. No, I do not like it. I do not like it at all. England, in these times, needs a man on the throne. A strong man. Not a slip of a girl."

ૐ *Sunday, 9 April*

This morning, directly we had returned from church, I had Paley drive me to the flats where the Bootes family live. After

I had knocked on their door, it was opened by a little boy of some six or seven years.

"Hello," I said. "Let me guess: you are young Peter, I'll be bound."

He shook his head, eyes all wide with the wonder of me.

"You can't be little Guy," I said, "for you are much too big a chap. You must be Tom, then."

He nodded and smiled.

"My name is Pamela," I said, "and I am a friend of your mamma's."

I heard a boy's voice, in the flat, ask, " 'Oo is it, Tom?"

When Tom did not answer, the other boy appeared. Although he was but a year older than his six-year-old brother, he had the brusque and forceful air of a man. "Yes, mum?" he said, all business.

"I know your mother," I said. "I've just called to see how you are getting on. May I come in?"

He shrugged. "It's all the same to me," he replied, but he stepped aside to let me enter. "I must finish feedin' the baby," he added.

"Little Peggy?"

"That's right."

"May I see her?"

"If you like. She's in the kitchen."

I followed him into the kitchen, where I saw five-year-old Guy sitting cross-legged on the floor, spooning porridge into his mouth from a bowl, and getting the greater part of it on his face. Baby Peggy was strapped to a wooden chair with what appeared to be the leather belt from a pair of man's breeches. Young Pete resumed feeding her porridge with a spoon.

"Where is your father?" I asked him.

"Out."

"So you are the man of the family."

"I 'spect I am."

"Do you have enough food in the house?"

"Enough for a day or two."

"Who looks after Peggy when you and the other boys are working?"

"Ain't nobody. We takes 'er wif us."

"What! To the brewery?"

"She plays about and sleeps in a crate of shavin's. She ain't no trouble."

"But how awful!"

He shrugged and tipped another spoonful of porridge into the baby's mouth. "It ain't so bad. Can't leave 'er 'ere, what with me mum gone."

"I suppose not," I admitted. "Peter, do you have any idea where she may be?"

He shook his head.

At that moment, the door to the flat opened and his father came in. Fatigue and heart-ache made him appear older than he had looked when last I saw him, in my bedroom, the night he had unlawfully entered our house, intent on burglary. For a moment, he did not recognise me; then, smiling and removing his cap, he said, "Why, it's Miss Summerfield, ain't it?"

"Yes, Mr. Bootes. I hope you don't mind that I've looked in on the children?"

"Mind? Not likely, Miss! It's that good o' you, it is."

"Have you had any word of your wife?"

He shook his head glumly. "Not a scrap. It's as if the Earth swallowed 'er up."

"Perhaps she'll come back when she begins to miss you and her children."

With a toss of his head, he motioned me into the next room, where we would be out of earshot of the little ones. "I think she's gone for good, Miss," he said.

"Why do you say that, Mr. Bootes?"

"Well, for a bit, now, she's been fed-up like. Talkin' 'arsh to the nippers; nary a word or a kiss for me. Like she was — I don't know — tired o' life. Can't say as I blame 'er. One baby after another; old before 'er time; nothin' to look forward to; no 'ope . . ."

"Are you saying that you think she —"

He put a finger to his lips. "Hush, Miss. I wouldn't want *them* to 'ear. But I wouldn't be surprised if, one of these days soon, the longshoremen fished my Sally out o' the Thames."

"Mr. Bootes! No!"

He nodded ruefully. "She was that low, she was, in 'er mind. Talked about dyin' all the time. Sayin' as 'ow all of us would be better off dead — the nippers, in particular."

I wanted to ask about the recent child; I wanted to find a delicate way of determining if he was sure it had been truly still-born; I wanted to allay my own gnawing suspicions; but he spared me the effort in his next words:

"Then, when the latest one was born dead — a little girl, it was; we would 'ave called 'er Mary, after Sally's mum — that just seemed to take the 'eart out of 'er. She said it proved she was right — God 'ad answered 'er prayers — it was a sign, she said; an omen. We was meant for death. That was the way she put it, Miss: meant for death. She looked down at the little dead baby when she said it."

"We are all meant for death, Mr. Bootes."

"Ah, yes, Miss, but that warn't Sally's meanin'. I was right 'ere with her when the baby was born — well, not properly born, bein' dead, but when it came into the world. 'Born dead,' she said, Sally did, lookin' down at the poor thing. And she kept repeatin' it: 'Born dead. Born dead. Like I prayed for. Born dead, like all of us should've been. Me. You. All of our kind. Better to be dead than to drag through a livin' death, a livin' 'Ell. God was merciful to this little creetur, Pete,' she said. 'I wish 'E'd be merciful to us, as well. You, me, young Pete, Tom, Guy, Peggy. All of us in a bolt of lightnin' together.' She went on like that, Miss, until I couldn't bear it no more. I told 'er to stop, but she just kept on natterin' about death. So I ran out and got drunk. Fell down in an alley some-wheres and slept it off. When I come back 'ere, she was gone. I ain't seen 'er since. I won't never see 'er again. She's in the Thames, Miss, I know it — she went and drownded 'erself, and that's the truth of it!"

The poor man broke apart completely and sobbed like a child.

My heart shattered to see him so. "Oh, no, I am sure you are mistaken," I said. "She would have been found before this if she had thrown herself into the river. You must stop think-ing in this morbid way, Mr. Bootes; truly you must. Sally is alive; I know it! You must believe that. And I intend to help you find her."

"You, Miss?"

"Yes. I will find her; I swear to you. *I will find her.*"

But how I meant to proceed in my search, I could not tell him, for I did not — and still do not — know.

ॐ *Monday, 10 April*

Madame Stevens was still attracting throngs of the curious when I arrived at Cooke's Circus this afternoon to meet Rhys O'Connor.

"I continue to assert that she is a bear," he said, suddenly appearing behind me and handing me a strawberry jelly.

"Oh! You startled me!" I said. "Have you been here long?"

"Perhaps a quarter of an hour. I have found a wooden bench in an out-of-the-way place, where we may enjoy a quiet conversation. If you will just step this way . . ."

When we had seated ourselves on the bench and had finished our jellies, he said, "Now then, Miss Summerfield — that note I received from you this morning. I find it devilish intriguing. You say you need me help —"

"In finding somebody."

"I am not an enquiry agent."

"No, but you are inquisitive, investigative. You never let go until you have found what you are looking for. There is a good deal of the bull-dog and the bloodhound about you, Mr. O'Connor."

"I accept the comparison with those noble beasts," he said, with a quick smile. "Sure, and I've been called much worse: a snake, a jackal, a vulture . . ."

"There is another reason I have thought of you in this connexion," I went on. "Some weeks past, I read a piece of yours about the traffic in young girls. I was impressed, not only by the fire of your indignation, but by your assemblage of *data* on the subject."

"I am nothing if not thorough, Miss Summerfield. I never begin to write until I am certain of me facts."

"May I then assume that you are well acquainted with the world of these wretched slaves?"

He rubbed his chin. "If, by well acquainted, you are asking me if I avail myself of their services . . ."

"That is *not* my meaning, sir."

"Then the answer is yes."

"Good," I said. "I have reason to suspect that a young woman whom I know may now inhabit that world."

"How dreadful," he said. "Girls of your class are seldom in those straits. Has she been abducted?"

"She is not of my class," I replied, and proceeded to tell him all I know of Sally. I emphasised her strange, wistful longing for a life of shame, and how it seemed to her to be more attractive than the duties of a wife and mother. I told him of the still-born child, and of her husband's account of her sudden leave-taking of her home.

He was thoughtful, and said nothing for a time. Then: "She is twenty, you say?"

"Yes."

"This will amaze you, Miss Summerfield, but in the world we are discussing, a girl of twenty is counted old. Their debauched patrons prefer girls of fourteen, thirteen . . even younger."

"Good Heavens!"

"I quite understand your shock. This is not a pleasant subject."

"She *is* twenty," I said, "and so worn that she appears to be even older. But she is pretty. And she could be quite striking if she were fitted out in becoming frocks, and her hair was properly dressed, and she had a bit of paint. I thought only that you might make some discreet enquiries. Her name is Sally Bootes."

"The name is of no importance," he said, as if brushing it aside. "These poor creatures seldom are called by their true names. But — yes — I can do a bit of sniffing about. Like a bloodhound. It would be an enormous aid if I had a portrait of her, of course, but girls of that class are not accustomed to sit for painters."

"Do you have a note-book and pencil in your pocket?" I asked.

"I would be lost without them," he replied.

"Let me borrow them for the space of a minute, and I will sketch her face for you. I am considered to be better than passable at drawing."

He reached into his pocket and handed me the articles which I had requested. I turned to a blank page and began sketching quickly, from memory. I then handed the note-book and pencil back to him.

He studied my drawing. "You have a talent, Miss Summerfield. I have never seen your model, but this is very well executed, with good technique and a piquant style. If Sally is as pretty as this, she would indeed be of great interest to those who buy and sell human flesh. Dark eyes, dark hair, full lips — a sultry siren, entirely. Yes, this will be of help." He slipped the note-book into his pocket.

"How will you proceed?" I asked.

"You would not wish to know the details of such proceedings, I assure you," he replied. "But I can tell you this much: I will casually put it about in certain quarters that I require diversion. Before long, a particular stripe of spalpeen will introduce himself to me as the representative of persons skilled in such entertainments. He will describe his wares; he may even conduct me to a place where he can display those same wares, as one might display fruit at a greengrocer's stall. I will say, in effect, No, these are too green; I have a taste for something riper —"

"Please," I said, "do not go on."

He made as if to reach for my hand, but checked himself. "I warned you that it is not a pleasant subject," he said gently. "At any rate, by these methods, I will endeavour to find a 'new' girl — new to the clientele of depravity, that is to say — of about twenty years or thereabouts, and resembling the sketch you have given me."

"Thank you, Mr. O'Connor."

"But, Miss Summerfield," he said darkly, "do not raise up your hopes too high. London is a labyrinth; she may never be found. *If* found, she may have no wish to be brought back — not all women in that profession despise their lives. Then there is the possibility that she has already been shipped from these shores and is a prisoner in some French or German brothel —"

"Oh! Dear God! Do not say it!"

"Finally, you must resign yourself to the likelihood that her husband may be right. All unfortunates who cast themselves into the Thames are not so soon dredged from its waters. Your poor friend Sally may be dead."

"I will not believe it," I said firmly.

This time he did take my hand, and pressed it. "There are those who say that death is a kinder fate than the life which you fear she now leads."

"Stuff and nonsnse" was my response. "Life is always to be preferred over death."

"Life at any price?"

"At any price!"

He smiled. " 'Tis a spirited girl you are," he said. "Don't worry; I shall do all that I can." He released my hand, saying, "And now I insist that we watch the Fête of Pekin together. It is just about to start. I have seen it before — and so have you, I dare say — but it is a splendid show and well worth seeing again."

We rose from the bench and walked off, he boldly offering his arm, and I, just as boldly, linking mine in his. "Are you also fond of loftier amusements, Mr. O'Connor," I asked, "such as the opera?"

"I am but a recent convert to that 'exotick and irrational entertainment,' as Dr. Johnson called it, but I have indeed, on several occasions, gone to the Opera to hear Jenny Lind, with —" He appeared to hesitate.

"With whom?"

"With great enthusiasm," he replied. "She is a heavenly singer."

I enjoyed the Fête of Pekin even more this time.

ॐ *Tuesday, 11 April*

I took a hamper of food to the Bootses' flat to-day, thinking to leave it with a neighbour if no one was at home. When I knocked upon the door, it was opened by Mr. Bootes, himself. He was badly in need of a shave.

He stared at me. It was evident that he had been drinking. "Ah — the young Miss — come in, come in — "

I entered, and handed him the hamper. "You're a good soul," he said, taking it. "The nippers will be peckish when they comes 'ome from work, and there's nary a crumb in the place."

"You could do with a bite yourself, Mr. Bootes, from the look of you."

"No, don't worry your pretty little 'ead about me," he said. "We'll put by these vittles for the childer."

"Please eat something," I entreated him.

"Later, p'raps," he said. "I got no stomach for it now, Miss: truly I don't."

He reached for a gin bottle, but I pleaded with him: "Do not drink any more, Mr. Bootes, I beseech you!"

"And why not, Miss?" he said, with a grin. "It's jolly stuff. Makes a man feel all warm and content-like. Takes the place of food, wife, church. When I 'as a bellyful of this stuff, I almost forgets me troubles."

"No!" I said firmly, snatching the bottle from him.

He scowled at me. " 'Ere, now — what call do you 'ave to take me comfort away from me? I 'spect your father takes a drop of an evenin', don't 'e?"

"This is not evening," I rejoined, "and you have had far more than a drop."

"Gi' me that bottle!"

"I will not. Mr. Bootes, listen to me! Your children are working to support you! Your baby daughter wallows all day in a crate of shavings at the brewery! You must take hold of yourself. You must return to work."

He sneered. "Oh, your kind is good at lecturin', ain't you? Tellin' us what lazy swine we are. Go back to me pa's brewery, she says — sweat your ballocks off like a bleedin' dray-'orse! Never mind that my Sal is floatin' in the Thames wif the other turds. Never mind that she was drove to it by your damned pa and 'is kind. Go back to work, you scum, she says. Go back and fill me pa's pocket with tin so's I can live in a fine 'ouse in Berkeley Square and wear silk on me back."

He advanced towards me, hate flaming in his bleary eyes.

"And what would you be, me girl, if I was to tear that silk *off* your back, eh? What if you was mother-naked, without all your finery? You'd be no better than my Sal, then. Not all 'igh-an'-mighty. Just another wench. Two teats, an arse, and a cunt. *Let's 'ave a look at 'em, shall we?"*

He reached out and seized the front of my frock. I went hot and cold with fear, and came near to fainting.

"Mr. Bootes," I said quietly, "you are a good and decent man. You will do me no hurt. But the poisonous stuff in this bottle has the power to rape and kill. If harm comes to me here in your house, it will not be Peter Bootes who will have done it, but the devilish swill that has possessed you!"

He leered at me, his hand still clutching the bosom of my frock. Then he blinked, and let go his hand, and staggered backwards. He collapsed upon a wooden chair. I was shaking from head to foot.

"Pour it out," he said. "Pour out the filthy muck."

I walked into the kitchen and did precisely that. When I returned to him, he was holding his head in his hands and moaning. "Oh, please forgive me," he was saying. "Wot was I thinkin' of?"

"Put it out of your mind," I said. "We shall never speak of this again. I am going to brew a large pot of strong tea. You will drink it if I have to ladle it down your throat through a funnel. And you will eat, sir. I will stand here and watch you do so. Do you understand me?"

He nodded, avoiding my eyes.

After he had eaten and drunk the tea, he said, "I'm that ashamed, Miss. I should be 'orsewhipped."

"There is altogether too much horsewhipping in the world," I responded. "But you must promise me, Mr. Bootes, that you will never again drink that stuff and let it make a beast of you."

"Oh, I do promise you that," he said, earnestly.

"And you must promise me that to-morrow morning, bright and early, you will take yourself in hand and shave and go to work."

"Yes, Miss," he mumbled.

"And you must promise me yet another thing: that you will stop worrying about your wife and saying that she is dead.

You must have faith, Mr. Bootes, as I do: faith in the certain fact that she is alive. I have enlisted the aid of a very thorough and dedicated gentleman who is even now searching for Sally. I have great confidence in him, and so must you."

He nodded.

"And now I think you must rest," I said. "Then, when your children come home, all of you can have a good dinner together."

"Yes, a proper lie-down; that's what I needs, right enough," he agreed. "But, Miss —"

"What is it?"

He was like a child when he said, "I'm that afeared, I am, to be alone. Would you sit beside me bed and talk to me till I drops off?"

"Dear Mr. Bootes. Of course I will."

ခ။ *Thursday, 13 April*

Rutledge (bless the man) brought this note directly to me as soon as the post delivered it this morning:

"Dear Miss Summerfield, —

"I have no news, as yet, of your friend; but I have made the acquaintance of a man whose trade may put him in the way of her.

"Your bloodhound,
"Rhys O'Connor"

I have an idea of what manner of man he meant.

ခ။ *Friday, 14 April*

Am I unnatural? Is it perversity in me to expend so much concern upon a total stranger, Sally Bootes, when someone much closer and dearer to me, my own sister, may be in God knows what degree of danger to body and soul?

It may be that my efforts on behalf of Sally are no more than a surrogate — a second-best and substitution for what I wish I could do for Phoebe. The plain fact is that I am entirely

259

helpless as regards Phoebe's unknown plight; I can do *nothing* for her; whereas for Sally I can at least *try* to do something.

Forgive me, Phoebe, but, in my place, would you not do the same?

ॐ *Saturday, 15 April*

In the post to-day, this note:

"Dear Miss Summerfield, —

"Would it be entirely out of the question for you to visit me in my rooms to-morrow? After all, you have done so once before. I shall be here all day, working (it will come as no surprise to you that I do not keep the Sabbath holy). The fact is, I have news of your friend: she is alive, and she has not left England. But, I beg of you, say nothing of this to her husband or to anybody else until I tell you the details of my encounter with her.

"Until to-morrow,
"Rhys O'Connor"

Sally alive! Thank God!

ॐ *Sunday, 16 April*

I feel sick. I have just returned from Rhys O'Connor's rooms.

After church, I told Mamma and Papa that, rather than going home with them in our coach, I preferred (if permitted) to go off on my own in a hackney, for I was worried about the Bootes family and wanted to do all I could on their behalf. It was not actually a lie — I hate to tell my parents outright falsehoods — but I admit that my words were designed to give the impression that I was going to see Mr. Bootes and the children in their flat. At any rate, a hackney was hired and when I had been driven out of earshot of my parents, I told the coachman to ignore my earlier instructions and to take me, instead, to Chelsea.

"Thank you for coming, Miss Summerfield," said Mr. O'Connor, as he opened his door for me.

"Thank *you* for finding Sally," I said.

"You may not be so thankful when you have heard what I have to tell you," he murmured. "Please sit down."

I did so; but he — rather than sprawling in that *chaise-longue* with the defective arm-rest — paced restlessly back and forth for several moments without speaking another word.

"Well, sir?" I asked, impatiently. "What is your news? Surely it can not be so bad if she is alive and has not been shipped abroad. Her husband is certain that she was drowned in the Thames."

He turned to me suddenly. "You didn't tell him that I'd found her?"

"I did exactly as you bade me in your note. I told no one."

"Good, good. Well, then, here is the position —" He broke off to say, "Can I offer you tea? Brandy?"

"Nothing, thank you. *Please* go on."

He sat on the very edge of the *chaise-longue*. "After following some false scents —"

"Bloodhound that you are."

"Precisely. I finally came to a certain establishment in a street leading off Gray's Inn Road. It is known as Mrs. Jeffers's, after the name of the proprietress. I think you can guess what manner of place it is."

I nodded.

"I made it known that I was in the market for what is called 'damaged goods.' Allow me to explain. There are some men so degraded that they can not find pleasure unless they debauch innocent girls — children of twelve or thirteen. There are other men who demand the opposite — women who have been 'round the course a bit,' as they put it, 'broken to the saddle' — all metaphors of horseflesh, you see, which indicate the essential bestiality of such men. No dewy-eyed innocents for them; no smooth, uncorrupted flesh. Their pulses quicken at wrinkles and blemishes, eyes dulled by time or vile experience. Women in this category are known as 'damaged goods' — and, in a way, I find the taste for them almost more loathsome than that for unspoilt maidens, for the latter can be explained, though not condoned, as a distorted form of that which the best of men seek — purity and goodness. But the former is beyond understanding. Forgive me — I appear to be rambling —"

"Not at all," I assured him, although I was indeed hoping he would get to Sally soon. "Please tell it in your own way. I can see that it is difficult for you."

"Yes, it is. I had thought that I was a man of the world, hardened to such things; but I found myself revolted and shaken. But let me go on. I represented myself to Mrs. Jeffers as a man seeking somebody who'd been round the course a bit. She gave me to understand that she did very little custom in such merchandise, but, to oblige such a fine young gentleman — and more blarney of that order — she would do her best to meet me needs.

"Her exact words were: 'There *is* a girl — quite handsome, really, but not what you might call fresh. Seen a bit of life. Been buffeted about, I expect. She's to meet one of our regular gentlemen this evening — he's due at almost any time, now — but if you could call again to-morrow —' I immediately agreed to return the next day, but I added: 'If I could but *see* her now. For a moment, no more. I'll leave before your other client arrives, I promise you.' And I slipped a bank-note into her hand. 'Well,' she said, 'just for a minute. But you'll have to come up to the special room.' "

"The special room?"

"Yes," said Mr. O'Connor. "It was the mildest word she could have used to describe that room, but it was, indeed, special. She led me up the staircase and along a corridor, far beyond the other rooms in her establishment, to a door that was painted entirely black and fitted with an enormous padlock. She produced a large key from her bosom. 'Myself, I don't hold with this sort of thing,' she said, 'but some of the gentlemen are that partial to it, and they pay well for their entertainment. I'm a woman of business: I meet my customers' requirements. And don't it say in Scripture, sir, judge not that y' be not judged?' She inserted the key into the padlock and turned it."

Mr. O'Connor paused and looked directly at me. "Your education is about to be considerably broadened," he said, "but in a direction that may leave you wishing that you had remained ignorant. I know you have an enquiring mind, Miss Summerfield, and that is commendable; but I must warn you that what lay behind that door was of such a nature as to disgust you in a way you could have never imagined. Are you sure that you wish me to continue?"

"Quite sure."

"Very well. But before I do, let me say that, in my researches into these matters, I have heard things that turned my blood cold. Young English girls, abducted and drugged, then shipped abroad to Brussels or Paris, to be auctioned off like cattle to the proprietors of brothels from all over the Continent."

"I know about that from your article," I said.

"What you may not know, because I have not yet written of it, and learnt it but recently meself, is that most of those girls are fortunate —"

"Fortunate!"

"— when we compare their fate with that which befalls certain of their sisters."

"Whatever can you mean?"

"There are some few houses in Central Europe — be thankful that they are in the minority — which cater to a particular kind of man. These are men whose appearance and demeanour give no sign of the corruption within: prosperous industrialists, some of them; prominent statesmen, perhaps princes and kings — loving husbands and fathers, more than likely — and yet all of them the lowest and most loathsome kind of creature in the world, for they are insatiably addicted to the worst variety of perverted lust. In those houses, the poor abducted slaves are not treated as women; they are not treated as human beings at all. To be sent to such a place is a sentence of death — and I wish I could tell you that the death is quick and merciful, like that accorded by the gallows or the guillotine, but it is not. Have you ever seen small boys amuse themselves by tearing the wings off flies? Then let me say no more than this: in those houses, the condemned girls are treated like such flies; and their tormentors are not small boys, but grown men."

My throat was dry. I swallowed, but without relief. Seeing

this, he poured me a glass of brandy without my asking, and I drank it in one draught. It took away my breath; but when it returned, I said, "You can not mean — that they are — tortured to death?"

He nodded.

"Not literally?"

Again he nodded. "By the most various and mediæval of methods."

"Merciful God!"

"Exactly," he said dryly.

"But *why* are they punished so? — for what *reason* —"

"It is not punishment. It is sport. As with the boys and the flies. You are pale — will you have another drop of brandy?"

"No, thank you. I'm all right. Please go on. I want to hear about Sally."

"Sally," he said. "Yes." Now he poured himself an inch of brandy and swallowed it. "Miss Summerfield, I did not tell you of those Central European houses merely to horrify you."

"I'm sure you did not."

"I had a purpose. The purpose was to soften the blow. Now that you know the worst, let me assure you that there are no such houses in England."

"Thank Heaven!"

"Not to my knowledge, that is — and my knowledge in these matters has become regrettably large in pursuit of me profession and the search for Sally. But there *are* places in London that are pale approximations of those houses. One of them is the special room in Mrs. Jeffers's establishment.

"She opened the black door and we entered. It was dimly lit — I could scarcely see — but I was appalled. Metal manacles hung by chains from the ceiling. There were ladders and tables to which victims could be strapped. There was a pillory, with holes for the head and hands. On one wall, in notches, I could see the entire catalogue of flagellation: the common head-master's birch, and holly branches, and buggy-whips, and the cat-o'-nine-tails . . ."

"No! How ghastly!"

"Mrs. Jeffers assured me that the worst of these were 'only to make a show on the wall; stage properties, so to speak. The gentlemen don't use 'em — just the birches and such.' I wish I could be certain of that. At least, there was no rack or Iron Maiden. But otherwise, the room had every aspect of the torture chamber. My abominable guide seemed to be proud of it. 'In this room, sir,' she said, 'a gentleman can enjoy himself with the certainty that no one can hear a thing. The room is perfectly secure. The walls are thick, and there's a double carpet on the floor. A gentleman can do as he pleases. Not a sound'll be heard, I warrant you.' She turned up the gas.

"I turned to me left — and there, hanging from the ceiling by her wrists, her toes barely brushing the floor, was a dark-haired woman with a full, voluptuous figure. She was quite naked."

"Dear Christ, it can not be so," I said in a whisper.

" 'There she is, sir,' said Mrs. Jeffers. 'Is she to your liking?' I said I required a moment alone with her — 'To examine her,' I added with a wink, and gave the old harridan another bank-note. 'All right,' she said, 'but only a moment, mind. My other gentleman will be here soon.' She nodded towards the girl. 'He likes her to hang a bit before he gets here. Ripening, he calls it.'

"She left the room, and I walked up to the girl as she hung there by her wrists. I had seen only the back of her before this, but now I saw her face. Large dark eyes — ringed with suffering — and sensual red lips. She was your drawing, to the life! Quickly, I spoke: 'Are you Sally Bootes?' She looked at me with suspicion. 'Please tell me!' I begged her. 'You are Sally Bootes, are you not?' She groaned a little — it must have been intensely uncomfortable to hang there in that way — and then she said, 'I'm just plain Sal 'ere, Charlie. Come back tomorrow and I'll do you proud.' "

"Dear Heaven! Was it truly she?"

"Oh, yes," said Mr. O'Connor. "There can be no doubt of that. I said to her: 'You're not to worry, Sally. I'm going to take you out of this.'

"She became angry. She said, 'What do you mean? 'Oo are you? 'Oo sent you?'

" 'I was sent by Miss Summerfield, on behalf of your husband,' I told her. And then came the worst shock of all."

"What can be more shocking than what you've already told me?" I demanded, close to tears.

"Her next words. For she said: 'You just listen to me, Sir Knight-in-Shinin'-Armour. You tell little Miss Summerfield that if she wants to do me a good turn, she should keep 'er nose out of my affairs. I'm comin' along just fine, I am. You tell 'er that.'

"I could scarcely believe me ears. I tried to reason with her. But her voice became shrill.

" 'Leave me be!' she cried. 'Mrs. Jeffers is good to me! I eat better and more regular than I ever 'ave in me life! I'm makin' money and even puttin' a bit by. I sleep in a warm bed. We 'ave jolly parties 'ere. Champagne to drink! The girls are good friends. The gentlemen are not so bad, most of 'em. Oh, I may be strung up like a plucked goose, waitin' for some poor sod to come in 'ere and beat me arse — but, compared with the life I led with Pete and that brood of brats, gettin' me arse beat now and again is *a bed of roses!* Now get out of 'ere! And don't never come back! You understand me, mister? *Don't never come back!*'

"I left her like that, dangling by her wrists, shouting at me. I opened the black door just as Mrs. Jeffers was ushering in her regular client. The old bawd smiled at me. 'Spirited wench, ain't she? Got a nasty tongue. But you come back to-morrow evening, sir, and she'll shew you a good time.'

"The man quickly walked past me to the wall where the various implements hung in notches. As he deliberated upon his choice, he kept his face turned away from me, for fear that I might recognise him, I expect. No doubt he is some well-known public figure. Mrs. Jeffers and I left the room, and as we walked away from the closed door, I began to hear the sound of the lash, striking Sally's flesh. And her screams. 'Just play-acting,' Mrs. Jeffers said, but I was not so sure. 'He pays her a nice bonus,' she added. 'Very generous with the money, he is.' "

"Oh, God, how vile. How sad."

"But you *do* see why you mustn't tell Bootes where she is? She *prefers* that life. She doesn't *want* to go back to him. If we did take her out of that place, she would only run away again and return to Mrs. Jeffers."

"It is inconceivable!" I cried. "To leave her home, her husband, her children — for *that?* If she had become the pampered mistress of a nobleman, I might begin to comprehend it. But to be hung up like meat in a slaughter-house and *flogged?*" I shook my head. "I shall never understand." I got up. "Thank you for your efforts, Mr. O'Connor. You have proven to be a friend."

"I hope I shall always be your friend, Miss Summerfield. But I fear that you would have been happier without this news."

I nodded. "I shall not sleep well to-night," I said. "I shall see her before me, as you described her. I shall hear the sound of the whip."

He said, "I shall hear it — and see her white body stretched from that ceiling — for the rest of me life. But the reformer in me will reflect upon the greater horror."

"*Greater* horror?"

"Of how unbearable her former life must have been — if she prefers to stay with Mrs. Jeffers."

࿊ *Monday, 17 April*

God, in His inexplicable and all-too-rare mercy, has seen fit to cause the poppy of the East to flourish, that it may yield those precious ruby drops which, alone, have the power to cast out sorrow and despair from my heart.

If my writing is unsteady, it is because my hand, as well as my mind, has been set adrift by that medicine. I staggered from my bed — moving as if through cotton-wool — to my desk, to set down these few words; and now I shall take another drop or two and return to bed again.

࿊ *Tuesday, 18 April*

For the first time, my faithful panacea has failed me. All of yesterday, I was lost in dreams, to be sure — but *such* dreams! I thrashed about in bed, stewed in my sweat, seeing Sally, her flesh maggot-white, hanging from that ceiling; seeing her awful client raising the whip, his mouth twisted in a leer. I heard Sally scream as the whip came down on her naked back —

And then it was Phoebe hanging there, stripped to her skin, shrieking under the lash —

Looking upwards, I could see nothing but my own wrists — manacled — chains rivetted into the beams of the ceiling — and feel the lash as it struck my bare back, my buttocks. I heard myself scream —

I was in the special room for eternity. I know, now, what the souls in Hell must feel. Pain without end, time stretching out for ever, no hope of rescue or escape or mercy.

Treacherous poppy! When I have most need of you, you betray me!

Mr. O'Connor's disclosures have profoundly distressed me. Human cruelty and depravity are limitless, infinite. And for Sally to choose, of her own free will, to wallow in that depravity, is a thought that darkens my soul.

ಸಿ *Wednesday, 19 April*

To-morrow is again a night of the full moon.

Will the Fiend take yet a fourth life?

What manner of madness drives such a creature? I think it must be the ultimate form of the fit that grips those men who visit Mrs. Jeffers's special room.

ಸಿ *Thursday, 20 April*

Of course, I told Mamma nothing of Sally's plight. She thinks my distress is due only to the onslaught of my monthly Time.

"I am going out for a bit," she told me this afternoon. "Can I bring home anything that will improve your spirits? A book, perhaps?"

"No silly romances," I said, almost viciously.

"Something of more substance, then?"

"Perhaps, if Mr. Carlyle's new book has been published —it has been announced for this year."

"What is the title?"

"The French Revolution."

"Dear, dear, such heavy fare. Young girls are so much more serious than they were in my day. But I shall enquire in the shops."

When she returned, just a few minutes before Papa came in from the City, she handed me a paper-wrapped parcel, saying, "I could not find *The French Revolution,* so I brought you another of Mr. Carlyle's books instead."

I tore off the paper and groaned with disappointment.

"What's the matter?" she asked.

"*Sartor Resartus!* I read it three or more years ago in *Fraser's Magazine!*"

"Don't *whine* so, my dear. It is most annoying. I can not be expected to remember everything that has been published in *Fraser's.* Perhaps a 'silly romance' would have been best, after all."

"No," I said. "Life is not like a romance."

"Which is why we read romances," she replied.

꙾ *Friday, 21 April*

It was in the morning edition:

Another woman, this one called Hattie Morrison, was strangled and defiled yesterday in Hyde Park.

Mlle. La Grange, who dressed my hair to-day, clucked her tongue over this new murder. "*Pourquoi?*" she pondered, shuddering.

"*Pourquoi?*" I echoed. With bitterness, I said: "There is no mystery in it, Mam'selle. It is quite easily explained. The Full Moon Fiend does these things for the same reason that respectable men go to brothels and whip girls. For sport!"

Shocked at the extent of my knowledge, she asked, "Where do you learn of — these things?"

"From a friend." I sought her eyes. "You think I made it up, don't you?"

"*Non.*"

"You do not believe that such things go on?"

"*Ah, mais oui!* I know of this bad thing. But you — so young — *très innocente* —"

"I shall be eighteen next month!" I said firmly. Then, in a gentler tone, I asked, "Is it common?"

She shrugged. "Common? I think not so. But myself, I knew once a man —"

"He flogged you?" I said, incredulous.

She shook her head. "This sad man, he was — how do you say it — the different face of the money?"

"The other side of the coin."

"Oui! Exactement!"

"But — you cannot mean — that *you* —"

"Mais non! But he *wished* me to do this."

"Flog him?"

"On the *derrière."*

"Good Heavens!"

"It was, for him, the only way he could feel *le plaisir."* She sighed. *"Le pauvre homme.* But I refused him, *naturellement."*

"Men can be so odd, Mam'selle," I said.

"Ah, oui — but it is not only the men."

I turned round and looked at her. "You do *not* mean to say that there are *women* who like to be whipped?"

"Le plaisir, it is very strange," said Mlle. La Grange.

ಶಾ *Saturday, 22 April*

The latest killing of The Full Moon Fiend was nearly the only topic of conversation during to-day's at-home.

"It is outrageous," said Lady Merlyngton, "that the police have not captured this monster!"

Mr. Cargrave said, "The problem, I believe, is that this monster, as you call him, is monstrous only once a month. Don't ask me to explain *why* he is maddened by the full moon — the pathology of the mind is not my line of country — why do dogs howl at the deuced thing? — but the fact remains that he commits these atrocities on just a single night out of every month. At all other times, apparently, he walks amongst us and behaves quite normally."

"Normally!" exclaimed Mamma. "What a word to use for such a man!"

"I only meant, dear lady, that if he went about every day.

looking monstrous — frothing at the mouth and what-not — he would have been long since apprehended. He has eluded capture because — on every day save one — his demeanour attracts no attention. He might be any man. A costermonger or a cobbler. An Englishman or a foreigner. Why, he might even be"—and here, Mr. Cargrave turned to Lord Merlyngton — "a member of the House of Lords!"

"Eh? What did you say? Preposterous!"

"An interesting word, 'preposterous,' " I interjected. "Rutledge once told me that, in Ciceronian Latin, it means that one's backside is in front."

"Pamela!" said Mamma, looking severely at me, then at Rutledge — who, I do believe, was blushing! "I am surprised, Rutledge," she said; "I am truly surprised."

"With respect, ma'am," he said, "the expression loses something in translation."

"I should hope so."

But Papa was smiling. "Arse-to-front, is that what you meant by it, Lord Merlyngton?"

"Wilfrid!"

"Most certainly not," huffed Lord Merlyngton. "I meant to say that, whoever this Full Moon Fiend may be, I am certain of one thing. He can not possibly be a gentleman."

ॐ *Sunday, 23 April*

This morning, I truly went to see the Bootes family, in the family coach, after Paley first drove Mamma and Papa straight home.

They were all on hand — father and children — just finishing their morning meal. Mr. Bootes looked much better than when I had seen him last. He was shaven; his colour was improved; and it was apparent that he had not been drinking recently.

"Why, Miss!" he said. "It's good of you." Then, anxiously, he whispered, "Do you 'ave news o' — you know."

I nodded, and indicated, by my manner, that I wished to speak to him alone.

" 'Ere, Pete," he said to his oldest, "take the others outside to play."

"What about the dishes, Pa?" asked young Pete.

"I'll wash 'em. You nippers go an' 'ave a nice 'oliday."

When the children had left, I asked, "Shall I help you with the dishes, Mr. Bootes?"

"Ah, no, Miss, let 'em wait. Sit down; 'ere's a nice chair. That's it. Now, then, what do you 'ave to tell me?"

All this morning, in church, I had been planning this visit, and inwardly rehearsing what I would say to him. I knew that I should have to tell him something; and I agreed with Mr. O'Connor that it must *not* be the truth. I had finally decided upon what I considered to be the kindest falsehood.

"I fear that I do not have good news for you," I said.

He nodded and looked down at the floor. "I can guess at it," he said. "Me Sally's dead, ain't she?" I found that I could not answer, but when he looked up at me for a reply, I nodded.

"Well, Gawd 'ave mercy on 'er soul," he said. "She's better off, I 'spect. Out of this life she 'ated so much. Still, it's a shock to 'ear it." His voice trembled. "Such a pretty thing, she was. So young." Tears came to his eyes. "I didn't deserve 'er, Miss. I warn't good enough for 'er, not by 'arf."

"That's not true, Mr. Bootes."

"She was that sweet, she was, when she was in good spirits. Oh Gawd, what will I do wifout 'er? What will the nippers do? It's 'ard, Miss. It's perishin' 'ard!" He sobbed openly now.

Then he wiped his eyes on his shirt-sleeve and took hold of himself. "When might I see 'er?" he asked.

I was not prepared for this. "See her?"

"Where 'ave they put 'er?"

"I'm — afraid I don't know, actually," I said.

"That's all right, Miss; just tell me what you do know, and I'll find out the rest for meself."

"But, Mr. Bootes — I think it will be impossible for you to see her —"

He nodded. "Ah. I get your meanin'. Not a pretty sight. Drownded in the Thames, and in the water all this time. I see. But I must make arrangements, Miss."

"Arrangements?"

"For burial."

"Yes, of course. But — that is to say — she's already been buried, you see."

"So quick? In what graveyard?"

"Why — I —" (Oh, what a tangled web we weave, etc. Sir Walter, you were never more true!)

Peter Bootes looked at me closely. His eyes narrowed.

"Wot is it, Miss?"

"Nothing —"

"You've been 'oldin' somethin' back, 'aven't you?"

"No —"

"Ah, but you 'ave! I can tell! Somethin' too 'orrible for me to 'ear — that's it, ain't it?"

"Mr. Bootes —"

"Me Sally warn't drownded — she was murdered! By that Full Moon bloke! Was that the way of it?"

"No, no, I *assure* you she wasn't murdered —"

"Strangled! Raped!"

"No! —"

"Oh, Gawd! That poor little thing! 'Er last moments on Earth — strangled to death by that rotten blighter, and *then* — I can't bear it! I can't *bear* it, Miss! 'Ow can I go on through life, knowin' 'ow she suffered at the last?"

"She was not murdered!" I cried. *"She is alive!"*

(What have I done? I asked myself. The words were out of my mouth before I knew what I was saying.)

He looked at me. In a hoarse whisper, he echoed my last word: "Alive?"

I nodded, avoiding his eyes.

"Then why did you tell me she was —"

I shook my head. "I thought it better."

"Better? Better for me to think 'er *dead?"*

"She does not want to come back to you, Mr. Bootes."

"She told you so?"

"She told my friend."

"Well, Miss, she'll 'ave to tell *me* before I believe it! Where is she?"

"I may not tell you."

"You *will* tell me, by Gawd!"

"I promised not to."

"Damn your promise! Tell me!"

I shook my head.

"I'm 'er 'usband! I 'ave a right to know!"

"Oh, *please,* Mr. Bootes, do not force me to tell you! You would not wish to know it!"

"Where is she? *Where's my Sally?*"

"God forgive me — she's in a brothel!"

The word stunned him. "No . . . no . . ." Then, recovering somewhat from that blow, he asked, quietly, "Where?"

"Don't ask me that."

He seized both my shoulders and lifted me roughly to my feet. He shook me, savagely. I screamed.

"Tell — me — where!!!"

Sobbing, I said, "Off Gray's Inn Road — a place called Mrs. Jeffers's —"

He pushed me from him, and I fell back into the chair. Without another word, he turned and rushed from the flat.

What a frightful mess I have made of things.

ཉ *Monday, 24 April*

The newspaper to-day carried a brief account, in the back pages, which I herewith paste down:

DISTURBANCE OFF
GRAY'S INN ROAD

A disturbance took place on Sunday at the house of Winifred Jeffers, near Gray's Inn Road.

A man, whose name remains unknown, appeared there during the course of a luncheon party and caused considerable consternation among the guests. Mrs. Jeffers, a widow, was obliged to call in constables to deal with the intruder.

According to Mrs. Jeffers, he was "a coarse, labouring sort of person, not the kind I am accustomed to invite into my house."

The man refused to give his name to the constables, but insisted that he had come for his wife, who he claimed was a guest there at the time. "There she is," he said, identifying a young woman. When questioned by the constables, the woman denied knowing the man.

He is reported to have used offensive language in suggesting that Mrs. Jeffers presides over a house of accommodation. Calling his remarks slander, Mrs. Jeffers did not, however, press charges against him. He was led away by the constables and eventually released.

There was no damage to property.

৪৹ *Tuesday, 25 April*

The temperature had got up to 53 degrees by three o'clock this afternoon, and the day was fine, with fleecy clouds and a light wind; so I decided to enjoy a short stroll before tea.

I had not walked very long before I saw a shabbily dressed man standing at the next turning. He approached me, and I recognised Peter Bootes.

"Beggin' your pardon, Miss," he said, humbly, "but I was 'opin' to catch you up like this."

"You could have come to the kitchen entrance and asked one of the staff to fetch me," I told him. "How long have you been standing here?"

"It don't matter —"

"Here, you," said a constable, who suddenly hove into view. "I told you to be movin' on. Is this man annoyin' you, Miss?"

"That's all right, Constable. I know him."

"Very good, Miss."

When the constable had walked away, I said, "I read about you in the newspaper yesterday, Mr. Bootes."

He nodded, grimly. "Good job I didn't give the peelers me name."

"I'm very sorry you had to know about Sally."

"I just 'ad to tell somebody about it, Miss. Might I walk along wif you for a bit?"

"Of course."

"Well, it was 'orrible. I thought I 'ad some rights, as 'er 'usband, but when I come to that house, that Mrs. Jeffers woman — awful old tart, she is — why, she ordered me out.
Told me she accommodates only gentlemen. I told 'er I
wanted to see me Sally. So she fetches 'er, and there she is,
right enough. All painted and stinkin' o' scent, so's I could
scarcely recognise 'er. Not 'ardly dressed at all, she warn't;
more like 'arf-naked, beggin' your pardon — and that wif
men sittin' all about where they could see 'er. 'What in 'Ell do
you want?' she says.

" 'I come to take you out of this,' I said. She larfed. Just put
'er 'ands on 'er 'ips and threw back 'er 'ead and larfed at me.
'Not likely,' she says.

"I tried to take 'er in me arms, gentle-like, but she backs
off. 'None o' that,' she says. 'But I tell you wot — if you
come upstairs wif me, I'll let you do anythin' you like. Right,
Mrs. Jeffers? Providin' you got the tin to pay for it.' Then she
larfs again, and so does that old tart.

"That's when I lost me temper. *'Pay* for it?' I shouts. 'I'm
your *'usband,* and don't you forget it! Now get some decent
clothes on your back! You're comin' 'ome to your children!'
Well, I made a bit of a row, and Mrs. Jeffers tells some big
bloke of 'ers to fling me out — and I knocks 'im to the floor
wif one blow, and that's when she calls in the peelers. The rest
of it, I 'spect you read in the papers."

"I don't know what to say, Mr. Bootes."

"Ain't there nothin' to be done, Miss? Ain't I got no right
to 'er? I'm 'er 'usband!"

"I simply don't know."

"The peelers, they all know what kind of 'ouse that is. But
they winks at it. They push me about — because I ain't a gentleman. And they treats that old tart like she was Queen Adelaide 'erself! It ain't right, Miss. It ain't right at all."

"I agree with you, Mr. Bootes. But you must remember
that Sally isn't being held there against her will."

"Ah," he said, "an' that's the pity of it. That's what breaks
me 'eart." He shook his head.

"Poor Mr. Bootes. You must try to forget her. You will

find another to take her place and to be a mother to your children."

"Oh, I'll find somebody or other, I 'spect," he said. "But no one 'oo will take 'er place. And as for forgettin' 'er — no, Miss, it ain't likely. Not 'er. Not me Sally. I won't never forget 'er."

He touched his cap and walked quickly away, without even giving me a chance to say good-bye. I watched his departing figure — shabby, work-worn, shambling — and a grey cold sadness moved in like fog to surround my heart. The day no longer seemed fine.

࿔ *Wednesday, 26 April*

I wonder if Willy has reached Africa as yet? I rather imagine that he has. I hope he will not forget to write to us.

How does one teach the precepts of gentle Jesus to naked shoe-black savages who wear bones through their noses? How does one preach mercy to creatures who cook people in great pots and eat them? Do they kill the unfortunate folk before cooking them, or do they boil them alive? What does human meat taste like, I wonder? Is it tough or tender? Do women taste better than men? Do the savages use any sauces or seasonings? Do they have favourite cuts — sirloin, saddle, haunch?

Oh, dear. I am becoming positively morbid.

࿔ *Thursday, 27 April*

The weather has changed again. The temperature has fallen by several degrees, and there is heavy rain.

I am re-reading *Sartor Resartus*.

～〜✛

We had not quite finished our dinner when Rutledge, coming in with the sweet, said to me, "Miss Pamela, there is a boy in the kitchen, wanting to see you."

"A boy?"

"Drenched to the skin, in this rain. He came round to the

rear entrance, and keeps asking for 'the young Miss.' He answers to the name of Tom."

"That must be little Tom Bootes," I said. "Mamma, may I be excused?"

"Yes, my dear."

"Will you not be eating your sweet, Miss? It's your favourite — sherry trifle," said Rutledge.

"Save it for me. No — better yet, hand it to me. I'll take it down to Tom."

"He's had two helpings already, Miss," Rutledge said, with a smile.

"Oh, very well, I'll eat it later."

I dashed downstairs to the kitchen, to find six-year-old Tom wrapped in an enormous old dressing-gown of Rutledge's, and apparently quite naked save for that, sitting in a chair and tucking into his third helping of Mrs. Pruitt's trifle.

"Hello, Tom," I said. "What are you doing here?"

He looked up from the bowl. "Pa says, 'Please, Miss, come at once.' "

"Why? What's happened?"

He blinked at me. "Pa says, 'Please, Miss, come at once.' " Apparently he could say only what he'd learnt by rote.

"Right you are, Tom," I said.

By this time, Rutledge had joined us, and I bade him tell Paley to get the coach ready. "Where are the boy's clothes?" I asked Mrs. Pruitt.

"There they are, Miss Pam," she said, pointing. "Hanging by the fire to dry. But it will take for ever, they're that soaked. Mr. Rutledge took the liberty of looking up some clothes that belonged to Master Will when he was about the age of this'n. Here they are, on the counter, if you'll be wanting to dress him, Miss. Shall I help you?"

"I can manage. Come now, Tom, out of that dressing-gown and into these breeches."

"Can't I finish me sweet?"

"Well, you *do* have a tongue in your head, after all, don't you? All right, finish it up, but don't be too long about it."

He scraped the bowl clean, and I helped him wriggle into Willy's old clothes. "There!" I said. "You're quite the fine young gentleman."

As we rode through the pummeling rain towards Tom's home, I asked him, "How did you get to my house?"

"Walked."

"In all this wet? Heavens!"

I told Paley to wait for me, and we hurried from the coach, under my umbrella, and into the block of flats.

"Thank Gawd you've come, Miss," said Mr. Bootes as he opened the door. "I 'ated to ask you, in this weather, and seein' as 'ow you already done so much for us, but I didn't know where else to turn."

"What is it?" I asked.

"Come in 'ere, Miss, if you don't mind." I followed him into a bedroom, and he closed the door behind us. "Let me just turn up the bedside lamp a bit," he said.

"Why, it's Sally!" I exclaimed. "She's come back!" For it was, indeed, his wife, eyes closed, who lay on the bed, on her stomach, under the sheet.

"Not much more than an hour ago, it was. We was eatin' our dinner, and we 'eard this noise at the door — a weak sort of scratchin' it was — and I opened the door, and she just *fell* into me arms. I carried 'er in 'ere and put 'er on the bed. Then I sent Tom to fetch you, Miss."

He bent over the bed and spoke gently to her. "Sal? It's Miss Summerfield, come to see you."

Her eyes fluttered open. After a moment, she recognised me. "Oh, Miss," she said, in a voice so faint I could scarcely hear her. "Oh, Miss, I've been such a fool."

"You are home where you belong," I said. "Nothing else matters."

Her eyes rolled in the direction of her husband, who stood beside me. "Shew 'er, Pete," she said.

"No, Sal, it wouldn't be proper, not such a nice young lady as 'er, and meself bein' 'ere, an' all."

"Then you'd best quit the room," Sally said, "an' leave us two women together."

He nodded and, somewhat reluctantly, left the bedroom, closing the door.

"Now then, Sally," I asked, "what is it you want to shew me?"

"Pull off the sheet," she said.

I took hold of a corner of the sheet and drew it down to about as low as her shoulder-blades — where, to my horror, I saw a long, slanting gash that stretched all the way across her back. I gasped at the sight of it.

"Pull it *all* the way off!" she said, impatiently; and when I hesitated, she reached her hand round to the sheet, and herself flung it completely from her body, dropping it to the floor.

"My God!"

She was naked from head to foot. Her back was an obscenity of mutilation. Across her shoulder-blades, down the whole length of her spine, the small of her back, her buttocks, her thighs, I saw a glistening network of criss-crossing cuts, oozing with blood. No mere welts; these were hideous ragged fissures, deep, wide, gaping, stippled by pieces of minced flesh, and with strips of torn red skin hanging from them. It was not like a human body at all — it was a landscape in Hell, furrowed by fiends, sliced into scarlet ruts by the Devil's plough.

"Pretty, ain't it?"

I could not control my revulsion. I sprang to the basin that stood on the dresser, and vomited my dinner into it, retching and gagging in spasms of sickness that convulsed my whole body. Finally, my stomach emptied, my breath reeking, I reached for the towel that hung over the dresser and wiped my lips on it. I rinsed my mouth with water from the pitcher. I moistened a corner of the towel and held it to my face for a moment. I was pale and weak and shaking.

My legs unsteady, I walked back to the bed, where I picked up the sheet from the floor and placed it gently over Sally again. I knelt on the floor, at the head of the bed, and kissed Sally on the brow, and stroked her thick dark hair.

"Who did this to you?" I asked.

"Mr. Augustus," she replied, "the rotten, scar-faced bastard. The first time, 'e only used the birch. That was bad enough, but I was bein' well paid for it. I told meself: Well, schoolboys 'ave to suffer the same, and nary a farthin' to shew for it, so wot's the odds? If that's the only way the poor perisher can get 'is thing to stand up, why, 'e's to be pitied. Let 'im 'ave 'is bit o' fun. I'm a strong girl, I says to meself; I can take it. I've known worse; it ain't as bad as 'avin' babies. Gawd, *there's* torture, if you like; rips you apart! So I grits me teeth an' takes the birchin'.

"But when 'e come back the next time, an' Mrs. Jeffers leaves me wif 'im in the special room an' goes out an' locks the door — *this* time things is different. I'm 'angin' there by those shackle things, same as always, standin' on the tips o' me toes, wif me 'eels not touchin' the carpet. But that ain't good enough for Mr. Augustus. 'E cranks up the shackles another inch, so's me toes don't reach the carpet no more, and the weight o' me 'ole body is draggin' on me wrists. Just one little inch, but wot a bloody awful difference! 'That's better,' 'e says, smilin'-like. 'We don't want you to be *too* comfortable, do we?' But that was only the start of it.

"I watch 'im walk over to the wall, where the birches and such is. 'E takes the birch, an' 'e looks at it, an' 'e looks back at me, an' 'e smiles. Then 'e puts it back. 'E takes down a big black whip, then — cruel long thing it is — the gentlemen ain't allowed to use it, Mrs. Jeffers told me — and I says to 'im, 'None o' your teasin', Mr. Augustus. Don't be tryin' to frighten a poor girl, now.' So 'e smiles and 'e puts it back. 'That's a good gentleman,' I says. But then the filthy swine takes down the *cat*. That's the worst of 'em all — bunch o' stiff leather thongs, wif knots in 'em, an' sharp little metal 'ooks. An' this one 'e *don't* put back. This one 'e 'olds on to and walks over to me, where I'm 'angin' there, and 'e looks up into me face — tall as 'e is, 'e 'as to look *up,* because I'm 'angin' 'igher now, you see — an' 'e ain't smilin' any more.

"An' 'e says: 'It is time for you to learn a lesson, my girl. You must come to know your master. Your lord and master. You are proud. Pride is a sin. Sin must be punished. You are spirited. It is time to *break* that spirit. And break it I shall. Break you and tame you and bring you to submission, like the unruly mare that you are!'

"An' then 'e walked aroun' be'ind me an' — an' — 'e used the cat on me! Oh, Gawd, Miss, I never felt such awful pain before in me life! I begged 'im to stop, but 'e wouldn't. I screamed and screamed, at the top o' me lungs, but Mrs. Jeffers never come to 'elp me. Nobody come. 'E only stopped when 'is arm got tired. I 'spect I must 'ave fainted. When I come back to meself, I was still 'angin' there, wif me feet not touchin' the floor, and 'e was gone. I fainted again, and when I woke up, I was in me bed at Mrs. Jeffers's 'ouse, and the girls was tryin' to 'elp me. They told Mrs. Jeffers I needed a doctor, but she said: 'Are you mad? A doctor would report this to the police, and *then* where would we be? This ain't a thing they can wink at. They'd make me tell the name of the man. I can't do that to Mr. Augustus! Our best customer! We must care for the girl ourselves, the best way we can. And we must make sure she doesn't get out. Not in *that* condition. She must *not* be seen!'

"But the girls was that afeared I might die on 'em — they're good souls, good friends — so they 'elped me get out of that; give me money for the 'ackney. I didn't know where to go — so I come back 'ere."

"You came *home,*" I said. "Home, to your husband and children. No one will ever flog you again. And now, you must have a doctor. Just lie there and try to rest — I shall be back in a moment."

I ran downstairs, into the rain, and told Paley to go at once, with all possible speed, to Mr. Cargrave's house and to bring him back without delay. Then I returned to the Booteses' flat and sat in the bedroom, at Sally's side, until the doctor arrived.

When he had finished tending her, and left some medicines and ointments with her husband, we both left in the coach. As we rode, I asked him about Sally's condition.

"She will recover," he said. "But she will be scarred for the rest of her life. Physically, as well as in other ways. I was obliged to stitch some of the worst wounds. Made her breathe a bit of chloroform first. Worked like a charm. I'll remove the stiches in a few days. I assume she did not receive those tender attentions from her husband?" I shook my head. "In a house of ill-fame, then?" I nodded. "I thought as much," he said.

"Have you seen such things before, then, Mr. Cargrave?"

"My dear young lady," he replied, "if I were to tell you the things that I have seen in the course of my medical career, your hair would turn white." We had reached his house, and

Paley reined in the horses, bringing the coach to a stop. "This which we've seen to-night, Miss Summerfield, is as nothing, I assure you. Nothing at all. Of course, I speak relatively, you understand."

He climbed out of the coach and hurried through the rain to his door. Paley drove me home.

If it were my way to place an epigraph, like a head-stone, on each day of this diary, I think I would erect on the present day a fierce verse from Dante's *Inferno*. I have been struggling, of late, with that great work, in the original, and have made my own rough translation of certain passages, although not in the sublime *terza rima* of the author. My anger at those who trade in human females — profiting from their shame and bondage and worse — is reflected most aptly in these lines from Canto XVIII:

> The whips of his tormentors down in Hell
> Cracked on his back. He heard the demons yell:
> "Move on, you pimp! No women here to sell!"

ॐ *Saturday, 29 April*

Diary, I have a confession to make. I am beginning to find the day-to-day recording of my life to be less and less an anticipated joy, and more and more a tedious duty.

Like all new things, I was fascinated by you at first, and could not wait to set down, each day, all my thoughts and feelings; my questions about life; my fears and problems; my observations; my no-doubt-immature stirrings of philosophy. These gushed out of me in the first quarter of the year, as from an unstoppered keg in Papa's brewery, in a strong, steady stream, and were mixed with my reporting of events which I deemed to be worthy of note.

But I must acknowledge that I am, after all, a very young, and possibly shallow, person. I am not a great philosopher or an historian or even a journalist. If my living depended on writing a *feuilleton*, for the newspapers, every day for years and years, I should starve to death. My fund of philosophy is

283

spent; my store of knowledge is empty; the flowing keg is now quite dry.

I suspect that I am suffering from a common complaint among diarists, which might be called Attenuation of the Interest; the symptoms being a withering or wasting-away of the writing arm and a decline of the verbal appetite, following a prolonged period of unnaturally feverish activity.

The cure is simple: it is a strict reduction of diet. Beginning at once, only events of extraordinary interest will be set down in this book. By this practise,

I break off to report that the post has arrived, with a letter for Mamma from Aunt Esmie:

"My dear Melissa, —

"Come at once, all of you. Phoebe is with me — she has been for some little time — and she is now on the point of entering her confinement. It is her wish that you, her father, and her sister be present when the child is born.

"Your always devoted
"Esmeralda"

We leave for the Cotswolds at once. I shall not write more until we return.

May

§

"ARRESTED FOR MURDER"

We returned from the Cotswolds late last night, and we are all of us in the deepest distress. Mamma and Papa look as if they have aged ten years. Papa, in the few days between the time we left and the time of our return, has lost a shocking amount of weight: the flesh has left his body, not in the healthful way of exercise and abstemious diet, but as if it had been burnt away in some awful immolating flame.

When we arrived at Aunt Esmie's house, she met us with a face shrouded in sorrow. "Oh, my dears," she said. "My poor dears. You are too late."

"Too late!" Mamma cried. "Is Phoebe —"

Aunt Esmie nodded, embracing her sister. "Yes, Melissa. Not much above an hour ago, your dear child left this world."

Papa cried, "No!"

"Oh, God in Heaven!" groaned Mamma.

Stripped of words, I burst into a flood of tears.

After a moment, Papa — in a voice more hollow than any I had ever heard from him before — said, "May we see her?"

Aunt Esmie conducted us upstairs into a bedroom. There, in soft candlelight, lay Phoebe, her hands crossed on her breast, her eyes closed, her expression one of infinite peace. Mamma threw herself upon that lifeless form, sobbing uncontrollably.

Papa allowed her to continue thus for a time before he gently put his arms round her shoulders and attempted to lead her away from the bed. "Come, my dear," he said. "This is not Phoebe. Our girl is in the bosom of Abraham. Come away."

"*I will not leave her!*" Mamma cried in a voice of fire.

Aunt Esmie spoke softly to Papa: "Let her stay alone with her child for a time, Wilfrid. You and Pamela come down-stairs with me."

She served us tea. Papa and I discovered that we had been made ravenous by the journey. Whilst we ate and drank, Aunt Esmie answered all of our unasked questions.

"Phoebe came to me some few weeks past — I do not recall precisely when. She was great with child. She asked if she could stay here until the baby was born, and she swore me to secrecy. I agreed, of course — she was my dearly beloved niece — what else could I do? She told me the whole history of her marriage; she told me of her husband's inadequacy; she told me everything, I believe — except the name of her lover. When she felt her confinement approaching, she had a sudden change of heart about the secrecy. She wanted to see you again — both of you — and her mother. She wanted you to be here for the birth. She asked me to write to you. 'Shall I not write to *him* as well?' I asked her. 'He has a father's right.' But she said no. It was a long labour, and painful, but even in the extremity of it, she did not cry out his name. We did all that we could — there is an excellent midwife hereabouts — I called in a physician, too — but our efforts were in vain — God had willed otherwise — and, with a little sigh of . . . I should say contentment . . . her spirit left her body."

Aunt Esmie shook her head forlornly. "I had seen it all, many months ago, on the eve of her marriage. Or I *might* have seen it all, if I had read the signs more clearly. For it was surely there, to be read. It was *all* there, in the cards."

Papa and I chose to let this pass, for neither of us shares Aunt Esmie's faith in gipsy prophecies; and to speak darkly of foretellings *ex post facto,* as Aunt Esmie had just done, is an ac-complishment far too easily achieved.

Papa asked, "Before she died, did she not — say anything?"

"Almost nothing," replied Aunt Esmie. "But, just before the end, she asked about the child — if it was alive; if it was healthy and well formed; its sex. I assured her that she had given birth to a fine baby boy, and I shewed him to her. She smiled at him. I said, 'Tell me his name.' She said he must be called after his father. 'But what is *his* name?' I said. She smiled at me, weakly — and rather roguishly, I think — and said, 'Ah, Aunt Esmie, that would be telling!' Then she gave the little sigh, and was gone."

It was only after a short silence that Papa, as if just coming to a realisation, said, "Then the child — ?"

"Is here, of course," replied Aunt Esmie. "Your grandson is sound asleep, upstairs in my bedroom. He sleeps in the very crib that my dear husband carved for our first-born. But my babe lived for less than an hour, as you know, and no child has occupied that crib until now. It is as if it had been held in reserve — empty all these years — waiting for Phoebe's son. Life metes out such strange, bitter justice sometimes."

"I must see him at once!" Papa exclaimed.

"Naturally," said Aunt Esmie, "but you are *not* to disturb his sleep! We will go upstairs and bring Melissa away from Phoebe, and then all of you, together, will see the boy. Oh, he is a handsome young scamp!"

(Indeed he is, all wrinkled though he be, and fiercely ruddy, from his little toes to the rusty peach-down of his head.)

The funeral service was simple, and took place in the grave-yard of the quaint little rural church where Aunt Esmie worships. The name on the stone (its form decided upon only after much discussion) was: PHOEBE S. BRAITHWAITE. Papa had, at first, wanted it to read PHOEBE SUMMERFIELD, but we could not ignore the fact that her legal name, at the time of her death, had been Braithwaite. To use her maiden name as well as her married name would have been too cumbrous, and so the former was represented only by the initial.

We brought the child away with us, back here to London. He sleeps within range of my eye even at this moment, for I am writing this in our old nursery. We have engaged a good woman, called Penfold, to look after him and to wet-nurse him. She is a friend of Mrs. Pruitt's, and there can be no higher recommendation than that. The servants, of course, had to be told something — but they are "family," and may be trusted to remain discreet.

ॐ *Tuesday, 9 May*

Papa says that he will write to Mr. Braithwaite to-day, telling him of Phoebe's death but saying nothing of the child. "The boy is not his, nor did that poor ignorant man even suspect that Phoebe was carrying him. I see no reason to tell him something that should be kept within this family. Besides, it might distress the poor chap. He is decent enough — none of this was his doing — no point in making him suffer further. And I shall write to Roger; he must be told all, naturally. I would write to young Will if I knew where he was. I shall also place a notice of Phoebe's death in to-morrow's newspapers."

"But what of the baby, Wilfrid?" said Mamma. "He must be christened."

"Yes, he must," Papa agreed, "but not till we know his name. And we will not know that until we know his father's name."

"We may *never* know that," said Mamma.

"The truth will out," Papa insisted. "Somehow, some time, it will out."

"But, Wilfrid —"

Papa grew suddenly stern. "The boy will bear no name other than his father's. It was our daughter's final wish — *and we will honour it.*"

"Yes, Wilfrid," Mamma said, meekly. "To be sure, we will."

ॐ *Wednesday, 10 May*

The notice of Phoebe's death was in the morning edition.

Shortly after Papa had left for the City — a black band on his sleeve, his face lifeless with sorrow — Rutledge came to the drawing-room, where Mamma and I were sitting, still numb from the shock of recent events. "Beg pardon," he said quietly, "but Mr. O'Connor has called."

"O'Connor!" exclaimed Mamma. "That hateful person! What can he want of us, and at such a time?"

"I can not be sure, ma'am," replied Rutledge, "but I think he wishes to express his condolences."

"It is almost too much to bear," Mamma wailed. "Must that horrid scandal-monger mock us even at the moment of our greatest grief?"

"I can say you are receiving no one," Rutledge suggested.

"Mamma," I said, "perhaps we should receive him. If he is sincere, it would not be Christian to send him away."

"Very well, very well." She sighed. "Shew him in, Rutledge."

When Mr. O'Connor was ushered into the drawing-room, he was considerably altered from his customary posture of brusque insolence and ironic *hauteur*. He was quite pale; haggard; his eye was dull; his red hair hung wildly about his face; he seemed *smaller,* somehow, like a spent volcano, once seething and fiery, now collapsed upon itself to become a cold, dark, dead husk. Even Mamma appeared to mark the change in him.

"Will you sit down, Mr. O'Connor?" she said.

"Thank you, Madam, but I shall not impose meself upon you for very long." His voice was hoarse and subdued. "I saw the notice in the paper this morning. Because I have, in the past, caused your family some unpleasantness, I felt I could not allow this sad event to pass by without offering you me most profound sympathy."

Mamma nodded, wearily. "It is good of you," she said, "particularly in view of the fact that the departed person was a stranger to you."

Mr. O'Connor bowed stiffly, to both of us. "I will take me leave," he said. But he hesitated as he turned to the door, and appeared to be reluctant to go. "Mrs. Summerfield," he said, haltingly, "would it be too unseemly of me, too presumptuous, if I were to ask your permission to speak a few words privately to your daughter?"

"To Pamela?" Mamma turned to me. "Do you wish to speak privately with Mr. O'Connor?" she asked me.

"I am willing to hear what he has to say," I replied.

"Then I suppose it would be hopelessly old-fashioned of me to object. Very well, Mr. O'Connor. I think that you are not quite a gentleman, but I also think that you are not stupid enough to take an advantage which could have only disastrous consequences for you."

"You are correct on both counts, Madam," he said, without sarcasm, as if uttering a simple truth.

Mamma arose from her chair. "I must confer with Mrs. Pruitt about luncheon and dinner. Meals must be cooked and served, even when no one has the appetite to eat them. Thank you for calling, sir. It shews a commendable sensibility in you." With great dignity, like a galleon, she sailed slowly out of the room, as Mr. O'Connor opened the door for her.

No sooner had he closed it than his reserve broke and he turned to me in wild despair. "Oh, Miss Summerfield! How cruel, how unjust! How *unbelievable!* Can it be true? Am I not dreaming? Is this not some hideous nightmare from which I must surely awaken?"

I was completely dumbfounded by his behaviour.

"Oh, God!" he cried. "How can I endure it?"

In a flash of revelation, I knew the truth. I was stunned. Still, I felt constrained to say, "What can you mean, Mr. O'Connor? You had not even so much as *met* my sister."

"Met her?" He groaned. "I *loved* her! I loved her from the very deepest recesses of my soul. She was a bright star — a golden angel — the only good and blessed thing in me pathetic life — and now she is gone — for ever! Ah, no, it is too horrible — I will not believe it — it is not *she* who has died — it is somebody else — she is too young, too fair, too good. Say that she is not dead, Miss Summerfield — say that me beloved Phoebe is not dead!"

He had thrown himself into a chair, his face in his hands, and tears were now trickling between his fingers.

I could say only, "Oh, Mr. O'Connor — *dear* Mr. O'Connor —" I felt I must walk over to him and place my hand consolingly upon his bowed head. In his grief, he threw his arms round my waist and, still seated, buried his face in my bosom. I continued to stroke his blazing hair; and it was then that it became clear why he had come to see me last month, in such perturbation: a cryptic mention in a note of mine about a death

292

in our family had led him to fear it had been Phoebe — a fear that had foreshadowed the actual sad event. For him, it was as if she had died twice; he had suffered the agony twice. Poor, poor man.

"She is with God," I said, "and happier now than she has ever been before."

"If I could but believe that!" he said, feelingly, releasing me and rising from the chair. "I would give anything — even me life — if I could put me trust in that belief — if I could share your faith — if I could live in hope that one day, when life is over, I might see her again for an instant, in her heavenly radiance, her glory, just once before the demons drag me down. If only I could believe that!"

"You can," I assured him; "you *can*. And more: believe that you and she will be reunited in Heaven and will dwell together eternally. Turn to God. Open your heart to Him, and He will fill it to overflowing with that belief!"

"This heart!" He looked at me, with a bitter hint of his old ironic smile. "This calloused piece of goods? This dry, cold, hardened lump of leather? I fear it is not fertile soil, Miss Summerfield, if I may mix me metaphors. The seed of faith would not take root and thrive there. It would die."

"You place too low a value on that heart," I replied, "and on yourself. You are not the cynic you pretend to be. You are a man of deep feelings. You are outraged by injustice. You weep for the persecuted and the downtrodden. You fight for those who have not the strength or the spirit or the means to fight for themselves. You truly *believe,* more than anybody I know, that the meek will inherit the earth."

"Take care, Miss Summerfield," he said, "or you will have me canonised. But thank you for those words. To utter them is more than kindness. 'Tis the highest act of charity."

"Take care, or you will have *me* canonised," I said.

He smiled, sadly. "Perhaps the truth is that we are both no more than a pair of poor, bereft creatures — who loved the same sweet angel."

"Oh, yes, that is indeed so, Mr. O'Connor."

"I must not overstay me welcome," he said. "Please make me farewells to your mother. And I should be grateful if you would convey me condolences to your father. He may not accept them from me, for I have caused him much discomfiture, but — " He shrugged.

I could not let him go so soon, with so much unsaid. "How long did you know my sister?" I asked him.

"In terms of time, not long," he answered. "Two months and a little over, I think. But when we were together, all measurements of time and space dissolved — all universal laws were suspended — the planets stopped — we moved in a dimension of our own. You have seen me rooms — they are plain and cluttered; a scribbler's studio, serviceable, without beauty. But when she was there, those rooms became a palace — Eden — Paradise."

"Then *why*," I cried, "why did you not marry her?"

"I *pleaded* with her to marry me! I begged her again and again! It was *she* who refused."

"It can not be that she did not love you."

"No. That was not her reason — although I thought so for a time, 'tis true. She simply said that she could not marry me, and that we must stop seeing each other, because she was about to accept a proposal of marriage from another man. She would not even tell me his name. Some weeks after that — our last meeting — I saw the notice in the papers. She had married someone called Braithwaite. I came very near to killing meself. I took to drink. I became an insufferable boor — or perhaps I should say I became *more* of an insufferable boor than I already had been. I cursed her in me heart; I cursed all women. And then — only yesterday — I had a letter from her."

"Yesterday?"

"I know now that she was already dead by the time I received it." He reached into his pocket and handed me the letter. I recognised Phoebe's hand at once. "Please read it," he said. "She would have wished you to do so, I think."

I opened the letter and read it:

"My beloved Rhys, —

"I hesitated before writing this, because it is my hope that, by this time, you will have begun to forget me, and I should not wish to open old wounds and cause fresh pain.

"No, I tell a lie. Selfishly, I want you to remember me as vividly as I remember you. And oh, my dear, I have remembered you so very clearly — every second of every minute of every hour of every day since last we met.

"Those times we spent together — I cherish them, and guard jealously the memory of each detail. Do you remember how we would talk for hours, on every subject under the sun, lying side by side in your bed? And then, suddenly hungry, how we would crouch at your fire-place, wrapped only in blankets, toasting crumpets, great mountains of them, wolfing them down like savages, and licking the butter from each other's fingers? Then back to bed again?

"Do you remember, as I do, sharing a jelly at the circus? Applauding Jenny Lind at the Opera? Then back to your rooms, and reading poetry to each other — Byron, Shelley, Rochester? Do you remember my body, as I do yours? — that white Irish skin of yours, delicate as a girl's, so easily burnt by the sun; the lovely bristles of copper on your chest and limbs and elsewhere — I treasure and recall each several single hair.

"I know, dear Rhys, how cruelly I hurt you when I refused to be your wife. You thought I did not love you. I wanted you to think that. For a marriage between you and a Summerfield could never be. I know full well the earnestness and intensity with which you throw yourself into your work. You are no churl who pipes whatever tune is asked for by whatever man will pay. You are dedicated; indefatigable; relentless — and you are without mercy when you are hot on the scent of the merciless. You love me — but you hate my world, my family, my father, his business, the laws that protect him, the 'legally sanctioned conspiracy that squeezes the lower classes like so many grapes in a wine-press' — your words, my darling, and they are good words. They are the words of a fine and dedicated man, a man of purpose, a man who will never compromise or bend the knee. Married to me, you would not have then ceased to attack my father's world and all in which he believes (believes as strongly and sincerely as *you* believe in your own high principles, my sweet, intractable Rhys!).

"That is why I did not marry you. That is why I finally ac-

cepted — after many declinations — the proposal of a respectable and decent man who, in his own way, truly loves me,
even though I do not, and never could, love him.

"Forgive me, my own dear Rhys, for waiting so long to
reveal my reasons. I could not tell them to you whilst you held
me in your arms — for you are the most persuasive Welsh-
and-Irish spinner of blarney; the most irresistible of Gaelic
spell-binders — and you would have brushed aside my reasons as easily as you so often brushed a lock of hair from my
forehead, saying, 'The better to kiss you, me dear.'

"We probably shall not meet again in this world, my love;
and I know you think that we shall not meet in the next. You
have denied yourself the greatest comfort we poor mortals
have — and I admire the stern tenacity with which you reject
that comfort and 'go it alone' in the cold and frightening Godless universe you have chosen. When you, from time to time,
remember me, think of me as one who, although married to
another, has ever in her soul been true to you — only you.
And let those lines of Lord Rochester's which we both love
echo and re-echo in your heart:

> Then talk not of inconstancy,
>   False hearts and broken vows;
> If I, by miracle, can be
> This live-long minute true to thee,
>   'Tis all that Heav'n allows.

"The live-long minute of which that poet sings will be the
longest in the history of Creation; an unending instant; a moment that will stretch out to the utmost distant corner of eternity — and in that bright corner, I shall be waiting for you,
Rhys!

"Your true love,
"Phoebe"

My eyes were flooded with tears by the time I had read the
final line. I folded the letter and handed it back to him.

He kissed it and put it back in his pocket. Then another cry
of anguish was ripped from him: "The dear, *foolish* girl! Did

she not know that she was worth all the noble efforts and good causes in the world? One smile from her, one glance, was worth far more than any of them — I valued her smallest toe nail above the most high-minded purpose! Did she not *know* that? I would have scrapped it *all* for her! I would have taken the meanest job of work — sweeping chimneys, digging ditches. I'd have become a chartered accountant and trudged into the City every day in a silly hat with all the other drones, and sat on a high stool, slaving at a desk, doing the most stupid, pointless, dullest drudgery — if only, at the end of work, every day, I could have come home to *her.*"

He breathed deeply, to steady himself. He was silent for a moment before he said: "The notice in the morning edition gave no details. How did she die? What was the cause? No — don't tell me. If her death was lingering — if she suffered — if she was in terrible pain — I could not bear to know it."

I longed to tell him: It was a joyous pain; a mother's proud travail; the glorious pain of giving birth to the child of her own true love.

But I had not the right to tell him that. To the very end, she insisted that he must not know of the child. And yet the poor dear was so vacillating when she lay at the point of death — telling Aunt Esmie that the boy should be called after his father, but refusing to divulge the father's name — she was confused, contradictory. Oh, if only I could rend the veil of death and speak to her, plead with her, beg her to reveal her true wishes! If only her *revenant* spirit could come to me and tell me what to say! For does not Mr. O'Connor have rights? Does not a father deserve to know that he has a son?

I could not sort it out — not then — I needed time — I needed to think — and so I brazenly purloined those words Mamma had said to comfort me when Sophie died. I said to him:

"One moment, she was alive; in the next, she was dead. She could not have even known the point when she passed from the one state into the other."

"Thank you for telling me that," he said. "I will go now."

"Mr. O'Connor —"

"Yes?"

297

"Please do not be a stranger to this house. Come back — often — and speak to me about Phoebe. As you said, we both loved her."

"We must see about that," he said, indecisively, and took my hand and held it for a moment to his lips, not in that hungry, moaning manner of Signor Olivo's, but in a simple, manly way.

"Your hand," he said, softly. "Your strong little hand. It is just like hers."

I relieved Nurse Penfold for an hour or so to-day, in the nursery. Phoebe's little boy slept the whole time. Now that I know he is not the son of Cumberland, he looks even more beautiful to me, and the sparse strands of his head seem to have taken on a more pronouncedly reddish tint.

I passed most of the hour just looking at that dear tiny creature and admiring him. How I yearned to tell Mr. O'Connor that he is the father of this handsome fellow! I prayed for some sign to guide me.

Idly, I browsed among the old toys and books that used to occupy us when we were children. How long ago those days seem to me now. Our old music-box still played the "Greensleeves" tune, but a bit rustily — "Alas, my love, you . . . wrong to cast . . . 'teously" — with a limping gait and metallic wheezes in the place of missing notes. Here was my Mother Goose book, the pages still glued together, not by the maligned Ridgely twins, but by naughty Willy. And here was one of the many albums in which Phoebe and I had written our childish verses and word games. There I saw lines written in my hand, and other lines written in hers. My own has changed through the years, but Phoebe's fine hand remained curiously the same even into her adult life. That probably signifies something innately steadfast in her and changeable in me.

Here I read again my old sentence: "If lace over veils enhances prettiness, let's use more, surely." (I *still* love plums!) And here was one of Phoebe's that I had not remembered —

"Tearful eyes, loving lips, hearts in misery!" — which strangely seemed to foretell the tragedy of her last months in this world. How pointedly and poignantly those childhood words (no doubt inspired by some extravagant romance she had been reading) described Mr. O'Connor and herself; for indeed his heart is in misery, and his eyes were tearful yesterday. His heart would be lightened somewhat, I was certain, if he could but be told that a son born of his flesh and Phoebe's is resting safely under our roof.

I looked again at Phoebe's old sentence, and my spine froze suddenly into one long icicle. Somebody had entered the room without opening the door, and was standing directly behind me, I felt, looking over my shoulder. Deathly afraid, I none the less turned quickly — but there was no-one. I looked once more at the album page, and felt my scalp become alive. If there had been a mirror in the room, I know I should have seen the hairs of my head standing stiffly up; for, by the agency of miracle, or chance, or visitation, or some awesome twist in the mysterious texture of time, I now read Phoebe's childhood sentence as an acrostic, and saw, with a shock that stopped my heart, that "Tearful eyes, loving lips, hearts in misery!" harboured the urgent message —

Tell him!

ℬ *Friday, 12 May*

I knew, immediately I awoke this morning, what I must do. I dressed and breakfasted; and, as soon as Papa had left the house, I said — still sitting at table — that I wished Paley to ready the family coach for me at once. My tone must have seemed unusually mature, for Mamma said merely, "Very well." She rang for Rutledge. "Where are you going?"

I had prepared my answer to this question beforehand. "I could say that I am going shopping," I replied, "but I mean to tell no lie about this matter. And yet I can not reveal the whole of it, Mamma; not yet. I am going to see somebody by whose agency that innocent little boy upstairs may become christened, sooner than any of us expected that he might be."

"But who *is* this somebody?"

"If all goes as I plan, you will know that very soon, Mamma."

"I wish to know it now."

"I may not tell you now."

"You defy me?"

"Dear Mamma, reflect: in less than a fortnight, I will be eighteen years old. If I were of royal blood, I should then be of age."

"You are *not* of royal blood."

"Neither am I a child. You must trust me, Mamma. All will be made clear before long. May I have the use of the family coach — or must I hire a hackney?"

Rutledge entered the room just then, in response to Mamma's summons.

"Rutledge," she said, "how soon can Paley have the coach ready for Miss Pamela?"

"Beg pardon, ma'am, but Mr. Summerfield took the coach into the City this morning. However, Paley can ready one of the other carriages in no time."

"Please instruct him to do so."

"Yes, ma'am." He left the room.

"Thank you, Mamma," I said.

"You have asked me to trust you," she responded. "Very well; I shall. Please make certain that my trust is not misplaced."

"You have my word on that."

"It is all that I ask."

Soon after, Paley took me to Chelsea and, according to my instructions, waited for me as I paid a call on Rhys O'Connor.

"Miss Summerfield!" he said, as he opened his door. "I was not expecting you."

I wasted no time. After I had seated myself, and had declined his offer of tea, I said: "Mr. O'Connor, I have reason to believe that you are not repelled by me."

"Repelled? Indeed not," he said, settling into his decrepit *chaise-longue*.

"On a recent occasion, you told me that I am uncommonly attractive."

"And so you are."

"On a later occasion, you kissed my hand — most feelingly I think. Pray correct me if I am mistaken."

He could not suppress a small smile. "You are not mistaken."

"Excellent. Now, permit me to make a confession. My heart belongs to another. His name need not enter this conversation. He and I have — that is to say — I am no longer a maiden."

"My dear Miss Summerfield, why should I be made privy to these revelations? I beg of you —"

"No, hear me out, please. That other gentleman — although I freely own that my heart still yearns for him, and may continue to do so for quite some time to come — has left London. I probably shall not ever see him again. But I assure you that the proposal which I am about to make to you does not — I repeat emphatically, does *not* — mean that I am in any way 'in trouble,' as I believe the phrase is. Am I being clear to you, Mr. O'Connor?"

He scratched that unkempt mass of red hair. "I — *believe* so," he said. "That is to say — I know what the expression 'in trouble' signifies in this context, and I accept your assurance that you are *not* in that kind of trouble. What is the proposal you mean to make to me? I admit that I am consumed by curiosity."

"Mr. O'Connor," I said, sitting up with a very straight backbone, "it is my urgent desire that you and I be married."

"What?"

It is no exaggeration to say that Mr. O'Connor, at precisely this point in our conversation, fell off the *chaise-longue* — not entirely from force of his astonishment, perhaps, for the rickety wooden arm-rest, on which he had been placing most of his weight, suddenly gave way, sending him almost, though not quite, to the floor. Recovering his balance, he held the detached arm-rest in his hands, as if studying it. Looking up at me, he then said, "Would you be so kind as to repeat your last remark?"

"I want you to marry me," I said.

"You do me great honour, but why on earth should I marry you?"

"In order that a baby, now sleeping safely in our house, may enjoy the advantages of a full complement of parents; and so that he may be christened with the name that his mother wished him to have."

"I am covered with confusion," he said. "What baby? *What* name?"

"Rhys O'Connor."

"Rhys O —— *My* name? — but —"

"His dead mother wished him to be called after his father. Must I tell you more than that?"

He blinked. He appeared to be stupefied. And then his face became illuminated by understanding. "Phoebe? She had a child?"

"Your child."

"She said so?"

"She never spoke your name."

"Then —"

"Her husband is incapable of being a father. And you are the only man she ever loved." He was silent, and so I added, "Besides, you have but to see the red hair on the little nipper."

He seemed to be still stunned. At length, he spoke, quite softly: "A child . . ."

"An adorable child."

"A boy, you say?"

"A fine strong boy."

He smiled to himself. "A son," he said. "Phoebe's son."

"And yours."

"The child of our love."

"Yes. Of that great love. Mr. O'Connor, I know that I can not hope to usurp her place in your heart — indeed, I should not wish to — and I know that I am no match to her in beauty — but then, *you* are no match to my captain in beauty, and can never replace him in my affections — and yet I do not find you altogether displeasing — and I think you do not find me so. We can make a good marriage. We shall have other children. We may, with time, grow to love one another, a little. There would be a large marriage settlement. You should never again want for money. You told me that you would have been willing to abandon all your crusades and causes for

Phoebe's sake — will you not make a different sacrifice for her son? For your son?"

"My son," he said, as if he had heard no other word of mine. "I must see him."

"To be sure, but this matter of our marriage must be settled between us first."

He looked at me with amazement. "Marriage? That is quite out of the question."

"Indeed it is not, sir! Why do you say so?"

He reached for my hand and took it in his. He smiled. " 'Tis a fair colleen y'are," he said, lapsing into the brogue and then lapsing out of it again. "A dear, a *very* dear girl. But you must not make such a sacrifice. To marry a man whom you have so recently despised — may still somewhat despise — just to give your sister's child a name. It would never do, Miss Summerfield; it would never do at all. You would be throwing yourself away. It is good and generous of you; it is great-hearted — but it would be wrong — quite wrong — to repeat your sister's mistake and marry a man whom you do not love."

"Oh, Mr. O'Connor," I said, my eyes a-swim with tears, "I do not despise you; truly I do not. And as for love — I know I am a foolish girl — a child — but I know something of what love is — of what many forms it takes — how curiously it can flower from barren soil — and I tell you that, for what reason I can not say — whether it be that Phoebe loved you, and all she loved I must love, too — or whether it be the thought of that dear infant who resembles her and resembles you — and who is part of *me,* in a way, of my flesh, because my sister was part of my flesh — or whether it be the nobility and fairness of all that you do — or the unhesitating way you searched for Sally and found her — or the way you rhyme words so cleverly — or your blue eyes — or that unspeakable red bird's-nest that passes for your hair — whether it be all or none of these, you must believe me when I tell you, Mr. O'Connor, that I *do* love you — I love you very much!"

He stroked my hand. "Well, well," he said, "it is very fine of you to say it — and I will admit that you could melt a heart of stone when you speak like that, in that way that you have — such a pretty vixen you are! — but, for the moment, there is one thing, and one thing only, that you must do. You must take me to see me son."

I wiped my tears with my handkerchief. "Yes," I said, "of course you must see him."

"At once."

"No — not at once. You must give me time to prepare my parents. It will be a shock to them when I tell them that the father of Phoebe's child is Rhys O'Connor. We must do this gradually. I will tell them to-day — gently, by stages. And you will come dine with us to-morrow evening. At that time, we shall all have many matters to discuss. And you will meet young Rhys."

"Very well," he said. "Till to-morrow, then."

ॐ *Saturday, 13 May*

Yesterday evening, during dinner, I informed Mamma and Papa, as gently as I could, that the baby's father is Rhys O'Connor.

What cries of incredulity! What oaths (from Papa) of indignation! What long, chilling silences of numbed astonishment! The food before us went untouched and grew quite cold.

"You can not be serious," said Mamma.

"It is one of her little games," Papa assured her. "A riddle or conundrum of some sort. A jest. Come now, Princess, own up to it. I shan't scold. I enjoy a joke as much as the next man."

"It is a *kind* of joke," I began to say.

"There! You see? I knew it!"

"But not that kind. A joke played on us by Fate." Slowly, and only after a deal of talking, they came to believe, if not like, the truth about the child's paternity. I wanted them to think no ill of Mr. O'Connor — I insisted that he was not a calloused seducer; that he had begged to marry Phoebe; and I shewed them her last letter to him, which he had allowed me to borrow. I told them what he had told me — that he would have given up all his pamphleteering for her, if he had but known her reasons for refusing to marry him. I did *not* tell

304

them that I had made a proposal of marriage to him — and had been declined — but I did say that I had invited him here to dinner on the following night.

Papa expostulated, "To dinner! At this table? *That* chap?"

"He is not such a bad sort, really," I said, "when one begins to know him better."

"And," Mamma reminded him, "he is apparently the father of our grandson."

Papa shook his head in that spasmodic way I have seen dogs and cats do, when they have got a flea in the ear. "O'Connor!" he said. "Of all people! It ravages reason! But I suppose we must receive him."

And receive him we did, this evening.

He was extremely courteous to my parents, and uncharacteristically deferential. When Papa asked him if he would drink a drop of sherry before dinner, he replied, "Thank you, sir, but if you will forgive me impatience, I would first of all like to see me son."

"I suppose that is a reasonable request," said Papa. "Melissa?"

"I shall ask Nurse Penfold to bring him down," said Mamma.

"Oh, please, let us not disturb him," Mr. O'Connor said. "May I not visit the nursery?"

"Yes, if you wish. We shall all do so. Come."

Upstairs, in the nursery, Mr. O'Connor gazed fondly down on his sleeping son. He whispered to Nurse Penfold, "Do you think I might hold him?"

"If you promise not to drop him, sir," she said, picking up the baby and carefully transferring him to Mr. O'Connor's unaccustomed arms.

He smiled at the precious bundle; then, turning to us, he said, "I fear he looks irretrievably Celtic."

"Perhaps he'll grow out of it," said Papa, with a grunt.

Mr. O'Connor returned the sleeping infant to Nurse Penfold. "I'll take that sherry now, sir, if I may — or something a bit stronger, if it's to be got."

"As it happens," said Papa, "I have a bottle of Irish whisky downstairs."

"The wine of me country," said Mr. O'Connor.

During dinner, I reminded all of us that Phoebe had wished the boy to bear his father's name.

"And so he shall," said our guest, "for he will be an O'Connor."

"Not Rhys?" I said.

"Your sister, if I have understood you aright, did not specify the name Rhys. As she did not, I think O'Connor is sufficient."

Mamma asked, "And what of his Christian name?"

"I should like to call him Brian, after me father. In point of fact, I am bound to do so. When he was dying, I promised him that if I were ever to sire a son, I would call the boy after him."

"Brian O'Connor," said Papa, rolling the name about in his mouth and tasting it like a wine. "It has a good sound to it."

"I am glad that you think so, sir. And now, I wonder what you will think when I ask your permission to take the hand of your younger daughter in marriage?"

Papa dropped his fork. Mamma looked at me. For my part, I was not much less surprised than my parents.

"Pamela?" said Papa. "You want to marry *Pamela?*"

"If she will accept me, I can think of nobody on Earth whom I should liefer have as me wife and as the mother of me children."

"But this is most precipitately sudden!" said Papa. "We scarcely know you. Only yesterday, we learned that you are the father of Phoebe's child. Now you ask to marry her sister. My brain is reeling!" He turned for aid to Mamma. *"Melissa?"* he said, plaintively.

Mamma took all in stride. "Wilfrid, my dear, we must not forget that we are living in an advanced age. Things are no longer as they were in our youth. This is, after all, the Nineteenth Century. We have seen many marvels — gas-lighting, the railways — I need not name them all. Before long, we shall very probably have a monarch exactly as young as Pamela. This alone may have a profound influence upon our society. Youth will be served. The old must give way to the new. The time was when young persons did only what their parents dictated. Marriages were arranged for them. Perhaps it was a better way of doing things; perhaps it was not. *Autres temps, autres mœurs.* To-day, they will have their own way, no matter what we say. Therefore, what have you and I to do with it? The decision rests entirely with Pamela. However" — and here she smiled at me and at Mr. O'Connor — "if my opinion were to be solicited, I should say that I think it is an *excellent* match. In many ways, not the least of which is from the standpoint of the child."

"Thank you, Mrs. Summerfield," said our guest.

"Oh, a very pretty speech, indeed!" Papa growled. "But what am I to — that is — how the devil — ?" He threw his napkin to the table. His face was quite flushed. "Damn it all, Princess, do *you* want to marry this fellow?"

"I do, Papa — very, very much."

Papa seemed to be talking to himself: "These past few months — Willy — Phoebe — the baby — now *this* — how is a man expected to receive such shocks — such surprises?" Suddenly, a new thought entered his mind, and his eyes narrowed in suspicion. He pointed an accusing index finger at Rhys, as straight and as menacing as a pistol. "See here, O'Connor. Are the pair of you hiding something from me? Have you played fast and loose with Pamela, as well as with Phoebe? Have you put another daughter of mine in the family way, damn you?"

"Papa!" I exclaimed.

"Wilfrid, *please,*" said Mamma.

Rhys, turning to us, said, "Mr. Summerfield has every right to ask that question, considering me behaviour with Phoebe —"

"And considering your reputation for Godlessness and radicalism, as well!" shouted Papa. "A man like you knows no restraints. You flout religion, law, authority — you make your own rules of morality — you attack me and my business, and then, as the crowning touch in your plan to embarrass me, you seduce my daughter — *both* of my daughters, more than likely! You *kill* Phoebe — she lies dead in a churchyard because of you and your spawn — and then you have the insufferable arrogance to sit here at my own table and ask for

Pamela's hand — as calmly as you might ask me to pass the salt!" Papa smashed his fist down on the table, rattling every dish. *"No!"* he roared. "I won't have it! Do you hear me? I — will — not — *have it!"*

He leapt up from the table, upsetting his wine-glass, drenching the cloth; and stamped furiously out of the room, with a powerful slam of the door.

A span of painful silence ensued.

At last, Rhys stood to his feet and said, quietly, "I think I shall be leaving now. Thank you for dinner, Mrs. Summerfield."

Mamma was firm. "Nonsense, sir! We have scarcely touched the first course! Sit down . . . *sit down, I said!"* He did, like a shot. "The three of us will finish our dinner. We will chew each mouthful slowly and thoroughly, as the doctors tell us we should. We will enjoy every course. We will sip the appropriate wines. We will converse. We will endeavour to know each other. We will be in no hurry to get to the end of the meal. Then, in an hour or so, we will join Mr. Summerfield in the drawing-room and drink our coffee with him. By that time, I trust that his temper will have cooled. And now I shall summon Rutledge. I think he has been discreetly avoiding the dining-room." She fluttered the little bell near at hand.

She then turned to me. "Pamela, I shall ask you only one question. *Are* you pregnant?"

"No, Mamma! Mr. O'Connor and I have never —"

"You need say no more. If you are not pregnant, there is no need to rush into this marriage. I suggest, subject to your approval, that we set the date for the thirtieth of June. Does that suit you?"

"Oh, *yes,* Mamma."

"Do you agree, Mr. O'Connor?"

He could only nod submissively.

"Then that's settled. You will be a June bride, my dear. A small wedding, of course. We are, after all, in mourning. Ah, Rutledge, there you are. You may serve the *entrée.* And please pour our guest a glass of brandy. He appears to feel the need of it."

It was not *quite* as settled as Mama had supposed. Papa had retired to his bed, not to the drawing-room. Rhys was obliged to leave without resolving Papa's objections.

But this morning — during breakfast, before church —Papa and I had it out. He was the first to speak. "You attract the most objectionable young men, Princess. I can't think why. That Ormond chap — I liked him at first, but he soon revealed himself to be most unsuitable. And now this awful pamphleteer! This Nihilist, whose goal in life is to destroy the foundations of our society! This man without morals, without honour; this cynical seducer of your poor dead sister!"

"Rhys was Phoebe's lover, yes," I said, "and she was his dearly beloved. There was no seduction. He pleaded with her to become his wife — not because she was with child; he did not even know that until after she died, but because he loved her, honourably, deeply. As for his scruples, when his tests shewed Summerfield's lager to be free of impurities, he said so in the public prints. Those verses which caused you nearly to sue him — I have seen the early draughts, and I am convinced that they were not meant to refer to you. Yes, he is a critic of our society; yes, he is a sceptic — but he is not a cynic. There is a great difference. He detests injustice, with a fine, righteous anger. He is a dedicated man. And yet he was willing to give up all that for Phoebe's sake. Such was the sincerity of his love. As for myself, Papa, I shall not require him to throw his convictions into the dust-bin — I tell you that in all candour beforehand. I do not want to change him. I think he is a fine man, and I love him as he is."

Looking past me at Mamma, he said, "Why are the young so righteous?"

"Somebody must be," replied Mamma.

Papa arose from the table. "You will excuse me," he said, coldly. "And you need not expect me to escort you to church this morning. I am in no humour to sit still and listen to pious sermons — particularly not in the company of a girl who condones adultery, bastardy, and atheism."

He left the room. I made to follow him, but Mamma re

strained me, saying, "Not now, my dear. Allow him to smooth his ruffled feathers in his own good time. Finish your breakfast. We must not be late for worship."

Later, during luncheon, Papa was very cool and said nothing until I took up the thread of our earlier conversation. "Among other things," I began, "we must consider Brian."

"Who?"

"The *baby*, Papa. Little Brian. He needs parents — two in number, one of each sex, lawfully married to each other. What better solution than that those parents should be his true father and his aunt? The boy is half-Summerfield, after all, and his legal mother will be a Summerfield. In a few years' time, when other children will have come along, we shall have all but forgotten that he is only the *half*-brother of his siblings. Indeed, he will be better than half — a two-thirds brother or three-quarters brother — oh, *bother* the arithmetic! — because his mother and theirs will have been sisters. All will blend into one united, happy family." I reached for Papa's hand across the table. "Please be an old dear and give us your blessing."

He grumbled, "It is all so irregular — so sudden — so upsetting."

"I know it is, Papa, and I know how difficult it is for you, and I am sorry."

"How can you be sure that he isn't after your money, as Captain Ormond was?"

I then told Papa something Rhys had said last night, as he was leaving. "He said he would never take a farthing from you, Papa. He said he would not live on the sweat of children."

"*Did* he, by God! The impudent Irish ape! Does he think he can support you and the baby, and the babies to come, on the income from his damned seditious scribblings? Love in a garret? Bread and kisses? We shall see about that. He may starve himself if he chooses — it's no affair of mine — but my daughter and my grandchildren will not starve! He will take my money, like it or not!"

Once again, he stamped furiously out of the room and locked himself in his study. We did not set eyes on him until the evening meal.

There was no conversation during the soup or the *entrée* or the sweet, but during the savoury, I made bold to murmur, "Papa?" He merely grunted in acknowledgement. I went on: "At luncheon — and pray correct me if I misrender you — I do believe you implied that you stood ready to provide Mr. O'Connor with a generous dowry if he and I are wed." He grunted again, but did not deny it. "Am I then to assume, Papa, that you no longer object to our marriage?"

"Object? Of course I object! I object most strenuously! But —" He delivered himself up of a great sigh. "But you will have your own way, I expect. You usually do." There was the beginning of a twinkle in his eyes. Then he sobered again, and said, more to himself than to me, "My name. My family's name. A few years hence, it will cease to be. Your brother will not have issue. Roger, my only surviving male sibling, has never married. My name will die."

"But your line, your blood, will not die," I reminded him. "Brian, and the children I shall bear, will pass it on. 'What's in a name?' "

He smiled wanly. "You and your everlasting Shakespere," he said.

🌙 *Monday, 15 May*

Yesterday, I wrote to Rhys, telling him that Papa had come round and informing him of the strict conditions laid down by my parents relating to our conduct in the weeks ahead. We are never, not even once, to see each other alone, until after our wedding, on the thirtieth of June. He may come to tea, but there must always be others present; and he is not to call for me to take me riding or to the theatre or for any other reason. Needless to add, I am expressly forbidden to visit his rooms.

To-day, I received this brief reply from him:

"My dear, —
"I accept all conditions — grudgingly, and with a long face — provided that I am invited to tea as soon as possible. By return of post, perhaps?

"With love,
"Rhys

"P.S. Kiss Brian for me, please."

I immediately replied, inviting him to tea to-morrow. The same post that had brought his note also brought a missive addressed to Papa:

"My dear Mr. Summerfield, —

"I can not begin to tell you what a blow I suffered upon reading your letter about the passing of my young wife. I hope that you and your family can believe that I loved her deeply — not as other men love, it may be, and not in the way she wished and deserved to be loved — but deeply, none the less. Why else should I have married her? Why else should I have sought her hand for so long? Of all human emotions, love is surely the strangest. Those few months in which she shared my house I shall always remember as the happiest period of my life.

"Please know that my heart goes out to you and your family in this heavy time — the heaviest, I have no doubt, that you have yet endured. Please know, as well, that if any unhappiness suffered by Phoebe or by you was of my making, I most heartily repent of it and beg your forgiveness.

"I shall not intrude myself upon your lives any further. But when you visit that dear lady's grave and place flowers upon it, I hope you will lay down a blossom in the name of

"The sorrowful
"E. Braithwaite"

Tuesday, 16 May

Rhys came to tea. His hair was neatly brushed. He managed Mamma most admirably (considering his generally rough-hewn manners), although perhaps with not quite the polished charm Giles brought to bear in like circumstances. He appeared to be a trifle nervous, and at one point came very near to dropping his plate.

"Pamela," said Mamma shortly afterwards, "perhaps Mr. O'Connor would like to hear you play that lovely medley of Tom Moore's Irish songs: 'The Minstrel Boy,' 'The Harp That Once Through Tara's Halls,' 'Believe Me if All Those —' "

He laughed. "Pardon me, Mrs. Summerfield, but as much as I admire the skills of Tom Moore, I fear I lack loyalty to the tunes of me father's people. I would much prefer to hear something by Mozart or, better still, Beethoven."

"You would?" I asked, pleased. "Then you shall." I opened the pianoforte and played for him *Für Elise*.

He was most appreciative, clapping decorously and saying, "Very prettily played, Miss Summerfield."

"Thank you. I think, however, that there would be no objections raised if you were to call me Pamela."

"Ah," he said with a smile, "if I were to call you Pamela, what other familiarities might not follow? Your mother understands, I am sure, the reason for these forms. To say 'Miss Summerfield' at once puts a bridle on me aspirations, a restraint upon me natural feelings; whereas, when I utter the name 'Pamela,' all mental barricades dissolve, I feel a dangerous sense of freedom, even of licence, and I can not trust meself to remain at a respectful distance from you. Words are magical: they can be shackles of constraint; they can also be cudgels to strike off those shackles."

"Well said, Mr. O'Connor," purred Mamma. "And yet I think you may address my daughter by her Christian name without undue peril. Perhaps you over-estimate the value of formality."

"I do *not* over-estimate the strength of me own passions," he replied. "I use the less-familiar form, not to placate propriety — I care little for what society deems proper or improper — but because I know too well the powers pent up within me." He turned in my direction now, looking into my eyes. "And I know that the loosening of but a single shackle would send me headlong into your daughter's arms. For I love her. I love her more each day, and at night in the cheerless gloom of me lodgings, I long to be with her. If you have ever thought, Mrs. Summerfield, that I wish to marry her because it would be a convenient arrangement for me son, or because I see in her a reflection of her sister, I urge you to put by such thoughts entirely. I love her for herself; for her own dear, sweet, delightful, spirited self — and that love is so near to bursting the confines of me heart that I *dare* not, until she and I are alone on our wedding night, call her other than Miss Summerfield."

How clever of Rhys to make such an ardent avowal of love to me — under Mamma's very nose.

Fanny (which is the name I have given the orange tabby that has adopted us since the death of Sophie) has acquired a suitor. He is a motley fellow, mostly white, but with grey splotches here and there, and a tail completely ringed by alternating bands of dark and light grey. He slinks about, with a furtive bent-leg crouch, and dashes off whenever a human approaches him; but Fanny holds him in slavish enchantment.

I think of him as The White Knight, because his behaviour towards her is so chivalric. He is not rudely familiar, but keeps a respectful distance between him and his beloved. Sometimes, if he forgetfully draws an inch too near to her in the garden, offending her sense of propriety, she will turn and hiss at him in regal reprimand, and he will back off, like a courtier bowing his way backwards out of his queen's presence.

He makes no demands of her; he seems content to sit by the hour, sometimes with the windows of the garden door between them, watching her, no doubt admiring her, possibly protecting her from other, grosser admirers. For her part, she gives him no encouragement, and is all haughtiness and cold disdain. His plaintive, love-lorn cries of "Ao? Ao?" would thaw the iciest heart; but not hers.

I feel sorry for the poor fellow. Such a totality of devotion, with no reward whatsoever. I am minded of the lines of Mr. Keats —

> Oh what can ail thee, knight-at-arms,
> Alone and palely loitering?

(He *is* pale, and he *does* sit alone as he loiters.) I feel like crying out to him — in words from the same poem — "La Belle Dame sans Merci hath thee in thrall!"

Perhaps I shall change Fanny's name to La Belle Dame. It is much more appropriate to her character.

The King is planning a gala birthday ball for Princess Victoria, to take place on the 24th of this month — which is, of course, my birthday as well. And the most exciting thing about it is that — *I am invited!*

(Along with Mamma and Papa, of course.)

The invitation came about through the good offices of Lord Merlyngton, who, in talking with His Majesty, happened to mention that he knew a young lady who had been born on the same day as the Princess, and who is the daughter of one of his most prominent subjects. King William's interest was aroused: he said that he would like to meet me, and expressed the opinion that the Princess might also be pleased to make my acquaintance. Lord Merlyngton said, "Then perhaps the Summerfields and their charming daughter — whose birthday it will also be — might be invited to the ball?" The King is reported to have replied, "A splendid notion, my dear fellow! Please see to it."

Bless Lord Merlyngton! I have never liked him very much, but with this one kindness he has redeemed himself in my eyes.

Mamma and I will require new gowns, of course, and Mrs. Forbes has been duly notified.

(Dearest Phoebe, forgive us for accepting this invitation in our period of mourning — but we can not refuse the *King!*)

I am in an absolute state about the coming ball!

Rhys teases me about it. At tea to-day, he said, "I quite understand why the *Princess* is celebrating her eighteenth birthday. But why are you? She will reach her majority on that day — but you will not. Each birthday brings her closer to the throne — not so you. In your life, each birthday brings you closer only to the grave. Is that sufficient cause for celebration?"

I tapped his knuckles, scoldingly. "You are merely envious that *you* have not been invited!"

"Envious? Not likely. All that bowing and scraping? No,

thank you! Still — if my presence *were* to be commanded, what a scalding article I should write about the silly shindig."

⅌ *Saturday, 20 May*

Mamma returned from an afternoon outing scarcely in time to change and receive our guests for to-day's at-home; so I was obliged to work with Mrs. Pruitt in selecting and approving refreshments. Even Rutledge, so knowledgeable about such matters, was temporarily absent on some errand or other, and the entire task fell upon me.

"It is good for you," said Mamma. "You are almost eighteen, and you have never known a moment's responsibility. Next month, you will become a wife — and a hostess. High time that you learned a few things, don't you agree?"

"Yes, Mamma," I said — and, of course, she is right (but is a woman's most important duty that of deciding whether cucumber or watercress sandwiches shall be served for tea?).

⅌ *Sunday, 21 May*

As we were riding home from church this morning, Mamma said: "I understand that Mr. O'Connor is some variety of freethinker. I hope that his beliefs — or lack of them — will not cause him to refuse a church ceremony when you and he are married? Perhaps his idea of a wedding is simply jumping over a broomstick, like gipsies?"

"I have never discussed it with him, Mamma."

"Then I suggest that you do so at the first opportunity. It will not *do* that a bishop's granddaughter should be married in some pagan rite."

The happy news of the birthday ball, and my last-minute flurry of responsibility yesterday, quite took my mind off the calendar, and I completely forgot that last night was a time of the full moon.

We were all horribly reminded of the fact, however, by this morning's newspapers. Last night, a woman named Maude Bates was murdered in Hyde Park. The crime bore every sign of having been done by The Full Moon Fiend.

Mrs. Forbes, our dress-maker, came to-day, with her fabric samples and her pins and tape-measure. I mean to be positively stunning at the birthday ball, so I chose the Levantine *folicé,* which is an exquisitely soft, yet very rich silk, patterned all over with the most cunning arabesque designs. Mamma selected a rich, shaded satin with intricate floral embroidery.

Asserting my new-found authority as a lady soon to be married, I defiantly instructed Mrs. Forbes — in Mamma's presence — to cut my frock low enough in front so as to display one of (that is to say, two of) my best features. Mamma sensibly voiced no objection.

In the post this morning, a dear verse from Rhys:

> I know a certain fair colleen
> Who will to-morrow be eighteen;
> And who, next month, will be a bride,
> And stand, refulgently, beside
> This undeserving *parvenu*
> Who is not fit to kiss her shoe:
> A wretch without good looks or pelf —
> Who loves her more than life itself.

A few minutes after midnight, I became eighteen years old. At a quarter past four this morning, Princess Victoria reached the same age. She is a woman. I am not. (But has *she* been plumbed to her depths by a lusty lover like Giles? I think not. Therefore, which of us is the woman, truly?)

Still, it is jolly for me that my birthday is made a public holiday — even though I know that it is in her honour, not mine. All along the country roads leading to London, mail-coaches, post-chaises, and carriages headed for Kensington

Palace to-day. The merry-makers from Devonshire and Dorsetshire decorated their horses' heads with sprays of lilac; those from the North used hawthorn buds. And bunting has been nailed up by the landlords of all those little taverns that surround the palace — the Adam and Eve, The Black Lion, The Hoop and Toy, and so on. I have not seen these festive decorations myself, but we have been told of them by various of our friends, such as Rhys, and Lord and Lady Merlyngton, and Mr. Randall.

The Princess awakened this morning to the sound of serenaders below in the garden. Thirty-seven of them in all, says Lady Merlyngton, and the Princess greeted them from her window. Later, accoutred in her birthday-ball frock and hat, and accompanied by her mother, the Duchess, she came down to receive the deputations from the towns and shires, and to hear the various addresses in her honour. The joy must have been mingled with monotony for her, I imagine.

Mr. Randall said, "What most struck me was the hopefulness that pervaded the assembled well-wishers. The breath of Spring was in the air outside; the breath of a moral and political Spring, of renovation and resurrection, buoyed us up within." When I asked him how the Princess looked, he replied, "Quite grown up, but no height."

I had flowers from Rhys, and many other lovely little gifts from Mamma and Papa, as well as from Uncle Roger, Aunt Esmie, et al. — but I am much too excited to list them, for to-night is the birthday ball, and it is all that I can do to contain myself. I will quieten my nerves with a drop of soothing medicine and try to compose my spirit for the wonderful event.

No more in these pages to-day, then; but to-morrow, I will recount all.

ᘐ *Thursday, 25 May*

Per te immenso giubilo! — For thee, immense rejoicing! How fitting that the musicians at the ball last night should have played those joyous, invigorating strains from *Lucia di Lammermoor;* for, in both the bracing, heart-lifting music of Donizetti, and the well-wishing words of his librettist, the tune could not have been more happily chosen.

Papa, Mamma, and I arrived at St. James's Palace well before the Princess, and *she* arrived well before her mother — an odd state of affairs, I thought. Lord Merlyngton thought so, too, and murmured to us: "The Duchess decreed that her daughter should set out from Kensington Palace in a separate carriage, and that she would follow in another. Most improper, in my view, to allow the Princess to arrive alone in this way."

"How is His Majesty's health?" Papa asked him.

"Slightly improved," Lord Merlyngton replied. "He is well enough, at least, that it was not necessary to cancel the plans for this ball. But he is not feeling strong enough to attend the festivities, I fear."

"I am sorry that I shall miss seeing him," I said, for I was so much looking forward to being presented to the King.

Mamma, gazing over the heads of the many guests, said, "Ah, the Duchess of Kent has arrived — at long last."

"Accompanied by 'King John,' " I said, referring, of course, to Sir John Conroy.

Lady Merlyngton sniffed in disapproval, and said, "Sir John is displaying an unusually defiant air to-night. One might almost describe it as triumphant."

"Bravado," said Lord Merlyngton, with a snort. "In truth, he is desperate. He sees power slipping through his fingers. He had hoped for a Regency so that he could rule the country through the Duchess, but now those hopes are blasted. The Princess is of age. When His Majesty dies — which may be sooner than we expect — she will be Queen, and Sir John will revert to being nothing more than the Duchess of Kent's lowly equerry."

I said, "He can not be happy to see the Princess seated on the King's chair of state, as she is now."

"It was His Majesty's express wish that she sit there," said Lord Merlyngton, "whether King John likes it or no."

The musicians played a variety of pieces. Everybody danced. I danced a waltz with Papa, a quadrille with Lord Merlyngton, and a very lively galop with Count Waldstein, quite handsome in his Hungarian uniform. But the crown of the evening, for me, was when Lord Merlyngton presented me to the Princess.

She was extremely gracious. "I am told that to-day is the

eighteenth anniversary of *your* birth, too, Miss Summerfield."

"That is so, Your Highness," I replied, trembling just a little with excitement. "May I wish you many more returnings of this anniversary?"

"Thank you, Miss Summerfield, and I wish the same to you. Come, let us walk a little together and talk, whilst the musicians are resting from their labours. It is not often that I have an opportunity to speak to young ladies of my own age — in this case, of *exactly* my own age."

And so we strolled and conversed, in the way that girls will do, with very little feeling of rank between us, and I was able to observe her closely. She is of shorter stature than I, as has been noted before, and has plump cheeks that slope back like the sides of a vase. Her eyes are very blue, and, I think, very intelligent. The nose is a bit beaky. Her mouth is small, near to being triangular in shape, and is always a bit ajar, due to her upper lip's being hitched up, as it were, in the centre. There is a pleasing air of softness and eagerness about her, and these qualities, with her quick-flushing colour, make her appear to be almost pretty. Her hair is light brown. The rumour that she irretrievably lost some of her hair due to an attack of typhus can not be true, unless she wore false tresses last night; and, if so, they looked remarkably genuine. As to her figure, it might be described as girlish — what I could see of it — although her shoulders, which were displayed (as were mine, and more) are quite fashionably round and full.

At one point, I said, "I am sorry to hear that His Majesty will not attend the ball."

Victoria sighed. "Dear Uncle Willy. He is not at all well, I fear. I wish that he may live for ever — I am so fond of him."

"I have a dear uncle, too," I said, "whom I adore; and he is elderly, also; and I worry about him for that reason."

"I am sure that you do, Miss Summerfield, and that you love him no less than I do mine. But when your uncle dies, you will not be suddenly laden with heavy responsibilities."

"True — but Your Highness has been trained all her life to deal with those responsibilities, and she will be more than a match for them."

"I am grateful for your confidence," she said. "But let us

320

talk no further of death. Tell me, does your mother often speak of the unseasonable hot weather that prevailed before your birth, breaking in honour of your arrival?"

"Why, to be sure she does! And the Duchess, does she —"

"Incessantly!" said the Princess, and we both laughed. We continued to stroll together, she nodding pleasantly to the ladies and gentlemen whom we passed.

"Do you not think that Count Zichy is very good-looking in his uniform, Miss Summerfield?" she asked, as we walked by that personage. I agreed that he was, and she then observed, "He is less so in plain clothing."

"Count Waldstein also looks quite nice in uniform," I said.

She nodded. "Remarkably well. I saw you dancing the galop with him. I should have liked to, but the peculiarities of my station prohibit me from dancing the more energetic steps, such as the galop and the waltz, as much as I should like to. And, such a pity, Count Waldstein does not know how to dance the quadrille —"

"But *I* do, my dear niece," said a deep voice behind us, "and I humbly pray that you will deign to be my partner in the next one."

"You were never humble in your life, Uncle Ernest," replied the Princess, as I turned to see a tall, lean figure smiling down at us from a fiercely bearded, hideously scarred face which I remembered well. His one useful eye flashed from the Princess to me and back again. "May I present Miss Summerfield, Uncle," the Princess said. "Miss Summerfield, this is my wicked, whiskered uncle, the Duke of Cumberland."

He bowed. "A great pleasure, Miss. I have seen you at the Opera, I believe. I could not forget such a pretty young lady."

"Your Grace is most kind," I said, coolly, and added, "I remember the occasion."

Speaking once more to the Princess, he said, "I shall leave you two to your feminine gossip — but remember, Drina, the next quadrille is mine." Flashing his lizard smile again, he turned and walked away, his great cadaverous height slicing through the crowd like a sabre.

"Uncle Ernest *will* call me by that childhood name," the Princess said, peevishly. Then she quite surprised me by taking both of my hands in hers and saying, on a sudden impulse, "Oh, Miss Summerfield, I am *so* pleased to have met you! I hope that we shall meet again. I hope that we may become friends. I have so few of my own sex and age; and later — when I — that is to say, I shall have even *fewer* then. I should like to know that I shall be able to have pleasant talks like this with you, always."

Her words overwhelmed me. "Your Highness," I said, my affection for her colouring my voice, "you can not know how happy you have made me by saying that! Please think of me at all times as your loyal subject and faithful friend!"

She smiled, with that darling little triangular mouth, and said, "Thank you, Miss Summerfield, and bless you. And now" — she sighed deeply — "I see that my mother is watching me, and no doubt wishes to present somebody to me. I must leave you. But we shall meet again and talk again — soon, *soon!*"

I was in a state of elation as I watched her return to her mother's side. What a dear, charming person she is! How sweet and warm! And what a fortunate girl am I, that she should take such an immediate liking to me. Without a doubt, I am destined to be the friend, the intimate, the confidante of the Queen of England!

That knowledge is the most beautiful, most cherished of all my birthday gifts.

୨୭ *Friday, 26 May*

A terrible, terrible thing:

We were all of us seated in the drawing-room this evening, after dinner, when Rutledge entered and told Papa that three gentlemen wished to see him. We were expecting no callers.

"Three gentlemen?" said Papa, surprised.

"More precisely, sir, one gentleman and two of his associates. The gentleman is Colonel Charles Rowan."

"Good Heavens!" Mamma exclaimed.

"The police commissioner?" asked Papa.

"I believe so," replied Rutledge.

"What on earth can he want of *me?*" Papa wondered. "Well,

well, I expect we shall have to receive him. Shew him in, Rutledge."

"Very good, sir."

As Rutledge opened the drawing-room doors again, our three callers were revealed to be standing just outside, not having waited to be conducted from the entrance hall. It struck me as rude.

Rutledge announced Colonel Rowan, who immediately entered with his two men. The constables wore long, dark blue coats, with blue-and-white striped armlets, and each carried a short wooden truncheon at his side.

"Mr. Summerfield," said Colonel Rowan, "I hope you will forgive this intrusion. These are Constables Buckley and Smither."

"May I present my wife; my daughter, Pamela."

"Ladies," said Colonel Rowan, "I wish we had met under more pleasant circumstances."

"Will you take some refreshment, Colonel?" asked Mamma.

"Thank you, no, Mrs. Summerfield."

Papa said, "You are here officially, I assume."

"I fear so," the commissioner replied.

"It must be a matter of some importance, if you take charge of it yourself."

"It is."

Papa turned to Rutledge. "That will be all, I think."

"Permit me," said Colonel Rowan, "but your man must be present."

"Indeed," said Papa, with raised eyebrows. He indicated with a nod to Rutledge that he should remain. "Now then, Colonel," he said, "perhaps you will be good enough to state the nature of your business?"

The commissioner did not answer Papa. He turned away from him and spoke to Rutledge: "I am required to ask your name."

"Rutledge, sir."

"Your full name."

"Henry Rutledge."

"Henry Rutledge," said Colonel Rowan, "it is my duty to

place you under arrest for the murders of Mary Wood, Emma Davis, Ada Wilkes, Hattie Morrison, and Maude Bates. Men, take him in charge."

The pair of constables seized Rutledge by the arms and ushered him roughly from the room. The poor man's face was ashen. He said nothing.

But Papa did. "See here, Colonel! This is absurd! I have known that man for years! He has lived in this house, with my wife, my children. I would trust him with our very lives!"

"I am sorry, Mr. Summerfield."

"You can not seriously believe that he is the person whom the newspapers call The Full Moon Fiend?"

"A court of law will decide that," the colonel replied, "but I may tell you that the evidence against the man is substantial. I must now ask your permission to search his room. I trust you will not impede our investigation?"

"Search and be damned, sir!" Papa roared. "You'll find nothing there to incriminate him!"

"Thank you. I quite understand your feelings. Please understand, in return, that I am doing no more than my sworn duty."

"Yes, yes," growled Papa, and threw open the drawing-room doors, as if curtly dismissing Colonel Rowan.

We could see Rutledge, standing outside the room, in the charge of the two constables. Papa walked up to him and clapped him warmly on the shoulder.

"What an absurd business, eh?" he said. "Never fear, old fellow. St. John Barstow will set to work at once. You'll be a free man again in no time."

"Thank you, sir," said Rutledge in a faded voice.

Later, after Rutledge's room had been searched, Papa sarcastically asked the colonel, "And have your ransackings turned up any blood-smeared axes or grisly human parts? A severed head, perhaps?"

"The murderer in this case," replied Colonel Rowan coolly, "despatches his victims by strangulation. Bloody axes and severed parts are not at issue. I will tell you this much, at least, Mr. Summerfield: we have found in your butler's room two articles — well hidden — which will furnish emphatic confirmation of his guilt."

"What are they?"

"I am not bound to say more. The articles will be produced in evidence at his trial. And now I bid you good evening."

Colonel Rowan bowed to Mamma and me, then left the house with his two constables and poor, pale Rutledge.

"I must go to see Barstow at once," said Papa, reaching for the bell-cord. "Confound it," he grumbled, "I was about to ring for Rutledge." And he walked off in a great rush.

Of course, there has been some outrageous mistake. Rutledge, *our* Rutledge, a multiple murderer? Reason rejects the idea. And yet, we are, all of us, in an extremity of distress. The awful episode appears to have hit Mamma the hardest.

And now I must say that, to-night, here at my desk, whilst I was taking out my inkpot and pen and preparing to set down these words, the pack of *tarot* cards from Aunt Esmie fell to the floor, spreading out all over the carpet. I was obliged to get down on my hands and knees to pick them up. All of them were face down, save one: The Hanged Man.

It is a good job that I am not superstitious — but what a positively *ghastly* coincidence!

⁊ Saturday, 27 May

"Barstow told me last night not to worry," Papa said this morning at breakfast (which was served by Crewe and one of the maids). " 'Your butler is patently innocent,' is the way he put it. 'Everybody in Mayfair knows Rutledge. There's not a man or woman who has ever been a guest in your house who will not swear to his unblemished character. The charge is absurd. The trouble is, you see, that the police have been under the gun to catch this Full Moon fellow, and they have been notably unsuccessful thus far. So they are clutching at straws.' "

"Where is Rutledge now?" Mamma asked, with deep concern.

"In Newgate Prison."

"How horrible." She shuddered.

Papa patted her hand. "He'll come to no harm there — although I expect he will be glad to return home to Berkeley Square. And he will do, my dear. Trust Barstow."

"What barrister will Mr. Barstow engage?" I asked.

"I told him to spare no expense, and he said that he feels certain he can get a King's Counsel, Sir Joel Hemming. 'A fire-breather,' he called him. 'Probably the best trial lawyer in England — save one.' "

"And who is that one?" asked Mamma. "And why does not Mr. Barstow engage *him?*"

"He is Sir Beowulf Gill, K.C.," Papa replied, "and his services are not available to us, for he is a prosecutor for the Crown."

"If he is superior to Sir Joel," I said, "I certainly hope that he does not draw the task of prosecuting Rutledge."

"My words to Barstow exactly," said Papa.

"And what did Mr. Barstow reply?" Mamma asked.

"I'm afraid that he replied: 'These murders have aroused the populace. They demand that this Full Moon Fiend be caught and tried and sentenced and hanged as soon as is humanly possible. The Crown will, therefore, call upon its heaviest artillery. And Sir Beowulf is a very, *very* large-bore cannon, indeed.' "

ॐ *Sunday, 28 May*

Rhys was waiting for us at home when we returned from church this morning.

"I won't detain you," he said to us, "but I had to commiserate with you in this outlandishly ridiculous affair of your butler. Sure, and they'll be finding Full Moon Fiends under their beds before long, I'm thinking. As for your man, why, I'll wager he's never even *been* to Hyde Park!"

"Certainly not to kill young ladies," Mamma assured him.

"If there'll be anything that I can do to help? —"

"It's good of you to call, O'Connor," said Papa, "but we have the situation well in hand. My solicitor has engaged Sir Joel Hemming to represent Rutledge."

"Sir Joel has an excellent reputation," said Rhys. "I will bid good morning to you, then."

But I said, "Will you not stay to luncheon, Rhys?"

"Faith, and I thought you'd never ask me," he replied, with a devilish smile.

This evening, after dinner, Mr. Barstow called — accompanied, *mirabile dictu,* by Sir Joel Hemming in the flesh! I had not known that barristers paid visits to the houses of their solicitors' clients (and, indeed, Sir Joel commented on the matter, citing *force majeure*). He is a man not much past fifty, I expect, stout as a barrel, with a ruddy complexion. Papa, sensible of the gravity of the occasion and the exceptional nature of this call, did not offer brandy and cigars. We all sat down in the drawing-room.

Mr. Barstow said, "We have learned that the trial has been set for the fifth of next month, at the Central Criminal Court."

"So soon?" said Mamma.

"Yes, Madam," Sir Joel replied, in the fine, deep, resonant voice of an actor. "There has been a great public outcry. Surely you have seen the newspapers this morning?"

Papa nodded. "Libelous rags — calling Rutledge a murderer and sexual degenerate before he's even come to trial. It's disgraceful. Murderer? Rutledge? Why, the man wouldn't harm a flea. As for the other, I doubt that he has ever touched a woman. Very cool-blooded fellow –– not the sort to let his passions get out of hand. If he has passions."

"Yes, yes," said Sir Joel, "but the press are clamouring for his blood, cool though it may be, and that is why an early date has been set for the trial."

"But surely that is a good thing?" Mamma said. "The sooner this dreadful business is over, the better, and the less time poor Rutledge will have to sit in Newgate."

"That is true, Mrs. Summerfield," said Mr. Barstow, "but the early date provides us with very little time in which to prepare his defence."

"But he is innocent!" I cried.

Sir Joel smiled at me and winked an eye. "That is what we hope to establish in court, my dear young lady."

Papa asked Mr. Barstow, "Do you know who will be acting for the Crown?"

Mr. Barstow nodded, glumly. "Gill, I'm afraid. As I predicted."

"Sir Beowulf doesn't frighten me," Sir Joel said. "I've bested him more than once — and, to be candid, he's bested *me* a time or two, as well. The chap I must look out for is not the prosecutor, but the judge."

"Who will he be?" asked Papa.

"Palmer," said Sir Joel. "The Right Honourable Lord Sydney Palmer. A gentleman advanced in years, but not in thinking. He is known in my profession as a 'hanging judge.' He is very religious, which is commendable, but he seems to consider himself to be God's good right arm here on Earth. Therefore, the Biblical words 'Vengeance is mine' Lord Palmer appears to believe to have been uttered by *him*. He deplores the leniency of our modern laws, and has often said that he yearns for a return to 'other, better days,' when a man could be sentenced to stand in the pillory for trifling crimes, and disembowelled for greater ones."

"Good Heavens!" I exclaimed.

"However, we must not be disheartened," Sir Joel concluded, rising to his feet. "I paid a visit to Rutledge to-day, in Newgate, and talked at some length with him. I am satisfied that he is innocent."

"Innocent men have been hanged before this!" Mamma said with sudden fierceness. "Hanged by the neck until they were dead!"

Sir Joel blinked with surprise at her outburst. "No doubt, Madam. And guilty men have gone free. But I beg you to have faith in Mr. Barstow's skill and in my own. We, for our part, will place our faith in English justice, English law, and God."

            ℬ *Tuesday, 30 May*

Mamma was out of the house this afternoon, and had not yet returned when Papa came in from the City. However, she did return some few minutes later.

"Where have you been, my dear?" he asked.

She sighed. "You must promise not to be cross with me, Wilfrid. I did not discuss it with you because I feared you might forbid me to go."

328

"Go where?"

"To Newgate."

"My word, woman, what a thing to do!"

"There, you see? You are cross."

"I am not cross; I am surprised. A lady of your station, to be seen entering a gaol —"

"But I was so sorry for poor Rutledge. Sitting in a cell. Accused of foul crimes. I wanted to assure him that we know he is innocent and that we stand behind him."

"Yes, that is so," said Papa. "but I have gone to see him, as you know, with Barstow and Sir Joel, and I gave him every assurance. There was no need for you to enter that awful place."

"Perhaps not, but I cannot see what harm it will do. A woman's voice; a woman's smile. You men do seem to set such great store by them. The members of my sex are expected to be ministering angels to men in times of distress, and I was doing only what might be expected of any woman. Besides, I believe that the prisoners of Newgate do not dine very well, so I brought him a hamper of food from Mrs. Pruitt."

"Is that permitted?" I asked.

"I bribed the warder."

"My *dear!*" exclaimed Papa. Then, softening, he said, "Well, it is all quite irregular, but I'll own that it was very good of you. And if anybody did take note of your visit — the press, for example — it will shew them that the Summerfields stand staunchly behind Rutledge."

"How *is* Rutledge, Mamma?" I asked.

"His spirits are very low," she replied. "Nothing that I said appeared to cheer him. But there was a treacle pudding in the hamper, and perhaps that will make him feel better. Mrs. Pruitt says that it is his favourite."

ॐ *Wednesday, 31 May*

Mr. Barstow burst, unexpected, into our house this evening whilst we were in the midst of our dinner. He was as white as a sheet.

"I am sorry to disturb you," he said, "but —"

329

"Sit down, man," said Papa. "A glass of brandy?"

"I'd be glad of a drop," said Mr. Barstow, and drained the glass in one swallow when Crewe brought it to him.

"What the devil is *wrong?*" Papa demanded.

"It is not a pleasant subject for the dinner-table," Mr. Barstow said, "but it must be told. I'm afraid that — Rutledge hanged himself this evening."

"Dear God!" Mamma cried.

"No!" I said.

"Pardon me," Mr. Barstow quickly added. "I should have said that he attempted to hang himself. They discovered him in his cell, and cut him down."

"Then he is alive?" said Mamma.

"For the moment, at least. But the prison doctor says that he is suspended between life and death. I sent for Mr. Cargrave — he's the only medical man I trust completely — and obtained permission for him to conduct his own examination. His opinion agrees with the prison doctor's: Rutledge may not last the night."

"Oh, merciful Heaven, *no!*" wailed Mamma.

"Can nothing else be done for him?" Papa asked.

"Apparently not. We can but wait and pray. I will be in continual contact with the prison authorities, and I will notify you immediately of any change, whether it is for the better or —" He left the rest unsaid.

After a moment, Papa asked, "Does Sir Joel know of this?" Mr. Barstow nodded. "And what does he say of it?"

"He says that it does our client no good. It is tantamount to an admission of guilt — in any event, that is the construction that will be put upon it by the press, by the Crown prosecutor, by everybody."

"And by you?" asked Papa.

"I do not know what to say," Mr. Barstow replied. "Prior to this evening, I had thought him innocent. But now — even if he lives — I am not confident that Sir Joel and I shall be able to save him from the gallows."

June

❦

"THE MESSAGE OF THE RAVENS"

Rutledge will live: that is the message we received this morning from Mr. Barstow. Thank God!

Would it have been better he had died? "He will live to stand trial" were Mr. Barstow's exact words — but for how long *after* that trial will he live? How long before the public hangman finishes the job which Rutledge started yesterday in his prison cell?

Rhys was here to-day, briefly, and we stole a few moments alone to kiss and fondle each other. (O ever-living unicorn, thou lurkest in the warmth and darkness of many a pair of breeches, to this I can attest!).

I unburdened to him my fears on Rutledge's account, finishing with "Why would an innocent man choose to end his own life in that way? Does it not all but *prove* that he is guilty?"

"Do *you* think him guilty?" Rhys asked.

"No — I do not — and yet —"

"Then trust your heart," he said, "and trust your feelings for this man whom you've known all of your life, this man who is like a second father to you. If your father, indeed, were accused of these crimes, and if he had tried to hang himself last night — would that persuade you of his guilt?"

"No," I admitted. "You are right. But why did Rutledge —"

"Pure black despair, perhaps," said Rhys. "Here is a man

who has lived a great part of his life in a gracious house, going about his work serenely, never a word to be heard in censure against him, eating well, sleeping well of nights. Suddenly, he is wrenched from his warm home by the law — accused of ghastly crimes — thrown into a cold dark cell — attacked by the press — Ah, my dear, the mills of justice can be frightening when one is ground up in them. Things appear to be hopeless — 'I am only an insignificant little man,' he tells himself, 'and a servant at that, with the whole weight of the Crown pressing down to crush me like a beetle. 'Tis futile to resist — the powerful always will prevail.' Reason crumbles, melancholy overwhelms him, and —"

"Yes," I said, "I can understand it, now. How wise you are, my darling."

"Wise, is it?" He laughed. "Would it were so! No, 'tis not wisdom. 'Tis just that I've seen a bit of life — and have learnt, as every Celt has learnt, that the law is rarely a man's friend, but often his bitterest enemy."

ૐ *Friday, 2 June*

The King is reported to be mending after a recent illness. That is welcome news, but we are all so upset over Rutledge and the impending trial that it is difficult to be as thankful as we should. God protect our dear and gentle King — and please, God, protect Rutledge, too.

ૐ *Saturday, 3 June*

A letter from Willy to-day! All the way from Africa! I shall paste it down:

My Dear Ones, —
I have been here for only a few days, but I will dash off this letter now so that an Arab trader, who is leaving this locality to-morrow morning, can take it with him and post it at his first opportunity. I have paid him well for the service.
This place is called Bakama — at least, that is the closest I can render it in the letters of our alphabet. It is very hot during

the sunlit hours, but quite cool, even chilly, at night. I do not mind the heat — I bask in it — I feel that it has curative powers. And you would not believe how *green* this country is! Such green was never seen in England. It is heart-breakingly beautiful. Pamela, if only you were here, with your paint-box!

I live in a little thatched hut that belonged to my predecessor. His grave, on which the natives have erected a rough wooden cross, is near by. I am in luck, for a few words of English are spoken by the people here, who learnt them from the man whose mortal shell lies in that grave.

The name of the king is Matuba. He is a strong, very black young chap whose word is, quite literally, law; and his bearing is more dignified than that of most European monarchs. His court numbers over three thousand! And each of these is totally submissive to his whim.

The royal enclosure covers very nearly a full square mile at the crest of a hill — I can see it now, in the middle distance against the setting sun, as I write — and is completely surrounded by a fence of reeds, vertical and untrimmed. This area contains close to six hundred buildings, made of reeds and roofed with tiger grass. Naturally enough, the largest part of this area is reserved for Matuba and his women. These include over eighty wives and about a thousand concubines. I do not exaggerate. Not Solomon in all his glory was wived and concubined as is Matuba! And yet not even they can slake his boundless appetite, as I will later explain.

In his audience hall — a building larger than all of the others — King Matuba sits on a throne of ivory, his feet resting on a pair of immense crossed elephant tusks. He wears a black tunic of Turkish origin, white trousers bound in red, shoes of red leather, and a red cap on his head. Those subjects who would approach this fearsome being must prostrate themselves before him, grovelling in the dry grass with which the floor is strewn.

Of course, I refuse to do so, explaining that I kneel only to my God. Matuba accepts this behaviour, no doubt because my predecessor accustomed him to it.

Unfortunately, we of the True Faith have been preceded in this region by followers of Mahomet — wily Arabs who brought with them such good things as cotton cloth, and such bad things as the slave-trade, fire-arms, smoking, and a predilection for the sin of Sodom.

The last-named is an evil to which King Matuba is particularly addicted. That is what I meant when I said that not even all of his wives and concubines can meet his needs. The giggling chocolate-coloured page-boys of his court are grist to the mill of his lust, which grinds unceasingly, insatiably.

As you see, I have a difficult job of work cut out for me here, for not only is Matuba steeped in sin and vice; he is on the verge of embracing the faith of Islam — partly because he covets Arab guns, and partly because Islam does not frown upon a multitude of wives and concubines, nor on a taste for boys.

And yet, your son and brother has a card or two up his sleeve. I have come to be as wily as an Arab. Only to-day, for example, in a private audience with Matuba, I told him of an Islamic custom which he had not previously encountered. If he is to become a Moslem, I assured him, he must needs allow himself to be circumcised. He had not heard the word before, and he asked me to explain its meaning. I obliged His Majesty — most graphically. He winced in pain at my description. He was horrified. I believe that he will think twice before bowing to Mahomet.

I must close now, for the light is going. Please convey my love to Phoebe and Uncle Roger and Aunt Esmie, et al. — I can not write to everybody — and remember me to Rutledge and Mrs. Pruitt and the rest of the staff. Pamela, scratch Sophie behind the ears for me. And, all of you, when you can, please write to me in care of the mission in Whitechapel (Pam knows the address), and they will endeavour to forward your letters to me. I long to hear from you. I pray for you all, and I ask that you, in turn, pray for

Your devoted
Will

℘ *Sunday, 4 June*

Write to Willy? How can we? What can we say?

Shall we tell him that Phoebe is dead?

336

That she died giving birth to a child not sired by her husband?

That the child's father is the very man whom Willy called "a cynical atheist," and who attacked one of Willy's tracts?

That I am about to marry that "cynical atheist?"

That even little Sophie is dead and will never again be scratched behind the ears?

That Rutledge has been arrested for the murders of five women, and to-morrow will go on trial for his life?

How can we burden Willy with such news?

ᵖᵉ *Monday, 5 June*

This was the first day of Rutledge's trial.

I had never been inside a court of law before, and I am ashamed to say that, from the very moment I walked into the Old Bailey with my parents, I felt elated and excited. I should have felt downcast and gloomy, I know, but I could not help myself. Besides, I was so certain that Rutledge would be proved innocent that I was not deeply worried on that account.

As many of the staff as could be spared were also present for the proceedings: Mrs. Pruitt, for example, who kept a handkerchief perpetually at her streaming eyes (moaning, "Oh dear, oh dear" the while), and Hester and one or two others.

We were on hand, not merely as spectators, but also as witnesses to Rutledge's good character, if Sir Joel had need to call upon us.

I must tell you that much of court procedure is dull ritual, and I do not intend to fill these pages with leaden details of the "Oyez! Oyez! Oyez!" and our rising to our feet when the judge made his slow, stately entrance; or the repetitious swearing-in of the witnesses; or the way in which the voices echoed hollowly in the vast cavern of the Old Bailey.

The judge, the Right Honourable Lord Sydney Palmer, is an elderly peer with heavy-lidded eyes and a somnolent manner. He seemed to be weighted down by his robes and his immense wig. Seeing his eyes blinking from under that great absurd piece of head-gear, I was minded of the American President Mr. Jefferson who decreed that the judges of his young country should wear no wigs lest they look as English judges do — like rats peeping out from under bunches of oakum.

The prosecutor was the feared Sir Beowulf Gill, a man of reptilian coolness and calm, who looked neither to the left nor to the right, but kept his eyes fixed on the sheaf of papers before him. He was tall and about fifty-five, I guessed. Occasionally, one of several young assistants would lean over and whisper something in his ear and he would nod curtly, without replying.

Sir Joel Hemming exuded a jovial, cheerful air which I suspected was false. Mr. Barstow sat at a table to the rear.

When the preliminary rituals had been duly observed, Sir Beowulf Gill rose to his feet. He began to speak, low but clearly, in a kind of monotone, as if he were bored: there was nothing of the theatrical about him:

"May it please you, m'lud. Gentlemen of the jury. This is an extraordinarily unpleasant case. We do not mean to dwell upon unsavoury details any more than will be absolutely necessary to the efficient administration of justice. At this time, let it suffice for us to say only this: that five women, in five months, have been brutally murdered and ravaged — murdered and ravaged *in that order* — in the Hyde Park area of London; that witnesses, all of them residents of Hyde Park, will be brought forth to swear, under solemn oath, that they observed the accused, Henry Rutledge, a stranger to that neighbourhood, appear there, once every month, on the dates of the murders. Other evidence, *physical* evidence, found by the police, will also be produced at the proper time."

As Sir Beowulf sat down, I saw Rhys surreptitiously enter the court-room. He quietly made his way to the section where we were sitting. Nodding to my parents, he squeezed in beside me without a word.

In due course, the witnesses were sworn in and questioned, first by Sir Beowulf, then by Sir Joel. There were seven of them in all, five women and two men, and their stories were essentially the same. I will not tediously record here the testimony of all seven. One will serve, the first of them, a middle-aged woman named Olivia Higgins.

"Miss Higgins —" Sir Beowulf began.

"*Mrs.* Higgins, sir. I am a widow."

"Of course. I beg your pardon, Madam. Mrs. Higgins, do you live within visible distance of a block of apartments known as The Alroy, located in Strathmore Street, Hyde Park?"

"I do. Just across the road."

"And did you observe a stranger to that area, a man, visit that place in the late afternoon or early evening of Saturday, the twenty-first of January, this year?"

"I did, sir."

"Did you observe the same man visit the same place on Monday, the twentieth of February; on Wednesday, the twenty-second of March; on Thursday, the twentieth of April; and on Saturday, the twentieth of May?"

"Yes, I did."

"M'lud," said Sir Beowulf, "I would direct the attention of the court to the fact that those dates coincide with the dates of the full moon, as verified by the *Meteorological Journal* kept by the Assistant Secretary, at the apartments of the Royal Society, by the order of the President and Council. I would further remind the court that, on those same dates, Mary Wood, Emma Davis, Ada Wilkes, Hattie Morrison, and Maude Bates were first strangled to death and then perversely debauched —"

"M'lud, with respect," said Sir Joel, rising to his feet. "I believe that I heard learned counsel state, not many minutes ago, that he did not mean to dwell unnecessarily upon unsavoury details? In view of that laudable announcement, may I say that I find the term 'perversely debauched' to be excessively colourful?"

Sir Beowulf turned to his opponent, acknowledging his existence with a slight bow. "I apologise to my esteemed colleague, and assure him that no colouring was intended. A man may debauch a woman without being perverse. The act may be immoral, indelicate, or in other ways reprehensible, but if it is conducted along the lines prescribed by Nature, it can not be considered to be perversity. If, on the other hand, a man commits such an act, not with a living woman, but with a *cadaver* — as was, lamentably, the case with each of the five victims of the so-called Full Moon Fiend (that colouring, Sir Joel, is not mine, but that of the popular press) — then those acts of debauchery surely may be described as *perverse* in the interests not of colour but of simple accuracy."

"Score one for old Gill," Rhys whispered to me. "Your man committed a tactical error by bringing up that trivial matter. He opened a door that Gill slammed in his face."

I nodded in rueful agreement, then asked, also in a whisper, "Rhys, are you reporting this trial for the newspapers?"

"No, not my line of country, but others are. And a pretty scandal they'll make of it."

Lord Palmer peered wearily at the prosecutor, saying, "Please resume your questioning, Sir Beowulf."

"Thank you, m'lud." He turned again to the witness. "Mrs. Higgins, the man whom you observed on those occasions — is he here, in this courtroom?"

"Yes, sir, he is."

"Will you point him out, please?"

"That's the man," she said. "The prisoner in the dock. Henry Rutledge."

"Are you quite certain?"

"I am. Except for being clean-shaven, he is the same man."

"One more question, Madam. Why did you take particular note of Henry Rutledge when he visited The Alroy? Do not many men, and women, too, come in and out of those apartments? What was it about Henry Rutledge that attracted unusual attention?"

"Well, it's hard to say, exactly. It was as if he wasn't *right,* somehow."

"Wasn't right?"

"As if he felt himself to be out of place. Ill at ease. Trying too hard *not* to attract attention, if you know what I mean."

Lord Palmer addressed the witness: "Mrs. Higgins, would you say that 'furtive' describes his attitude?"

"Yes, m'lord! Furtive! That's just the word!"

Sir Joel sprang to his feet. "M'lud, I do protest the court's putting words in the mouth of the witness!"

"The court," replied Lord Palmer, "was doing no such thing, Sir Joel. It was merely helping an inarticulate lady to express herself more clearly. Sir Beowulf, are you finished with this witness?"

"I am, m'lud. Thank you, Mrs. Higgins."

"Sir Joel, do you have questions for this witness?"

"Yes, indeed, m'lud. Madam, you have said that the defendant resembles the man whom you saw, *except for being clean-shaven*. Is that correct?"

"Yes, sir, that's right."

"The man whom you observed was bearded, then?"

"He wore a small moustache."

"A small moustache! Indeed! But large enough to be observed from your window, across the way?"

"Yes, sir."

"How very interesting," said Sir Joel. "M'lud, gentlemen — the defence will bring forth witnesses, in due course, to swear that Henry Rutledge has *never* worn a moustache in his life, and *certainly* has not been in the habit of growing a moustache once every month, shaving it off, and then growing it again! Thank you, Mrs. Higgins; you may step down."

The other six witnesses said much the same as Mrs. Higgins, and Sir Joel, each time, triumphantly iterated his point about the moustache.

The next witness called by the Crown was Colonel Charles Rowan. "Colonel Rowan," said Sir Beowulf, "I shew you this article, which will be marked as Exhibit A. Do you recognise it?" (From where I sat, I could not see the small object that he held up. It might have been a strip of ribbon.)

"I do," replied the Colonel.

"Will you tell the court, please, when and where you first saw it?"

"On the evening of the twenty-sixth of May, when I discovered it, during the course of an investigation, in the house of Mr. Wilfrid Summerfield."

"In what room of that house?"

"The room of the butler, Henry Rutledge."

"And will you describe the article, please, for the benefit of those who can not see it?"

"It is a false moustache." (A murmur went round the courtroom.)

"Of the kind worn by actors on the stage?"

"Yes."

"Like *this?*" And here, Sir Beowulf affixed the moustache to his own upper lip and turned slowly in all directions so that he could be seen by everybody — thus putting paid to my earlier thought that there was nothing of the theatrical about him. "Thank you, Colonel Rowan," he said, ripping off the moustache quickly and easily.

"Sir Joel," said the judge, "do you wish to question this witness?"

Sir Joel replied, "No questions at this time, m'lud."

"Then, the hour being late, the court will adjourn until to-morrow morning," said Lord Palmer.

"I'm afraid that it looks very bad for Rutledge," Rhys remarked.

Papa replied, "I am forced to agree with you."

ع๏ *Tuesday, 6 June*

"Not at all," said Sir Joel this morning, when Papa expressed those same misgivings just before the trial was resumed. "No, no, not at all. The prosecution's evidence, so-called, is as thin as gauze. It is all circumstantial. There is nothing wrong in visiting a block of apartments. Wearing a false moustache is not a crime. The first witness whom I call to-day will clarify everything and shew it all to be not in the least sinister."

"What witness is that?" asked Papa.

"Why, Rutledge himself. The good man is the very picture of honesty. Written all over his face, plain as a pikestaff. Looking at him, who could believe him capable of such ghastly crimes? Moreover, he will tell us the true reason for his visits. They were not precisely 'innocent' in all meanings of that word, perhaps; but they had nothing to do with murder." Sir Joel chuckled. "No, my dear chap, nothing to do with murder at all. Do not worry. Sit down and enjoy the show. Sir Beowulf has come a cropper this time, mark my word!"

Rutledge was not the confident, ramrod-straight man I have known all my life. He seemed to be broken, unsure, afraid. Perhaps he is not fully recovered from his hanging attempt. When he was sworn in, he mumbled, and had to be told by Lord Palmer to speak up.

Sir Joel beamed at him. "Now then, Henry," he said, brightly. "Form requires that I ask you a foolish question. Did you murder Mary Wood?"

"No, sir. I did not."

"Did you murder Emma Davis?"

"No, sir."

"Did you murder Ada Wilkes, Hattie Morrison, or Maude Bates?"

"No, sir! I never murdered anybody in my life!"

"That's all right, Henry; no need to upset yourself. Tell us, if you please, how long you have been employed as butler to the Summerfield family?"

"Twenty-two years, sir. Going on twenty-three."

"Really. And are you a good butler, Henry?"

"That's not for me to say, sir."

"Quite. Others there are, in plenty — m'lud, gentlemen — who will testify to this man's industriousness, reliability, and impeccability of character. Now, Henry, tell us this: Are you a married man?"

"No, sir."

"A widower, perhaps?"

"No, sir; I've never been married."

"I see. Is that not a lonely life, Henry?"

"I don't complain, sir."

"Of course you don't. But are you a man like other men? That is to say, do you have the usual masculine appetites?"

"I'm not sure that I know what you mean, sir."

"Oh, Henry, do not be bashful! Of course you know what I mean. Do you *like the ladies?*"

"Yes, sir. Mind you, I'm no rake." (Subdued laughter from the court-room.)

"No, no, of course you're not. But do you occasionally visit a member of the fair sex?" Rutledge hesitated. "Come, come, Henry; there's not a man here who will condemn a fellow for seeing a female friend. Answer the question: Do you, on occasion, pay visits to a woman at The Alroy in Hyde Park?"

"Yes, sir."

"For amorous purposes? Come — this is no time to be shy."

"Yes, sir."

Sir Joel smiled. "So! The *horrible truth* is finally revealed! Henry Rutledge knows a woman! How perfectly awful! How shocking! How unprecedented!"

Lord Palmer murmured, "Sir Joel, if we may forgo the pleasure of your vaunted irony . . ."

"Forgive me, m'lud. Now, Henry — if you will be so good as to satisfy our curiosity about that false moustache: Is it yours?"

"Yes, sir."

"And do you wear it when you visit your friend?"

"Yes, sir."

"And on no other occasions?"

"No, sir."

"And just *why* do you wear it?"

"Well, sir — to disguise myself — so that I won't be recognised —"

"By your friends' neighbours."

"Yes, sir."

"To spare yourself and your friend embarrassment. To prevent gossip. Is that correct?"

"Learned counsel is leading the witness," muttered Sir Beowulf.

"Learned counsel is doing no such thing," snapped Sir Joel. "Learned counsel is merely *helping an inarticulate man to express himself more clearly.*" He looked straight at Lord Palmer on those words. "Now then, Henry, I am going to ask you a question which I have asked you before. I think you know what it is, and I think you know how important it is that you answer it. You have declined to answer it in our private discussions; but now I must ask that you answer it here in open court. This woman, what is her name?"

Rutledge was in agony.

"What is her name, Henry?"

"I can not tell you."

"Rubbish, my good fellow. You mean you *will* not tell me, and that is not wise. It may be good; it may be noble; but it is not wise. Tell us her name, that she may be brought here to corroborate what you have already told us."

"I'm sorry, sir," said Rutledge, "but I can not."

"Henry," said Sir Joel, pleading with him, "you are accused of a series of capital crimes. You are facing the gallows. This woman, if she has any affection for you, do you think that *she* wants to see you hanged? Tell us her *name, man!*"

"Counsel is badgering his own witness, m'lud," drawled the prosecutor.

"Be quiet, Sir Beowulf," said the judge. "Mr. Rutledge, it is my duty to remind you that you are under oath. You have sworn to answer all questions and answer them truthfully. In your own interest, if this servant-girl exists, you *must* disclose her identity."

"I'm sorry, m'lord, but I simply can not," said Rutledge.

Lord Palmer sighed. "Are you quite finished, Sir Joel?"

Drained, Sir Joel sat down heavily. "Yes, m'lud."

"Sir Beowulf?"

The prosecutor stood up and said, "I think that your lordship arrived at the crux of this matter a moment ago and expressed it succinctly. The witness was advised that he must reveal the identity of his phantom paramour, if she exists. *If she exists!*" Sir Beowulf wheeled towards Rutledge and pointed his finger at him. "Henry Rutledge, I put it to you that your testimony is a tissue of lies!"

"No, sir! I told the truth!"

"I put it to you that there is no such woman! I put it to you that your visits to Hyde Park were for the sole purpose of foully murdering and defiling —"

"No! No!"

"Do you deny that you killed Emma Davis?"

"Of course I deny it!"

"Do you deny that you killed Ada Wilkes? Hattie Morrison? Maude Bates?"

"I did not kill them!"

"And what of Mary Wood? Did you kill her?"

"*No!*"

"Did you *know* Mary Wood?"

"I did not!"

"Then tell us, Henry Rutledge," cried Sir Beowulf, suddenly producing a square of white cloth and waving it in the air like a banner, "tell us, if you please, why this handkerchief, which will be marked Exhibit B — this *lady's lace handkerchief* — which bears the *embroidered initials M.W.* — was found *hidden* in your room!"

Rutledge went white. He was speechless.

"Hidden!" the prosecutor repeated. "Like the guilty secret it is! Tell us why!"

"I . . . don't . . ."

"I suggest that you took it from the poor, murdered body of Mary Wood —"

"No!"

"— as a vile memento of your crime, a grim souvenir!"

"No, no, I swear it!"

"Perhaps there are other such souvenirs? Hidden in other places? In the kitchen of the Summerfield house, in the butler's pantry, in the wine-cellar —"

"No — please —"

"Something from each of the murdered women? A bit of ribbon, perhaps, from Emma Davis?"

"No!"

"A string of glass beads from Ada Wilkes?"

"No!"

"Locks of hair from the heads of Hattie Morrison and Maude Bates?"

"No! No! No!"

"Do you *deny* that this handkerchief was hidden in your room?"

"It — I —"

"Do — you — deny it?"

"No . . . I do not . . ." said Rutledge, all but collapsing.

Sir Beowulf turned away from him, throwing the handkerchief upon the table and drawling, with contempt in his voice, "M'lud, I am through with this witness."

Rhys was unable to attend the trial to-day. He may find time to do so to-morrow.

ଚ୬ *Wednesday, 7 June*

"I hope that things will go better for Rutledge this morning," Rhys said to all of us as we seated ourselves in the court-room.

346

"That handkerchief old Gill pulled out of thin air yesterday must have been a bit of a shocker. One of me journalist-friends told me about it. Incidentally, there is a rumour going round that Princess Victoria has been taken ill. I do not know how much truth there may be in it, or, if true, how serious her illness may be, but —"

The court was being called to order. After the preliminaries had been dispensed with, Sir Joel began the procedure of calling upon witnesses to attest to the high character of Rutledge. I should have liked to give testimony, but, as a minor, I required Papa's permission. He said that he preferred not to drag me into the distasteful business. However, he testified on Rutledge's behalf, as did Mamma and Mrs. Pruitt and Hester.

Papa's testimony was the longest: he described Rutledge's earlier life as a climbing-boy for his chimney-sweep father; his successful efforts to raise himself up; his knowledge of Latin; and his record of irreproachable service in our house for over two decades. It was an effective, impassioned speech. Mamma's testimony was the shortest: with hushed voice, and face still hidden by mourning-veil, she merely said that Rutledge was a fine man who had never given her cause for disappointment. Mrs. Pruitt and Hester said that they had never worked for a better man; and that, in all the years that they had known him, there had never been the slightest hint of impropriety in his conduct towards them or towards any of the other female members of the staff.

Although I have condensed this into a paragraph, the actuality took up a great deal of time, particularly with the calling-up and swearing-in, and the questions put by Sir Joel. Sir Beowulf asked no questions of any of these witnesses.

Sir Joel then said: "It can not have escaped notice that this lady and gentleman — he, a prominent man of commerce; his wife, a bishop's daughter — that these good people and their servants, as well, are dressed in garments of mourning. A beloved family member — a young woman with her whole life before her — passed from the world only last month. I think no one will rebuke me if I commend their sense of duty in coming forth voluntarily at such a time, and putting aside their grief, to give testimony."

Sir Beowulf got to his feet and said, "We join our colleague in commending the generosity of these witnesses, and we offer our own inadequate condolences on their loss. We would remind the court, however, that some of the most shocking murders in history have been committed by persons of unimpeachable reputation. If pressed, I might recite an endless anthology of such examples — but I should prefer to spare your ears and my voice that ordeal."

"The court is grateful for that mercy, Sir Beowulf," said his lordship, "and takes your point that a horrifying crime, or even series of crimes, may be committed by a person whose prior life has been blameless."

There was now a short recess. Sir Joel and Mr. Barstow had an intense, whispered, frowning consultation with Rutledge and my parents, during which Rutledge kept shaking his head in firm negation. At one point, his voice rose, and I heard him say, "I won't allow it," and then Sir Joel replied, "Damn it, man, I don't like it any more than you do, but we are on our beam-ends! This is your last chance to save your life!" Rutledge looked at Papa, as if for guidance, his face twisted with shame, and Papa curtly nodded, as if to say: "You have no choice. You must permit it."

The consultation over, Mamma now murmured to me and Papa, "Pamela looks to be fatigued." She smiled, with great effort, at Rhys. "Perhaps Mr. O'Connor will escort her home now?"

I expostulated so loudly that the whole court turned to look in my direction: *"No,* Mamma! I wish to *stay!"*

"Let her stay," Papa said, in a tired voice. "Why should she know only the distorted accounts in the newspapers?"

The recess ended. Sir Joel, addressing the judge, said, "M'lud, I wish to re-call an earlier witness, to present new testimony, relating to facts which have only now come to my attention."

"Will this testimony be of substantial significance?"

"It is my belief, m'lud, that it will completely clear Henry Rutledge and cause the charges against him to be dismissed."

"Indeed?" Lord Palmer responded, raising his eyebrows. "Does the Crown have any objection?"

Sir Beowulf replied, "The Crown objects to nothing that is

in the interest of justice, m'lud. One hopes only that learned counsel's well-known optimism has not led him to exaggerate his expectations."

"I share that hope," said the judge. "Sir Joel, is this testimony likely to be of some length?"

"I will endeavour to conduct it in the shortest possible time, m'lud, but I can not predict the amplitude of my worthy colleague's questions." Here, Sir Joel bowed sardonically to Sir Beowulf, who, with a thin smile, returned the bow.

"Then we will adjourn until to-morrow morning," said Lord Palmer, "when we shall all of us be rested and refreshed and better able to endure such — er — amplitude."

❧ *Thursday, 8 June*

Rhys met us again at the court-room door. "I shouldn't want to miss the last act," he murmured to me. "The tragedy promises to have a happy ending. Sir Joel seems to think that he will win to-day. I wonder what the old fox has up his sleeve?"

We soon found out.

Lord Palmer asked Sir Joel, "Is defence counsel ready to call the next witness?"

"Yes, m'lud. We call again Mrs. Wilfrid Summerfield."

I stared with considerable surprise as Mamma arose, walked forwards, and was reminded that she was still under oath. I whispered, "Papa? What on earth —" But he touched a finger to his lips and gently held my hand. His grip was as cold as that of a corpse.

When Mamma lifted her veil (which she had not done during her brief appearance as a character witness), I saw that she was very pallid. Some may have attributed it to powder, but I knew better: Mamma has never powdered heavily. Despite her pallour, I think that she never looked more beautiful.

Rhys seemed almost to be reading my thoughts. "What a lovely woman she is," he said, softly; and in his tone I told myself that I could hear an unspoken addition: "How much Phoebe resembled her."

"M'lud," said Sir Joel, "I wish the court to know that this

witness has *volunteered* to give further testimony. Indeed, she has insisted."

"The court takes note," said His Lordship. "Carry on."

Sir Joel turned to Mamma. "Mrs. Summerfield," he said, "I will do my utmost not to prolong your testimony. Permit me to ask you, first, for your Christian name."

Her voice, when she replied, was surprisingly strong and resolute: "Melissa."

"And what was your maiden name?"

"Worthing."

"I shew you Exhibit B, a lady's handkerchief, embroidered with the initials M.W. Is it, in fact, yours?"

"Yes." (A rumble of astonishment went round the court.)

"Mrs. Summerfield," Sir Joel went on, "are you the occasional occupant of a domicile other than your husband's house in Berkeley Square?"

"Yes."

"Please tell us the address of that place."

"It is an apartment in The Alroy, in Strathmore Street, Hyde Park."

This time, the response from the court-room was a thunder of uproar, and the usher was forced to demand order. My heart felt squeezed as by a vise. Papa gripped my hand more tightly. Rhys tenderly took my other hand.

"M'lud," said Sir Joel, "gentlemen of the jury, need we detain this courageous lady any longer? The defence rests."

"The Crown does *not* rest," said Sir Beowulf, springing to his feet. "Defence counsel has clumsily attempted to join together two unrelated statements, implying that they are connected, and hoping that this court will draw from them certain inferences that will clear his client. I applaud my worthy colleague's audacity. I admire the courage it required for him to rest his entire case on such flimsy stuff. But I am shocked and sorry to learn that he considers this court to be composed of blockheads who will be taken in by his tactics. This lady tells us that she keeps rooms at The Alroy. Many people keep such rooms, in addition to their houses, as convenient way-stations, havens where they may rest or bathe or otherwise freshen themselves during a day's shopping, perhaps; or as studios where they may write or paint, undisturbed. It is a costly luxury, but the cost is a trifle to a wealthy person such as this witness. And yet defence counsel hopes to stun us into stupefaction by this unremarkable fact; he seeks to pull the wool over our eyes. Then there is the matter of the handkerchief. Again, he would amaze us with the knowledge that it is the property of this lady — but I am amazed only by his enormous presumption. Mrs. Summerfield, is it not true that Henry Rutledge purloined this old handkerchief of yours without your knowledge — no doubt for some bizarre pleasure it afforded his abnormal mind?"

Mamma licked her lips and swallowed visibly. "No," she said. "I gave it him."

"At his request?"

"Yes."

"He exerted some power over you, then; some spell; some threat, perhaps?"

"No. I gave him the handkerchief willingly."

"For what purpose?"

"As a keepsake. A token."

"A token of what?"

"Affection."

"Aff —— For your *butler?*"

Sir Joel said, "Witness has already answered the question."

"I withdraw it," said Sir Beowulf. "Madam, defence counsel has tried to establish a connexion between the fact that you keep certain rooms at The Alroy and the fact that the accused has been seen entering that block of flats. But surely there are many apartments in The Alroy other than yours?"

"Of course."

"And surely the accused may have been visiting any one of them; may indeed have been the tenant of one, from which he carried out his degraded crimes, unknown to you. I suggest, Mrs. Summerfield, that the accused never met you at The Alroy."

"That is untrue. He did."

"My dear lady," said Sir Beowulf, "we must all admire the unselfishness of your effort to help a faithful servant — but do you expect us to believe that, by the most absurd of coincidences, you met Henry Rutledge at The Alroy only on the specific dates of January twenty-one, February twenty, March twenty-two, April twenty, and May twenty — on which dates the moon *just happened* to be full, and five women *just happened* to be murdered?"

"Why, no," said Mamma; "not *only* on those dates, and not always at The Alroy."

"Will you please elucidate?"

"We have been meeting at The Alroy for only the past five or six years. Prior to that, we met in other rooms, in Knightsbridge and in Chelsea."

Amazed at these statements, Sir Beowulf murmured, as if to himself, "For only five or six years . . ." Then he turned to Mamma again. "Madam, may I ask how long you have been meeting the accused, in various apartments?"

"I think it must be close to fifteen years, now," she replied. (I glanced at Papa. Tears were tric..ling down his cheeks.)

"Fifteen years!" echoed Sir Beowulf, his composure shattered. "And always, purely by chance, on the night of the full moon?"

"Not by chance," said Mamma. "By design."

"May we know that design?"

"It is a simple one. We wished to have some set time every month, when we should agree to meet without the necessity of further discussion. We wished, also, to avoid too obvious a pattern, which might draw suspicious attention; and, for that reason, we rejected a set date of the month or a set day of the week, settling instead on the night of the full moon, which falls on different days and dates."

"I see," said Sir Beowulf, clearly stunned. "And there was no other reason?"

"What other reason should there be?"

"The witness," said Lord Palmer, "must answer questions, not ask them, Madam."

"I beg your pardon, my lord."

"Proceed, Sir Beowulf — with velocity, if possible."

I looked at Rutledge in the dock. He was staring at the floor, covered with shame.

"Mrs. Summerfield," said Sir Beowulf, recovering some of

his former aplomb, "do you expect this court to believe that, although Henry Rutledge has been meeting you in Hyde Park for the past five or six years, it is only in the past five *months* that residents of Hyde Park have taken notice of him?"

"I expect you to have the good sense, Sir Beowulf, to realise that his comings and goings, if seen, were of no interest to anybody, and therefore were not impressed upon the memory — *until* the murders made everybody in Hyde Park unusually alert to any variance or anomaly."

Sir Beowulf was silent, searching for words. The judge, taking advantage of this hiatus, said, "To satisfy what I hope is not a frivolous curiosity, Madam, may I ask why such an elaborate arrangement was designed? I mean to say, if the two principals in this matter desired to form such a *liaison*, would it not have been simpler for them to — er — come together in some snuggery or other of the no-doubt commodious house in which they both lived?"

Mamma turned and looked sternly at him. "My lord," she said, "I think I am a woman of some character. I hope you do not believe that I am so coarse, so calloused, so vulgar and unfeeling, that I would form such an attachment under my husband's very roof? In the same house with my children?"

"I apologise for the question, Madam. Sir Beowulf, do you have any further questions of this witness?"

Sir Beowulf looked at Mamma. His mouth opened. It closed again. "I do not, m'lud," he said. Then, obviously with great pain and effort, he added, "The Crown moves for dismissal of the charges against Henry Rutledge."

"You may step down, Mrs. Summerfield," said Lord Palmer.

Mamma turned, chin up like a queen, and then quietly fainted, falling out of our sight.

"Melissa!"

It was not Papa who called out, but Rutledge, who sprang from the dock and rushed to her side, saying, "Some water, please!"

When she had been revived, and Rutledge had helped her to a chair, Lord Palmer spoke:

"I can not make an end of these proceedings without remarking on the lesson which they have taught us. We are all human, and made of weak, corruptible flesh; but, just as there is a hierarchy in Heaven — with its angels and archangels, cherubim and seraphim, and an Omnipotent Deity over all — so there is a hierarchy here below. The society of men, emulating that of Heaven, is arranged in layers, from the highest to the lowest — and rightly so, else all were Chaos. Between each of these layers, there is a great gulf fixed. Woe betide those who would disregard those gulfs! In to-day's disclosures, we have learnt what havoc can be wrought when a person of one class bestows intimacy on a person of another. Think of the anguish and humiliation which this otherwise respectable woman has brought upon herself, her husband, her children, by descending beneath her class in this lamentable affair. Reflect upon her disgrace, and profit by the horror of her example. Mrs. Summerfield, you are a foolish woman, afflicted by the frailties of your sex, and are no more than ridiculous and disreputable. But *you,* Henry Rutledge, are infamous. You are contemptible. You are an upstart, an ingrate, a lecherous bounder; and were it in my power, I would order you to be flogged through the streets. However, because judicial powers in this lax age are regrettably limited, I am constrained to say — against my will — that all charges against you are dismissed, and this court is adjourned."

"Insufferable old ass," muttered Rhys.

ፄ *Friday, 9 June*

The journey home from the Central Criminal Court yesterday lasted for an unbearable eternity. Not one of the three of us uttered a word. Papa looked as if he had been bludgeoned. Mamma appeared to be on the point of fainting again. God alone knows what *I* looked like.

As we left the court-room, Rhys asked me if I wished him to accompany me home. I told him that I did not, and he went his way.

When our coach arrived home, Mamma and I climbed out, but Papa told Paley to drive on to his club. Mamma went directly to her room, and I to mine.

It was all so grim and silent and horrid — worse, *much* worse than the aftermath of a funeral — for after the burial of a dear one, there is always a great release, and everybody has a keen appetite, and enormous quantities of food are eaten, "the funeral bak'd meats." There is conversation about the departed — fond remembrances — amusing anecdotes — even laughter ("Do you recall the hilarious way he had of . . ." etc.).

But the house yesterday, after the trial, was not at all like a funeral — it was like a tomb. When I came down to dinner yesterday evening, I was the only one seated at table. A moment later, the tureen of soup was carried in by Crewe.

"Where is Rutledge?" I asked him. "Has he not come back?"

"Come and gone, Miss."

"Gone?"

"Packed his bags and left, Miss. I believe he left behind a note for your parents."

"Where *are* my parents? Are they not dining?"

"Mrs. Summerfield will have a tray in her room, she says. Mr. Summerfield will dine at his club. Turtle soup, Miss?"

"No, thank you, Crewe. I'll not be dining, after all."

"Are you certain, Miss? Mrs. Pruitt's done a nice joint of beef."

"Quite certain. You may clear."

This morning, I arose early and wrote this letter:

"My dear Rhys, —

"By this letter, I am absolving you of your obligation to marry me.

"My affection for you has not changed; but, in good conscience, I can not bind you to marriage into a family which you must now consider to be iniquitous.

"As for Brian, I entreat you to let me rear him in this house as my own. People will point the finger at me, but what does a little more scandal matter, in a household already scandalous?

355

"Of course, you may demand that I relinquish the child into your care. You are his father, and you have that right. I ask only that you let me know your decision soon.

"Your ever-grateful
"Pamela"

I gave the letter to Crewe for an early posting, and then I knocked on Mamma's door. Entering her room, I saw her sitting up in bed, reading a letter. A breakfast tray had been set to one side.

"Are you not coming down to breakfast, Mamma?"

"I've had coffee and a bit of toast. But *you* must eat a good breakfast, my dear. I understand that you had no dinner at all last night. It will not do."

"I shall eat, Mamma."

"You appear to have something on your mind, Pam. I am not surprised. Do you wish to talk?"

"Do you?"

"I don't mind. I'm feeling much better this morning." She patted the bed at her side. "Come, sit down." I did so.

"Crewe told me that Rutledge has left," I said.

Mamma nodded and sighed. "He thought it best. And your father stayed at his club last night."

I told Mamma, "I wrote to Rhys, breaking off our engagement."

"Oh, dear. Was that wise, do you think? Was it necessary?"

"I do not want to put him in the position of going through with a marriage that may now be repugnant to him, merely because of a prior promise that he is too honourable to break."

"Yes, I understand," said Mamma. "But are you sure that you are not misjudging him? Is he the kind of man who would think you tarnished by *my* peccadillos? The truth of it, I believe, is that *you* feel somehow tarnished by yesterday's revelations."

"No, Mamma —"

"I'm afraid that my testimony shocked you very much."

"It — surprised me."

"I dare say. And it hurt your father most cruelly, of course. But what a good man he is. The night before we revealed it to

356

Sir Joel, I confessed all to your father. It was as if I had stabbed his heart with a dagger. Another man might have struck me. But he said, 'You must tell this in open court.' I said, 'How can I? It would tear apart our family.' He replied, 'The life of an innocent man is at stake. That is all that matters.' "

"What will happen now, Mamma?"

"I am uncertain," she said, glancing idly at the letter in her lap.

"Is that from Aunt Esmie?" I asked, although I knew it was not in my aunt's hand.

"No, it's from Henry. That is, Rutledge. He left it behind for me." She paused. "I expect that you find me contemptible."

"I could *never* think you contemptible, Mamma! But I do find the whole matter so terribly difficult to understand."

"In some ways, so do I," she said. "My father, the bishop, was fond of a passage from the Book of Jeremiah. He used to quote it, often: 'The heart is deceitful above all things, and desperately wicked: who can know it?' "

"Did you actually — love — Rutledge? For fifteen years?"

"What is strange about that? I have loved your father for a much longer time."

"You loved them both — at once?"

"I did, and do. Good Heavens, child, there is nothing peculiar in that. Do you not love Mr. O'Connor? And — confess, now! — do you not still love Giles Ormond?"

I nodded, somewhat sheepishly.

"I expect," said Mamma, "that what actually bewilders you is what attracted me to Rutledge."

I nodded again.

"He is not much younger than your father, and he is less handsome. He is of low station. He is excessively proper; one might almost say prim — nothing of the rogue about him. I am not sure that I can put it into words. As you know, your birth was a great travail for me, and after it, I was told that I could no longer bear children. This had an effect on me. Although neither your father nor I felt obliged to enlarge our family any further, I felt an unreasonable guilt, as if I had, somehow, failed him. I felt as if I were no longer a woman —

not a complete woman, at any rate — and when your father would turn to me in the natural way of a husband, I was cold towards him. In my foolishness, I told myself that he did not truly desire me; that he was going through a pretence to spare my feelings; fulfilling an obligation to perform his conjugal duties. I am sure now that I was wrong: his feelings had not changed — not, that is, till my continued coldness finally was the cause of a coldness in him. Some time passed. A year, two years, more. We still loved each other, but that part of our life, we tacitly agreed, was now over. If your father had sought solace elsewhere, I could not have condemned him, but I do not believe that he did.

"One day whilst he was in the City, I caught the tip of my shoe in a carpet edge on the landing, and would have fallen down the stairs and been injured — had not Rutledge reached out and caught me in time. I felt the strength of his arms round me, like bands of steel. I realised how long it had been since a man had held me so. I had not known, till that moment, how much I had missed it. I had been dead for such a long time; but now, in his arms, I felt life flooding through me again, in waves of delightful warmth. He said, in such a gentle voice, 'You've not hurt yourself, ma'am?' I said, 'I don't know — perhaps my ankle — please help me to my bedroom, Rutledge.' I had meant for him only to lend me his arm as far as the door, and I was surprised when he lifted me up as if I were a feather and carried me into my room and placed me upon my bed.

" 'Which ankle is it, ma'am?' he asked. 'The right one,' I said. He removed my shoe. I felt his fingers on my ankle, my foot, delicately massaging through the stocking. Desire welled up in me. I had no control of myself. I reached out my hand and stroked his lovely thick hair. As I did so, I was shocked at my action, and feared that he would be shocked, too — that he would recoil in surprise and embarrassment. But his response was entirely unexpected. At first, there was no response at all; and then, he pressed his lips to my foot in a kiss of unmistakable ardour. In the next moment, and with the most urgent willingness on my part, he took me, here on this bed. It was the only time it ever happened in your father's house. From that time on, having been thawed, so to speak, my life with your father also bloomed again. We became like young lovers once more, and I went from one extreme to another — from a desiccated, half-dead creature to a lusty lady with an embarrassment of carnal riches to enjoy.

"Rutledge is a remarkable man, Pamela. I had always admired him. The way he educated himself, by sheer strength of will, without help from anybody. The masterful way he took charge of things. He was so very masculine. For the rest — all I can say is, when he touched me, I burst into flame like dry tinder and became a different person — a person whom you, whom even your father, would not have recognised — a creature completely without restraint, willing to do anything he might ask of me. Anything — no matter how degenerate or outlandish. It is to his credit that his demands — how can I even call them demands? — his attentions were always of the tenderest and most decorous kind."

Tears came to my eyes. "I do understand, Mamma. Truly I do. When Giles touched me — I felt exactly the same."

She gripped my hand. "Don't fret. Things will sort themselves out. And now you must go down and eat breakfast, and allow me to get dressed. We shall meet again at luncheon."

Shortly after luncheon, when Mamma and I were in the drawing-room, Crewe announced Rhys — who burst in upon us impatiently, even before Crewe had finished uttering his name. My letter was in his hand.

"Pamela!" he cried. "What snobbish, pompous balderdash is this? I beg your pardon, Mrs. Summerfield, but this silly daughter of yours has written the most absurd letter I have ever received!"

"Do come in, Mr. O'Connor," said Mamma, coolly, "and sit down. May we offer you something?"

He did not sit down. "Pamela — you dear, foolish child — what can you think of me? Am I, in your eyes, some priggish country curate? Do you think I care a fig for what the newspapers are saying? They are all disgusting rags, the lot of them — and I know that full well, having written for some of them meself! But nothing that has ever been written for any of those fish-wrappings is half as nonsensical as *this!*" He tore my letter into shreds and flung the pieces into the grate, where, if there had been a fire, they would have been soon reduced to ashes.

Then, without so much as a by-your-leave, he pulled me out of the chair, to my feet, and crushed me in his arms, squeezing the breath out of my lungs and pressing his mouth to mine so brutally — yet so deliciously — that I feared my lips would be swollen and bruised. At length, he released my lips, though not my body, and — with the brogue rising thick in his voice like a mist in a bog — he said: "We'll be havin' no more o' that, me girl. No more o' that, at-all, at-all. 'Tis yourself I'll be for marryin', and no other."

"Well said, Mr. O'Connor," Mamma murmured, "albeit in that exotic accent that seems to come and go without warning, like the showers of Spring. But you will now unhand my daughter, if you please."

"Forgive me, Madam," he said (in perfect English again), letting me go. "But I had to shew the addled little ninny that I love her."

"I am sure that your demonstration has succeeded," she said. "I, for one, never doubted your love; and, if I had been *you,* sir, I think I should have taken her over my knee and spanked her, into the bargain. Not that I am suggesting that you do so."

Rhys bowed to her, and said, "I'll be off now, Madam, but I hope that I may come to tea to-morrow?"

"Come to tea, by all means, Mr. O'Connor. You will be our only guest. This is the house of a scarlet woman, you know."

" 'Tis a lovely colour," said Rhys, with a smile. "It matches me hair. Till to-morrow, then." He bowed, and left.

Papa again did not come home for dinner, but much later, shortly after I had got into bed, I heard his step on the landing, and then I heard him enter Mamma's room. I threw off the bed-clothes and, holding a water tumbler to my ear and pressing it to the wall (unforgivable behaviour!), I heard enough to reconstruct the following conversation:

"I came to collect a few of my things. I shall send for the rest of my effects later. I am going to move into my club until I can find rooms."

"No, Wilfrid."

"What do you mean, 'No'?"

"It is out of the question that you should quit your own house. You are not the transgressor. *I* am. I have done you a grievous wrong. You have never wronged anybody. You must stay."

"That is impossible. We can not continue to live together."

"I know that. It is *I* who must leave."

"You? Where would you go?"

"To Paris."

"That is unthinkable! You don't know a soul there. How would you live?"

"I hope that you will not deny me my father's money? Legally, of course, you can —"

"No, of course I shall not. But —"

"And, as for not knowing a soul in Paris — I shall know Henry."

"Rutledge?"

"He has already gone there and has asked me to join him."

"My God!"

"I love you, Wilfrid. I always shall. But it is my curse to love two fine men — in somewhat different ways, it may be — and now I am faced with a choice."

"And you choose him."

"That is not the point. You have just said that you and I can no longer live together. I have lost you. I know that. Must I lose both of my men? I am not choosing one man over the other — I am trying to salvage something — some small pathetic fragment — out of the wreckage I have made of my life. Of all our lives."

"Will you be requiring a divorce?" Papa asked.

"Will you?"

"Good Lord, no. There is enough scandal as it is. I have no wish to marry again. But you — and Rutledge —"

"We shall — I believe the expression is 'live in sin.' We are not known in Paris. Possibly we shall change our names."

There was a long silence, and then I heard Mamma say, "Oh, Wilfrid, my dear, do not weep. You will break my heart."

Finally, in a choked voice, Papa said, "When will you leave?"

"To-morrow."

"So soon?"

"What would be the point in delay?"

Another moment of silence, and Papa said, "I shall sleep in Will's room to-night."

"If that is your wish."

"My *wish?!* What have my wishes to do with it? My *wish* is to sleep here with you!"

"Even now?"

"Even now."

"You would — use me — one last time, then?"

"Use you? What a dreadful thing to say!"

"What else *can* I say? What am I to think?"

"Melissa, it is not just this one night that I wish to to be with you. It is all the nights to come."

"But you said we can not live together."

"Damn what I said! A man says many things when he is hurt! But if you find my attentions loathsome —"

"Loathsome! Oh, you poor darling man! I was a child — an aging child, I admit — presented with two kinds of cake. I could not choose between them, and so I gorged myself on both."

"Do you truly mean that?"

"With all of my heart."

"Do you love me? Do you swear it?"

"By the Almighty God Who is my judge."

"Then do not leave me, Melissa. Do not go to him. *Choose* this time. And, I beg of you, choose *me.*"

There was another silence, much longer than any of the others, and then Mamma spoke — so softly that I could scarcely hear — saying what I *think* were these words:

"Remarkable. And at your age."

That is when I put down the water tumbler.

I will not say that all the clouds have blown away and that everything is once more as it was. For one thing, Rutledge is gone, and that seems very strange, indeed, for he has been an important part of this household all of my life. We catch ourselves saying, "Tell Rutledge —" or "Call Rutledge —" or "Rutledge will see to it —"

And there is another oddness in the air — an unnaturally over-courteous, over-solicitous manner between Mamma and Papa; a straining to behave as if nothing had happened.

Of course, there are the newspapers — and the less said of them, the better. Papa refuses to take them into the house, and I do not blame him.

Our true friends remain still true. The Cargraves, for example, continue to call upon us, with no change whatever in their behaviour. Mamma's friend the Widow Ridgely also calls, with her detestable daughters, but in all of their faces is such a look of pity and pain and condescension and righteous superiority that I am sorely tempted to pour the tea into their laps. Those twins have always been little beasts, the pair of them, and they always will be. I hate their thin lips and their watery eyes. I have always hated those particular features of theirs, just as I have hated their drab minds and priggish manners. I shall persist in my belief that one or both of them *did* glue together the pages of my Mother Goose book — no matter *what* Willy may say to the contrary.

Lord and Lady Merlyngton have cut us completely. Good riddance, I say. But I fear that Papa's knighthood is now lost to him. He would have liked to be called Sir Wilfrid, I think, and I know that I should have been terribly proud, for his sake. His faithful friend and business associate, Mr. Randall, remains staunch and true.

As for this diarist, all my cherished hopes of becoming a friend and confidante of our future Queen have been dashed to the ground. No matter how generous and sensible she may be (and I believe her to be both), her station will never allow her to be familiar with any member of such a scandalous family.

I think occasionally of Giles. If he were still courting me, what would his attitude now be? Would he bravely ignore the gossips and stay at my side? It is wrong to judge him hypothetically, but I think he would not. Giles has an eye ever fixed on the main chance, and a concern for appearance and propriety and the good opinion of so-called good people. I do think that he would not remain true.

As I sat down to write these lines, I first leafed idly through the pages of earlier months; and my curiosity led me to seek out those dates of the full moon, so significant to this family. There, indelibly written in bold black ink, is corroborative evidence of Mamma's secret life:

On 21 January, I wrote: "Mamma returned from shopping to-day just in time to preside over our at-home." On 20 February, I wrote that she "left the house on business of her own." On 22 March, I wrote nothing in these pages, for I spent the whole of that day in bed. April 20 was the day that "she returned, just a few minutes before Papa came in from the City," bringing me Mr. Carlyle's *Sartor Resartus,* instead of his *French Revolution.* And just three weeks ago, on 20 May: "Mamma returned from an afternoon outing scarcely in time to change and receive our guests . . ." How queer: it was all there, all the time, in my own hand — those hours of absence and late returnings — but I never took especial note of them. Eyes had I but I saw not.

ॐ *Sunday, 11 June*

In the coach this morning, returning from worship, Mamma again brought up the question of Rhys and his attitude towards a church wedding.

"Have you broached the subject to him yet?"

"I'm afraid I quite forgot."

"Further delay would not be wise! The wedding is less than three weeks away!"

"Rhys is coming to tea to-morrow," I said. "I shall bring up the matter then."

"See that you do, my dear; for if you do not, *I will.*"

Before Rhys arrived this afternoon, I begged Mamma to sound him out on the church question herself. "You are a bishop's daughter, Mamma; you will know exactly what to say and how to say it." Reluctantly, she agreed to take on the task.

"Mr. O'Connor," she said, after tea had been poured and Madeira cake served, "I have some notion of your present opinion of churches, but I am wondering if, as a child, you had a religious upbringing."

"Well, this was the way of it, Mrs. Summerfield," he said. "I was brought up in Dublin — although I left it as soon as I could and came to London to make me fortune. Father's people were Irish Catholics, but himself did not take it all that seriously. He went to Mass only on certain holidays — Easter, Christmas, and what-not. Mother was a good deal more steady in her church-going and took me with her every Sunday for many years — but she, you see, was Welsh and a Protestant. I'm called after her father. As a result of this patchy sort of religious upbringing, very little of it stuck to me, saving a deep respect for the fine language of King James's Bible, one of the glories of our literature, along with your daughter's favourite, Mr. Shakespere. Then, later, I shed it all off, like a snake shedding its skin, and became, for a time, inimical to religion of all varieties. This has simmered down, now, to a kind of indifference or neutrality — except when there's talk of enforcing the fine for not attending Sunday worship; then, of course, me principles compel me to speak out."

"Most interesting," said Mamma. "This is a religious household, you should know. Church of England. We attend worship every Sunday and on all the important holidays. So do our staff. We used to have a scullery-maid who was a Roman Catholic; we allowed her to attend Mass. You remember her, Pamela: Bridget. My father was a bishop; my son is a missionary in Africa."

"I know most of that already, Madam," said Rhys.

"My purpose in bringing up these matters," Mamma went on, "is to make certain that you understand that Pamela will be married in a religious ceremony. I trust you will present no obstacle to that?"

"May I have another cup of tea?" Rhys asked. "And just a drop of milk. Thank you." He sipped and then said: "I am a man of certain principles, Mrs. Summerfield. I like to think that I am no hypocrite. When I was a bit younger, I would have considered it a breach of my convictions to go through a religious ceremony of any kind. But I think I have learnt something of — I will not say compromise, but — call it tact or good manners or common courtesy. I am willing to go through all the motions of the wedding service, Madam, and if I can not, in good conscience, say that I believe every single word of it, let me assure you that I will not disdain or mock it. And let me say something further. I have not been inside a church for many years. The last time was when I was but a boy, when Mother took me. On the thirtieth of this month, when I step into that church and stand at Pamela's side, who is to say what memories of childhood may not flood me? what sentiments? what tears, perhaps? what cherished remembrance of Mother's face, long lost to me through death? Be certain, Madam, that in no way will I desecrate the faith that she held dear."

"Thank you, sir," said Mamma. "I am satisfied. More cake?"

ఞ *Tuesday, 13 June*

The King is continuing to be very bad in his health, it is said. We hear that Lord Palmerston believes all hope to be gone. I pray for our dear King and ask God to spare that good man suffering in his final days — for it seems futile to pray now for his life.

ఞ *Wednesday, 14 June*

Even more disturbing than yesterday's news about King William is the rumour abroad to-day that the Princess has been taken ill — *quite* ill, it seems.

I remember Rhys, at some point during Rutledge's trial,

telling us that she had been ailing, but now her condition appears to have worsened — and nobody will say precisely what the illness is. Perhaps they do not know? Could it be the dread hæmophilia that afflicts so many royal families?

Our monarch and his successor, both gravely ill: we must all pray for them, and for England.

ঙ *Thursday, 15 June*

Papa seemed to be rather glum when he returned from the City this afternoon. At dinner, he said very little. I thought that he was, perhaps, worried about the illnesses of King William and Princess Victoria — and, of course, he is; we are, all of us, worried — or that he was possibly still in low spirits because of the trial and the disclosures about Mamma. Or even pining still for Phoebe.

I did not wish to ask him "Is anything wrong?" — for he could, with justice, reply, "Is not *everything* wrong? You would do better to ask me: Is anything *right*?" So I held my peace and left it up to Mamma to say, as she did, "You are very silent this evening, Wilfrid."

"What? Yes, I expect that I am. Sorry, my dear. But there was the most curious rumour going about the City to-day. It was Mr. Randall who first heard it and passed it on to me. Apparently, the whole town is buzzing with it."

"Well, what *is* it, Papa?" I asked, with great lack of patience.

"I could not believe it, at first. Stuff and nonsense, I said. But later, after leaving my office to return home, I made a point of stopping by the Tower to find out for myself —"

"The Tower?" Mamma interjected. "What has the Tower to do with it?"

"Everything, in fact," said Papa. "It's the ravens. They're gone."

"*Gone?*" I repeated.

"Vanished. Flown the coop. Every man jack of 'em."

"God in Heaven!" I said.

"There is no need for profanity," Mamma admonished.

"But the old legend —" I began to say.

367

"Is simply an absurd superstition," said Mamma, "and you are not a superstitious young lady. England will not fall merely because some birds have flown away from the Tower of London — no matter *how* many centuries they have been there. Am I not right, Wilfrid?"

"Right about what, my dear?"

"The nation will not fall in ruin because a few ravens have flown off."

"No, of course not. It's all rubbish."

None the less, he had no appetite for his dinner. Nor did I. Nor — I could not but notice — did Mamma.

After dinner, I wished to be alone, so I came up here to my sitting-room. "Old wives' tales," I kept muttering, over and over again. I reminded myself of the way in which Aunt Esmie's *tarot* cards had fallen to the floor on the very night Rutledge had been arrested for murder — all of them face down, save for The Hanged Man. *There* was an awful omen, if you please — but Rutledge had been found innocent and had gone free, his neck untouched by the hangman's hemp. So much for prophecy! (Although Rutledge *did* attempt to hang himself . . .)

In a spirit of defiance, or bravado, I took out the pack of *tarot* cards and dealt out several draws.

The first time, I drew the Death card, followed by that seemingly persistent Hanged Man. Death is represented as a skeleton with a scythe, standing on a blackened field littered with severed heads and hands and feet. Not a picture to inspire confidence, but I stuck out my tongue at it and referred to Aunt Esmie's letter, the one that had accompanied the cards. In a part of that letter, she explained the alleged "meanings" of various combinations.

According to her, the Death card followed by The Hanged Man predicts "death with bad consequences." How gloomy.

Nothing daunted, I shuffled the cards and laid out another draw. I drew the *same two cards* — which somewhat took me aback — but in reverse order: The Hanged Man, followed by Death. Aunt Esmie's letter says that this foretells "death by criminal means." Worse and worse!

Still, I pressed on, and on the third draw, I drew Death

again! — followed by the card of Force. On this card, a lady is shewn, prying open the jaws of a golden-maned lion. (The British lion? Can the lady be Victoria?) Aunt Esmie says that the Death card, followed by the card of Force, is "a prophecy of *brutal* death" and "an abrupt break-up of matter," whatever *that* may mean. What cryptic words!

And what relentlessly gruesome cards! I am *not* superstitious and will pay them no heed.

But I fear that I shall dream of them to-night.

೫ *Friday, 16 June*

This is the blackest day that England has ever known.

I still can not believe it; I can not come to grips with the full horror of what has happened. And the far greater horror of what is yet to come. (How curiously those words echo certain fear-filled words in an old letter of Phoebe's: *what is yet to come.*)

It was Rhys who brought the awful news, banging our door-knocker at an unseemly hour this morning, rousing the staff, demanding to see me, to see us all. Crewe was uncertain that he should admit him, and bade him wait till Papa could be awakened. But impetuous Rhys, tossing propriety to the wind, pushed past him and ran up the staircase, pounding on our doors and shouting: "Wake up! Wake up, all of you!"

I thought that the house was afire. We all stumbled out of our bedrooms, to the landing, blear-eyed, struggling into our dressing-gowns. Papa was furious. He roared at Rhys, "Damn it, sir! Do you know the hour? What are you playing at?"

Rhys was extremely distrait: his face was flushed, his dress in disarray, his hair uncombed.

"What *is* it, my dear?" I asked.

"Doomed," he said; "we are all doomed!"

"Explain yourself!" Papa demanded. "Doomed? What do you mean by it? Who is doomed?"

"England," said Rhys, in what was very near a wail or a keening.

"Is it — war?" I asked.

"I wish it were." He groaned.

"Out with it, man," said Papa. "What has happened?"

"The most dreadful thing that could possibly have happened," Rhys replied. "We are at the mercy of a man far worse than any tyrant in all of English history! We must measure him against Nero, Caligula, Ivan of Russia, to find his equal!"

"What can you mean, Mr. O'Connor?" asked Mamma.

"Cumberland is King!" Rhys cried.

"Absurd," said Papa. "What hoax is this?"

"It is no hoax, sir," Rhys replied, shaking his head woefully. "The Duke of Cumberland — that incestuous, murdering madman — is King. Or he will be, in a matter of mere days."

"Rhys!" I exclaimed, taking his hand. "What are you saying? Is King William —"

"The King still lives, but can not live much longer. It is a catastrophe that many have feared but have not dared to think of. It is the Princess!"

"Victoria?"

He nodded.

"What about her?" I demanded.

"She is dead!"

I felt as if I had been struck in the stomach by a cannon-ball. Time froze. Sound stopped. My parents' lips were moving, but I could hear nothing that they said. They and Rhys all turned to me suddenly, with shock in their faces — Rhys reached out for me — the carpeted floor of the landing sprang up and struck me in the face — I was sucked down into a giant's inkpot —

A revolting pungency filled my nostrils, my head, made my eyes burn — I pulled away from it — and I came to the realisation that I was lying on the landing and that Mamma was holding spirits of ammonia under my nose. I pushed her hand away — gagged and coughed — and allowed Rhys to help me to my feet.

"My dear," he asked, "are you better?"

I nodded. "A glass of water?" I said weakly, and tried to walk, but my knees gave way and he held me up.

"Take her into her bedroom," said Mamma.

Rhys picked me up and carried me into my room and placed

me gently upon my bed. Mamma poured out a tumbler of water and held it to my lips. I took but a small sip, and then I looked up at Rhys and said, "It can not be — true?"

"There is no doubt of it," he replied.

"Oh, my God!"

Papa, quietly now, said, "How did you learn of this? When did she die?"

"A bit past four this morning," Rhys said, misery darkening his voice. "I heard it from a journalist-friend, who heard it from one of the staff at Kensingston Palace — an informant of his."

"But — how —" That was Mamma.

"No-one knows how. She was ailing for several days. No apparent cause. Then she took a turn for the worse — and now —"

I said, hollowly: "Poison. I'm sure of it. That beast, Cumberland, poisoned her! He finally succeeded! All those old stories — they were true!"

Papa put his arm about me. "Now, now, Princess. You must not leap to conclusions. The Duke is of the blood royal. Victoria was his niece. He will soon be our King. You must not say such things. Besides, how could such a poisoning be managed? The Princess seldom leaves — seldom left — Kensington Palace."

"That rambling place!" I responded, scornfully. "It's casually guarded — a dozen people can hide there without fear of detection. And if a journalist can keep an informant there, why not Cumberland a poisoner?" I looked up fiercely at Rhys. "*You* believe he poisoned her, don't you?"

"I do not know what to believe," he said. "I only know that Cumberland is a foul, perverted swine who is not fit to *live* — let alone be King of England!"

"Come, Mr. O'Connor," said Papa. "Those are strong words. The Duke has been much maligned by his enemies — rascals like Conroy, with their own axes to grind —"

"I have little love or respect for King John," said Rhys, "but he is Jesus Himself next to Cumberland. I tell you, sir, this country — this empire — can not endure, with such a man on the throne."

Mamma asked, "Is it not possible that your friend, or his informant, was mistaken? Perhaps the Princess is alive, after all, and we are all making ourselves upset for no cause."

In reply, Rhys strode to the nearest window and threw it open. " 'Tis all over London by now," he said. "Listen."

We heard a boy in the street, selling papers, bawling:

"Death of 'Er 'Ighness! Death of Victoria! Buy a paper, sir? Death of Princess Victoria! . . ."

I clasped my hands together in despairing fervour. "Dear God in Heaven!" I prayed. "Protect us! Protect our people! God save England from that unspeakable monster!"

It was only later that I remembered to pray, as well, for the soul of our dead Victoria.

৪৬ *Saturday, 17 June*

Stunned. Numb. That is my condition. It is the condition of all in this house; all in this country, I do not doubt. That good young lady, my age to the day, gone for ever. It is too much for the mind to encompass. I have been aware of her for as far back as my memory will stretch; she has always been part of my life; I have always sensed the parallel on which our two lives were lived — hers, royal; mine, common — she, my future Queen; I, her future subject. She seemed to be a piece of me, like an arm or a chamber of my heart; and when at last I had the great privilege of meeting her face to face last month, I felt myself to be the most fortunate of creatures. Now she is dead, and a piece of me is dead, and our country faces a period of unimaginable strife.

৪৬ *Sunday, 18 June*

The King is too ill to be told of Victoria's death. That awful news alone could kill him on the spot, says Mr. Cargrave, who has been called in to assist the King's physician. Even so, he can not live much longer. This is Waterloo Day, of course, and the dear old man's mind is clear enough to know it. Although he was almost suffocating with asthma, he said, "This is the eighteenth of June. I should like to live to see the sun of Waterloo set." We have heard from Mr. Cargrave that the

Duke of Wellington sent the Tricolour to the royal bed-side. King William was moved: "Right, right," he whispered to Lord Munster. "Unfurl it and let me feel it. Glorious day!"

All of England was on its knees in church to-day, praying for him. In many hearts, I am certain, another prayer was offered, for England herself.

ॐ *Monday, 19 June*

This is a cutting from the morning edition:

FULL MOON ATTACK
IN HYDE PARK

Last night, in Hyde Park, a woman narrowly escaped serious harm and possible death at the hands of an assailant.

Violet Muncie, a parlour-maid employed by a family of the area, fought her attacker so resolutely, and shouted so loudly, that he fled, probably for fear that her shouts would attract constables.

Constables did arrive upon the scene, in response to her cries, although they were too late to apprehend the malefactor.

"He put his hands around my throat and tried to strangle me," Miss Muncie told the constables. This mode of attack, coupled with the fact that last night was a time of the full moon, suggest that the man may well have been "The Full Moon Fiend" who is responsible for the murders of five women in Hyde Park. Miss Muncie might have been the sixth such victim had she not resisted him so strenuously and frightened him off with her cries.

The sky being heavily overcast last night, Miss Muncie was unable to furnish the constables with a good description of the culprit, despite the full moon. She could say only, "He was a tall man, and very strong. I did not see his features clearly, but when I put my hands on his face to push him away, I could feel that he was not only bearded but disfigured, as it may be by the scar of an old wound."

The police are continuing their investigation, although they are not sanguine about the possibility of an early solution. In the words of Colonel Charles Rowan: "There are hundreds, even thousands, of men in London who might fit that description."

True — but need I add my own unswerving suspicion regarding the Fiend's identity?

The King is much worse, although he still clings to life.

ᘒ *Tuesday, 20 June*

The King is dead.

Our dear King William departed this world at twelve minutes past two this morning, in the Blue Room of Buckingham Palace. To the end, Mr. Cargrave tells us, he knew nothing of the death of Victoria.

The King is dead. But I will not hypocritically add, Long live the King.

ᘒ *Wednesday, 21 June*

Rhys joined us at the dinner-table this evening, and he was full of stories of the new King, gleaned from divers sources and filtered through his friends in the world of journalism.

"He has chosen to be called Augustus the First," he said.

"How very — Augustan," Mamma remarked.

"'Tis that," said Rhys. "He undoubtedly relishes the Imperial Caesar sound of it; and his names *are* Ernest Augustus, which provides him with some justification."

(The bleeding, mutilated flesh of Sally Bootes burnt a path through my mind. If I had harboured suspicions before about the identity of her "Mr. Augustus," they were now firmed as I was reminded of Cumberland's full name. Fond of flogging, he and his brother Kent! A family pastime, it seems!)

"There is an interesting story circulating," Rhys went on. "If we are to believe it, Cumberland was in the midst of ordering his breakfast when the news reached him of Victoria's death. He had been saying something on the order of 'I shall start off with a bit of haddock. Then I'll have a large portion of buttered eggs —' At that point, the news was brought him. After hearing it, he concluded his breakfast order: 'We shall then take some kidneys, and we shall finish with coffee and fruits.' Virtually in mid-sentence, you see, he changed from the first person singular to the royal 'we.' "

"There was no sign of grief?" I asked.

"Nor of surprise, apparently. He received the news with less emotion than he might have received the result of a cricket match. And instantly, by his change of pronoun, he made it known that he was due the respect and deference one gives a king. With William still alive!"

"Arrogant bounder," Papa muttered.

"To-day," Rhys continues, "he called together all of King William's councillors: the archbishops; the Prime Minister, Lord Melbourne; the Duke of Wellington; your friend Lord Merlyngton —"

"Former friend," murmured Mamma.

"— Lord Grey, Lord Brougham, Sir Robert Peel, and the only remaining royal Duke, his brother, Sussex. Peel told a friend of mine that the King said to them:

" 'Saving Lord Merlyngton, with whom we desire private conversation after this audience, you may all start seeking other employment, for you are to be replaced. We prefer to sweep with a new broom, and to appoint in your posts men with whom we have enjoyed long associations. You are excused, with our thanks for your loyal service to our late brother, William.' Then, as all save Merlyngton began to leave the royal presence, the King singled out Sussex. 'Stay, brother,' he said. 'You are to be conducted, under close guard, to the Tower.' "

Papa cried, "The Tower?! His own brother? Why?"

"Those were, apparently, the Duke's own words, according to Sir Robert. 'This is an outrage!' Sussex said.

" 'Not at all,' the King replied. 'As next in line to the throne, dear brother, your life is very precious. We must keep you safe, under lock and key, so that no harm may come to you.' Of course, what he really meant was 'so that no harm may come to *me,* from you' — for so suspicious is he of everybody that he fears his brother will attempt to kill him, to seize the throne."

"He judges others by his own example," I said.

"But to imprison a royal Duke!" said Mamma. "On no charge! Surely it is illegal!"

"Of course," said Rhys, "and yet the Duke of Sussex sits in the Tower at this very moment, forbidden all contact with the outside world."

I said, "How is it possible for the King to do this — to ride roughshod over laws and restraints?"

Rhys replied: "It would seem that he has been in readiness for this *coup* for some long time past. He has bided his time, made his plans, and prepared himself thoroughly for this eventuality. Whether he is responsible for the death of Victoria, he was certainly ready for it. Through the years, he has slowly gathered loyal followers around him, men to whom he has made grand promises and who will do his bidding and deny him nothing. They are men of all ranks: high, like Merlyngton —"

I said, "I am not surprised that *he* is one of them!"

"— who will no doubt be the new Prime Minister," Rhys continued, "and of lesser rank, like the officers and men who make up his private army."

Papa said, "Army?! Surely not!"

"It amounts to that," said Rhys. "A small but dedicated corps, calling itself the Augustan Guard. They are fiercely loyal to him — and plain fierce to any who oppose him."

Mamma waxed indignant: "The man must be mad to think that this will be tolerated!"

"Mad he assuredly is, in many ways," Rhys agreed, "but with method. Think: King William is but one day dead, and this despot has already seized control of the nation. There is talk of his dissolving Parliament — as a 'temporary emergency measure.' And anybody whom he suspects may be his enemy is in danger of unceremonious arrest by his Augustans."

"But what of the police?" asked Papa.

"Colonel Rowan has been dismissed, I am told," replied Rhys. "No doubt the King's toadies will be put in charge — or are already in charge."

"I can not believe this!" Mamma exclaimed. "It is like a nightmare!"

"One from which we will not soon awaken," Rhys morosely added.

ꝍ *Thursday, 22 June*

I arrived at a decision this morning, and when Rhys came to tea this afternoon — he is our guest for tea or dinner almost every day now — I announced my decision to him and to Mamma.

"The wedding must be postponed," I said.

"Pamela," Mamma retorted sharply, "this vacillation must stop! First, you accept Mr. O'Connor; then you write him a letter calling off the marriage; then he kisses you and all is mended again; and now you tell us that the wedding must be postponed. In the name of all that is reasonable, *why?*"

"I think Rhys understands why," I said, looking at him.

"I believe I may," he said. "The country is in too unsettled a state. There are new outrages daily. The late King's widow, Adelaide, has been trundled off to Kensington Palace, where she is virtually a prisoner, not permitted to leave. Victoria's mother, the Duchess of Kent, is likewise shut up there. Any solace or protection she might have enjoyed from her friend, Conroy, is denied her; Sir John has been taken to the Tower. He and Augustus have long despised each other: I dread to think what fate is in store for him. In such times as these, personal matters must take second place. I assume that those are your reasons, Pamela?"

I nodded.

Mamma said, "But life goes on, no matter what tempests may rage around us. It always has done. It always will. People marry and raise families in the most parlous of times."

"I know, Mamma, but I could not be happy were we to be married now. I am much too distressed. Things *must* sort themselves out — isn't that so, Rhys? — in one way or another?"

"In one way or another," he said, in a tone that invested the words with more meaning than they had contained when I had spoken them.

"And when they are resolved," I said, "and the country is on an even keel again, the wedding can take place."

Mamma sighed. "It is so tiresome. And so *very* irregular."

ॐ *Friday, 23 June*

St. John Barstow was our dinner-guest this evening. After a few glasses of wine, he became loquacious.

"My greatest fear," he said, "is that Augustus will tamper with our system of laws."

"How is that possible?" asked Papa. "We are a constitutional monarchy. The days of a king's absolute power are long past."

"Are they?" responded Mr. Barstow. "His influence is more wide-spread than we had believed; more pervasive; more deeply embedded. You will recall that, last year, the radical Hume suggested in the House that upon the death of William, the Orange Lodges were ready to rise for Cumberland, their Grand Master, and declare him monarch in place of Victoria. A powerful body, those Lodges. More than three hundred thousand Englishmen, stout Tories and anti-Papists, all."

"But Cumberland dissociated himself from their views," said Papa.

"Oh, indeed," Mr. Barstow responded, "and quite dramatically, too. He assured the House of Lords that he was prepared to fight to the death, if need be, in defence of 'that innocent person,' as he called Victoria. Even so, he received a strong hint from the Government that he should completely sever his connection with the Orange association. He ignored the hint, so the Government sent an address to the King, praying that His Majesty would take such measures as should be effectual for the suppression of the Orange Lodges. Well, of course, Cumberland then had no choice but to dissolve the Orange societies. I believe that they were *never* dissolved, but were merely rendered invisible, and that they now constitute his strongest supporters and defenders. His people are everywhere — have been for some time — waiting for his signal to act. They occupy positions of great power. They are in government certainly, and I strongly suspect that they are also in commerce, the press, the military, even the clergy."

The bishop's daughter was taken aback at this last. "Surely not the clergy, Mr. Barstow!"

"Madam," he said, "the garter episcopal is not a guarantee of wisdom or even of goodness. I fear that some highly placed members of our Church are bigots. If Augustus were to promise them that he will institute stern measures to repress Catholics and Jews, they might well flock to his camp. We know the views of Lord Merlyngton, for one, on the subject of Jews. I think that Disraeli and the Rothschilds will begin to feel the effect of the new *régime* very soon, and very sharply."

Papa asked, "In what way will the laws be fiddled, do you think, Barstow?"

"In my opinion, he will begin by re-defining the meaning of the word 'sedition.' The description will become so broad, so loose, that it will cover almost anything that Augustus may wish it to cover. All acts or attitudes not to his liking will be called seditious — and probably made punishable by death."

"Good Heavens!" I said. (I thought of Rhys. For how long would Augustus tolerate critics of his *régime?*)

"We sometimes forget," Mr. Barstow went on, "that our English monarchs have prerogatives not often used. Why, less than three years ago, King William was able to impose an unpopular ministry on the majority of Parliament — you remember it, Summerfield?"

Papa nodded. "November, '34. He dismissed the Melbourne ministry on a mere pretext —"

"But in reality because he disapproved of their Irish Church policy," said Mr. Barstow. "He brought in Sir Robert Peel and established him in Melbourne's stead, against enormous opposition. True, the new ministry did not last long —

dissolution followed soon after, and Melbourne was reinstated — but if William had been stronger, more ruthless, his
ministry might well have prevailed. Well, then. We may disagree about the merits of King William, rest his soul — many
of us considered him to be a bit of a blunderer, rather indecisive and timid — but no one disputes the fact that he was a
good man, genial, warm of heart, of decent intentions. If even
he was able to bring about such a *coup d'état,* think what may
be done by an unscrupulous man like Augustus!"

ఇ *Saturday, 24 June*

Waiting for a moment when Mamma was out of the room,
Rhys said to-day at tea, "I wonder if you can guess what person I saw, accompanied by retinue, admitted to the Palace last
night?"

"I have no idea."

"Mrs. Jeffers and several of her girls."

"To the *Palace?* I can not believe it!"

"I think you can," said Rhys, "when you consider the character of the man who is now our King, and what we know of
him. Stories seep out of the Palace — accounts of orgies —"

"Merciful Heaven! Do such things take place in the presence
of the Queen?"

"There are some who say that she — takes part in the festivities."

At this point, Mamma returned, and he could not say more.

ఇ *Sunday, 25 June*

"And what of the succession?"

That was the theme of the buzzing talk outside the church
this morning.

"The King and his Queen are childless," Mr. Randall
pointed out.

Mrs. Randall added, "A daughter of theirs was born dead,
twenty years ago, and . . ."

"Sussex is the next in line," said Papa.

"He is also a prisoner in the Tower," I reminded him.

"If, indeed, he is still alive," murmured Mr. Randall, not too loudly.

Lord and Lady Merlyngton passed by, ignoring us as if we were not there, which has been their wont of late. But a glint came into Papa's eyes at this insult, and he responded to Mr. Randall's remark with the resonantly enunciated words "Perhaps Lord Merlyngton can enlighten us on that score."

At the sound of his name, so loudly spoken, Lord Merlyngton could no longer ignore us. He turned to Papa and regarded him coldly, saying nothing.

"My lord," said Papa, "we were discussing the unusual situation of the Duke of Sussex. He seemed to have disappeared, and there is a rumour that he has been imprisoned in the Tower by his brother, Cumberland — excuse me, *His Majesty*. Seeing that you are so close to His Majesty, I wonder if you can verify this rumour?"

"I can not, sir," Lord Merlyngton said gruffly, and turned to go.

"Can you deny it, then?" said Papa, persisting. When Lord Merlyngton could not find words for a reply, Papa added, raising his voice so that it could be heard by everybody who stood on the church steps, "Can you give us assurance that the Duke is *alive?*"

Lord Merlyngton's face was suffused now with a purple flush. "The personal relationships between His Majesty and the other members of the royal family are none of my business. I may add that they are likewise none of yours."

"I think that they are, my lord," said Papa. "I think that they are the business of every Englishman worthy of the name."

"Good morning, sir," said Lord Merlyngton, and quickly walked away, virtually dragging his wife after him by the arm.

"Wilfrid!" said Mamma. "That was most injudicious! And dangerous!"

"Very like," said Papa, his face glowing. "But it did me more good than a dose of salts."

"Speaking of the succession, as we were," said Mr. Randall, "if the Queen is unable to bear children, which appears to be

381

the case, and if Sussex is either dead or doomed to die, then the King may choose to divorce her."

"Divorce!" said Mamma, horrified. "There has been no divorce in the royal family since Henry the Eighth divorced Anne of Cleves! The scandal would be unthinkable!"

"Then it may be," said Mr. Randall with some delicacy, "that the King will take another course."

"What course is that?" asked Papa.

"He may follow yet another example of Henry the Eighth," Mr. Randall replied, drawing a finger across his throat.

I, who had been almost silent, said spiritedly, "It would be simple justice — she is reputed to have murdered one of her earlier husbands!"

"Hush, child," said Mamma, guiding me towards the church portal. "Awful woman that she is, we must pray for her safety, and for the safety of the Duke of Sussex, as well."

ঌ *Monday, 26 June*

"Billy-Be-Damned's been taken to the Tower," Rhys said today, with deep concern in his voice.

"Billy — who?"

"Billy Maginn, the editor of *Fraser's*. A good friend of mine. I think I've mentioned his name before. He's a merciless critic of the aristocracy, along with all the rest of his Round Table — meself, Jack Churchill, Peter Walburne, Alexander Fontaine, Thackeray, Gleig, Tom Croker, Lockhart, Hook, and the rest. Our satires have been published, as I once told you, under a fictitious name, 'Oliver Yorke,' but if Billy reveals our identities —"

"Is it likely he will do that?"

"Billy's a brave man, and Irish into the bargain. 'A randy, bandy, brandy, no Dandy, Rollicking jig of an Irishman' — that's the way he describes himself. And he can hold his tongue as well as he can hold his liquor, which is very well, indeed."

"Then surely he will not betray you or the others."

"I hope that he does not. But, as I've said, he has been taken to the Tower. And there are rumours —" His voice trailed off.

"What sort of rumours, Rhys?"

"One hesitates to give them credence, but I fear that they may be true: rumours that Augustus has introduced an aid to the interrogation of prisoners; or, rather, revived one that has been idle for centuries. The rack."

𝕘𝕖 Tuesday, 27 June

After dinner this evening, Crewe announced a completely unexpected caller — Lord Merlyngton!

"What?" said Papa, astounded. "Merlyngton? Most extraordinary. Shew him in, Crewe."

When Lord Merlyngton was ushered into the drawing-room and offered refreshment, he declined, but sat down, avoiding our eyes, giving the appearance of profound embarrassment. At last, he said, "I am here on behalf of His Majesty."

"Then we should be honoured," said Papa, not without a touch of sarcasm.

"There is an entertainment to-night at the Palace," Lord Merlyngton went on, "and I am instructed to proffer His Majesty's invitation —"

"More likely, a royal command for our presence," said Papa.

"If you wish to put it so."

"How very singular, my lord, that he should send a peer of the realm on such a lackey's errand," said Papa. "But I fear that you must make my excuses to His Majesty" — I swear that Papa's lip positively *curled!* — "and tell him that an indisposition regrettably prevents me from obeying his gracious command."

Lord Merlyngton cleared his throat. "See here, Summerfield," he grumbled, "I have no taste for this, but, damn it, the man is my sovereign, after all, and — well — that is to say — it is not *your* presence that is desired at the Palace."

"Whose, then?"

"Your wife's. And your daughter's."

383

Papa, who had been smoking a cigar, removed it from his mouth, and slowly, carefully crushed it out in the tray at his elbow. "I find that curious," he said. "My wife and my daughter — but not —"

"None of this is my idea, Summerfield," Lord Merlyngton said, blushing.

"I think I am entitled to an explanation of the King's breach of courtesy."

Lord Merlyngton merely said, "I have no further instructions. I can not tell you more."

"That will not do, my lord," said Papa, sharply. "I *demand* to know more!"

Mamma spoke: "I think I can attempt to elucidate this situation for you, Wilfrid. No doubt I came to the King's attention during the recent trial. He read a great deal about me. He heard me described in the newspapers as 'a handsome woman,' perhaps. Also a shameless one. An adulteress —"

"Melissa, please —" said Papa; but Mamma continued, as if he had not interrupted:

"And so he said to himself: 'How amusing it would be to have this hussy *perform* for us at to-night's little *fête*. One grows weary of harlots; let us see how a bishop's daughter compares with professional bawds —' "

"Madam!" croaked Lord Merlyngton.

" 'And let us have that pretty child of hers, as well,' no doubt he added. 'A tempting little morsel she looked to be, at my late niece's birthday ball. Let us have them both here to-night and put them through their paces.' "

Lord Merlyngton was crushed by humiliation. "Madam, I assure you, I have no knowledge of —"

"Your face gives you the lie, my lord," said Papa. "You know full well the true character of your mission to this house. It seems that you are not only the King's lackey, but also his *procurer!*"

"Summerfield, please —"

"Is this the same Lord Merlyngton who hitherto has been so active in the suppression of vice?" said Papa. "The same man who used to be shocked at the prevalence of prostitutes? The same man who cut my wife dead in the street because of her

384

bravery in divulging an indiscretion to save a servant's life? How the mighty have fallen, my lord."

Papa rose from his chair and pulled the bell-cord. "I must ask you to leave my house," he said. "Tell the monster whose minion you are that we are not at home, or that these ladies are ill, or any other lie you may choose. Offer him, instead, some depraved wretch who will commit the foulest act for gain — *offer him yourself!* But never again, my lord, come to this house; for if you do, you will be met by a *pistol* — and shot like any trespasser!"

Crewe entered the room, in response to the bell. "Lord Merlyngton is leaving," said Papa.

> *Wednesday, 28 June*

To-night, we dined at the house of Mr. and Mrs. Cargrave. Papa told them of Lord Merlyngton's visit last night. They expressed the shock that one would expect of them, and then the doctor said, "Obviously, the King's mind has deteriorated much more rapidly than I should have predicted."

"Predicted?" said Papa. "Can insanity be predicted?"

"Sometimes it can be, when it has a physical cause," Mr. Cargrave replied. "The man's brain is rotted by syphilis. He contracted it many years ago, as a young chap, and he has never ceased to associate with the lowest, most diseased type of women. The illness lay dormant for a rather long time — a characteristic of it — but apparently it has returned with a vengeance. Mind you, I am not saying that he would have been a saint were it not for the disease. No doubt there were always flaws in his character. But the illness has deepened those flaws, made him reckless, causing him to throw aside all caution."

Mamma said, "This illness of his has been a closely guarded secret, apparently. How do you come to know of it, Mr. Cargrave?"

"I treated him for it. Such treatment as we have. There is no effective treatment, no cure. Ordinarily, I am bound by ethics to say nothing of this, of course, but under the present circumstances, I no longer feel that obligation to be binding."

"What may we expect of him in future?" Papa asked. "What course will the disease take?"

"He will become more and more unpredictable and irascible. He will begin to suspect everybody — even shadows. He will laugh one moment and strike out in anger in the next. He will scream for no reason. He will weep like a baby. He will go blind. He will babble. He will soil himself. He will crawl about on the floor like an animal. In time, he will die."

"In how *much* time?" asked Papa.

"That, only God can foretell. But I fear, my friends, that we may have a very long wait."

৪৩ *Thursday, 29 June*

Horrid events have been piled upon me so heavily in the past fortnight that I have had no choice but to deaden myself with large administrations of dream-drops. To lie for hours, as insensible as a log, in a stupor as thick and impenetrable as stone walls: that is the only way I know to shut out the world.

৪৩ *Friday, 30 June*

This was to have been my wedding day. I wonder if Rhys and I shall *ever* be married?

To-night, Mr. Cargrave suddenly appeared at our door. We had not expected to see him again so soon, for we dined at his house on Wednesday.

"I could do with a brandy," he said, as he sat down in the drawing-room; and when he had drained his glass in one swallow and indicated his need for another, he swore us to absolute secrecy ("Else my life will be forfeit") and began a story that kept Mamma, Papa, and me engrossed to the very end.

He told how he and several other prominent physicians had been summoned, this evening, to a private audience with the King. "Mr. Partridge was there, Mr. Hood, Mr. Bell, Mr. Brodie, Mr. Addison, and others. The King's demeanour was extremely grave. He remained standing, and so, of course, did we.

" 'Gentlemen,' he said, 'what takes place in this room to-night you must consider as a secret of state — a secret so closely guarded that, if word should ever reach our ears that it has been bruited about, all of you will be under *sentence of death*. We think you know that we do not issue idle threats or warnings.'

"There was a moment of silent discomfiture; and then Mr. Addison said, 'If I may be permitted to speak, sir?' The King nodded. 'I believe that I speak for my colleagues, as well as for myself, when I say that if Your Majesty imposes such secrecy, and such stringent measures of punishing its breach, it can only be for the good of the realm.' We all murmured our assent.

" 'Thank you, Mr. Addison,' said the King. 'Now then: we shall not need to remind you of the Asiatic Cholera epidemic that reached our shores in 1831, and continued until '33. Some sixty thousand people died, about eight thousand of them in London alone, chiefly in the poorest districts.

" 'We have called you here because you are the foremost members of our medical profession. Many of you devote a great deal of your time to research experimentation and to the writing of learned treatises. We are giving you a royal command to unite your efforts to *find the cause* of the Cholera and its mode of spreading. No expense need be spared; the Crown will provide unlimited funds. You will work diligently, in mutual co-operation, and, we repeat, in the utmost secrecy. Do you wish to put any questions to us?'

"I was encouraged to hear the King speak with such firmness of purpose on that subject. His concern for the poor did much to vindicate him in my eyes. I felt at once that I — that many of us — had misjudged him, and that, whatever he may have been guilty of in his past, he had been purified by kingship and had risen, almost miraculously, to a higher level of manhood, which had made him worthy of the crown. Indeed, it has been said that small-spirited men, mean men, can *grow* by taking on high office; can improve and elevate their abilities and their very souls, as if to fill and dignify their new stations — and this seemed to be true of the King. Perhaps even the natural course of his disease had been suspended or reversed by a Divine Hand?

"One of our number said, 'Your Majesty, the reason for the spread of the disease is believed to be a miasmatic vapour, which is inhaled . . .' Another interrupted him to say 'Begging your pardon, Your Majesty, but many of us believe that this plague is waterborne . . .' Here, the King held up his hand and spoke sternly:

" 'Resolve your conflicting theories amongst yourselves. *Find the cause.* And when it is found, report your findings, in secret, directly to us and to no other.'

"It was then that I stepped forth. 'With your permission, sir, I think that all of us admire the Crown's interest in this terrible disease which has ravaged our country once before and may do so again unless the cause is found. I wish to suggest only that our goal may be achieved more quickly if we are permitted to communicate with colleagues other than those in this room; particularly certain men of accomplishment in other countries — Germany, for example, and —'

" '*Sentence of death,* Mr. Cargrave,' the King said sharply. 'Those were our words. You will communicate the subject of this audience to *no-one.* We think we speak clearly?'

" 'Yes, Your Majesty,' I replied. 'May I ask the reason for such unusual secrecy?'

"The King looked steadily at me. The scar on his face took on a deeper colour, it seemed. 'Very well,' he said. 'You may remember that before the Cholera reached England, it had already devastated Russia and spread through the Baltic ports, until most of the capitals of Europe were affected. The disease appeared to afflict only the poor — the aristocracy and the rich of those countries seemed to be immune. The same proved to be largely true here in England. This circumstance led to a shocking rumour amongst the European peasantry; namely, that the high-born had bribed doctors deliberately to spread the plague amongst the poor so that they might be more conveniently governed. It was even said that the British had used this method of thinning the ranks of the population in India. It was further intimated that the bribed doctors were, in truth, the delegates of a central committee with headquarters here in London. Have you heard that story before, Mr. Cargrave?'

" 'Yes, Your Majesty,' I said, 'but it is entirely false. The only committee involved in any way with the Cholera was a Board of Health which was rather hastily assembled in June of '31. I was on the Board — so were many of these gentlemen.

It was purely an advisory board, without executive power, and responsible to the Privy Council. We were asked to draw up a sanitary code and to suggest measures that might be taken should the plague reach as far as Great Britain, which, of course, it did, but —'

" 'We think what you say to be true,' said the King. 'We think that the rumours abroad at that time were false — at least as far as British involvement was concerned. They may have been true as regards Russia and other countries; they may not have been; it is no matter. Even if they were entirely false, however, it can not be denied that there is the seed of a splendid idea in them. Do you grasp our meaning?'

" 'With respect, sir, I think I do not.'

" 'Oh, come, come,' said the King. 'One of the most vexing problems of modern life is the burgeoning ranks of paupers. They breed like flies. They threaten to overwhelm us all — we shall stand shoulder-deep in them before long. Work can not be found for all of them. They starve and grow bitter. When they grow bitter enough, they will revolt. They outnumber their betters already — all they require is a fire-brand to unite them and lead them, and they will overthrow all of us. Remember the French Revolution, gentlemen. Remember the guillotine. Remember the slaughter of whole families of gentry — men, women, children. Remember the anarchy and chaos that followed. Do you wish that to happen here? It will — unless preventative measures are taken.'

"Some of us still had great difficulty in believing the evidence of our ears. Surely the King could not mean what he seemed to be implying? But then he leaned forwards, speaking slowly and with emphasis; and his words crushed and stupefied us as if they had been cudgels:

" 'The plague of '31 rid England of *only* sixty thousand of that rabble,' said the King. 'We expect the *next* plague to be *much better managed*. Unlimited funds, remember. And an unlimited supply of human subjects for your experiments.'

" '*Human* subjects, sir?' I said.

" 'Why, yes,' he replied. 'From the prisons. You understand the reason for this unusual secrecy now, do you not, Mr. Cargrave?' Then he turned his back to us, and said, 'This audience is over.' "

July

"A DUEL TO THE DEATH"

The enormity of last night's disclosure prevented me from sleeping. At length, I was obliged to have recourse to my ruby drops — although I dislike to be indebted to them — for it was only through their agency that I was able to close my eyes.

The result was that I slept far past my customary waking hour, and staggered downstairs only in time for luncheon. Mamma and Rhys (who had been invited — I had forgotten) were already seated at table and were almost finished when I entered the room.

"I was just telling your mother," said Rhys, "that there is one small particle of good news, at least. I have learned that the Duke of Sussex is alive and is being cared for well enough in the Tower. Even Augustus dares not harm him."

"I am glad to hear it," I said, but my voice seemed to emanate from another person, so dull was I still from my sleeping-draught.

"I wish that I had such good news of Billy Maginn," Rhys added, "but we've had no word at all of him."

Crewe offered me food, but I declined it and took only tea. Mamma said, "Come, my dear, you must eat something, for you did not come down to breakfast."

"I have no appetite, Mamma."

She sighed. "Very well. Perhaps you can persuade her, Mr. O'Connor. You must excuse me now, for household duties await."

When she and Crewe had left the room, Rhys walked over to where I was seated and took my face in his hands. I thought he was about to kiss me, but I was mistaken. He looked into my eyes, analytically, probingly. He frowned. "How long have you been taking the vile stuff?" he said, sternly.

I pretended innocence. "Stuff?"

"You know full well what I mean. Laudanum, is it? I've seen its effects before." He seized my shoulders and shook me; my head wobbled like a doll's. "Damnation, girl, you're half-dead with it! How much did you take?"

"Just — a few drops —"

He snarled in his exasperation. "I've known many silly women, and silly men, to ruin their brains and bodies with that muck — but I thought you were wiser. It seems that you are not. It seems that you are as silly as the worst of them."

"Please, my darling, do not scold! Life is so hard — sometimes the only way I can endure it is to numb myself with that medicine."

"Medicine! A pretty name for it! *Poison* would be more apt! Pamela, you must promise me that you will leave off taking it, *at once*. Not a bit at a time, but immediately and completely. Pour it out. Every drop of it. Do you understand me? Do you promise — in the name of that God whom you fear?"

"Rhys —"

"Do you promise?"

"Yes — my dear — I promise."

He smiled then and kissed my forehead. "Now, what do you say to a bite of luncheon?"

I shook my head. "I can not. Rhys, I must tell you something —"

"Very well."

"It is a secret — a secret so strict that should it ever be let out, several good men will lose their lives."

"You're certain this is no opium dream?"

I responded fiercely: "I wish that it were! I wish to *God* that it were! But it is all too monstrously true! I must swear you to secrecy, Rhys."

"You have my word," he said.

I then related to him everything that Mr. Cargrave had told us last night. When I had finished, he looked away from me, past me, his face paler even than its usual milky hue: it had gone all chalky and sickened.

"Mad — hopelessly mad —" he whispered.

"Rhys," I said, "I swear to you, I am in complete control of my reason."

"What? Bless you, girl! I meant Augustus!"

I then told him the other thing, about the King's disease, that Mr. Cargrave had divulged to us on Wednesday evening.

Rhys got up and paced. "Then we must move faster than we had thought necessary," he muttered.

"Move? What do you mean, Rhys?"

"There are a few of us — Billy Maginn was our leader, but I have taken his place since he was arrested — who are working *sub rosa* to depose Augustus. We have scarcely started to make our plans — do you realize that he has been King for only a dozen days? — but I see that we must accelerate our efforts. This Cholera madness, and the crumbling condition of his mind, force us to act quickly."

"What will you do?"

He shook his head. "I am not sure. I must meet with the others as soon as possible." As if I were not in the room, he droned softly to himself, "Caesar had his Brutus, Charles the First his —"

"What are you saying?"

"Nothing. Some words another wild Celt spouted, years ago. Treason, it was called. Well, so be it."

My thoughts were still clouded, and I could not understand him.

"I must leave now, me love," he said, taking my hands and squeezing them fondly. "There is much to be done, and the devil's own scarcity of time in which to do it." He kissed my lips, and then he walked quickly to the door.

"Rhys! When will I see you?" I cried. But he was already gone.

Later, I kept my promise to him, and poured out every drop of my laudanum. Dear God, give me the strength to live in this fearful world of Yours without its help.

Half a year ago, when I (No, Diary, I shall turn back to the fly-leaf and set down the rest of to-day's thoughts there, at a point before the beginning).

ॐ Sunday, 2 July

As we climbed into our coach this morning, to return home after church, an uninvited party leapt in after us: Rhys. "Tell your coachman to drive on — quickly!" he said.

Papa called out, "Directly home, Paley." With a clip-clop of hoofs, the coach moved forwards.

"Rhys, what is it?" I asked, fearful.

"Thackeray and Carlyle have been arrested," he said. "On charges of 'sedition,' if you please!"

"Great Heavens, Mr. O'Connor," said Mamma, "even *I* have read those writers, and I am not a friend of sedition."

"They are contributors to *Fraser's,*" Rhys explained, "and that is the reason they have been arrested. The Augustans are looking for Jimmy Fraser, the publisher, and Churchill and Croker, too, I hear; but they have so far eluded capture. So has Tom Moore. Cumberland has hated him ever since he wrote that poem for *The Times,* a few years ago, about the 'dreary Duke.' Billy must have divulged our names, or the names of some of us. Those filth must have ripped him apart — else he'd never have told them." Rhys smiled grimly. "Perhaps the only reason he hasn't given them my name as yet — if indeed he hasn't — is out of loyalty to a fellow-Hibernian. But how long can he hold out? They'll stick at no foul torture to make him talk."

"The poor man," I said. "Is there nothing that can be done to help him?"

Rhys shook his head. "Billy's past help. Hopelessly crippled by now, I have no doubt, if he's not already dead. I met with the remnants of the Round Table in the early hours this morning. We have agreed that we must go into hiding — some of us here in the British Isles; others abroad — and continue our

396

'seditious' work there, in relative safety, until Augustus can be deposed or killed."

"Killed!" said Papa. "You would advocate regicide?"

"In the present circumstance — yes," Rhys replied. "Do not forget, sir, that Augustus plans to annihilate half of his subjects with deadly pestilence."

Papa nodded in tight-lipped, grudging agreement.

Mamma added, "And if he *were* to — expire suddenly — the succession would pass immediately to Sussex, who you tell us is alive."

Rhys nodded. "And a good enough man he is, by all accounts. But I have not finished telling you about the Round Table's plans. We drew lots this morning to determine which of us shall go whither. Churchill will leave for America; Lockhart will go to Germany; and so on. I will cross the Channel to France."

"When?" I asked.

"To-morrow night. All arrangements for passage have been made."

"You shall not go alone!" I insisted.

Rhys sighed. "I had anticipated this difficulty," he said. "But you can not come with me, Pamela. I shall be a hunted man. Even in France, I shall not be free from danger."

"I *will* go with you, Rhys!" I cried.

He looked from Mamma to Papa, and said, "Can you not talk sense to her?"

Papa, who had said almost nothing through all of this, now spoke: "I am not so sure that she would be safer here than in France with you, O'Connor. The King has a certain — interest in her." And he told Rhys of Lord Merlyngton's despicable mission to our house on Tuesday night.

When he had finished, Rhys said, through clenched teeth, "The abominable swine. Assassination is too good for him. He should be burnt at the stake."

"Then you will take me with you?"

"I must."

"And Brian?"

Rhys hesitated but finally said, "Yes."

"And La Belle Dame?"

397

"*Who?*"

"My dear tabby. Oh, *please,* Rhys — I can not leave her behind!"

He sighed deeply. "Very well, very well."

"But you will *not* live unmarried in France," Mamma said firmly.

"We'll be married as soon as we get our land-legs back," Rhys assured her, "and as soon as I've recovered from me sea-sickness. I expect I'll be green with it by the time we reach France. And the ceremony, Mrs. Summerfield, will be as religious as you'd wish. Now the problem is this, Pamela: Where shall we meet before embarking? I'm avoiding me rooms in Chelsea, for I fear they may be watched by the Augustans. I dare not come to your house: if I am seen there, the King's wrath may fall on your family. We must meet somewhere to-morrow night. But where?"

"Cooke's Circus?" I suggested.

He shook his head. "Too many people about."

"Perhaps I can supply the solution to your problem," said Mamma. "A discreet apartment, completely vacant, paid up to the end of the year, to which I have the only key." We all knew, without the necessity of her saying anything more, that she meant her rooms at The Alroy.

"Perfection," said Rhys. "Then, Pamela, I shall arrive there precisely at a quarter past eight to-morrow night. You will already be there — no later than eight — and will have let yourself in with the key. Do not admit *anybody* other than meself."

"How shall I know it is you?"

"I shall knock — like this." He tapped with his knuckles on the coach door: three raps, in the form of an amphibrach: da-*dum*-da. "It's the same metre as 'O'Connor,' " he said, with a smile. Turning to Papa, he added, "Stop the coach at the next turning and let me off there, please. I don't want you to be seen in my company." The two men shook hands. Rhys kissed my cheek. "Till to-morrow night," he said, and repeated the knock: da-*dum*-da.

Paley reined in the horses at Papa's order, and Rhys slipped nimbly out of the coach. As his feet touched the cobblestones, Mamma, suddenly remembering a vital detail, called out to him: "Apartment B-Four!"

He blew her a kiss and dashed away. We drove straight home.

I took a hackney to Hyde Park this evening. Papa thought it best to involve none of our servants in my clandestine departure. Why endanger them with secrets that might put them on the rack? I arrived early in Strathmore Street, about half past seven, burdened down with bags and Brian and a hat-box, punctured with air-holes, containing La Belle Dame. The hackney coachman helped me to carry my impedimenta into Apartment B-Four of The Alroy. After he left, I locked the door securely.

Brian, such a good little boy, had slept in the hackney and continued to sleep, on a small velvet-covered couch. La Belle Dame squawled to be let out of the hat-box. I obeyed her command. These things done, I sat down and waited.

So these were the rooms in which Mamma and Rutledge had met. How strange it seemed to be here, knowing what had gone on within these prettily papered walls. The place was decorated simply, but with Mamma's good taste. There were a few prints on the walls, and the absolute minimum of furniture. There were no decanters of wine or spirits. There was nothing to read. The apartment was for one purpose only. There was a sitting-room, and a privy, and a bedroom. I peeped into the latter and studied the serviceable bed that stood there, trying to imagine Rutledge and Mamma upon it. I could not. But, for the matter of that, I have never been able to conjure up a mind-picture of even Mamma and Papa doing the deed. And yet, imaginable or no, that bed at which I stared had rocked and groaned, once every month for the past five years, under the weight of my mother and our butler — naked, no doubt; she with her thighs inelegantly spread and her feet locked behind his back; he pounding away at her again and again with his great truncheon — those two middle-aged people! It was an unseemly picture. But is not the act of love always an unseemly picture, and a bit absurd, except to the enraptured lovers?

I closed the bedroom door and returned to the sitting-room.

Brian still slept soundly. La Belle Dame was busy giving herself a tongue-wash. I put my watch on the table, where it would be constantly before my eyes (Papa gave it to me last year, for my seventeenth birthday): it was just one minute past eight. Rhys would not be here for almost another quarter of an hour. I sighed. I was restless. I wanted it all to be over; I wanted to be on the choppy Channel; I wanted to be in France; I wanted to be married to Rhys; I wanted to be in bed with him and to spread *my* thighs and hook *my* feet behind *his* back and feel the pounding rhythm of *his* truncheon. The thought occurred in my naughty mind: Would there be time for us to make use of that sturdy bed in the next room? Must we wait till we had reached France and had gone through a ceremony? I had not stood on such ceremony with Giles. Why must I do so with Rhys?

Aunt Esmie's *tarot* cards were among the effects I had packed for the journey, I know not why. To pass the time, I took them out and placed them on the table. I looked at the pack as it lay before me, face down. I was afraid to touch it. Those cards had been disturbingly prophetic — they had seemed to predict that Rutledge would hang himself in his cell; and, even more fearfully, they had uncannily foretold the murder of Victoria and the fall of England. Or so it had appeared, at least. I continue to tell myself that I am not superstitious. And yet, I do believe in Almighty God, and in His power, and in the miracles He has made to happen. Is it not illogical of me to believe in one kind of supernaturalism and not in another? Shutting my eyes, I reached out and divided the cards. I opened my eyes: the pack had divided at The Hanged Man.

I gasped — but, in the next instant, I was angry with myself for allowing the silly bits of pasteboard to frighten me. I put them away.

Da-*dum*-da.

A knock at the door! Rhys was early — it was only five minutes past eight. What a welcome sound! Almost giggling in my delight, I ran to the door, quickly unlocked it with the key, and threw it open. "Rhys! —"

But, although the landing was dark and I could not clearly

see the face of the man who stood there, I knew at once that he was not Rhys. He wore a colonel's braid and the black uniform of the Augustan Guard.

I cried out in fear and attempted to slam the door shut, but his booted foot prevented me. Still, I tried, but to no avail, and although I leant on the door with all my strength, he easily pushed it open. My heart went cold with despair. As he entered the room, I turned and ran — but where could I go? I was trapped. I picked up little Brian and held him closely to me, to protect him.

"Don't be afraid, Pam," said the Augustan.

I turned to him, struck dumb by that familiar voice.

"Do you think I would hurt you, my dear?" he said.

"Giles!"

He smiled charmingly and touched his helmet in a mock salute. "Colonel Ormond of His Majesty's Guard, at your service, Miss."

"But — why are you here?"

"Is that all you can say to me, after all this time? Are you not happy to see me?"

"Giles — I —"

He looked down at the baby. "What a fine-looking little chap," he said. "How-de-do, Brian."

"You — know his name?"

He chuckled, good-naturedly. "To be sure. I know whose child he is, as well. O'Connor's. And your sister's."

"You know a good deal," I said, growing more perplexed and uncomfortable.

"Yes, I do. I knew, for instance, that you would be here this evening, and at what time. I know also that O'Connor will be here in a little less than ten minutes. I even know this —" He rapped on the table: da-*dum*-da.

"But *how* do you know these things?"

"It is no matter. I am here. You are here. We are together again. Nothing else signifies. Now, why don't you put that little fellow down and come over here and greet me properly?"

I did exactly as he bade me. I have never been able to resist him. I put Brian on the velvet couch again and walked over to

401

Giles and let him take my face tenderly in his hands and let him kiss me. I wish I could say that I felt no emotion at the touch of his lips; but the truth is that I felt a tingle of the old love, starting at the tips of my toes and flashing up my body. Then he put his arms about me and kissed me again, crushing my body to his. My own arms encircled him. Our tongues kissed each other. I moaned softly — faithless, shameless, lewd little beast that I am!

At last, he released me, and my breath returned. I said, in a small, hoarse voice, "You've shaven off your moustache."

He stroked his naked upper lip. "A bit too un-Roman for His Majesty." He looked longingly at me. "Oh, Pam, my sweet love, how much I've missed you! Do you remember the lock of your hair which you sent to me on Saint Valentine's Day? Look — I carry it still — I shall carry it for ever." He reached inside his tunic and took out a small cloth sack, drawn closed by a string. Opening it, he carefully shook its contents into the palm of his hand: my curl.

I said softly, "And I still carry the locket you sent me that same day." I reached into my bosom and shewed it him: his boyhood portrait on one side; a lock from his five-year-old head on the other.

"How much I want you!" he said, and began to take me in his arms again, but this time I delicately eluded him.

"Things are not as they were, Giles," I said.

"Quite right. Things are *better* than they were. I am a colonel, with a colonel's pay and bright expectations for advancement. I have the good opinion of the King. We can be married now, and —"

"No, Giles," I said, firmly, "we can not be married. I am about to marry another man."

He laughed lightly. "I know all about that. A convenient arrangement, for the sake of the child. But it is no longer necessary. I shall adopt the boy and love him as if he were my own. Call him Brian, if you wish — Brian Ormond."

"Giles, you do not understand! I am marrying Rhys O'Connor!"

"A man whom you hate. A man who attacked your father, who ruined *my* father. A Godless radical. A traitor, who will soon be hanged."

"Hanged?"

Giles shrugged. "Oh, there'll be some form of trial, I expect, but the verdict is certain. That scoundrel, Maginn, gave testimony in plenty before he died."

"Maginn is dead?"

"Dead as a door-nail. Good riddance, I say."

"*Tortured* to death by your fine King!"

"No, not really. He was — treated rather roughly, I'll be bound, there in the Tower; but the filthy traitor deserved it, and he refused to give evidence until he was persuaded. The King's men didn't kill him, however. He hanged himself in his cell. Ashamed of betraying his friends."

(The Hanged Man! Again the cards had spoken true!)

"These radicals are all alike," Giles added; "men of straw; no iron to them. They break apart and screech like rats if you do no more than tread on their toes."

"The rack!" I cried. "Is that what you call treading on toes?"

"I know nothing of any rack," he said. "A bit old-fashioned, wouldn't you say? Sounds like some radical's fairy-story." He smiled. "The wild imagination of O'Connor, I'll wager. Well, that imagination will soon be held in check. The moment he arrives." Giles looked at my watch, lying on the table. "That should be almost any second now." The hands stood at precisely 8:15.

I would have to keep Giles talking. The sound of our conversation would be heard by Rhys on the other side of the door, and he would be warned.

"Please, Giles," I said, "you must tell me how you came to know our plans. I am so frightfully curious."

That disarming smile again. "I suppose you may as well know, as we shan't be using that informant again."

"What informant?"

"Can't you guess? Come now; try. Who knew of your plan? Who knew every detail — the time, the place, the very number of the apartment, the special knock? Who was present when the plan was made yesterday morning, after church, in your family coach?"

"Rhys and I. And my parents. Oh, Giles! It can not have been Mamma or Papa!"

He laughed. "There was a fifth person present."

403

"No," I said, "there were only four of us." Then my hand flew to my mouth. "It wasn't — Paley?"

Giles nodded. "Your faithful coachman. It's surprising how much can be accomplished with a few coins of the realm."

"How much did you pay him?" I said, bitterly, as tears crept into my eyes and my voice. "Thirty pieces of silver?"

"Not near so much," he replied.

My watch now read 8:20. Rhys was late. I took heart — perhaps my scheme had worked — perhaps he had heard our voices through the door and had fled. But I could not be sure, so I was determined to keep talking.

"Giles," I demanded, "tell me all that you've done since you boarded that train out of London."

"Well, actually," he said, "what I couldn't entirely tell you, that day in Whitechapel — because it was a closely kept secret — was that I had accepted an undertaking to help organise groups of Army officers who supported Cumberland's cause. Of course, if you had come with me, as I wished you to do, I should have been obliged to tell you. I admit that, at the time, I didn't place much importance in it. That was why I was in such a sour temper that day. It was only a job, I thought, a way of putting my military skills to some use and making a bit of money till something better came along. As it was, I travelled from regiment to regiment under the pretext of inspecting equipment, but really to form the Centurion Clubs, so-called. You probably don't know, my dear — no reason you should — that the Duke was the Grand Master of —"

"The Orange Lodges. Yes, I know."

"Ah. Well, thanks to chaps like your humble servant here, the Orange Lodge supporters in the Army began to grow — first among the Household Guards regiments, and then throughout the whole Army."

"Then Mr. Barstow was right," I said, more to myself than to him.

"What's that?"

"The Lodges were never really disbanded."

Giles nodded. "Oh, the Duke made a great show last year of dissolving the Lodges, but their work went on in secret, you see. In any case, the Centurion Clubs took in the majority of the officers in most of the regiments, and — are you *quite* sure you're interested in all this, Pamela?"

"Avidly," I replied.

"Very well. Each Club conceived a plan for seizing control of its regiment in the event an opportunity should arise to place the Duke on the throne."

"You were very well prepared," I observed, frostily.

"Indeed we were!" he said, with a proud smile. "And, if you don't mind my saying so, it's all turned out for the better, don't you agree? — a return to the best English principles, and a monarch who'll resist to the death all those damned Jacobin ideas . . ."

"To whose death? Billy Maginn's? And who will be next? Mr. Carlyle? The Duke of Sussex?"

"Come now, Pam, don't strike that attitude." He quickly changed the subject. "What do you think of my new uniform?" He stood up straight and threw out his chest, the better to display the grim black costume with silver facings, and he clapped the round, helmet-like cap over his heart in a mock salute.

"You have always been most handsome in uniform," I assured him. "But I don't understand the purpose of it."

"Well, you see," he explained, "the Duke was not entirely trustful of the household troops, and he felt need for his own. So he formed the Augustan Guard. New Guard; new uniform. The really new thing, though, is that our duties are just as much civil as military."

"And you think that to be good?"

"Of course! As you can see for yourself, we're not just strutting about the parade-ground — we're in the cities, doing useful work, taking all necessary measures against traitors and sedition."

My watch now read 8:25. My mind darted about, searching for a new subject of conversation, because I had to keep him talking. Raising my voice, I said, "What of your father and the tea affair? Is he —"

"Pam, Pam," he interrupted with a fond shake of his head, "there's no need for you to keep nattering on in that loud voice. You shan't warn off O'Connor. My men will seize him

405

before he reaches the landing. They may have already capt——"

A rifle shot! Another! Shouts and running feet! My heart was stabbed by fear. "Rhys!" I cried.

The door burst open. A sergeant of the Augustan Guard dashed in and saluted Giles. "He's — he's —" the man stammered.

"*Dead?*" Giles shouted. "You damned fool, I told you to take him alive!"

"Yes, sir — that is, *no,* sir —" said the embarrassed sergeant.

"No *what,* you idiot?"

"No, he ain't dead, sir. He's — got away."

"*Got — away?*" Giles slapped the sergeant's face so viciously that the man's helmet flew off and fell with a dull *clang* to the carpet.

"You'll go to the Tower for this!" Giles screamed. "I promise you that! I'll *personally* tear you limb from limb, as we did Mag ——"

He stopped, looked quickly at me, then mumbled to his trembling sergeant, "Get out. I'll deal with you later."

As the sergeant hurried away, I said, "So you know nothing of any rack, Giles? It's all a radical's fairy-story? You said *'we'* just now — 'as *we* did.' You were there, weren't you? You looked on as they racked poor Billy Maginn. *Or did you turn the crank yourself?*"

"I do my duty," he said, quietly. "At least, I am not a traitor and an assassin, like your fine friend O'Connor. Come, I'll take you home."

"No, you will not. If I decide to leave these rooms, I shall take myself home."

"I'm afraid that will not be possible," he said, and there was true sadness in his voice. "I — I must ask you your name," he said.

"My — name? What nonsense is this?"

"Please, Pam. Simply state your name."

"You are behaving like a lunatic, Giles! You know full well that my name is Pamela Summerfield!"

"Pamela Summerfield," said Giles, "it is my duty to place

you under arrest as an accomplice in sedition and treason." He offered me his arm, in a courtly manner.

"Ever the gentleman," I said, "even when escorting a lady to the Tower and the rack!"

༄ *Tuesday, 4 July*

Needless to say, I was not conducted to the Tower or the rack last night by Giles. I was courteously escorted home to Berkeley Square, along with Brian and La Belle Dame, where I was told that I was confined to my domicile.

"What?" roared Papa when he heard Giles use the expression.

"Merely a technicality, sir," Giles assured him. "It's for Pamela's own good. What it actually means is that I'm placing her under my personal protection. There will, in fact, be no hindrance of her freedom. She may leave the house to go shopping or to the theatre or wherever she may wish, provided that one of my men accompanies her. There will be Augustans stationed outside the house day and night."

"For how long?"

"Only until these assassins are apprehended. They are dangerous men, sir, and your daughter does herself no good by associating with them. I will take my leave now, and bid you all a good night; but I hope I may return to-morrow evening and have some words with Pamela on certain personal matters."

"It seems that I have no choice," I said.

"You do," he replied. "I hope only that you make the right one."

When he had left, Mamma and Papa cannonaded me with questions, and I told them everything that I knew. I could not tell them what I did not know — where Rhys was, and whether he had been wounded by Augustan fire-arms.

Then I sought the refuge of my rooms, where I dutifully wrote down yesterday's entry, and fell, exhausted and despairing, into bed. I longed for some of my drops to ease my anxious mind; but so drained was I that I fell asleep soon enough without them.

This morning, when I awoke, my thoughts were in the past, as if they had not been able to catch me up; and for the space of a few moments, I had no awareness of the tragedies and horrors of this half-year. Then, one by one, they bobbed up to the surface of my mind, like horrid bloated corpses bobbing up out of the dark depths of the river. Phoebe's unhappiness in marriage — her illicit pregnancy — her disappearance — her death. Willy's disgrace and self-banishment. The death of Sophie. The ghastly mutilation of Sally Bootes. The Full Moon murders. The arrest of Rutledge. The trial and Mamma's shame. The death of the Princess. The despotic *régime* of Augustus. Billy Maginn, spread-eagled on the rack. The collapse of our escape plans. And Rhys! — where was he? lying wounded somewhere, bleeding to death, perhaps already dead? — all these past and present blows buffeted me anew till my mind reeled under them.

Next, I heard noises, deep in the house, muffled but unmistakable: someone was being beaten! I could hear the sound of fists striking flesh, and the cries of a man in pain. The cries diminished to whimpers, then stopped, and were followed by the loud slam of our front door.

I leapt from my bed and wrapped my dressing-gown about me. I ran out of my bedroom and saw Papa, already dressed, climbing the staircase to the landing. "Papa!" I said. "What were those cries?"

"Paley," he told me. "I gave him a hiding he'll not soon forget, and threw him out of the house." Papa rubbed his knuckles, which were red from their task.

"Good for you, Papa!"

"Disgusting turncoat. I think I may have broken his jaw. I hope I did. He deserves hanging."

The word "hanging" reminded me instantly of Rhys, who stood in danger of that fate; and I asked, "Has there been any word — from anybody?"

He shook his head. "I'm afraid not, Princess. The morning post has not arrived — no doubt it's being held up by your friend Colonel Ormond, and scrutinised for possible seditious content. There is no news of O'Connor. I expect he's smart enough to stay away from this house. I sincerely hope so; there are Augustans posted everywhere one turns."

The day was spent in distressing anxiety. I could not read nor eat; I was too worried about Rhys. After dinner, during which I could take only a few spoonfuls of soup, Giles came to the house and was ushered into the drawing-room, where I sat with Mamma and Papa.

"With your permission, sir," he said politely to Papa, "I should like to interrogate Pamela, and I would appreciate the use of this room for the purpose."

"But, Giles," I said, "there are no thumb-screws or pincers here. I suppose we might make a fire and heat up some coals?"

He ignored my attempt at satire, and spoke again to Papa: "It should take only a few minutes, sir."

"And if I were to refuse you permission, Colonel?" said Papa. "What then?"

"Why, then, sir," Giles responded with a smile, "I should feel quite downcast to be sent away by a gentleman who, I hope, will one day be my father-in-law."

"You still entertain that ambition?" asked Mamma.

"I do, Madam," said Giles. "And I think I am in a better position now than ever before. I hold a post of great trust. I am well paid. I have influence and authority. I am respected. I can not believe that Pamela will throw herself away on a traitor to the Crown. And I will not believe that her old feeling for me has changed. Mine for her has not."

"You are a persistent young man," said Mamma.

"I am told that persistence is a virtue."

Papa said, "If Pamela wishes to be interrogated, as you call it, I have no objection." He looked at me.

"I possess no information that would interest the Colonel," I said, "but I shall not refuse to converse with him."

"Then the drawing-room is yours, Colonel Ormond," said Papa, rising from his chair. "Mrs. Summerfield and I shall leave you to your duties."

When Mamma and Papa had left, Giles casually bolted the drawing-room doors. "To prevent my escape?" I asked.

"To prevent intrusion," he replied. He then sat next to me on the sofa and took my hand.

"There is a Bible in the library," I said. "Shall we send for it so that I may swear to tell the truth?"

Still holding my hand — which I had not the power to pull away, so sweet it felt to be touched by him — he said, "I would prefer that we use it to read together from the Book of Ruth: 'Intreat me not to leave thee, or to return from following after thee: for whither thou goest, I will go; and where thou lodgest, I will lodge . . .' "

"Prettily spoken, Giles," I said, "but you were ever a pretty speaker of others' words. And they *do* say that the Devil can quote Scripture to his purpose."

"A devil? Is that what you think me?"

"N-no . . ." I admitted. "But the sovereign whom you serve is surely one."

"You misjudge him. Many do. You listen to slander and scandal. He is strong and strict, but he is just. King William was soft and shilly-shallying, too lenient with sedition and rebellion. Augustus will make this nation toe the mark. And I will help him. Why, Pamela, he's taken a liking to me! I've had private audiences with him. Of course, to-day he's upset with me, and rightly so, because I let O'Connor get away. But when I capture him, and the others of his rebel band, the King will reinstate me in his esteem. I mean to be an important man in this country, Pam. I fully expect to be knighted before long, for services rendered the Crown. Think of it, my darling: Lady Ormond — how does that sound to you?"

"It sounds very nice, indeed," I said, "and I hope that you will find a jolly girl on whom to bestow it."

"You are the only girl on whom I shall ever bestow it," he replied. "But, first, of course, I must become Sir Giles; and before that can come to pass, I must catch O'Connor. That is why you must tell me everything that you know about his habits and hiding-places."

"If I knew, I should not tell you — unless you broke my body on the rack. God knows I can not blame any poor soul for divulging secrets under such torture."

"Don't be a silly goose, Pam. You know you stand in no danger of torture."

"As it happens, you could take me to the Tower and tear me into a hundred pieces and still I could tell you nothing. Not because I am brave, but because I do not know. I know his Chelsea address, and that is all. I assume you know that already."

He nodded. "And James Fraser's house, in Regent Street, where Maginn's so-called Round Table met to plot and scribble. Fraser has fled, but we are watching his house. Do you truly not know any other place where he might go?"

I shook my head.

"Very well," Giles said, resigned. "I think that you would not lie to me. We shall have to use stern measures on Carlyle and Thackeray — no doubt they'll be able to tell us something. Let's say no more of these matters, however, for I know that they distress you. Let us move to more pleasant things."

He put his free hand on my bosom and gently squeezed. I own that it felt exceedingly pleasant, but I brushed his hand away. He chuckled and stroked my upper thigh. Again, I pushed away his hand.

"Why so coy?" he said, softly. "You still love me; I know it."

"Love can die," I said.

"My love for you has lived, healthy as ever, through all these long months. You have never been out of my thoughts or my dreams. I have ached for you — physically *ached,* Pamela."

"It was an ache easily assuaged, surely? There can have been no lack of ladies to relieve a handsome officer of his pain."

"There have been no others."

"Oh, Giles, what a little fool you must think me if you expect me to believe that!"

"No others, I swear it. No other woman in my heart, my arms, my bed, since that blessed afternoon in Whitechapel. I have longed for your sweet body —" And again he kneaded my breast.

I slapped his hand sharply. "*No,* Giles! There will never again be anything like that between us!" But he continued to press my bosom under his palm. "Giles, I warn you! I shall scream — and Papa will beat you black and blue, as he did Paley!"

411

He frowned now, confused and angry. "What are you play-ing at?" he said, quietly.

"I am not playing — nor am I your plaything."

A hard glint came into his eyes. "Don't come that tone," he said, low but fiercely. "Don't play the fine lady with me, Pam. I know you for what you are. I felt the way you melted into me like hot wax last night when I kissed you. I heard you whimper like a bitch —"

"Giles!" I got up abruptly from the sofa and walked to the pianoforte. He followed me. I stood facing him, the keyboard at my back.

"I know what you like," he went on. "There's a hungry little mouth of you that can't do without a part of me." He pointed to the bulge of his breeches. "This part!" he coarsely added.

"You are offensive!"

"Offensive, am I?" he said, still in a fierce near-whisper, as he began to unhook my frock. "Not when you're having a bit of my third leg. *Then* you're not offended. Oh, not at all. 'Don't stop yet, Giles, not yet, not yet, dear Christ not yet.' You love it. All of you Summerfields love it. Runs in the blood, I expect —"

"Please, Giles!" I pulled back from him, awkwardly striking a number of keys with my backside and bringing forth a thorny dissonance from the assaulted strings.

His hands were on my flesh now, and my frock hung half off my body. "Your sister had a taste for it, hadn't she? Dearly adored O'Connor's Irish shillelagh — took every inch of it, deep and true —"

"You're vile!" We had both sunk down to the carpet, and he was astride me, throwing off his tunic.

"Not as vile as your saintly missionary brother — he has a taste for it, too, I gather, the filthy pervert. As for your mother —"

"Don't speak of my mother!"

"Why not?" he whispered, peeling down his tight breeches. "She's a whore, isn't she?" I slapped his face. He laughed. "You're all of you whores, you Summerfields. Hot-breathing, holier-than-thou whores — bishop's daughters and divinity students and prim little prigs — swiving soldiers, butlers, schoolboys, scurvy rebels, anything with ballocks. Fairly frothing at the mouth for the old rail-spike, every one of you. Well, I'm willing to oblige you. I know how to bring you down from your high-and-mighty pedestal. I know how to make you crawl on your hands and knees and beg for what you crave. You do crave it, don't you, my girl? You'd die without it. Very well, here it is, as you like it, hot as a new loaf, done to a turn!"

"Gi——!!"

But my shout turned into a sigh of purest piercing ecstasy as he drove that heavenly tusk deep into my vitals. Dear God, how I had missed it! How maddeningly sweet to feel its dear hard fine long loveliness plumb me to the depths, again and again, building pleasure so high, so keen, so blinding-bright, that I would have given my immortal soul to Satan if it could have gone on for ever and ever and ever!

"Oh, my love, my king, my god, my soul!" I breathed huskily into his ear, as my eyes, through tears of joy, studied the carved oaken beams of the ceiling. "Yes, yes, ah yes, I am a little whore, it's true, your own adoring whore, yes, yes, oh yes, yes, yes —"

"Sweet — suffering — flesh — of — Christ — *Almighty!*" Giles exclaimed in shivering rapture as the too-long-pent imposthume of his desire burst like a rocket in my guts.

Spent, limp, panting, sweating like horses in the July heat and the tightly closed-off room, we lay there on the carpet in the tangle of our half-removed clothing, Giles with his leather boots still on but his breeches hanging off his beautiful alabaster backside, as firm and smooth and rounded as that of Michael Angelo's "David."

"Oh, my dear," I moaned, "I *do* love you."

"My sweet beloved," he said, between gasps, "I am frightfully sorry for those dreadful things I said."

"They're all forgotten."

"You did provoke me so."

"Oh, yes, I am to blame; I was so foolish. I am a despicable little wretch."

"You are the dearest girl alive."

Clumsily, we disengaged and pulled ourselves to our feet and began to put our clothes in order.

"Is my hair a sight?"

"No, remarkably neat, you vain creature, all things considered," I said. "And mine?"

"Most becoming," he replied.

We had recovered our composure not a moment too soon, for now there was a knock at the drawing-room door. Smoothing my frock, I walked over, drew back the bolt, and flung wide the doors. "Yes, Lieutenant?" I said, for an Augustan of that rank stood there. But in the next instant, I recognised him: *"Rhys!"*

He stepped quickly into the room and closed the doors.

"O'Connor!" cried Giles. "What are you doing in that uniform? How did you slip past my men?"

"Faith, and I didn't slip past them," Rhys replied. "I put the dear boys to sleep. They're all piled like a cord of wood in the wine-cellar, snoring peacefully. I took the liberty of relieving one lad of his fine feathers. This new chloroform is marvelous stuff. A few drops on a handkerchief, and —"

"Oh, Rhys, I was so afraid that you'd been wounded!"

He smiled. "One of their bullets came near to taking off the lobe of me left ear, but I'm very fit, as you can see."

Giles was fuming. He faced Rhys, his face as red as a lobster with anger and his recent exertions. "Sir," he said, "I must ask your name!"

"Oh, dear," I murmured.

"Sure, and what would you be thinkin' it is, you great loon?" said Rhys, spreading on the brogue as thick as jam, merely to irritate Giles.

"Your *name,* sir, damn you!"

"Now, now, Ormond," Rhys said, soothingly, "let's have no more of that. Let's talk this matter over, man to man. Pamela, dear, would there be a drop of your da's whisky to be had? It's that thirsty I am."

I poured a tumbler of whisky for him, asking Giles if he wished any.

"A touch, perhaps," he said.

"And I will join you both," I announced, pouring three glasses in all.

"Shall we sit down, like civilised folk?" Rhys suggested, setting an example by perching on the pianoforte stool.

I sat in Papa's chair, and Giles sullenly threw himself upon the sofa, grumbling, "As long as you understand that you are under arrest, O'Connor."

"Arrest, is it? Do you not see this thing in my right hand, pointed straight at your belly? 'Tis no clay pipe. 'Tis a pistol I've borrowed from me future father-in-law."

"*Your* future father-in-law! What damned infernal gall!"

"Cool your temper, Colonel," said Rhys. "Affairs have reached an *impasse*. You want to arrest me, but I have the upper hand at the moment. You want to marry this dear young lady, and so do I. It's in me mind that she is torn betwixt and between. She loves you, Ormond. I see it in her face and in the softness of her eyes. And 'tis true that you have the prior claim. But I believe that she loves me, as well. The poor girl is impaled on the horns of a dilemma as old as time itself.

"Now, I think that you place great importance in a certain code of conduct. You style yourself a gentleman, an *English* gentleman, and far be it from me to deny that. You are a loyal soldier of the King, sworn to serve him, bound by duty to obey him. I, on the other hand, am considered a traitor to your King, and I dare say 'tis true that I am. You therefore have a duty to bring me in. But — and here is where your own dilemma raises its horns, Colonel — your gentleman's code is in conflict with your duty."

"How so?" Giles interjected.

"I think that you already know that. I can see it in your discomfiture, your indecisive behaviour. You realise that 'tis a bit too suited to your personal convenience to arrest and hang me — 'twould be too easy a way to be rid of a rival for this lady's affections — too churlish of you to take advantage of your authority and power. It troubles your sense of chivalry. 'Tis at odds with your gentleman's code of honour. Moreover — and perhaps a bit closer to the point — you fear that this lady would think less of you should you press your advantage unfairly."

Giles glanced at me; then looked steadily at Rhys. "There is something in what you say," he admitted.

"Ah, good, then we agree! Now, let us further agree —

with no hypocrisy — that each of us would be the better were the other dead. I should not grieve to learn of your demise; you would shed no tears over mine. Given this state of things, here is what I propose:

"You and I shall meet to-morrow at dawn, on what I believe is called the field of honour. There we shall fight a gentleman's duel — a duel to the death — the choice of weapons is yours. If I am killed, England will be rid of one traitor, and Pamela will be free to marry you if she so chooses. If *you* are killed, she will marry me — but before the wedding takes place, another important event will occur: I will hasten directly from the field of honour to the Palace, disguised in this handsome uniform, and there I will shoot Augustus dead and proclaim the Duke of Sussex King."

"What!"

"Rhys! You'll be hanged as a regicide!"

"Sussex will grant me amnesty; I shall probably be declared a national hero; and this wild melodrama in which we all are players will come to a happy ending — save for the Colonel and Augustus, that is."

Rhys paused and finished his whisky. Then he said to Giles, "What is your answer?"

"If it should be no?"

"Then, Colonel, I shall be obliged to blow out your brains here and now. But I prefer not to soil this lovely wall-paper."

Giles shifted his weight uneasily on the sofa. "It's deuced odd," he said. "Damned if I've ever heard a more zany proposal."

"Can you think of a better?" Rhys asked him.

After a moment, Giles replied, "I confess I can not."

"Then you agree?"

"I agree."

"No, *no!*" I cried, leaping up. "You shall not do this foolish thing! The two men I love most in this world — killing each other like savages! I will not stand by and let you do it!"

Rhys said, "We shan't be killing each other. One of us will survive and return to claim your pretty little hand."

Giles said, "He's right, damn it. There is no other way."

"Look upon it," said Rhys, "as a kind of knightly test, a

trial by fire, a weeding-out process. The man who is less fit will lose. The fitter one — smarter, quicker, cleverer, or plain luckier, for the ability to attract luck is a kind of fitness — will win the privilege of blending his blood-line with your own. Faith, and I'm thinking that we poor benighted males have never been much more than a kind of enormous breeding experiment — presided over by females. You pick out the best breeders and providers and protectors, all for the sake of the cubs, and discard the rest of us. Tough, hard, practical little baggages you women are, the lot of you!" But he smiled when he said it, and then took me in his arms and kissed me — without letting his eyes or his pistol waver from Giles.

Giles then embraced and kissed me, too. "I will return to you," he said.

"*I* will return to you," added Rhys. "Come, Colonel, let us leave this house together, and on the way we'll settle the details of time and place. Farewell, Pamela, until to-morrow."

"Until to-morrow," echoed Giles.

And I, echoing both of them, said in a choked voice, as they left the room, "Until to-morrow — my dear ones."

La Belle Dame is curled up under my chair, asleep. Outside somewhere, in the otherwise silent darkness, her faithful White Knight sends up his pathetic, hopeless "Ao? Ao?"

I sit here at my writing-desk, waiting for the dawn. I pray that God will somehow spare the lives of both of my men. I remember something that Papa once said: "The flesh. How it trips us up and traps us. Beckons to us with promises of pleasure beyond price . . . but always, without fail, there is a price." I think of the price exacted from Phoebe by the flesh; and from Willy; and Mamma and Rutledge. I listen to the White Knight's heart-rending "Ao? Ao?" and pity him, for he is enchained and enslaved by his flesh. I think of Cumberland, whose flesh led him to torture Sally Bootes and God knows how many others. I wring my hands in anguish for Rhys and Giles, one of whom will die because of his thirst for my flesh; and I think, with envy, of Uncle Roger, who has never yearned for flesh of woman or man, and is the most serene person I have ever known.

I curse myself for a fickle, contemptible, miserable miscreant. I tell myself that Giles was right to call me a whore. No harlot ever shifted her allegiance from man to man faster than I did from Giles to Rhys and back to Giles again. Rhys is the better of the two, my good sense tells me; for if he is victorious in the duel, he will not only make a fine husband, he will also perform a needed act of execution, ridding our country of a degenerate tyrant and restoring England to its equilibrium. Yes, that is what my good sense tells me, and my heart, as well — or a part of it.

But another part of it — or is it that hungry nether mouth Giles spoke of? — hopes for my colonel to return and take me in his arms again. Oh, God, yes, what a beastly little whore I am, indeed!

And a scheming one, as well; for I have just decided that, should Rhys be the one to return, I shall lose no time in granting him my favours — not waiting for the nuptial night, but offering him the gift of my flesh at once, seducing him if need be; and not out of simple lust, but cunning prudence. That afternoon in Whitechapel, when Giles took me for the first time, I was extremely lucky, for, although I later suffered several days of anxiety when my Time was late, all had come right, and there had been no consequence of our act. It would be folly to think that I shall always be so lucky; and if this evening's coupling with Giles should have a living result nine months hence, I am determined that Rhys (should he, as I say, be the returning victor) will never suspect that he was not the cause.

In this connexion, I must ask myself a question about my own birth. Ever since the trial, and my long talk with Mamma the day after, I have wondered if she has been entirely accurate and completely candid. My birth, so difficult for her and so disastrous in its physical toll: May it not have taken place *after* she started her *affaire* with Rutledge, rather than before? The *affaire* began fifteen years ago, she said — but may it not, in truth, have started three or more years earlier? Rhys once referred to Rutledge as my second father. Is it not possible that he is my *true* father? If Mamma had been alternately bedding both him and Papa, perhaps not even she knows the answer. Certainly, I can not bluntly ask her; indeed, I think I do not want to know.

> *Qui tollis*
> *peccata mundi*
> *miserere nobis!*

౩౦ *Wednesday, 5 July*

The King is

Afterword

So ends Pamela Summerfield's diary, abruptly, in midsentence, on 5 July 1837. The pages that follow are blank. Why did she never return to the journal? Did she suddenly die? Did she vacate her father's house at a moment's notice, leaving behind this diary? Did she, perhaps, continue it elsewhere, in another volume? No such volume has been discovered. Nor has any diary of hers for earlier or later years been found.

The one we are fortunate enough to have was uncovered three years ago by S. A. Mocine while he was working as "a.d." (assistant director) on a Hollywood-financed motion picture being filmed in Suffolk, England. The interior and exterior of a beautiful but decaying mansion, designed by the great James Wyatt, had been leased for location-shooting of a costume drama. I was present, as the last of the script's several writers, to provide eleventh-hour revisions if they were needed. The magnificent old house required some revisions itself, a certain amount of renovation and set-dressing, before the cameras could roll, and, in the course of this work, Mocine had found the diary in the library, wedged between the two massive volumes of Samuel Johnson's famous dictionary. He handed it to me — with some wry comment about my affection for flowery dialogue — and, in spare moments, I began to read it.

I was fascinated by its vivid picture of 19th-Century English life, and particularly by its detailed description (in the entry of 22 January) of the very house in which we were billeted. As I drew near the end, I was baffled by its strange deviation from history as we know it. The diary cried out for publication. After some intricate negotiations between my agent and the mansion's present owner, Sheikh Abu Sadi, an arrangement was eventually reached.

A search of the Summerfield family plot in the local church-yard yielded several gravestones bearing that name (including Roger, an early occupant of the mansion), but none with the name of Pamela. It was nothing more nor less than a happy accident that, while leaving the churchyard (and what an at-mospheric old place it was — moss-blanketed and silent under lowering clouds, headstones of antique style leaning awry in all directions, the perfect location for a Frankenstein film!), I passed through the family plot of the Royces. The name rang a bell, or a very soft gong, for I was sure I had run across it somewhere in the diary (the entry of 11 March, as it turned out). My pulse quickening, I walked among the graves, peer-ing at names, until I almost literally stumbled over a weather-worn gravestone bearing this simple inscription:

Here Lieth in Eternal Rest
PAMELA S. O. ROYCE
Beloved Wife and Mother
24 May 1819
26 September 1898

I had found Pamela! "My" Pamela! Or had I? To this day, I am not sure, and can say only this:

There may well have been other Pamelas born on the same day as Victoria. The long-lived lady buried under that stone may not be the Pamela who wrote this diary, but her two initials lend credence to the idea that she was. The S may well stand for a maiden name, Summerfield. The O could easily denote the surname of a first husband, who may have left her widowed while she was still in the prime of her beauty and vigor — but whether it stands for Ormond, O'Connor, or some other name (a waggish colleague suggests Olivo) has not, as yet, been determined.

About this journal's most curious element — the accession of Augustus I — we can only speculate. Was it merely the product of a vivid, somewhat operatic, imagination; a girlish prank? Or was it something darker: a morbid, neurotic fantasy? Were her thoughts colored and distorted by tincture of opium, commonly called laudanum? Her chronicling of historical events is conventional before 16 June, where it suddenly and radically differs from recorded history. Are there other anomalies in these pages, before or after that date, relating to her personal life or lives of her family members? We have no way of knowing. In her first entry, 1 January, she questions her own ability to distinguish truth from its counterfeit and admits to certain undefined "wilder, whirling fancies." She is a confessed "dramatiser," too; witness her verse playlet about Phoebe's possible plight (19 March) and her rhapsody on the death of Beethoven (26 March). Before we dismiss this aspect of the diary with an airy *Se non è vero, è ben trovato,* however, we must remind ourselves that many respected members of today's scientific community by no means scorn the "parallel universe" or "multiple universe" theory. "Black holes," "white holes," "event horizons," "naked singularities," and other strange terms have entered the language of science. So has "breakdown of causality," which, in the argot of quantum theory, is the result of the "collapse of the state vector." For example, if I toss a coin, it lands both heads *and* tails, in different universes; at any rate, that is the substance of what Princeton University physicists Hugh Everett, John Archibald Wheeler, and Neil Graham seem to be telling us. In other words, the "state vector" collapses in an infinite number of directions, but we see only one of many results because, as R. A. Wilson explains, "We are in only one universe: but in the universe next door, another you and I will see a different result. And there are an incredible number of such . . . alternative universes." Bryce DeWitt, another physicist, says, "I still recall vividly the shock I experienced on first encountering this multiworld concept." And yet, in Wilson's words, "DeWitt and others have accepted it." Our universe, as John G. Taylor has written, may have "all started as a white hole, from someone else's universe." He goes on to describe the uncanny phenomena, previously considered absurd, that now, in the light of new understandings, must be thought of seriously as plain, if not simple, possibilities: "We can go on time voyages, and so make many copies of ourselves . . . meet ourselves setting out on our circular trip. But then the world is bizarre, for which of these copies is the real one, if any?" He does not attempt to answer that question, nor shall I; but we would be bigots, indeed, flatly to deny that Pamela, as some have suggested, had a valid, if paranormal, glimpse into a world of alternative possibility, like that imagined by her in the entries of 9 February and 1 March. Laudanum, instead of dulling her mind, may have sharpened it, sensitized it, rendered it capable of receiving perceptions beyond the reach of mundane personalities. Of interest, at least to me, are certain words written by Pamela's contemporary De Quincey (not in his famous *Confessions of an English Opium Eater,* with which we know she was familiar, but in its sequel, *Suspiria de Profundis,* which postdates her diary, having first appeared in 1845 in *Blackwood's Magazine*): "The machinery for dreaming planted in the human brain was not planted for nothing. That faculty, in alliance with the mystery of darkness, is the one great tube through which man communicates with the shadowy. And the dreaming organ, in connexion with the heart, the eye, and the ear, compose the magnificent apparatus which forces the infinite into the chambers of a human brain, and throws dark reflexions from eternities below all life upon the mirrors of the mind." Even a judgment of madness would not necessarily invalidate her vision; for, as Professor Harold C. Goddard said (in an essay written around 1920, but not published until 1957, posthumously): "Whether the insane man creates his hallucinations or whether insanity is precisely the power to perceive objective existences of another order . . . no open-minded person can possibly pretend to say."

I am not a psychiatrist, and am far from sure what the best definition of a term like "paranoia" may be, so I must ask those who consider themselves qualified to answer: Is there a disorder the opposite of "delusions of grandeur" — a thing we may call delusions of humble origins? A not-uncommon day-dream, we're told, is the fancy that one is not the offspring of one's ostensible father, but of a radiant hero or mighty prince who enjoyed one's mother's favor for a pleasant hour. Do the annals of aberration contain any examples of the contrary? I ask because of Pamela's suspicions, voiced in the entry of 4 July, that she may have been sired by Rutledge. If those suspicions are the product of an unstable mind, am I incorrect in thinking them unique — or, at least, exceptional? On the other hand, her suspicions may have been well grounded: compare her self-descriptions (3 January and 13 March) with her description of Rutledge (8 January) and note the strong resemblance between them. But, of course, the author of those descriptions is the very person whose respect for accuracy is in question, and it would be foolish to accept them without challenge.

Most of those who have studied these pages agree that the truncated final entry ("The King is") would have read, if completed, "The King is dead." Those who hold that view cite as support O'Connor's vow to assassinate Augustus, and the opening words of an earlier entry, that of 20 June, telling of the death of William IV, which does begin, "The King is dead." There is certainly a great deal to recommend that interpretation, and no doubt many of us would prefer to believe that the perverted syphilitic despot here described was shot like a mad dog, whether in this world or a "parallel" one.

Nevertheless, one feels duty-bound to draw attention to several other entries, all beginning with those same three words ("The King is"), that go on to chronicle less momentous events: "The King is not well . . ." (3 February); "The King is planning a gala birthday ball . . ." (18 May); "The King is reported to be mending . . ." (2 June); "The King is continuing to be very bad in his health . . ." (13 June); "The King is too ill . . ." (18 June).

A note on Anthony Trollope: his insistence, recorded more than once in these pages, that he was not a novelist was by no means a pose, for his first novel, *The Macdermots of Ballycloran,* was not published until 1847, fully a decade after this diary was written. His fascination (25 February) with William Huskisson and death-by-railway bore fruit much later, when, in his novel *The Prime Minister,* the distraught Ferdinand Lopez became the first character in world literature to commit suicide by stepping deliberately into the path of a train. Tolstoy, who called *The Prime Minister* "a beautiful book," borrowed the idea when he did away with his own Anna Karenina. "Trollope kills me, kills me with his excellence," the Russian novelist confessed.

The physical dimensions of the original diary are 12 3/4 by 7 3/4 inches. It contains 500 leaves, or 1000 (unnumbered) pages. Its other features are exactly as described in the entry of 1 January. Pamela's once-black ink (see 10 June) has aged to a kind of dark, rusty, dried-blood umber, owing to oxidation's natural toll; but the pages themselves are free of foxmarks or any other variety of deterioration. For this, we may thank the method of paper-manufacturing prevalent before the 1850s. Its product was a fine, handmade stuff based on cotton and linen rags. As the 19th Century reached its half-point, and commercialism reared its horned head, quantity replaced quality, manufacturers began using wood pulp instead of rags, and printers added chemicals to make the papers more readily absorb ink. The result is that, for over a century, most of the paper used for books has had an acid content that drastically reduces its life span; which means, ironically, that the pages of the volume you now hold in your hands will probably turn yellow, then brittle, and finally crumble into dry brown powder long before time has wrought similar ravages on Pamela's original, much older, book of days.

R.R.

Because flesh houses spirit
and because the flesh we spring from
and which springs from us
is our link with past and future
this book is dedicated to

WILLIAM RUSSELL

and the memory of

MARGARET RUSSELL

from their loving and grateful son
and to
MARC *and* AMANDA
from their loving and imperfect father